Leadership and Organizational Culture

Edited by
Thomas J. Sergiovanni and John E. Corbally

LEADERSHIP AND ORGANIZATIONAL CULTURE

New Perspectives
on Administrative Theory
and Practice

University of Illinois Press

Urbana and Chicago

Illini Books edition, 1986

©1984 by the Board of Trustees of the University of Illinois
Manufactured in the United States of America
P 5 4 3 2 1

This book is printed on acid-free paper.

Library of Congress Cataloging in Publication Data

Main entry under title:

Leadership and organizational culture.

Bibliography: p.
1. School management and organization—Addresses,
essays, lectures. 2. Universities and colleges—Admin-
istration—Addresses, essays, lectures. 3. Leadership—
Addresses, essays, lectures. I. Sergiovanni, Thomas J.
II. Corbally, John E. (John Edward), 1924–
LB2805.A425 1984   378.73   83–1338
ISBN 0-252-01347-6

CONTENTS

PREFACE

New Perspectives on Theory and Practice is the auspicious subtitle for this book. It communicates rather well, however, hopeful new developments in understanding administrative theory and practice. Recently the literature on administrative theory and leadership theory has cast a shadow of doubt and growing dissatisfaction. At the heart of this shadow is frustration with the inability of traditional scientific inquiry to account for practical knowledge and indeed to inform practice in administration. In part, dissatisfaction with traditional administrative theory is merely a reflection of a larger dissatisfaction with social science conceived of as a first cousin to the natural sciences. It is not the intent of this book to restate these issues or to add to this continuing critique of traditional social science. Instead, we attempt to move on to more hopeful ways of viewing administrative theory and leadership behavior.

The armature for this book is a report of a conference on the topic of administrative leadership held at the University of Illinois at Urbana-Champaign in July 1981. Indeed, nine of the chapters which comprise the book are based on papers presented at this conference. Six chapters were specially prepared for the book by individuals who attended this conference. Three additional papers were added to the collection, bringing the total number of chapters to eighteen. The chapter by James G. March deserves special comment. His is the seventh David D. Henry Lecture on administration given at the University of Illinois at Urbana-Champaign in September 1980. March's chapter is particularly significant, for it was as a result of this lecture that the conference was planned.

March gave a stimulating and challenging critique of the differences between actual administrative behavior and grander conceptions gleaned from theory. In some respects he painted a gloomy portrait of leadership in action and illustrated the inability of traditional theoretical concepts to account for the real world. He suggested that the world of administrative effort could be better appreciated if viewed as a class of activities beyond individual actors. He dangled a few other intellectual carrots as well by highlighting the importance of more symbolic aspects of leadership and of meaning within organizations. The book picks up at this point. We are not concerned with administrative behavior, leadership styles, organizational behavior, and other instrumental aspects of organizational life. Instead, attention is given to the more cultural aspects of administrative and organizational activity; to the more substantive and qualitative aspects of leadership; and to theoretical constructs which can help us understand better administrative and organizational phenomena.

In Chapter 9 Thomas B. Greenfield suggests that "the cultural world is one of man-made reality and its creation is like a conjuror's trick." What is this stuff of culture which comprises organizations and from which organizational living derives meaning? A standard definition of culture would include the system of values, symbols, and shared meanings of a group including the embodiment of these values, symbols, and meanings into material objects and ritualized practices. Culture governs what is of worth for a particular group and how group members should think, feel, and behave. The "stuff" of culture includes customs and traditions, historical accounts be they mythical or actual, tacit understandings, habits, norms and expectations, common meanings associated with fixed objects and established rites, shared assumptions, and intersubjective meanings. Intersubjective meanings are dynamic and suggest that culture in organizations is continually in process. As Herbert Blumer suggests, humans act toward events and objects on the basis of the meanings these things have for them; the meanings of such things derive from the social interactions one has with others; and these meanings evolve and are modified by individuals through an interpretive process (Blumer 1969, 2).

Within a cultural framework, leadership gives more attention to the informal, subtle, and symbolic aspects of reality. Symbols evoke and bring to the forefront one's history. Meanings are raised to one's consciousness and through meanings one is able to link onto aspects of his or her organizational world. Evoked meanings, however, are not the same for everyone and thus need to be woven together into persistent cultural strands which define the organization's mission and activities. Organizational members need answers to such questions as: What is this organization about? What is of value here? What do we believe in? Why do we function the way we do? How are we unique? How do I fit into the scheme of things? The answers come from definitions of the organization's cultural strands. These strands introduce an orderliness to one's organizational life, provide one with a sense of purpose, and enrich one's meanings. In this sense, quoting Thomas Greenfield, "The task of leaders is to create the moral order that binds them and the people around them." It is in this sense as well that purposing emerges as a paramount leadership concern. Peter Vaill, in Chapter 6, describes purposing as "that continuous stream of actions by an organization's formal leadership which have the effect of inducing clarity, consensus, and commitment regarding the organization's basic purpose." Leadership is viewed as a form of cultural expression. This view gives more importance to what leaders believe, stand for, and communicate to others than to behavioral styles or management strategies.

The cultural perspective is particularly important in understanding loosely structured organizations. Such organizations are characterized by a great deal of breathing room for individuals and units despite managerial attempts to tighten and structure things by applying conventional management theories. In loosely structured organizations coordination is difficult, controls are adhered to more by letter than spirit with little actual effect, and, whether intended or not, individuals enjoy a great deal of discretion. Workers operate independent of each other and are frequently invisible to each other; thus close supervision is difficult to practice. Many public organizations, organizations in the private sector of the R & D genre, and educational organizations are readily characterized as loosely structured. They share as well the characteristic of ambiguous goals which makes individual, unit, and organizational accountability difficult.

The breathing room which characterizes loosely structured organizations allows cultural factors to come into play more readily and thus symbolic aspects of leadership become more important. In tightly structured organizations, by contrast, traditional management controls are able to take hold more forcefully and thus to overcome or "suffocate" the impact of cultural factors. Regardless of cultural nuances, quality control in tightly structured organizations can be achieved by monitoring performance closely, by specifying in detail what routines will be followed, and by developing specific operational plans. The battle for quality in loosely structured organizations, however, is won or lost on the basis of individual commitment — a cultural matter and not one of bureaucratic regulation or management technique.

These are examples of the themes addressed in this book. They are discussed within the context of leadership theory and practice, organizations as cultural systems, theory of practice, and putting theory into practice. The intellectual heritage for this discussion is far-reaching and includes symbolic interactionism, cultural anthropology, phenomenology, normative discourse, hermeneutics, and critical theory. Despite these biases, leadership and organizational analysis is viewed as a multiple-perspective field and integrative frameworks are sought. At issue here is not scientific and technical rationality, but its universalization. The plea here is for restoring balance among a variety of perspectives; for achieving harmony among the descriptive, normative, and interpretive sciences; and for a renewed appreciation of the practical.

Contributing authors represent a variety of academic and professional fields including sociology, social psychology, organizational behavior, political science, business administration, public administration, educational administration, and higher education. They include well-known scholars and respected practitioners. They represent Australia, Canada, the United Kingdom, and the United States. Throughout, we stress the public administration context with particular emphasis on educational administration. Thus, this is a book which will be of direct relevance to scholars and practitioners concerned with the organization and administration of schools and universities. But, as suggested by the credentials of contributors, its relevance reaches beyond this context to wherever administration and leadership is studied and practiced. Scholars and practitioners in public and business administration, therefore, will be served well by its contents.

Our list of acknowledgments is long as can be imagined when one considers the nature of this project. Special attention, however, goes to professors Louis Pondy and Jack Culbertson who helped us in initially planning the conference. The support of Dean Joe Burnett and our colleagues in the College of Education at the University of Illinois, Urbana–Champaign, was uniformly enthusiastic. David Leslie of the president's office and President Stanley O. Ikenberry were helpful during the initial development of the book's perspectus. Barb Lucas did all of the vital work by serving as the conference coordinator. Special appreciation goes to Harold Enarson, William Toombs, John Keiser, James Lipham, Robert Silverman, Robin Farquhar, Phil Piele, Ernest House, Kenneth Mortimer, Hugh Petrie, Michael Moch, Louis Pondy, Francis Trusty, Suzanne Jacobbitti, JoAnn Fley, Robert Cope, John LaTourette, Kim Cameron, and Gerald Salancik for serving as moderators and discussants at the conference. Finally, we express our appreciation to all of the contributing authors for joining us in this enterprise.

Thomas J. Sergiovanni
John E. Corbally

REFERENCE

Blumer, Herbert (1969). *Symbolic Interactionism Perspective and Method.* Englewood Cliffs, N. J.: Prentice Hall.

Leadership and Organizational Culture

CHAPTER 1

Cultural and Competing Perspectives in Administrative Theory and Practice

Thomas J. Sergiovanni

A number of perspectives in administration and organizational behavior compete for the attention of professionals involved in the leading and managing of educational organizations. The most well known reflect a high concern for efficiency, the person, and politics. Newest and most controversial are cultural perspectives. Controversy stems in part from cultural perspectives adopting assumptions that depart from other views, from the suspicion in which they hold norms of traditional science, and from their emphasis on understanding as well as explanation. Each of these four perspectives provides administrators with a framework for actions and decisions. Since determined reality and sensible events in organizational life differ depending upon the view adopted, actions and decisions differ accordingly. Perspectives, be they explicit or implicit, are the means by which actions and decisions are rationalized as legitimate and sensible.

In this introductory chapter the four perspectives are described with greater attention given to the cultural view. The cultural perspective provides the theme thread for subsequent chapters. A basic assumption of the book is that administrative and organizational analysis in schools and universities, and in other public organizations, should best be viewed as a multiple-perspective activity. Theories of administration, therefore, should not be viewed as competing, with the thought that one best view might emerge. Instead, the alternate and overlapping lenses metaphor is offered. When viewed in this way, each theory of administration is better able to illuminate and explain certain aspects of the problems administrators face but not others. Increased understanding depends upon the use of several theories, preferably in an integrated fashion.

Heretofore, cultural perspectives have been neglected and the other perspectives have typically been used singularly as separate truths in competition with an array of assumed falsehoods. The singular use of a particular perspective or brand of theory stems in part from viewing administration as an applied science. When this occurs, principles of action are determined by the direct—either implicit or explicit—application of laws presumed to be established by social science. Neglected is the extent to which this applied knowledge fits the particular characteristics of the problem and its context. When several theoretical perspectives are brought together to bear on a problem, the administration of educational organizations is viewed as an art where principles of action result from the judgments of administrators at work. The role of the various social sciences and related administrative theories in this case is not that of surrogate to the administrator's intuition, but serves instead to inform this intuition. Intuition allows the artful application of knowledge in a setting where particulars of the situation are taken into account.

Explicit and Background Assumptions

Theoretical perspectives in administration are comprised of at least two distinguishable components. One component is the explicitly formulated and stated assumptions which give a particular perspective structure, form, and definition. The other component is the background assumptions which are tacit (Gouldner 1970). Background assumptions define how events ought to be interpreted and what events are to be accepted as fact and real.

Explicitly formulated and stated assumptions central to any theoretical perspective are influenced as much by the prevailing background assumptions as by the properties of events and situations under study. In administrative practice, for example, how problems are defined, what factors are to be considered, how events are to be evaluated, which decision-making strategies are to be used, and what the standards are by which truth is to be determined can all be traced to the prevailing background assumptions of the administrator and the group in question. As the assumptions change so do the characteristics of practice. In this sense there is no separate reality in organizational behavior and administrative functioning. Objectivity and truth are evasive and no order exists beyond that which is created in the minds of persons and that which is imposed upon the organization by persons. It is in this sense, as well, that the study of organizational behavior and administrative functioning might well be considered as "artificial" sciences (Simon 1969).

In the artificial sciences, reality is created by human conventions rather than by being inherent in the nature of the universe. Chemical elements and genetic characteristics, for example, respond according to natural laws. Traditional science aims to discover these laws and to test them by predicting natural behavior. The human sciences, by contrast, are unique. Except for instinctive and other low-level functioning, humans do not behave; they *act.* Actions differ from behavior in that they are born of preconceptions, assumptions, and motives. Actions have meaning in the sense that as preconditions change, meanings change regardless of the sameness of recorded behavior.

To bring order to this apparent confusion, conventions are invented to help determine what is true, to guide appropriate action, and to establish standards by which action might be evaluated. It is the scholar's perception of the dominant conventions that governs the nature of knowledge production and the professional's perception of dominant perspectives that governs professional practice. Among Kant's many contributions was his idea that knowledge is not a passive mirror of reality; its nature and substance is determined by the ways in which people comprehend (Bleicher 1980).

The efficiency perspective is reflected in the commonly accepted principles of "good" management which characterize the organization and operation of schools and universities. A division of labor exists whereby instructional and coordinative tasks are allocated to specific roles. Roles are defined by job descriptions which are clearly linked to some overall conception of what the organization is to accomplish. Certain guides, such as span of control and student/faculty ratio, have been accepted to help decide the number of faculty needed and how they should be assigned. Tasks are subdivided and specialists are hired for various functions. Roles are ordered according to rank, with some enjoying more authority and privilege than others. Day-by-day decisions are routinized and controlled by establishing and monitoring a system of policies and rules. These in turn ensure more reliable behavior on behalf of organizational goals. Proper communication channels are established and objective mechanisms are developed for handling disputes, allocating resources, monitoring quality, and evaluating personnel. Good management, defined in this sense, is directed at the efficient achievement of certain ends. But efficiency cannot be accidental; it requires deliberate and calculated planning. The ends must be clearly defined and the means carefully determined and stipulated. If means are implemented precisely according to plan, ends are likely to be accomplished efficiently.

Much of what is taken for granted as good management can be traced to an era of development in administration referred to as scientific management (Taylor 1911). Scientific management did not offer a theory of administration and organization as such, but a set of principles and injunctions for administrators to follow. Efficiency was to be maximized by defining objectives clearly, by specializing task through division of labor, and, once the *best way* was identified, by introducing a system of controls to ensure uniformity, reliability, and standardization of product.

Efficiency principles persevere today as strong considerations in curriculum development, selecting educational materials, developing instructional systems, and in other aspects of educational administration. This continued interest in scientific management can be attributed to a period of economic instability and to demands for accountability felt by all public organizations. But its strength is derived from the attractiveness of efficiency and technical rationality valued in Western thought.

Historically scientific management principles were applied directly. Traditional control mechanisms such as face-to-face supervision, however, have now been replaced by more impersonal, technical, or rational control mechanisms. It is assumed that if visible standards of performance, objectives, or competencies can be identified and measured, then the work of teachers and that of students can be better controlled by holding them accountable to these standards thus ensuring greater reliability, effectiveness, and efficiency in performance. These standards are reflected in the attention university administrators give to such "quality" indicators as grades distributed by curricula, admissions scores by program major, number of students taught by faculty FTE (Full Time Equivalent), and number of books and paper published.

Karl Weick (1982) suggests that efficiency management principles assume the existence of four properties for the organizations in question: the presence of a self-correcting rational system among closely linked and interdependent people, consensus on goals and means, coordination by dissemination of information, and predictability of problems and problem responses. Schools and universities, by contrast, are loosely structured with ambiguous goals and large spans of control. Weick notes that when the efficiency principles are applied to schools and universities and other loosely structured organizations "effectiveness declines, people become confused, and work doesn't get done." With respect to schools he concludes that "they are managed with the wrong model in mind" (Weick 1982, 673).

When viewing administrative theory and practice from a single perspective, certain aspects of organization and administration are emphasized and better understood but other aspects are neglected or given secondary status. The efficiency perspective did not give adequate attention to the human side of life in educational organizations. Such issues as individual personality and human needs and such conditions as job satisfaction, motivation, and morale seemed to be clearly secondary.

By 1930 an effective counterforce on behalf of the human side of enterprise was to emerge. This force was later to evolve into a distinct pattern of thought about administration with a strong emphasis on the person. The metaphor "organic" is often used to describe the person perspective. The analogy is to that of a biological organism capable of feeling and growing but also capable of ill health if not properly nurtured. The building blocks to organizational health are individuals and their needs as groups of individuals. According to this view, an ideal school department or unit is one characterized by highly motivated individuals who are committed to objectives from which they derive satisfaction. These individuals are linked together into highly effective work groups. The work groups are characterized by commitment to common objectives, group loyalty, and mutual support. Efficiency views emphasized specialization by tasks; personal views emphasized specialization by people. Specialization by people permits individuals to function as experts who enjoy discretionary prerogatives and who are influenced more by client needs and their own expert abilities than by carefully delineated duties and tasks. The concepts of collegiality in universities and shared decision-making in schools are allied with this view.

The person perspective is reflected in human relations and human resources management theories. The bench mark most frequently mentioned as the beginning of the human relations movement in administration is the work of the research team which functioned from 1924 to 1933 at the Hawthorn plant of the Western Electric Company in Cicero, Illinois (Roethlisberger and Dickson 1939). Elton Mayo (1945), a prominent pioneer in this movement, offered a set of assumptions to characterize people which was quite different from that of efficiency management. He suggested that persons are primarily motivated by social needs and obtain their basic satisfactions from relationships with others. He maintained that management had robbed work of meaning, and therefore meaning must be provided in the social relationships of the job. Mayo also concluded that persons were more responsive to the social forces of their peer group than to extrinsic incentives and management controls. Finally, a person's identity and loyalty to management and organization depended upon the extent to which interaction and acceptance needs were provided for at work.

Human resources theory represented a maturation of earlier human relations principles (Miles 1965). Both human relations and human resources lamented the loss of meaning in work. But in human resources this loss was not attributed to neglect of a person's social needs as much as to inability to use talents fully. A person's presumed capacity for growth received the greatest attention by human resources theorists. They urged that shared decision-making, joint planning, common goals, increased responsibility, and positive provision for more autonomy were the sorts of strategies to be developed by administrators. Motivation was to be intrinsic because jobs were to become interesting and challenging. Human resources theorists reflected not only an interest in people at work but a new regard for their potential. A great deal of emphasis was placed on autonomy, inner direction, and the desire for maximum self-development at work (McGregor 1960; Likert 1967; Argyris 1964).

The political perspective represents a recent and important development in the literature of educational administration. Four critical emphases distinguish the political perspective from those which emphasized efficiency or the person.

Each of the other views is primarily concerned with forces, events, and activities internal to the organization. The political perspective is concerned with the dynamic interplay of the organization with forces in its external environment. Schools and universities, for example, are viewed as open rather than closed systems, as integral parts of a larger environment not as bounded entities isolated from their environment. They receive inputs, process them, and return outputs to the environment. Inputs are presumed to be diverse and output demands often conflicting. As a result there is constant interplay between school and environment. The university is expected to meet its commitments to teaching but at the same time to win enough research contracts to help maintain financial solvency. The high school is expected to maintain tight control over students but at the same time to teach them self-responsibility and initiative. The nature of this interplay is political. As issues are resolved, bargains are struck and agreements reached. Internally, schools and universities are comprised of interdependent subunits and groups with self-interests which compete with each other.

The emphasis in other views is on the administration of policy decisions. In the political perspective the emphasis is on policy development. Political views do not consider goals as given to be administered. Goals are considered to be highly unstable and constantly changing. Therefore, understanding the process of bargaining in the development of consensus and understanding that sensitivity of such agreements to external forces are considered important.

The other views seek to suppress, program, gloss-over, or resolve conflict. In the political perspective conflict is considered as both natural and necessary. Conflict resolution is an important concern to administrators who work from the person perspective for they view conflict as unnatural and pathological. Since finding and using the "one best way" are characteristics of the efficiency perspective, conflict is regarded as a deviation to be corrected. The emphasis in the political perspective is on policy formulation. This emphasis requires debates over appropriate goals, values, and strategies and is naturally accompanied by conflict.

Each of the other views assumes norms of rationality in decision-making. The political perspective is not based on similar interpretations of rationality. For example, since it is assumed that goals are not givens but negotiated, and since the interplay within the organization and between the organization and its environment is viewed as bargaining, then the rational pattern of establishing clear goals and subsequently programming individual and organizational behavior to maximize these goals is suspect. Instead, a "satisficing" image of person and organization is offered as a substitute for more traditional rational images. Administrators do not seek optimal solutions to the problems they face but seek solutions that will satisfy a variety of demands. The "best" research program is not adopted but the one that is easier to implement and which costs less is chosen. In the schools the "best" reading program is not selected for children but the one which teachers will accept and implement with the minimum amount of difficulty is chosen.

The political perspective began to receive attention by administrators in the late fifties as scholars from political science and the decision sciences systematically began to study the problems of organization and administration. Herbert A. Simon's now classic work *Administrative Behavior: A Study of Decision-Making Processes in Administrative Organization* (1945) is considered by many as the forerunner of this movement. In recent years James G. March and his colleagues have turned their attention to the analysis of educational organizations (Cohen and March 1974), coining the label "organized anarchies" to characterize the way these organizations function (March and Olsen 1976).

The Cultural Perspective

Within the cultural perspective organizations are viewed as artificial entities subject to the whims of human predispositions and conventions, and within organizations administrative activity is viewed as a cultural artifact. The emphasis in analysis and practice is more on understanding than explaining and on making sense of events and activities than on describing.

The cultural perspective is the most recent view of theory and practice among the four and the view likely to receive more attention in the near future. This view looks to phenomenology, symbolic-interactionism, anthropology, ecology, hermeneutics, and critical theory as relevant scholarly traditions. More particularistic in focus and with a higher regard for the practical and the practitioner's way of knowing than the other three views, the cultural is concerned with the unique aspects of issues and situations and with grass-roots approaches to studying educational organizations and environments. Individuals, for example, are studied in context where both context and individual are assumed to be relatively equal. According to this view individuals are not masters of context but integral parts. Thus the study of human behavior separate from the unique characteristics of the specific organizational context is viewed with suspicion.

Underlying the cultural perspective is the concept of community and the importance of shared meanings and shared values. Within the university there exist several subcultures each seeking to promote and maintain its values. To understand the university is to understand the nature of multicultural societies, and to administer the university requires that one deal with the web of conflict and tension which exists as several subcultures try to protect their way of life. The administrator accepts the fact that differences among subgroups are greater than values shared in common; that often administrative practices represent the intrusion of one culture on another; that how people interpret events is very important; and that normative and persistent qualities of each subculture are sacrosanct. The need exists, nonetheless, to identify and articulate those cultural strands which can evoke enough common human consciousness among groups to enable concerted action.

Leadership within the cultural perspective takes on a more qualitative image; of less concern is the leader's behavioral style, and leadership effectiveness is not viewed merely as the instrumental summation of the link between behavior and objectives. Instead, what the leader stands for and communicates to others is considered important. The object of leadership is the stirring of human consciousness, the interpretation and enhancement of meanings, the articulation of key cultural strands, and the linking of organizational members to them. As Pondy suggests, "What kind of insights can we get if we say that the effectiveness of a leader lies in his ability to make activity meaningful for those in his role set — not to change behaviors but to give others a sense of understanding what they are doing, and especially to articulate it so they can communicate about the meanings of their behavior" (1978, 94). He characterizes the difference between behavior and meaning as the difference between "playing notes" and "making music." Within the cultural perspective concern is greater for the music-making aspects of leadership than note-playing aspects.

The concept of "center" is important to the cultural perspective. Organizational and societal centers represent the locus of values, sentiments, and beliefs which provide the cultural cement for holding together human groups. As Edward A. Shils states:

Society has a center. There is a central zone in the structure of society. This central zone impinges in various ways on those who live within the ecological domain in which the society exists. Membership in the society, in more than the ecological sense of being located in a bounded territory and of adapting to an environment affected or made up by other persons located in the same territory, is constituted by a relationship to this zone.

The center, or the central zone, is a phenomenon of the realm of values and beliefs. It is the center of the order of symbols, of values and beliefs, which govern the society. It is the center because it is the ultimate and irreducible, and it is felt to be such by many who cannot give explicit articulation to its irreducibility. The central zone partakes of the nature of the sacred. In this sense, every society has an official "religion" even when that society or its exponents and interpreters conceive of it, more or less correctly, as a secular, pluralistic, and tolerant society. . . . The center is also a phenomenon of the realm of action. It is a structure of activities, of roles and persons, within the network of institutions. It is in these roles that the values and beliefs which are central are embodied and propounded [1961, 119].

As repositories of values, organizational and group centers are sources of identity for individuals and groups from which their organizational lives become meaningful. Developing and nurturing center value patterns and accepting center norms which dictate what one should believe and how one should behave represent a response to felt needs of individuals and groups for stability and order and for a mechanism whereby the new and varied can be absorbed in a meaningful fashion. Centers provide a sense of purpose to seemingly ordinary events and bring worth and dignity to human activity within organizations. Centers, therefore, are cultural imperatives—normal and necessary for establishing social order and providing meaning.

Since the development of centers within organizations occurs naturally in response to human needs, left unattended several "wild" centers may develop with only accidental congruence with official organizational purposes and ideals. Further, "wild" centers developed by various subgroups within an organization may not only contradict administrative and organizational aspirations but may conflict as well among themselves. Thus the "domestication" of centers becomes an important leadership responsibility of administrators who work within the cultural perspective. To this effort, leaders consciously work to build unity, order, and meaning within the organization as a whole by giving attention to organizational purposes, the philosophical and historical traditions of the organization, and the ideals and norms which define the way of life in the organization for purposes of socialization and of obtaining compliance.

Summary

Perspectives are images of reality and not truths in themselves. Since educational administration and organizational behavior are linked to human conventions, perspectives of practice are not truth seeking in the traditional sense but rather serve to enhance one's understanding and to illuminate one's view of the world.

Though it is natural to debate the relative usefulness of various perspectives, some scholars continue to emulate the more exact sciences by seeking the replacement of one perspective with another. An assumption basic to this book is that multiple-perspective and integrative views are more appropriate in fields such as public and educational administration. A multiple-perspective view requires that technical and practical matters, explanation and understanding, be brought together. In analyzing Habermas's (1970) views on the nature of knowledge and its integration, McCarty notes "the real problem . . . is not technical reasons as such but universalization, the forfeiture of a more comprehensive concept of reason in favor of the exclusive validity of scientific and technological thought, the reduction of *praxis* to *techne* and the extension of purposive-rational action to all spheres of life. The proper response, then, lies not in a radical break with technical reason but in properly locating it within a comprehensive theory of rationality" (1978, 22).

It should be clear, then, that our argument is not with other views of administrative theory and practice, only with their universalization. A multiple-perspective view cannot be realized, however, in the absence of parity for the cultural perspective, a problem we seek to remedy with this book.

REFERENCES

Argyris, Chris (1964). *Integrating the Individual and the Organization*. New York: John Wiley & Sons.

Bleicher, Josef (1980). *Contemporary Hermeneutics: Hermeneutics as Method, Philosophy and Critique*. London: Routledge & Kegan Paul.

Cohen, Michael D., and James G. March (1974). *Leadership and Ambiguity: The American College President*. New York: McGraw-Hill.

Gouldner, Alvin (1970). *The Coming Crisis of Western Sociology*. New York: Avon Press.

Habermas, Jurgen (1970). "Technology and Science as Ideology." *Toward a Rational Society*. Translated by Jeremy J. Shapiro. Boston: Beacon Press.

Likert, Rensis (1967). *The Human Organization: Its Management and Value*. New York: McGraw-Hill.

McCarthy, Thomas (1978). *The Critical Theory of Jurgen Habermas*. Cambridge, Mass.: MIT Press.

McGregor, Douglas (1960). *The Human Side of Enterprise.* New York: McGraw-Hill.

March, James G., and Johan P. Olsen (1976). *Ambiguity and Choice in Organizations.* Bergen: Universitetsforlaget.

Mayo, Elton (1945). *The Social Problems of an Industrial Civilization.* Boston: Harvard Graduate School of Business.

Miles, Raymond E. (1965). "Human Relations or Human Resources?" *Harvard Business Review* 43(4), 148–56.

Pondy, Louis R. (1978). "Leadership as a Language Game." In Morgan W. McCall, Jr., and Michael M. Lombardo, eds. *Leadership: Where Else Can We Go?* Durham: Duke University Press.

Roethlisberger, Frederick, and William Dickson (1939). *Management and the Worker.* Cambridge, Mass.: Harvard University Press.

Shils, Edward A. (1961). "Centre and Periphery." In *The Logic of Personal Knowledge: Essays Presented to Michael Polanyi.* London: Routledge & Kegan Paul, pp. 117–31.

Simon, Herbert A. (1945). *Administrative Behavior: A Study of the Decision-Making Processes in Administrative Organization.* New York: Macmillan Co.

_____ (1969). *The Sciences of the Artificial.* Cambridge, Mass.: MIT Press.

Taylor, Frederick (1911). *The Principles of Scientific Management.* New York: Harper & Row.

Weick, Karl E. (1982). "Administering Education in Loosely Coupled Schools." *Phi Delta Kappan* (June), 673–76.

PART I

Reconceptions of Leadership Theory and Practice

Dissatisfaction among scholars with progress in understanding leadership and in helping practitioners increase leadership artistry and skill is legendary. Often quoted to reflect this state of affairs is Bennis's comment, "Of all the hazy and confounding areas in social psychology, leadership theory undoubtedly contends for top nomination. Probably more has been written and less is known about leadership than any other topic in the behavioral sciences" (1959, 259). Eleven years later Stogdill writes, "Four decades of research on leadership has produced a bewildering mass of findings . . . it is difficult to know what, if anything, has been convincingly demonstrated by replicated research. The endless accumulation of empirical data has not produced an integrated understanding of leadership" (1974, vii). Is there a relationship between these conclusions and dominant conceptualizations of leadership? Does how one looks at the phenomenon of leadership determine what one sees? Has too much attention been given to the study of leadership in its scientific, instrumental, and behavioral senses? Might we get a different view of leadership by concentrating on qualitative aspects? If leadership is viewed more as a performing art and a human act than as a behavioral response or a series of management techniques, would our understanding be improved?

The chapters in Part I seek to move beyond current understanding of the instrumental in leadership to the symbolic; from viewing leadership as a "rational" set of actions directed at clearly focused and well-defined objectives to leadership as a much more uncertain process with a kind of "rationality" which is real in its own right, but less understood; from a focus on leaders who behave to leaders who act in accordance with certain predispositions such as needs, beliefs, and perceptions; and from a conception of leadership where effectiveness is defined as accomplishing objectives to one of building identity, increasing understanding, and making the work of others more meaningful.

In Chapter 2, James G. March compares administrative theory with administrative life noting little resemblance between the formally explicit, more rational conceptions of theory and the ordinary, tacit, less rational realities of life. Studies of administrative life, he maintains, consistently challenge the clarity, order, and linear relationships characteristic of theory, revealing instead a leadership world characterized by a concern for minor things and a puzzlement over ambiguous goals and preferences.

From his portrayal of theory and life March proposes three estimates of the worth of leaders. Estimate one, gleaned from theory, attributes the major portion of variance in organizational success to specific qualities of individual leaders. Administrative leadership, in this estimate, is reassuringly significant and this view endures despite contrary portrayals of leadership found in studies of administrative life. The second estimate, derived from accounts of administrative life, views the setting for leadership as characterized by the metaphors "loose coupling," "organized anarchy," and "garbage can" decision-making. Life in this setting leads to a pessimistic estimate of the significance of leadership — a source of consternation for administrators. In the third estimate, leadership is viewed as a significant class of activities where no one leader is considered more significant than others. Success results from the density of administrative competence within the organization, not from unique qualities of individual leaders. Within this estimate the honor of administration is left intact but its glory is vanquished.

At issue throughout March's discussion is how administrative life is to be studied and defined. Chapter 2 raises the possibility that too much emphasis has been given to studying administrative leadership on the lines and not enough to between the lines. On the lines focuses attention on what administrators do and how they behave. Between the lines is concerned with interpretations and meanings derived from actions and behaviors. When leadership is studied between the lines, symbolic aspects receive primary attention. The true value of leadership beyond competence may well be found in these symbolic aspects. This possibility is charted in March's discussion of organizational rituals and symbols.

Intuitive artistry is the leadership theme discussed by Donald A. Schön in Chapter 3. Administrators recognize the importance of intuition over technique when confronted with unique situations, when they must respond under stress, and when extended calculation and analysis is not possible. Less recognized is the importance of intuition under more stable conditions where routine management practices prevail. Schön suggests that even management technique relies on intuitive artistry.

Intuitive judgment and skill come to mind easily when one speaks of the art of management. Schön argues that reflection is a necessary but neglected part of this art. Reflection takes place when an administrator puzzles thoughtfully on a phenonomenon he or she perceives is not congruent with intuitive understandings. Reflection-in-action consists of surfacing, examining, criticizing, reformulating, and testing of intuitive understandings of a problem or situation. Schön aptly describes reflection-in-action as "a reflective conversation with the situation." Throughout his chapter Schön allows us to eavesdrop on reflective conversations by providing examples and cases drawn from several settings including university administration.

Warren Bennis, in Chapter 4, asks the question, "What are the components of an organization that can translate intention into reality and sustain it?" The components he identifies are leaders, a set of symbolic forms which communicate intents, and individuals who comprise the organization. The means to transformation within this triad are implicit in the "compelling vision" of leaders which is artfully communicated into a set of precepts, standards, and cultural imperatives for organizational members. This transformation power of the leader, Bennis maintains, is found in his or her vision; capacity to communicate this vision meaningfully and convincingly; fortitude comprised of persistence, consistency, and focus; and enpowerment defined as the leader's ability to tap and harness the energy and commitment of others on behalf of the organization.

Bennis does not arrive at these conclusions by mere speculation. Instead, this portrayal of leadership as transformation power emerges from his extensive study of eighty chief executive officers representing a variety of public and private organizations.

Chapter 5, "Leadership and Persistence" by Barry Staw, takes a different tack in examining the concept of leadership. Staw points out that there are hazards in attributing mystical qualities to leaders that elevate them above the frailties of human nature. He examines leadership behavior as one of many ordinary organizational activities and explores limitations and judgments of leaders as a common human characteristic. Thus, as ordinary mortals, leaders are subject to the same problems of perception, information processing, and preference identification as others despite recognition that leader shortcomings are typically harder felt on the organization.

Using the example of persisting in a course of action, Staw documents the human tendency to increase one's commitment to a course of action in the face of failure, as a means to recover past psychological and material investments, rather than to cease participation in an effort to cut future losses. He then explains the human tendency to seek, indeed often to invent, internal and external justification for one's actions. Justification, in turn, provides a rationale for a renewed commitment to failure. In addition to the need for justification Staw points out that norms of consistency drive the individual further along a course of action. Consistency in management is highly prized by theorists and practitioners alike and is expressed in the precept that if one sticks to a course of action long enough success will follow.

Staw provides a detailed accounting of research which supports his assertions and weaves this information into a model of the determinants of persistence in escalation situations. This chapter concludes by providing an analysis of the implications of this problem for leadership and organizational life.

Recall the most effective, high-performing, excellent organization to which you have belonged in your history as an organizational member. How did life in this system differ from the more ordinary of its genre? In particular, what unique leadership qualities characterized this system? These are the questions raised and explored by Peter Vaill in Chapter 6 as he analyzes the nature and characteristics of leadership in high-performing systems. The following criteria distinguish high- from ordinary-performing organizations: excellent performance against a known standard; excellent performance against assumed potential; excellent performance relative to previous performance levels; judged qualitatively by informed observers to be substantially better than comparable systems; performing with significantly fewer resources than assumed to be necessary; and perceived as a source of ideas and inspiration.

Vaill's studies lead him to conclude that high-performing systems know why they exist and what they are trying to accomplish. Members, he maintains, "have pictures in their heads which are strikingly congruent." This strong sense of commitment to purpose within the organization points to "purposing" as the key concomitant quality of leadership found common to high-performing systems. Purposing refers to "that continuous stream of actions by an organization's formal leadership which has the effect of inducing clarity, consensus, and commitment regarding the organization's basic purposes." Vaill then provides an analysis of the functions of purposing and how they are expressed.

What are the characteristics of leadership action which contribute to purposing? Vaill finds that leaders express purposing by investing extra amounts of time; by having strong feelings about the system, its purposes, and achievement; and by focusing attention and energy on key issues and variables. It is time, feeling, and focus, he concludes, that communicate to others what the organization is about and that build commitment to these images. Leadership, then, is less a matter of style expressed in one's behavior and more a matter of communicating standards, ideals, and meanings.

Leadership as a form of cultural expression is the theme of Chapter 7 by Thomas J. Sergiovanni. Bringing together the major strands of previous chapters, he proposes ten principles of quality leadership. The principles are grouped into four categories: leadership skills, antecedents, meanings, and culture. Taken together they provide the conceptual balance needed to guide future inquiry in leadership theory and research. Articulated together, they represent the celebration of the art of leadership in practice.

Leadership skills represent the important tactical requirements of leadership expressed as instrumental behavior guided by management theory and research. Leadership antecedents, meanings, and culture, by contrast, are more subtle, qualitative, and symbolic. They represent the more enduring and far-reaching value of leadership and thus are considered as important strategic requirements.

Leadership antecedents represent conditions, feelings, assumptions, cognitive maps, and attitudes of leaders which determine reality and guide action. Meanings are the sense-making aspects of leadership intended to breathe life, understanding, and significance into day-by-day activities of people and to help people interpret their contributions, successes, and failures in light of organizational purposes. When leadership skills, antecedents, and meanings are successfully articulated, leadership becomes less a management technique or behavioral set and more a form of cultural expression. Relying on the reader's tacit understanding of excellence, Sergiovanni tests each of the ten principles against the realities of organizational life.

REFERENCES

Bennis, W. G. (1959). "Leadership Theory and Administrative Behavior: The Problem of Authority." *Administrative Science Quarterly* 4(2), 259–69.
Stogdill, R. M. (1974). *Handbook of Leadership*. New York: Free Press.

CHAPTER 2

How We Talk and How We Act:
Administrative Theory and Administrative Life

James G. March

I am not an administrator. I believe I am only the second person without experience as a college president to be invited to deliver the David D. Henry Lecture. I am a student of organizations and administration, and it is from that point of view that I talk. Nevertheless, I hope that some comments from the ivory tower may be marginally useful to the real world of administration. Students of organizations are secretaries to people who live in organizations. Much of our time is spent talking to people in administrative roles, recording their behavior, and trying to develop descriptions of organizational life that fit common administrative experiences into a larger metaphor of organizational theory. As best we can, we try to make sense of what we see.

Making sense of organizational life is complicated by the fact that organizations exist on two levels. The first is the level of action where we cope with the environment we face; the second is the level of interpretation where we fit our history into an understanding of life. The level of action is dominated by experience and learned routines; the level of interpretation is dominated by intellect and the metaphors of theory. Ordinary administrative life is a delicate combination of the two levels. Managers act. They make decisions, establish rules, issue directives. At the same time, they interpret the events they see. They try to understand their own behavior, as well as that of others, in terms of theories that they (and others) accept. They try to present themselves in understandable, even favorable, terms. They try to improve the way they act by

This paper was given as the David D. Henry Lecture on Administration at the University of Illinois, Urbana–Champaign, 25 September 1980. It is based, in part, on work done jointly with Michael Cohen, Martha Feldman, Daniel Levinthal, James C. March, and Johan P. Olson, and supported by grants from the Spencer Foundation, the National Institute of Education, and the Hoover Institution.

contemplating its relation to the way they talk, and they try to modify their talk by considering how they act.

The process has elegance, but it also has traps. The interweaving of experience and theory often makes it difficult for the student of administration to disentangle the events of organizational life from the theories about those events that participants have. The same interweaving complicates the ways in which administrators learn from their experience to improve their organizations. I want to explore some aspects of those complications today. My intentions are not grand. I want to talk about some parts of administrative theory and administrative life, about the implications of recent thinking on organizations, and particularly about the possibility that some of our administrative precepts — the way we talk — may sometimes be less sensible than our administrative behavior — the way we act.

Classical perspectives on administrative leadership are rich enough and varied enough to make any effort to describe them in broad terms ill informed. Nevertheless, there is a relatively standard portrayal of organizations and their leaders that is easily recognized and is implicit in most of our administrative theories. Without attempting to represent those theories in a comprehensive way, I want to focus on four assumptions of administrative thought that are important both to contemporary administrative action and to recent research on administrative life:

Assumption 1: The rigidity of organizations. In the absence of decisive and imaginative action by administrative leaders, organizations resist change.

Assumption 2: The heterogeneity of managers. Top managers vary substantially in their capabilities, and organizations that identify and reward distinctively able administrative leaders prosper.

Assumption 3: The clarity of objectives. Intelligent administrative action presupposes clear goals, precise plans, and unambiguous criteria for evaluation.

Assumption 4: The instrumentality of action. The justification for administrative action lies in the substantive outcomes it produces.

These assumptions permeate both our writings and our talk about organizations and administration. Although it is certainly possible to find counterexamples in the literature, they are part of generally received administrative doctrine. Moreover, they are not foolish. They reflect considerable good sense. One difficulty with them, however, is that they appear to capture only part of our experience. Most studies of administrative life present a somewhat different vision of administrative roles. Although there is a tendency for some biographers of particular leaders to surround administrative life with grandeur, most studies and most reports from administrators present a different picture of what administrators do. Administrative life seems to be filled with minor things, short-time horizons, and seemingly pointless (and endless) commitments. The goals of an organization seem to be unclear and changing. Experience seems to be obscure. Life is filled with events of little apparent instrumental consequence. The ways in which administrative theory leads us to talk about administrative life seem to be partially inconsistent with the ways in which we have experienced and observed it.

Such an inconsistency is neither surprising nor, by itself, disturbing. Tensions between theory and experience are important sources of development for both. But in this case, I think our theories lead us astray in some important ways. In order to examine that thought, I want to note some observations about organizational life drawn from recent research. First, some observations about change; second, some observations about clarity; third, some observations about managers and managerial incentives; and fourth, some observations about instrumentality in administrative life. Taken together, these observations suggest some modest modifications in our assumptions of management.

Organizations and Change

Recent literature on organizations often details the ways that hopes for change are frustrated by organizational behavior. The contrariness of organizations in confronting sensible efforts to change them fills our stories and our research. What most of those experiences tell us, however, is not that organizations are rigid and inflexible. Rather, they picture organizations as impressively imaginative. Organizations change in response to their environments, including their managements, but they rarely change in a way that fulfills the intentional plan of a single group of actors. Sometimes organizations ignore clear policies; sometimes they pursue them more forcefully than was intended. Sometimes they protect policymakers from the follies of foolish policies; sometimes they do not. Sometimes they stand still when we want them to move. Sometimes they move when we want them to stand still.

Organizational tendencies to frustrate arbitrary administrative intention, however, should not be confused with rigidity. Organizations change frequently. They adopt new products, new procedures, new objectives, new postures, new styles, new personnel, new beliefs. Even in a short perspective, the changes are often large. Some of them are sensible; some are not. Bureaucratic organizations are not always efficient. They can be exceptionally obtuse. Change is ubiquitous in organizations; and most change is the result neither of extraordinary organizational processes or forces, nor of uncommon imagination, persistence, or skill. It is a result of relatively stable processes that relate organizations to their environments. Organizational histories are written in dramatic form, and the drama reflects something important about the orchestration and mythology of organizational life, but substantial change results easily from the fact that many of the actions by an organization follow standard rules that are conditional on the environment. If economic, political, or social contexts change rapidly, organizations will change rapidly and routinely.

In such a spirit, recent efforts to understand organizations as routine adaptive systems emphasize six basic perspectives for interpreting organizational action:

1. Action can be seen as the application of standard operating procedures or other rules to appropriate situations. The terms of reference are duties, obligations, and roles. The model is a model of evolutionary selection.

2. Action can be seen as problem solving. The terms of reference are alternatives, consequences, and preferences. The model is one of intended rational choice.

3. Action can be seen as stemming from past learning. The terms of reference are actions and experiences. The model is one of trial and error learning.

4. Action can be seen as resulting from conflict among individuals or groups. The terms of reference are interests, activation, and resources. The model is one of politics—bargaining and power.

5. Action can be seen as spreading from one organization to another. The terms of reference are exposure and susceptibility. The model is one of diffusion.

6. Action can be seen as stemming from the mix of intentions and competencies found in organizational actors. The terms of reference are attitudes, abilities, and turnover. The model is one of regeneration.

These standard processes of organizational action are understandable and mostly reliable. Much of the time they are adaptive. They facilitate organizational survival. Sometimes organizations decline, and sometimes they die. Sometimes the changes that are produced seem little connected either to the intentions of organizational actors or to the manifest problems facing an organization. A propensity to change does not assure survival, and the processes of change are complicated by a variety of confusions and surprises. Solutions sometimes discover problems rather than the other way around. Organizations imitate each other, but innovations and organizations change in the process. Environments are responded to, but they are also affected. The efforts of organizations to adapt are entangled with the simultaneous efforts of individuals and larger systems of organizations. In these ways, the same processes that sustain the dull day-to-day activities of an organization produce unusual events.

These six perspectives portray an organization as coping with the environment routinely, actively adapting to it, avoiding it, seeking to change it, comprehend it, and contain it. An organization is neither unconditionally rigid nor unconditionally malleable; it is a relatively complicated collection of interests and beliefs acting in response to conflicting and ambiguous signals received from the environment and from the organization, acting in a manner that often makes sense and usually is intelligent. Organizations evolve, solve problems, learn, bargain, imitate, and regenerate. Under a variety of circumstances, the processes are conservative. That is, they tend to maintain stable relations, sustain existing rules, and reduce differences among similar organizations. But the fundamental logic is not one of stability in behavior; it is one of adaptation. The processes are stable; the resulting actions are not.

Organizations change routinely and continually, and the effectiveness of an organization in responding to its environment, as well as much of the effectiveness of management, is linked to the effectiveness of routine processes. As a result, much of the job of an administrator involves the mundane work of making a bureaucracy work. It is filled with activities quite distant from those implied in a conception of administration as heroic leadership. It profits from ordinary competence and a recognition of the ways in which organizations change by modest modifications of routines rather than by massive mucking around. Studies of managerial time and behavior consistently show an implicit managerial recognition of the importance of these activities. The daily activities of a manager are rather distant from grand conceptions of organizational leadership. Administrators spend time talking to people about minor things, making trivial decisions, holding meetings with unimportant agendas, and responding to the little irritants of organizational life. Memoirs of administrators confirm the picture of a rewarding life made busy by large numbers of inconsequential things.

These observations describe administrative life as uncomfortably distant from the precepts of administrative theory and from hopes for personal significance. They have led to efforts to change the ways managers behave. Numerous training programs attempt to teach managers to bring their personal time allocation closer to the ideal. They provide procedures designed to increase the time for decision making, planning, thinking, and the other things that appear more characteristic of theories of administration than of administrative jobs. These efforts may be mistakes. Making bureaucracy work involves effectiveness in executing a large number of little things. Making bureaucracies change involves attention to the minor routines by which things happen. Rules need to be understood in order to be interpreted or broken; simple breakdowns in the flow of supplies need to be minimized; telephones and letters need to be answered; accounts and records need to be maintained.

The importance of simple competence in the routines of organizational life is often overlooked when we sing the grand arias of management, but effective bureaucracies are rarely dramatic. They are administrative organizations that require elementary efficiency as a necessary condition for quality. Efficiency as a concept has been subject to considerable sensible criticism on the grounds that it is either meaningless or misleading if we treat it independent of the objectives being pursued. The point is well taken as a critique of the "cult of efficiency," but it is much too simple if we take it as an assertion that all, or even most, efforts in an administrative organization need a clear specification of global goals to be done well. An administrative organization combines large numbers of tasks into some kinds of meaningful combinations, but much of the effectiveness of the combination depends on the relatively automatic, local correction of local inefficiencies without continuous attention to the "big picture."

Much of what distinguishes a good bureaucracy from a bad one is how well it accomplishes the trivia of day-to-day relations with clients and day-to-day problems in maintaining and operating its technology. Accomplishing these trivia may involve considerable planning, complex coordination, and central direction, but it is more commonly linked to the effectiveness of large numbers of people doing minor things competently. As a result, it is probably true that the conspicuous differences around the world in the quality of bureaucratic performance are due primarily to variance in the competence of the ordinary clerk, bureaucrat, and lower manager, and to the effectiveness of routine procedures for dealing with problems at a local level. This appears to be true of armies, factories, postal services, hotels, and universities.

Organizations and Ambiguous Preferences

The classical administrator acts on the basis of knowledge about objectives. Goals are presumed to be clear — or it is presumed to be a responsibility of administration to make them clear. Administrative life often seems to be filled with ambiguous preferences and goals, and this becomes particularly conspicuous as one nears the top of an organization. Objectives are hard to specify in a way that provides precise guidance. That is not to say that they are completely unknown or that all parts are equally obscure. Administrative goals are often unclear; when we try to make them clear, they often seem unacceptable.

Goal ambiguity is particularly troubling to a conception of rational administrative action. As we normally conceive it, rational action involves two kinds of guesses: guesses about future consequences and guesses about future preferences for those consequences. We try to imagine the future outcomes that will result from our present actions, and we try to imagine how we will evaluate those outcomes when they occur. Neither guess is necessarily easy. Anticipating future consequences of present decisions is often subject to substantial error. Anticipating future preferences is often confusing. Theories of rational choice are primarily theories of these two guesses and how we deal with their complications. Theories of choice under uncertainty emphasize the complications of guessing future consequences. Theories of choice under ambiguity emphasize the complications of guessing future preferences.

In standard prescriptive theories of choice:

Preferences are relevant. Prescriptive theories of choice require that action be taken in terms of preferences, that decisions be consistent with objectives in the light of information about the probable consequences of alternatives for valued outcomes.

Preferences are stable. With few exceptions, prescriptive theories of choice require that tastes be stable. Current action is taken in terms of current preferences. The implicit assumption is that preferences will be unchanged when the outcomes of current actions are realized.

Preferences are consistent. Prescriptive theories of choice allow mutually inconsistent preferences only insofar as they can be made irrelevant by the absence of scarcity or by the specification of trade-offs.

Preferences are precise. Prescriptive theories of choice eliminate ambiguity about the extent to which a particular outcome will satisfy preferences, at least insofar as possible resolutions of ambiguity might affect the choice.

Preferences are exogenous. Prescriptive theories of choice presume that preferences, by whatever process they may be created, are not themselves affected by the choices they control.

Each of these theoretical features of proper preferences seems inconsistent with some observations of administrative behavior. Administrators often ignore their own, fully conscious preferences in making decisions. They follow rules, traditions, hunches, and the advice and actions of others. Preferences often change over time in such a way that predicting future preferences is often difficult. Preferences are often inconsistent. Managers and others in organizations are often aware of the extent to which some of their preferences conflict with others of their preferences, yet they do nothing to resolve the conflict. Many preferences are stated in forms that lack precision. It is difficult to make them reliably operational in evaluating possible outcomes. While preferences are used to choose among actions, it is often also true that actions and experiences with their consequences affect preferences. Preferences are determined partly endogenously.

It is possible, of course, that such portrayals of administrative behavior are perverse. They may be perverse because they systematically misrepresent the actual behavior of administrators, or they may be perverse because the administrators they describe are, insofar as the description applies, stupid. It is also possible that the description is accurate and the behavior is intelligent, that the ambiguous way administrators sometimes deal with preferences is, in fact, sensible. If such a thing can be imagined, then perhaps we treat preferences inadequately in administrative theory.

The disparity between administrative objectives, as they appear in administrative theory, and administrative objectives, as we observe them in organizational life, has led to efforts to "improve" the way administrators act. These characteristically emphasize the importance of goal clarity and of tying actions clearly to prior objectives. Deviations from the goal precision anticipated by decision theory have been treated as errors to be corrected. The strategy has led to important advances in management, and it has had its successes. But it also has had failures. Stories of disasters attributable to the introduction of decision technology are clichés of recent administrative experience.

As a result, students of administrative theory have been led to ask whether it is possible that goal ambiguity is not always a defect to be eliminated from administration, whether perhaps it may sometimes reflect a form of intelligence that is obscured by our models of rationality. For example, there are good reasons for moderating an enthusiasm for precise performance measures in organizations. The introduction of precision into the evaluation of performance involves a trade-off between the gains in outcomes attributable to closer articulation between action and measured objectives and the losses attributable to misrepresentation of goals, reduced motivation for development of goals, and concentration of effort on irrelevant ways of beating the index. Whether we are considering a performance evaluation scheme for managers or a testing procedure for students, there is likely to be a difference between the *maximum* clarity of goals and the *optimum* clarity.

The complications of performance measures are, however, only an illustration of the general issue of goal ambiguity in administrative action. In order to examine the more general issue, we probably need to ask why an intelligent administrator might deliberately choose — or sensibly learn — to have ambiguous goals. In fact, rationalizing ambiguity is neither difficult nor novel, but it depends on perspectives somewhat more familiar to human understanding as it is found in literature, philosophy, and ordinary experience than as we see it in our theories of administration and choice. For example:

1. Many administrators engage in activities designed to manage their own preferences. These activities make little sense from the point of view of a conception of action that assumes administrators know what they want and will want, or a conception that assumes wants are morally equivalent. But ordinary human actors sense that they might come to want something they should not, or that they might make unwise or inappropriate choices under the influence of fleeting, but powerful, desires if they do not control the development of preferences or buffer action from preferences.

2. Many administrators are both proponents for preferences and observers of the process by which preferences are developed and acted upon. As observers of the process by which their beliefs have been formed and evoked, they recognize the good sense in perceptual and moral modesty.

3. Many administrators maintain a lack of coherence both within and among personal desires, social demands, and moral codes. Though they seek some consistency, they appear to see inconsistency as a normal, and necessary, aspect of the development and clarification of values.

4. Many administrators are conscious of the importance of preferences as beliefs independent of their immediate action consequences. They accept a degree of personal and social wisdom in ordinary hypocrisy.

5. Many administrators recognize the political nature of rational argument more clearly than the theory of choice does. They are unwilling to gamble that God made clever people uniquely virtuous. They protect themselves from cleverness by obscuring the nature of their preferences; they exploit cleverness by asking others to construct reasons for actions they wish to take.

If these characteristics of ambiguous preferences processing by administrators make sense under rather general circumstances, our administrative theories based on ideas of clarity in objectives do not make as much sense as we sometimes attribute to them. Not only are they descriptively inadequate, they lead to attempts to clarify things that serve us better unclarified. Some of our standard dicta that managers should define and pursue clear objectives need to be qualified by a recognition that clarity is sometimes a mistake.

Organizations, Managerial Ambitions, and Managerial Incentives

In most conceptions of administration, administrators are assumed to be ambitious for promotion, position, and success. Managerial incentive schemes are efforts to link such personal ambitions of managers with the goals of the organization so that the behavior of self-interested managers contributes to achieving organizational objectives. As you move toward the top of an organization, however, some things happen that confuse ambition. Promotions are filters through which successful managers pass. Assuming that all promotions are based on similar attributes, each successive filter further refines the pool, reducing variation among managers. On attributes the organization considers important, vice-presidents are likely to be significantly more homogeneous than first-level managers. In addition, as we move up the organization, objectives usually become more conflicting and more ambiguous. Exactly what is expected of a manager sometimes seems obscure and changing, and it becomes harder to attribute specific outcomes to specific managerial actions.

Thus, as we move up the organization, evaluation procedures become less and less reliable, and the population of managers becomes more and more homogeneous. The joint result is that the noise level in evaluation approaches the variance in the pool of managers. At the limit, one vice-president cannot be reliably distinguished from another; quality distinctions among top executives, however consistent with their records, are less likely to be justified than distinctions made at a lower level. Toward the top of an organization, it is difficult to know unambiguously that a particular manager makes a difference. Notice that this is not the same as suggesting that management is unimportant. Management may be extremely important even though managers are indistinguishable. It is hard to tell the difference between two different light bulbs also; but if you take all light bulbs away, it is difficult to read in the dark. What is hard to demonstrate is the extent to which high-performing managers (or light bulbs that endure for an exceptionally long time) are something more than one extreme end of a probability distribution of results generated by essentially equivalent individuals.

Because it has such properties, a mobility system in an organization is a hierarchy of partial lotteries in which the expected values of the lotteries increase as we move up the organization, but control over their outcomes declines. Of course, if the objective is to recruit ambitious and talented people into management, it may not matter whether potential managers are able to control outcomes precisely, as long as the expected values of the games are higher than other opportunities. Ambitious people will seek such careers even if they believe — which they may not — that the outcomes are chance. What is less clear is exactly what kind of managerial behavior will be stimulated by management lotteries.

At the heart of a managerial promotion and reward scheme is normally some measure of managerial performance. Managers are seen as improving organizational outcomes by trying to improve their own measured performance, but every index of performance is an invitation to cleverness. Long before reaching the top, an intelligent manager learns

that some of the more effective ways of improving measured performance have little to do with improving product, service, or technology. A
system of rewards linked to precise measures is not an incentive to perform well; it is an incentive to obtain a good score. At the same time,
since managers are engaged in a lottery in which it is difficult to associate
specific outcomes with specific managerial behavior, it becomes important to be able to say, "I did the things a good manager should do." We
develop a language for describing good managers and bad ones, and
individual managers are able to learn social norms of management. Not
all managers behave in exactly the same way, but they all learn the language, expectations, and styles. They are socialized into managerial
roles.

These analyses of the consequences of managerial incentives at the top
seem inconsistent with the way we talk about leadership in organizations. In effect, we now have two contending theories of how things happen in organizations. The first is considerably influenced by stories of
great figures — Catherine the Great, Bismarck, Alfred Sloan — and elaborated by the drama of success and failure of individuals in bureaucratic
settings. It portrays administration in relatively heroic ways. Such portrayals lead us to attribute a large share of the variance in organizational
outcomes to special properties of specific individual managers. They are
comfortably reassuring in the major role they assign to administrative
leadership, but they seem to describe a world rather far from administrative experience or research.

The second theory (filled with metaphors of loose coupling, organized
anarchy, and garbage can decision processes) seems to describe administrative reality better, but it appears uncomfortably pessimistic about the
significance of administrators. Indeed, it seems potentially pernicious
even if correct. Consider two general types of errors a manager might
make in assessing the importance of intentional actions in controlling organizational outcomes. A manager might come to believe in considerable
personal control over outcomes when, in fact, that control does not exist. A "false positive" error. Such a belief would lead to (futile) attempts
to control events, but it would not otherwise affect results. Alternatively, a manager might come to believe that significant personal control is
not possible when, in fact, it is. A "false negative" error. Such a belief
would lead to self-confirming withdrawal from efforts to be effective.
Either type of error is possible, but the social costs of the first seem small,
relative to the second. Given a choice, we would generally prefer to err
on the side of making false positive errors in assessing human significance, rather than false negative errors.

Perhaps fortunately, organizational life assures a managerial bias
toward belief in managerial importance. Top managers are not random

managers; they are successful managers. They rise to the top on the basis of a series of successful experiences. We know that individuals often find it easy to believe that successes in their lives are attributable to their talents and choices, while failures are more due to bad luck or malevolence. Promotion to the top on the basis of successes at lower levels results in top-level executives believing in the possibility of substantial intentional control over organizational events. Even though their experiences might have led managers to such beliefs erroneously, managerial experience is likely to be subjectively very persuasive. In effect, the system of managerial mobility is designed to make managers much more resistant to false beliefs in impotence than to false beliefs in control. Administrative experience, as well as managerial self-esteem, will usually give managers a greater sense of personal importance and uniqueness than the second theory suggests.

In fact, there is a third theory, and it is probably closer to the truth than either of the others. In this third view, managers *do* affect the ways in which organizations function. But as a result of the process by which managers are selected, motivated, and trained, variations in managers do not reliably produce variations in organizational outcomes. In such a conception, administrators are vital as a class but not as individuals. Administration *is* important, and the many things that administrators do are essential to keeping the organization functioning; but if those vital things are only done when there is an unusually gifted individual at the top, the organization will not thrive. What makes an organization function well is the density of administrative competence, the kind of selection procedures that make all vice-presidents look alike from the point of view of their probable success, and the motivation that leads managers to push themselves to the limit.

Earlier, I used the analogy of a light bulb. I think it is a good analogy. If the manufacture of light bulbs is so unreliable that only a few actually work, you will not be able to do much reading. On the other hand, if light bulbs are reliable, you can read whenever you want to, but you won't much care which light bulb you use. One problem with some conventional administrative thought is that it encourages us to glorify an organization that finds the unique working light bulb in a large shipment of defective bulbs, rather than an organization that persistently produces a supply of nearly indistinguishable good bulbs. It is the latter organization that functions better.

Organizations, Rituals, and Symbols

Administrators and administrative decisions allocate scarce resources and are thereby of considerable social and individual importance, but decisions in organizations and the administration of them are important beyond their outcomes. They are also arenas for exercising social values, for displaying authority and position, and for exhibiting proper behavior and attitudes with respect to a central ideological construct of modern Western civilization — the concept of intelligent choice. Bureaucratic organizations are built on ideas of rationality, and rationality is built on ideas about the way decisions should be made. Indeed, it would be hard to find any institution in modern society more prototypically committed to systematic, rational action than a formal organization.

Thus, administrative action in an organization is a performance in which administrators try to behave in a normatively praiseworthy way. Making intelligent decisions is important, but the verification of intelligence in decision-making is often difficult. As a result, it often becomes heavily procedural. For example, in the usual scenario for administrative performance, the gathering of information is not simply a basis for action; it is a representation of competence and a reaffirmation of personal virtue. Command of information and information sources enhances perceived competence and inspires confidence. The belief that more information characterizes better decisions and defensible decision processes engenders a conspicuous consumption of information. Information is flaunted but not used, collected but not considered.

Ideas about proper administrative behavior diffuse through a population of organizations and change over time. What makes a particular procedure appropriate for one manager is that it is being used in other successful organizations by other successful managers. What makes an administrative innovation new and promising is that it has been adopted by other organizations that are viewed as being intelligently innovative. Managerial procedures spread from successful organizations to unsuccessful ones, as the latter try to present themselves as equivalent to the former; the signal a particular procedure provides is gradually degraded by its adoption by organizations that are not "well managed" or "progressive," thus stimulating the invention of new procedures.

This competition among managers and organizations for legitimacy and standing is endless. As managers attempt to establish and maintain reputations through the symbols of good management, social values are sustained and elaborated. For symbols of administrative competence are, of course, symbols simultaneously of social efficacy. Belief in the appropriateness of administrative actions, the process by which they are taken, and the roles played by the various actors involved is a key part of a social structure. It is not only important to decision-makers that they be viewed as legitimate; it is also useful to society that leaders be imagined to control organizational outcomes and to act in a way that can be reconciled with a sense of human control over human destiny.

Ritual acknowledgement of managerial importance and appropriateness is part of a social ceremony by which social life is made meaningful and acceptable under conditions that would otherwise be problematic. For example, managerial capabilities for controlling events are likely to be more immediately obvious to managers than to others in the organization. Since most of the managers with whom managers must deal are themselves successful managers, the problem is somewhat concealed from daily managerial experience. Many of the people whom we see in administration, particularly in a growing organization, are people who see themselves as successful; but there are others, less conspicuous, who do not derive the same prejudices from their own experience. So, we construct various myths of management. The same mobility process that encourages top managers in a belief in their own control over events tends to teach some others that managerial successes and the events associated with them are more due to luck or corruption.

The stories, myths, and rituals of management are not merely ways some people fool other people or a waste of time. They are fundamental to our lives. We embrace the mythologies and symbols of life and could not otherwise easily endure. Executive behavior and management procedures contribute to myths about management that become the reality of managerial life and reinforce a belief in a human destiny subject to intentional human control. They may not be essential to such a belief—it is reinforced in many subtle ways throughout society—but executive rituals and executive life are parts of that large mosaic of mutually supporting myths by which an instrumental society brings hope and frustration to individual lives. Since managerial rituals are important to our faith, and our faith is important to the functioning of organizations as well as to the broader social and political order, these symbolic activities of administration are central to its success.

Most administrators seem ambivalent about symbol management. On the one hand, they recognize that they spend considerable time trying to sustain beliefs in the intelligence, coherence, importance, and uniqueness of their organizations (and themselves). At the same time, however, they seem to view the activity as either somewhat illegitimate or as an imposition on more important things—such as decision-making, directing, or coordinating. They treat the rituals of administration as necessary, but they talk about them as a waste of time.

Partly, of course, the ambivalence is itself socially dictated. In a society that emphasizes instrumentality as much as Western society does, leaders would be less acceptable if they were to acknowledge the ritual activities of their jobs as central. One of their key symbolic responsibilities is to maintain an ideology that denies the legitimacy of symbol maintenance. Thus, they tend to do it but to deny they do it, or to bemoan the fact that they must do it. It is a careful dance along a narrow beam, and there is the possibility of much grace in it. But the elegance of the dance probably depends on a fine modulation between talk and action, as well as some administrative consciousness of the meaning of the dance. In order to achieve that consciousness, we probably need to recognize the ambivalence and to encourage administrators to see how the activities in which they participate are an essential part of a larger social ritual by which they, as well as others in society, reaffirm purpose and order in a potentially disorderly world.

Many managers, of course, recognize the many elements of storytelling by which they present themselves. Successful managers are usually adept at managing their own reputations. They know how to manage symbols for that purpose. The self-serving character of managerial symbol manipulation is easily seen as unattractive, and few would want to legitimize the self-aggrandizement and self-delusion that are its corollaries. Nor would many observers welcome an unconditional enthusiasm for using symbols to sustain the existing social order against all counterclaims. Critics of the establishment cannot be expected to embrace symbolic performances that have as their main consequence the reinforcement of an unacceptable social system.

These reasonable concerns about symbol manipulation are reminders of its administrative importance. Life is not just choice. It is also poetry. We live by the interpretations we make, becoming better or worse through the meanings we impute to events and institutions. Our lives change when our beliefs change. Administrators manage the way the sentiments, expectations, commitments, and faiths of individuals concerned with the organization fit into a structure of social beliefs about organizational life. Administrative theory probably underestimates the significance of this belief structure for effective organizations. As a result, it probably underestimates the extent to which the management of symbols is a part of effective administration. If we want to identify one single way in which administrators can affect organizations, it is through their effect on the world views that surround organizational life; those effects are managed through attention to the ritual and symbolic characteristics of organizations and their administration. Whether we wish to sustain the system or change it, management is a way of making a symbolic statement.

Round Theories and Flat Experience

In general, these observations are not particularly surprising. In most ways, they are familiar to our experience. They are less familiar, however, to the way we talk about administration. I have tried to list four emphases of administrative theory that seem to be relatively distant from our observations and experience. First, the theoretical emphasis on change as produced by heroic leader action and the consequent emphasis on effectiveness (goal-oriented action) rather than efficiency (goal-free actions), on *leadership* rather than *management.* The theoretical rhetoric of change seems antithetical to routine, but I have argued that effective systems of routine behavior are the primary bases of organizational adaptation to an environment.

Second, the theoretical emphasis on problem-solving of a classical sort in which alternatives are assessed in terms of their consequences for prior goals that are stable, precise, and exogenous. I have argued that many situations in administration involve goals that are (and ought to be) ambiguous.

Third, the theoretical emphasis on explaining variations in organizational outcomes is due to variations in top leadership skills and commitment. I have argued that when an organizational system is working well, variations in outcomes will be due largely to variables unrelated to variations in attributes of top leaders. Where top leadership affects variation in outcomes, the system is probably not functioning well.

Fourth, the theoretical emphasis on administrative action as instrumental, as being justified by the way it produces substantive consequences for important outcomes. I have argued that much of administration is symbolic, a way of interpreting organizational life in a way that allows individuals in organizations to fit their experience to their visions of human existence. Administrative processes are sacred rituals at least as much as they are instrumental acts.

If informed opinion says the earth is round but we experience it as flat, we are in danger of having to choose between our senses and our intellect. If we can, we want to discover behavior that is sensible but at the same time confirms our conventional probity — in the face of their apparent inconsistency. The usual procedure, of course, is to talk about a round world and use a flat map. In the case of the map and the earth, we are confident enough of the round theory to be willing to make a fairly precise rationalization of the map. In other cases, the issues are in greater doubt. If you experience planning as something you rarely do yet all the people you admire report that it is important, you might plausibly come to echo their comments without a clear understanding of why you talk about planning so much yet do it so little.

Like a person contemplating a naked emperor amidst courtiers exclaiming over the royal clothing, an administrator must simultaneously act intelligently and sustain a reputation for intelligence. Since theories of administration — and the talk that they generate — are part of the basis for reputation, their distance from ordinary administrative experience poses a problem. For most administrators, the difficulties are not likely to be seen as stemming from failures in administrative theory. What I have called "administrative theory" is not some set of esoteric axioms propagated by a few high priests of academe; rather, it is an elaboration of very general cultural beliefs about organizations, change, leadership, and administration. Most reasonable people accept them with as much confidence as they accept the notion that the earth is round, even while at the same time finding them inconsistent with important parts of organizational life.

The argument is not that administrative theory and administrative life should coincide. In general, they should not. The criterion for good normative theory is not its descriptive accuracy. It is not necessary that the theory be correct, consistent, or even meaningful in conventional terms. It is not necessary that the theory resolve all the difficult trade-offs that impinge on administrative life. In most human domains, we maintain the maxims of a good life by violating them judiciously without claims of virtue; we pursue goals we would not want to achieve in hopes thereby of becoming better than we are. For our theories of administration to be useful in administrative life, we require that *pursuing* (without necessarily fulfilling) the precepts of the theory improves organizations and administration. In such a spirit, administrators may struggle to follow the precepts of administrative thought, even though they are impossible, inconsistent, or unwise. Intelligent administrators might well do such a thing in full consciousness, not in hopes of fulfilling the precepts — for they would not want to do that — but in hopes of acting in a better way than they would without the struggle.

Much of standard administrative theory, including parts that have long been criticized by behavioral students of organizations, seems to me to meet such criteria. There are numerous elementary — but vital — rules of thumb that help improve the management of an organization when applied with intelligence, even though they seem either trivial or contradictory. For example, the dictum that managers should minimize the span of control *and* minimize the number of levels of the organization is obviously nonsensical as a statement of an optimization problem. It is, however, not foolish as a statement of contradictory complications in organizing. Many of the things that ancient texts on administration say seem to me similarly sensible — but not all of them. The fact that administrative theory, like a moral code, does not have to be prima facie sensible in order to be useful should not lead us to assume immediately that incomplete, inconsistent, or incorrect maxims are *necessarily* helpful.

Sometimes our assumptions are wrong, and the worlds we experience as flat actually are, if not entirely flat, not entirely round either. Administrators who feel that their experiences with the way organizations change, with ambiguity in objectives and experience, with management incentives and careers, and with symbolic action are consistent with the kinds of reseach observations I have noted may well want to question conventional administrative thought and welcome alternative formulations. If these research observations capture a part of organizational truth, some of the apparently strange things that an administrator does are probably more sensible than administrative theory recognizes, and the struggle to fulfill the expectations of administrative virtue may result in actions that are less intelligent than they would have been in the absence of administrative dogma. Sometimes our theories are misleading, and the way we talk confuses the way we act.

I) Orgs work on 2 levels
  A) action
  b) Interpretation
II) 4 Assumptions of goal L
  1) Orgs resist change w/o strong L
  2) Mangers are heterogeneous
  3) Clear obj
  4)

II) Org + change
    &orgs change selves to deal w/ envir.

III) Org + Ambiguous Preferences
I) Org, Mang Ambitions + Mang Incentives
II) Org, Returns + Symb

CHAPTER 3

Leadership as Reflection-in-Action

Donald A. Schön

Leadership and management are not synonymous terms. One can be a leader without being a manager. One can, for example, fulfill many of the symbolic, inspirational, educational and normative functions of a leader and thus represent what an organization stands for without carrying any of the formal burdens of management. Conversely, one can manage without leading. An individual can monitor and control organizational activities, make decisions, and allocate resources without fulfilling the symbolic, normative, inspirational, or educational functions of leadership. Whether this is perceived as a problem or not depends on features of the particular organizational context in question. There is no inherent reason why the separation of management and leadership functions need be problematic. Nevertheless, we generally expect managers to lead, and criticize them if they fail to do so. Hence, for the purposes of this essay, I shall treat management and leadership as though they were one.

The Split in the Field of Management

The field of management has long been marked by a conflict between two competing views of professional knowledge. In the first view, the manager is a technician whose practice consists in applying to the everyday problems of the organization the principles and methods derived from management science. In the second, the manager is a craftsman, a practitioner of an art of managing that cannot be reduced to explicit rules and theories. The first view dates from the early decades of the twentieth century when the idea of professional management first came into good currency. The second has an even longer history, management having been understood as an art, a matter of skill and wisdom, long before it began to be understood as a body of techniques. But the first view has gained steadily in power.

The idea of management science and the complementary idea of the manager as a technician have been carried by a social movement which has spread out from its center in the United States to encompass the whole of the industrialized world. The origins of this movement are difficult to identify, but a critically important milestone in its development was the work of Frederick Taylor (1911) who conceived of management as a form of human engineering based on a science of work. While Taylor may not have invented these ideas, he was certainly the first to embody them in a practice of industrial management and consultation, and he popularized them in a way that has had enormous influence in industry, in business, and in the administration of public agencies.

Taylor treated work as a man-machine process which could be separated into measurable units of activity. Every industrial process, from the shoveling of coal to the processing of steel, could be subjected to experimental analysis. The design of tools, the bodily movements of the worker, and the sequencing of production steps could be combined in an optimum configuration, a "one best way." Taylor saw the industrial manager as a designer of work, a controller and monitor of performance, and a distributor of rewards and punishments carefully selected and applied so as to yield optimally efficient production. Above all, he saw the manager as an on-line experimenter, a scientist in action, whose practice would consist of the trial and measurement of designs and methods aimed at the discovery and implementation of the one best way.

Taylor's views were by no means unique. Thorsten Veblen (1904), to take one extraordinary example, also perceived that industry had taken on the characteristics of an organizational machine within which managers of the business enterprise must be increasingly concerned with standards, measures of performance, and the articulation of interlocking activities. But it was Taylor who embodied these ideas in practice, and it was Taylor's version of the practice of industrial engineering, efficiency expertise, and time-and-motion study, which has evolved into the management science of the present day.

World War II gave an enormous impetus to the management science movement, first because of the general rise in prestige of science and technology and, second, because of the birth of operations research and systems theory. These disciplines, which grew out of the use of applied mathematics to solve problems of submarine search and bomb tracking, were later exported to industry, commerce, and government. In the wake of World War II, management science grew to maturity. Teachers and researchers in the new schools of management, in partnership with managers in public and private sectors, have engendered a plethora of new techniques. There is no field of management which has been immune to the incursions of management science. What was once true only of industrial production has now become true of sales, personnel selection and training, budgeting and financial control, marketing, business policy, and strategic planning. Technical panaceas have appeared on the scene with clock-like regularity, old ones making way for new. Value analysis, management by objectives, planning programming and budgeting, and zero-based budgeting are only a few of the better-known examples. Even the human relations movement, which had originated as a reaction against Taylorism, has tended increasingly to present itself as a body of techniques.

Yet in spite of the increasingly powerful status of management science and technique, managers have remained persistently aware of important areas of practice which fall outside the bounds of technical rationality. This awareness has taken two forms.

Managers have become increasingly sensitive to the phenomena of uncertainty, change, and uniqueness. In the last twenty years, "decision under uncertainty" has become a term of art. It has become commonplace for managers to speak of the "turbulent" environments in which problems do not lend themselves to the techniques of benefit-cost analysis or to probabilistic reasoning. At least at the level of espoused theory, managers have become used to the instability of patterns of competition, economic context, consumer interests, sources of raw materials, attitudes of the labor force, and regulatory climate. And managers have become acutely aware that they are often confronted with unique situations to which they must respond under conditions of stress and limited time which leave no room for extended calculation or analysis. Here, they tend to speak not of technique but of "intuition."

Quite apart from these exceptions to the day-to-day routine of management practice, managers have remained aware of a dimension of ordinary professional work, crucially important to effective performance, which cannot be reduced to technique. Indeed, they are sometimes aware that even management technique rests on a foundation of nonrational, intuitive artistry. That such knowing exists and is essential not only to extraordinary performance but to the skillful activities of everyday life, many authors of very different backgrounds and interests have attested.

In 1938, Chester Barnard appended to his *The Functions of the Executive* an essay on "Mind in Everyday Affairs." Here he deals with what he calls "non-logical processes," ". . . those not capable of being expressed in words or as reasoning, which are only made known by a judgement, decision or action. This may be because the processes are unconscious, or because they are so rapid, often approaching the instantaneous, that they could not be analyzed by the person within whose brain they take place" (p. 302). It is Barnard's purpose to "overcome the bias in favor of the thinking processes, and to develop an appreciation of the non-logical processes." His examples shift from golf, to algebra, to the reading of a balance sheet.

Take first judgment of distance in golf or for ball throwing. It is a matter of observation that some persons are fast and accurate judges of distance, that frequently their capacity for such judgment increases with practice, and that sometimes the measurement of distance by conscious comparison destroys the capacity for quick judgment. . . .

A second type of case might be the ability of a high school boy to solve a quadratic equation. Involved in this is a large part of the arithmetic and algebra learned through years from the time when his mother taught him to count, an intellectual process beyond many primitive people, to his last lesson in algebra. The discrimination and selection required to effect the solution would indicate the use or mental control of most of his acquired knowledge. Unless it could be marshaled and applied quickly, the problem could hardly be solved. Yet not only will the boy be unaware of what his brain actually does, but he will be unable to recall many of the broad steps that actually must have been taken. He could not write the text books which are registered in his mind.

There are many accountants and businessmen who can ordinarily take a comparative balance sheet of considerable complexity and within minutes or even seconds get a significant set of facts from it. These facts do not leap from the paper and strike the eye. They lie between the figures in the part filled by the mind out of years of experience and technical knowledge. That is what makes out of a set of figures something to which then reason can usefully be applied [pp. 305–6].

Chris Alexander, in his *Notes toward a Synthesis of Form* (1964), considers the knowing involved in processes of design and explores the question of the good or bad "fit" of a form to its context. He believes that we are often able to recognize "bad fit" and to correct it, usually without being able to describe the rules by which we find a fit bad or by which we recognize the corrected form to be good. In "unselfconscious cultures," traditional artifacts are made through successive detections and corrections of bad fit until the resulting forms are good. For example,

the Slovakian peasants used to be famous for the shawls they made. These shawls were wonderfully colored and patterned, woven of yarns which had been dipped in homemade dyes. Early in the twentieth century aniline dyes were made available to them. And at once the glory of the shawls was spoiled; they were now no longer delicate and subtle, but crude. This change cannot have come about because the new dyes were somehow inferior. They were as brilliant, and the variety of colors was much greater than before. Yet somehow the new shawls turned out vulgar and uninteresting.

Now if, as it is so pleasant to suppose, the shawlmakers had had some innate artistry, had been so gifted that they were simply "able" to make beautiful shawls, it would be almost impossible to explain their later clumsiness. But if we look at the situation differently, it is very easy to explain. The shawlmakers were simply able, as many of us are, to recognize bad shawls, and their own mistakes.

Over the generations . . . whenever a bad one was made, it was recognized as such, and therefore not repeated. And though nothing is to say that the change made would be for the better, it would still be a change. When the results of such changes were still bad, further changes would be made. The changes would go on until the shawls were good [pp. 53–54].

Geoffrey Vickers (1978) has extended Alexander's notion of the "bad fit" which we can recognize but not describe and has attributed this capacity to the "tacit norms" which underlie recognition, appreciation, and judgment in all domains of professional practice and everyday life.

Artists to-day are distinguished even from designers in that their work claims to be judged by purely "aesthetic" criteria, rather than by those criteria of utility which dominate our culture. Are they not a class apart?

I think not, and I choose a word which suggests this kind of art because the fine arts exhibit so clearly the problems which attach to judgments based on a sense of form which cannot be fully articulated. I shall argue that artists, so far from being alone in this, exhibit most clearly an oddity which is present in all such judgments. We can recognize and describe deviations from a norm very much more clearly than we can describe the norm itself [1978].

And Michael Polanyi, in his *The Tacit Dimension,* (1967) draws examples of tacit knowing from the recognition of faces and from the use of tools:

We know a person's face and can recognize it among a thousand, indeed among a million. Yet we usually cannot tell how we recognize a face we know. . . . We recognize the moods of the human face, without being able to tell, except quite vaguely, by what signs we know it . . . [p. 4].

Anyone who uses a probe for the first time will feel its impact against his fingers and palm. But as we learn to use a probe, or to use a stick for feeling our way, our awareness of its impact on our hand is transformed into a sense of its point touching the objects we are exploring. . . . This is so also when we use a tool. We are attending to the meaning of its impact on our hands in terms of its effect on the things to which we are applying it [p. 12].

Significantly, in this second example, Polanyi alludes to the process by which perceptions, once accessible to us, become tacit as we become skillful.

More recently a Canadian professor of management, Henry Mintzberg (1973) has caused a considerable stir with studies of the actual behavior of top managers that reveal a virtual absence of the methods that managers are "supposed to" use. In some of the most prestigious schools of management, where the curriculum depends on cases drawn from the actual experience of business firms, there is a widely held belief that managers learn to be effective not primarily through the study of theory and technique but through long and varied practice in the analysis of business problems, which builds up a generic, essentially unanalyzable capacity for problem-solving.

It is no exaggeration, then, to say that the field of management is split into two camps, each of which holds a different view of the nature of professional knowledge. At the same time that management science and technique have grown increasingly in power and prestige, there has been a persistent and growing awareness of the importance of an art of managing which reveals itself in both crucially important situations of uncertainty, instability, and uniqueness, and in those dimensions of everyday practice which depend upon the spontaneous exercise of intuitive artistry. One sign of this split is that in some schools of management, representatives of the two tendencies — the professors of management science and the practitioners of case-method — no longer speak to one another. The representatives of each school of thought go about their business as though the other school of thought did not exist.

But a split of this kind, which is barely tolerable in a professional school, creates for thoughtful students and practitioners a particularly painful variant of the dilemma of "rigor or relevance." For if rigorous management means the application of management science and technique, then "rigorous managers" must be selectively inattentive to the art which they bring to much of their day-to-day practice, and they must avoid situations — often the most important in organizational life — where they would find themselves confronted with uncertainty, instability, or uniqueness.

But if the art of managing can be described, at least in part, and can be shown to be rigorous in a way peculiar to itself, then the dilemma of rigor or relevance need not be so painful. Indeed, it may be possible to bring the art of managing into dialogue with management science.

The Art of Managing

In management as in other fields, "art" has a twofold meaning. It may mean intuitive judgment and skill, the feeling for phenomena and for action that I have called knowing-in-practice. But it may also designate a manager's reflection, in a context of action, on phenomena which are perceived as incongruent with intuitive understandings.

Managers do reflect-in-action. Sometimes, when reflection is triggered by uncertainty, the manager says, in effect, "This is puzzling; how can I understand it?" Sometimes, when a sense of opportunity provokes reflection, the manager asks, "What can I make of this?" Sometimes, when managers are surprised by the success of their own intuitive knowing, they ask themselves, "What have I really been doing?"

Whatever the triggering condition, a manager's reflection-in action is fundamentally similar to reflection-in-action in other professional fields. It consists of on-the-spot surfacing, criticizing, restructuring, and testing of intuitive understandings of experienced phenomena; often, it takes the form of a reflective conversation with the situation. A manager's reflection-in-action also has special features of its own. A manager's professional life is wholly concerned with an organization which is both the stage for his or her activity and the object of his or her inquiry. Hence, the phenomena on which a manager reflects-in-action are the phenomena of organizational life. Organizations, furthermore, are repositories of cumulatively built-up knowledge: principles and maxims of practice, images of mission and identity, facts about the task environment, techniques of operation, and stories of past experience which serve as exemplars for future action. When a manager reflects-in-action, he or she draws on this stock of organizational knowledge, adapting it to some present instance. The manager also functions as an agent of organizational learning, extending or restructuring, in the present inquiry, the stock of knowledge which will be available for future inquiry.

Finally, managers live in an organizational system which may promote or inhibit reflection-in-action. Organizational structures are more or less adaptable to new findings, more or less resistant to new tasks. The behavioral world of the organization, the characteristic pattern of interpersonal relations, is more or less open to reciprocal reflection-in-action — to the surfacing of negative information, the working out of conflicting views, and the public airing of organizational dilemmas. Insofar as organizational structure and behavioral world condition organizational inquiry, they make up what I will call the "learning system" of the organization. The scope and direction of a manager's reflection-in-action are strongly influenced, and may be severely limited, by the learning system of the organization in which he or she practices.

These distinctively organizational aspects of a manager's reflection-in-action must enter into any good description of the art of managing. In the examples that follow, I shall sample a range of organizational phenomena with which reflective managers concern themselves — the problem of interpreting the external environment's response to organizational action, the diagnosis of signs of trouble within an organization, the process by which an organization learns from its experience, and the effects of an organizational learning system on the way in which organizational problems are set and solved. I shall limit myself primarily to the experience of business firms, not because business managers are more reflective than others but because they are the source of my freshest examples, and I shall suggest briefly how management in the field of higher education presents phenomena similar to those encountered in the business context. In the business context, the kinds of organizational phenomena noted above may be illustrated by the behavior of a market, the problems of a production plant, the acquisition of knowledge about product development, and the learning system of a product development organization.

In all of these examples, I shall describe processes that managers often undertake but on which they seldom reflect. Managers do reflect-in-action but they seldom reflect on their reflection-in-action. Hence, this crucially important dimension of their art tends to remain private and inaccessible to others. Moreover, because awareness of one's intuitive thinking usually grows out of practice articulating it to others, managers often have little access to their own reflection-in-action. The resulting mysteriousness of the art of managing has several harmful consequences. It tends to perpetuate the split in the field of management, creating a misleading impression that practitioners must choose between practice based on management science and an essentially mysterious artistry. It also prevents the manager from helping others in the organization to learn to do what *the manager* can do. Since managers cannot describe their own reflection-in-action, they cannot teach others to do it. If others acquire the capacity for it, they do so by contagion. Yet one of a manager's most important functions is the education of his or her subordinates.

For all of these reasons, it seems to me critically important to begin to describe how managers do reflect-in-action and how their reflection-in-action is limited.

Interpreting Market Phenomena

A business firm is continually in interaction with its markets, and markets are often in a state of flux — some of which is induced by the action of the business firm itself. In the contemporary business setting, inquiry into market phenomena has become a specialized function in its own right. Market researchers and strategists have developed principles of marketing, models of market behavior, and techniques of market exploration and analysis. Nevertheless, much of what managers encounter in the market-place resists the application of ready-made theories and procedures.

Market research cannot say very much about consumer response to a radically new product. People cannot readily answer questions about their interest in something of which they have neither direct nor indirect experience. At best, if they are helped to carry out the imaginative feat of supposing themselves in possession of a nonexistent product, they may speculate on their future responses to it. But speculation of this sort is usually a very poor predictor of their behavior toward an actual product, more or less like the one described, which will appear one day, in a particular package and at a particular price, on supermarket shelves. If prototypes of the new product are produced (and it takes money to develop and produce them), then consumer panels may provide information from which managers can make inferences about actual market behavior. But the gap between panel response and market response is significant. Only with the introduction of large-scale market tests do manufacturers begin to get reliable information about market behavior, and regional market tests can also produce misleading results.

At each stage of the development of a radically new product, managers must make investment decisions in the absence of adequate information or rules for rational decision. Each such judgment is a unique case, and the market tests, which may reduce uncertainty, come only at the price of further investment.

The full-scale marketing of a product is also a test of sorts, and managers often find themselves confronted with surprising data that demand interpretation. Shortly after World War II, to take one rather celebrated example, the 3M corporation put on the market a clear, cellulose acetate tape coated on one side with pressure-sensitive adhesive, which they called "Scotch Tape." They had intended it for use as a book-mending material, a way of preserving things that would otherwise have to be thrown away, hence the name "Scotch." But in consumers' hands, the product came to be used in many different ways, most of which had nothing to do with mending books. It was used to wrap packages, to fasten pictures to the wall, to make labels, to decorate surfaces, even to curl hair. 3M's managers did not regard these surprising uses as a failure of their initial marketing plan, nor did they merely accept them as a happy accident. They *noticed* them and tried to make sense of them as a set of messages about potential markets. The company began to market types of Scotch Tape specially designed for use in such applications as packaging, decorating, and hair-curling.

3M's marketing managers treated their product as a projective test for consumers. They reflected on unanticipated signals from the marketplace, interpreted them, and then tested their interpretations by adapting the product to the uses that consumers had already discovered. But their tests were also moves aimed at strengthening market position and probes which might yield additional surprises. Their marketing process was a reflective conversation with consumers.

Interpreting Organizational Troubles

When a manager first gets signals that something is going wrong in the organization, he or she usually has no clear, consensual account of the trouble. Various members of the organization, who occupy different positions and have different interests, tell different and often conflicting stories. If the manager is to take action, he or she must make some sense of the organizational *Rashomon;** but by inquiring into the situation, the manager also influences it. Hence, any manager faces a twofold problem: how to find out what (if anything) is wrong, and how to do so in a way that enhances rather than reduces his or her ability to fix what is wrong.

Consider a case drawn from the recent experience of a manufacturer of scientific instruments.

The company, based in a developing country, was founded some fifteen years ago by a nuclear physicist who, with a small group of former students and colleagues, built a very narrow product line into a $100 million business. The company's main offices are in its home country, but it has sales and service facilities in thirteen foreign countries. It has captured about 15 percent of the market in its field.

The founder, now chairman of the board, attributes his success to two main principles: stay in close touch with the market and deliver fast responses to changes in the field.

From these two principles, many organizational consequences have been made to follow. In order to get product improvements to the market quickly, the company often puts instruments in the field before all development problems have been resolved. They depend on highly skilled technical service representatives to complete the development task. In order to achieve fast response to market demand, customers' orders are frequently changed. About 30 percent of all manufacturing orders are subject to engineering changes. As a result, manufacturing has become a highly sophisticated job-shop where speed and flexibility take precedence over efficiency, which depends on long production runs.

The company has deliberately refrained from establishing a fixed organizational structure. There are no organization charts. Roles are frequently overlapping and informal group problem-solving is the norm.

---

*A 1950 Japanese film which tells the story of a murder and rape from the point of view of four different people. The audience is left to decide which, if any, of the story versions approximates the truth. —Ed.

As the founder says, "This is no place for people who can't live with uncertainty."

Role-flexibility is carried to an extreme. The present vice-president for finance is a former nuclear physicist who has learned finance as he might have learned a new branch of physics, and every member of the top-management team has filled virtually every major corporate function. The president of the company, G, who began with the company fifteen years ago, has worked in budgeting, finance, sales, and manufacturing. He is still regarded as "the best engineer in the company." Along with the founder and the vice-president for finance, he regards work as "fun," likes to put "impossible" demands on himself, and expects others to do likewise. G is used to reaching down into the company to deal with whatever crisis presents itself. He has done this three or four times. Within the last year, for example, he spent three months at a computer console in order to resolve a critical software problem that threatened to stall a major new development.

The crisis presently facing G concerns a new production plant established a year ago to make metal parts for instruments manufactured in the two main production facilities. It is located in a development zone of the country, where it is eligible for generous government subsidies, although it lacks access to labor force and services which would have been available in one of the larger cities. The new manager of the plant, M, had been hired away from a large electronics firm. M has been in his position for a year, and during that time there have been increasingly troublesome production delays. Recently, one of the managers of the two main instrument plants brought the problem to G, who discussed it with the manager of the other instrument plant, the vice-president for manufacturing, and the manager of the new plant, M.

The manager of the first plant describes the situation as follows:

> I want the parts on time, and M wants efficiency! And I want 100 different kinds of parts. Opening the new plant caused a lot of crunches in our system. We worked night and day all last year to solve this problem. For a while, things were OK. Then, when the head of the metals section left because he couldn't get along with M, we had a big decline. M tried to manage the metals section by remote control. He should get in there and manage metals for himself. Or perhaps we should take the operation and bring it back to central, in a metals shop of our own. M lacks the capacity to manage the problem. I see no light at the end of the tunnel.

Manager of the second plant:

> M's is a new plant built around new people. There are communications problems, because people there don't adapt to flexible de-

mands. *M* is pressed between demands for efficiency and for fast response, and he's not solving the problem. They need new staff functions. They have problems with orders because they don't know what's going on. They must see their *raison d'être* as giving service to us, but they won't accept that definition. They are not equal. They feel second class.

M, manager of the new plant:

There's informal problem-solving at central, but between here and central, it can't work. You have to have more rules, even with less flexibility, because as you grow, without new rules, you have a mess. *G* prefers that we use 50 percent of our capacity and hold people on stand-by to respond to orders when they come in, but that teaches people to be inefficient. And so I sell to outsiders, but I have to give preference to the company. It's an axiom that you should produce efficiently, but I have to be inefficient in order to get the parts in on time. Management attention is split.

Vice-president for manufacturing:

Right now, the new plant is *G*'s crisis. First, we must clean up the channels of communication, providing better, more sophisticated management tools. And we must resolve the conflict of priorities. Most of the problems grow out of the frequent engineering changes which are vital to the company. Two-thirds of the problem is to get the right man in the right place. One of our main problems is a shortage of upper-middle management.

The first plant manager, who brought the problem to *G*, says,

I know *G* is working on the problem, because he hasn't erased all the figures we put on the blackboard!

And he is right; *G* is working on the problem.

G has listened to the several stories about the production delays at *M*'s plant, but he has chosen not to decide among them or even to try to put them all together to make a single coherent picture of the trouble. He has read the *Rashomon* as a sign of two main difficulties: a lack of effective communication among the several parties, and a split between the new plant and central operations. He has seen his problem as one of creating a process to deal with these two difficulties.

He has decided to treat the diagnosing of the problem as a central part of the resolution of the problem and has assigned the task of diagnosis to those who are most centrally concerned. He has asked the vice-president for manufacturing, together with his staff of three, to spend two days a week at the new plant over the next three months. They will work with their counterparts there to trace the sources of delays, to review and repair reporting systems, and to fix whatever problems in operations they discover.

G has followed company traditions in turning the full force of management attention onto the crisis point, but this time he has not gone down to deal with the problem himself. He has seen his role as one of designing and putting in place a process to identify and fix the problem, leaving to others the task of working out their conflicting views of it. He has set up an organizational experiment, the essence of which is to bring into close interaction those who have been distant from one another.

M has reacted favorably to this move. He says, "For the first time, I think they are learning what it is really like here. New capacity won't solve our problem; it will barely let us keep up with growth. But as the atmosphere improves and we get a better handle on the problems, we'll gradually remove the delays. I'm optimistic."

And G says, "Perhaps as M comes to feel that people here understand his situation better, he will begin to feel more a part of the company, and then he may commit more fully to his frame of reference."

G has responded to the organizational crisis by designing a process which will involve the key participants in collective reflection-in-action.

Learning about Product Development

A large American consumer products firm has an extraordinary reputation as a developer of new products. Inside the firm, individual managers are very well aware of their corporate reputation and attribute it to their success in learning about the process of conceiving, inventing, and commercializing new products.

What is remarkable about this firm is the consciousness that managers bring to this process, the sense they have of being members of a corporate culture which includes a great deal of knowledge about it, and the extent to which the managers see themselves both as users of the store of corporate knowledge and contributors to it. It is possible to dig down into the firm, at least four layers deep, without losing access to the corporate reservoir of knowledge about product development.

These are some examples of what product development managers believe they have learned.

(1) "The target is a variable."

One of the heads of technology remarks, "Product development is a game you can win, so long as you keep it open — so long as you remember you can redefine the target." Typically, a product development project is worked out among representatives of marketing, technology, and general management. Once a target has been defined, general management commits the necessary resources. As development proceeds, technical people learn more about the feasibility of the initial target and more about the properties of the materials with which they are working. They discover unexpected difficulties in achieving the target originally chosen, and they also discover technical possibilities they had not suspected at the outset. They can redefine targets to reflect these discoveries, so long as they also understand the marketing implications of their redefinition of the target.

Thus, in one project concerned with disposable paper products, the development director observes, "We found that the critical variable was not absorptive capacity but rate of absorption!" It was much more difficult to increase absorptive capacity than rate of absorption, but it was the latter that mattered most to the consumer. In the words of one researcher, "We knew we were on the right track when our panels no longer hated us!"

In order to treat the target as a variable, the development team must be able to see a technical property of materials in terms of its meaning to consumers, and they must be able to see a marketing target in terms of the technical demands that follow from it. Such a team cannot afford a "seesaw" between marketing and technology, in which marketing says to technology, "Make what we can sell!" or technology says to marketing, "Sell what we can make!" Technical and marketing specialists must be able to share the uncertainty which they convert to risk by redefining the development target. Like the marketing managers at *3M*, they must be willing to give up the assumption that they *know* the target, once and for all, at the beginning of the development process. As they discover new properties in the phenomena and new meanings in the responses of consumer panels, they learn to restructure not only the means but the ends of development.

(2) "The unit of development is not a new product but a game with the competition."

Members of the development team think of themselves as engaged in a game with the competition. For each major product line, there is a national market within which many companies struggle for position. Winning this game consists in establishing, maintaining, and extending market position at the expense of the competitors. Moves in the game consist of product improvements, advertising campaigns, and new product introductions. For every move, competitors make counter moves. The game lasts for the duration of the life cycle of the product line.

Playing the game well means forming and implementing a development *strategy*. A given development (a paper product with a higher rate of absorption, for example) is likely to trigger competitive developments, and good strategy includes anticipation of the likely countermoves. The development team tries to have, in the wings, a set of long-term develop-

ments which they can activate in response to competitors' moves when
the time is right. Thus, the unit of development is not an individual product but a full cycle of the competitive game.

Within the game, however, there is always the question, "What is the
situation now?" Depending on one's interpretation of the situation, construction of an appropriate strategy may vary significantly. In the case of
the paper product described above, for example, there was a period in
which the team believed that they had established the basic acceptability
of their product and needed mainly to get the price down. But a competi-
tor introduced a new product which came in at a higher price and
achieved greater consumer acceptance than theirs. How should they interpret their situation in the game? A corporate vice-president made the
suggestion, "Why don't you come up with a Cadillac?" This was surprising to the development team, because it ran counter to their strategy.
They did not reject it out of hand, however; they waited to see what the
market would do. Then, as they said, "When we discovered that our
product was holding its own among the low-priced brands, we were
freed up to work on the Cadillac. Had we brought out a low-priced improvement, we would have cannibalized our own brand."

The new signals from the marketplace enabled the development team
to construct a new picture of their situation, one which required them to
revise their understanding of their position relative to other brands.
From the new description of the situation, they evolved a new strategy
which they would test with the introduction of the "Cadillac," a familiar
metaphor which, like "cannibalizing," is a part of the repertoire they
bring to their inquiry.

(3) "The important thing is to keep the dialectic moving."

It is unusual to find the term "dialectic" in common usage within a corporate culture. But in this corporation, managers talk freely about dialectic, by which they mean the surfacing and working out of conflicting
views among participants in the development process.

The vice-president of technology goes so far as to define his role in
terms of the dialectic. He says, "I feel good when I see that engineering
and development, advertising and manufacturing, are really surfacing
and talking about their differences. It's my job to keep the dialectic alive."

And a general manager says, "You must keep the conflicts alive and on
the surface. Once you have identified the conflicts, you see to it that *they*
resolve them and that they let you know the results. If they agree ahead
of time, too quickly, that can shield you from legitimate conflict. It
breaks your heart when you see people have stopped talking about it."

The expectation is that "legitimate conflicts" will surface. The complexity of development situations is such that engineering and research, advertising and manufacturing, general management and finance, will have

different and conflicting views of situation and strategy, all of which are important to the organization. A manager's task is to make sure that such conflicts are neither suppressed nor circumvented. Organizational learning about a present situation, and about product development more generally, depends on the "working out" of such conflicts. But no one can say, ahead of time, *how* they will be worked out; that will depend on the reciprocal reflection-in-action of the parties to the conflict.

Limits of the Organizational Learning System

The very same company that is so conscious of organizational learning about product development also provides a very good example of the ways in which an organizational learning system may constrain reflection-in-action.

As a consultant to this organization, I was asked to address the problem of the "burn-out" of product development directors. These individuals, who work at the intersection of general management, advertising, and research, are hard to find, expensive to develop, and difficult to keep. They experience an unusually high incidence of alcoholism, health problems, divorce, and mental break-down, and the vice-president for technology wanted to know why.

We agreed that my study would take the form of an analysis of a case of product development — *Product X,* as I will call it, a product for use in household appliances. The story of *Product X* was already famous in the company when I began my study. Nearly everyone described it in the same way: "A case in which we nearly failed because of problems we ought to have anticipated and dealt with better than we did. But we came through and bailed ourselves out."

Initially, there were three questions about the case: Why were we so late in detecting and admitting the problems? Why were we so unwilling to ask for help and to accept help once it was offered? How did we bail ourselves out? The product had originated in a "brainstorming" session where development specialists had asked themselves, "What benefits can we deliver through products designed for use in household appliances?" When they had arrived at a basic product definition, they began to explore the technologies they would need, and they hit on a particular technology, owned by a private inventor, which they could turn to their purposes.

Their development process proceeded, as usual in this company, through a series of tests. They tested the product's effectiveness in delivering its intended benefit, and they tested it for possible harmful side effects. The testing process began in the laboratory where, for example, standard corrosion tests were performed by immersing steel plates in a bath made up of the product's components. The process continued through "blind" tests with consumer panels (a standard element in all of their development processes) and finally to regional test markets. It is important to note that a successful passage through such a sequence of standard tests functioned, in this company, as an essential part of the dialogue between technical development specialists and general managers. The general managers, who controlled the commitment of resources, depended on the results of standard tests to make their decisions.

The product performed very well in panel tests and was placed in its first regional test market. Two months into the test market, however, an appliance company, which had been asked to test the product, sent back word that "this product can get stuck in the machine, and if it does, you can get overheating. There is a risk of fire." Members of the development team at first said, "We don't think so," but the appliance company wrote a formal, threatening letter to general management: "If you market this product, we'll put stickers on our machines telling people not to use it."

With this exposure of the problem, everyone started to talk about it. General management, who had known nothing of the problem, were furious. Three different task groups were set up and they arrived at two different solutions. Both of these were subsequently accepted and incorporated in a new version of the product. But this created a new problem: what should be done with the existing test market? The old product had been successful in consumer panel blind-tests, and general management said, "We'll keep the old test market going. It's the original product we invested in. It passed our tests." The technical group nearly mutinied, but general management took the position that "we can assume a liability if we want to; your job is to tell us the odds."

The sense of general management's position was, "The product is a black box. We make decisions about things that pass our tests. But we don't take the cover off the box because we get confused." The sense of the technical group's position was, "We make decisions about particulars, not general probabilities. We understand what it is that makes a product pass tests. And we don't always trust the tests!" A year later, the first test market was dropped and a new one, based on the revised product, was instituted. But technical people felt that the issue had "put them into short pants." At this point; the development was some two years old, with $30 million invested.

A second major embarrassment occurred in the midst of the second test market. The product had been doing well when a sprinkling of complaints came in from the field to the effect that the product caused rust in appliances. These complaints came in after the "sticking" problem and after the laboratory immersion tests which had revealed no rusting. The technical team chose to ignore the complaints. The rusting detected by a few users of the product must have been produced by other causes.

Members of the corporate research laboratory, who heard about the problem, took a different view. One member of the research group lathered some of the product's ingredients on a tin can and left it overnight; in the morning the can had rusted. The researchers took the rusted can to the vice-president for technology who said, "There's no red light. Don't worry about it. We can handle it." But as letters from the field multiplied, the laboratory team became convinced that the rusting effect was real. They developed a model that would explain the rusting process, used X-ray spectroscopy to test the model, and brought in high-powered consultants from a university. The product development team reacted by asking, "Are you really sure of this? Why are you doing this to us? Why don't you do something constructive?"

The laboratory group was disillusioned. The head of the laboratory sent out a memo which forbade researchers to do more work on *Product X*. At this point, however, the vice-president for technology fired the head of the development team and appointed a researcher from the laboratory to become the new head. This man quickly satisfied himself, with the help of his former colleagues in the laboratory, that the rusting effect was real. This produced a new crisis.

The vice-president for technology then held a meeting with members of the two teams. At this meeting he said, "Are you guys man enough to keep this problem from general management and go ahead on faith, without knowing that you can really do it, to make an alternative work?" This set in motion a new process which led, eventually, to solution of the rusting problem. The laboratory group, who had been told not to work on the problem, continued to do so. They came up with a new ingredient which they believed not only solved the rusting problem but actually protected machines. The product development team criticized them for "shooting from the hip" and "overstepping their bounds." The new head of the laboratory team proposed a technical-political compromise — the new ingredient was to be combined with 10 percent of the old. New tests showed that the rusting effect had been overcome and the product worked as well as ever. As one member of the laboratory group said, "It was all played out under the tent, for fear of tipping off general management and breaking their commitment to the product. But at each replay of the problem, there was the same issue: Did the new element really work? What about negative side effects? It was a guerrilla war, and we used science as a weapon."

The interactions between product development team and research laboratory can be represented as a cycle of action and reaction, roughly as follows.

The product development team sought to protect themselves, to control the task and territory, and to win credit for their work and credibility with general management. To these ends, they

resisted the problems pointed out by the laboratory,

discredited the laboratory findings,

kept them in their place by confining them to narrow and unimporant problems,

kept their own work quiet.

The laboratory team became angry and frustrated, distrusted the product development team, and felt a low sense of their own worth. They retaliated by

taking an aggressive stance as they proved their points,

seeking to win through science,

continuing to work on the problem even when the boss told them not to,

trying to capture the task,

circumventing product development to get to management.

These strategies made the product development team angry, frustrated, fearful, and distrustful, and reinforced them in their efforts to win and protect themselves.

The consequences of the cycle were wasted effort, duplicated work, and delay in the recognition of problems. The product development team could not, under these circumstances, ask for help or use it when it was offered. As the cycle amplified, researchers and developers were less and less able to work together. Management injected only stopgap solutions. They shifted people around, and they intervened directly at moments of crisis. The pattern was one of "heroism under a tent." To quote some of the observations of the participants, "Three people told me not to work on *Product X*, but I wouldn't stop"; "Don't tell management what you're doing"; "Fix the problem first, then tell them about it."

What accounts for such a pattern? In order to answer this question, we must turn to the larger context in which the research/development cycle arose, for researchers and developers were involved in a more comprehensive process which I shall call "the product development game." The game has mainly to do with four variables — corporate commitment, credibility, confidence, and competence.

In order to set a new product in motion, general management must commit the necessary resources, but management commitment is deliberately made hard to win. This is partly a matter of thoroughness. As one of the managers said, "We're a very thorough company; we do our research well, and we don't accept just anything." But management commitment is also hard to win because managers tend to distrust research and development. As one manager said, "They are likely to flimflam and befool us if we're not careful." On the other hand, managers are aware of their dependence on research and development. They know that corporate growth depends on it.

Thus, managers must commit to a process which they distrust. They respond by making the commitment of resources hard to win; once resources are committed, they hold the product development director wholly accountable for performance, loading the director with the full burden of uncertainty. The maintenance of corporate commitment becomes touchier as investment in the product increases and the company becomes more exposed. Under these circumstances, product development people try to win the game by gaining and retaining management commitment while maintaining their own credibility within the company.

A participant's credibility behaves like a stock on the stock market, going up or down with the perception of success or failure. There is a corporate market for credibility. Employees strive to maintain their credibility at all costs, because a loss of credibility can make it impossible for them to perform. As the former head of the product development team reported, "When the problems hit the fan, my credibility was shot and I was dead in the company."

Confidence and competence are closely tied together. Individuals have "confidence tanks" whose levels rise or fall, depending on each individual's perception of his or her status in the company.

Credibility, commitment, confidence, and competence are interdependent in this sense:

"The more credibility I have, the more confident I can be";

"The more confident I am, the more confident I appear";

"The more confident I appear, the more I am seen as credible and competent."

Conversely,

"If I lose credibility, I may lose confidence";

"If I lose confidence, I appear to be incompetent and I lose more credibility."

As a result, the company is full of very confident-seeming people. It is seen as necessary to appear to be confident, no matter what the problems are, in order to maintain credibility. Indeed, old hands in technology management advise younger ones along the following lines: "Tell management enough of what you're doing to capture commitment, but not enough to make them uneasy. Commit yourself to do the things that are necessary, even if you're not sure you can do them. And do the work you see to be necessary, even if your boss says no." Thus heroism and secrecy (mastery and mystery) are essential elements of the strategy for winning the product development game.

The game, however, yields a double-bind, even for winners. It puts the players into a situation in which they lose, eventually, whatever the consequences. A participant may decide that "I must commit to what I'm not sure I can do, in order to secure corporate commitment. To this end, I lay my credibility on the line, without which I cannot function. So I must be heroic and secretive. If I fail, I lose big. But unless I play, I cannot win." But old-time managers say, "If you're up, you can stay up, and it's a winnable game, because there's plenty of resources and time and room for the redefinition of targets, if you have the competence and the confidence. But you must keep it up." So product development is a high-wire act in which you eventually fall. Moreover, you don't whine or complain because you would be seen to lack confidence. The effect is to put product development directors, those who occupy the pivotal position between general managers and the laboratory, under a great deal of strain. They strive to protect their own credibility, keeping problems "under a tent," with the result that in midstream problems tend to be ignored. In order to retain corporate commitment, the product is changed as little as possible. Once a problem has been exposed, however, they "climb all over it." They strive to retain ownership of the task which makes them treat offers of help as though they were threats to security.

In the light of this product development game, most of the questions with which the case study began can be given plausible answers. It is clear why problems encountered in midstream tend to be ignored until they are unavoidable, and it is also clear why, upon unavoidable exposure, they are "oversolved." It is clear how the corporation bails itself out of its crises, through stopgap, "patching" solutions which resolve the crisis at hand without affecting the underlying processes that produce crises. It is also clear how product development directors are placed under extraordinary stress which might well cause them to "burn out."

Considered more broadly as an organizational learning system, the product development game determines the directions and the limits of reflection-in-action. When crises present themselves, managers subject them to inquiry — often with successful results — but they do not reflect publicly on the processes which lead to such crises, for this would surface the games of deception by which product development deals with general management. While these games are "open secrets" within the organization, they are not publicly discussable.

Managers reflect on the strategies by which product development can be made into a "winnable game," but neither general managers nor product development directors reflect on the Model I theories-in-use which create the conditions for the game. Each participant tries to achieve his or her objectives as he or she sees them — general managers, to keep the burden of uncertainty on the shoulders of product development; product development directors, to retain corporate commitment while maintaining their own credibility. Each participant tries to avoid being tagged unilaterally with failure and the resulting loss of credibility. Each seeks to gain unilateral control over the situation, to win and avoid losing in a situation perceived as irretrievably win/lose. Each one withholds negative information from the other, as long as he or she believes it is a winning strategy to do so. Participants may be aware of these strategies, particularly as they are evinced by other players in the game, but they do not subject them to public reflection-in-action. To do so would be to make oneself vulnerable in an intensely win/lose world and, in the context of the product development game, might look like a failure of confidence.

This is not to say, however, that members of the organization are not able to recognize the game when it is described for them. When the results of the study of *Product X* were presented to those who had been involved in the story, there was a generally favorable reaction. Although most participants had never put the whole picture together for themselves, they recognized its validity. Some were highly amused. They seemed to feel that the study elaborated the open secret with which they were all familiar. But, with very few exceptions, they did not believe that the system was susceptible to change. The risks seemed too great, the stakes too high, and the chances of success too low.

The Art of Managing and Its Limits

Returning now to the questions with which we began this chapter, let us consider the lessons that may be drawn from the several examples of managerial practice which have occupied our attention.

It is clear that managers do sometimes reflect-in-action. Beginning with questions like, What do consumers really see in our product? What's really going on underneath the signs of trouble in our organization? What can we learn from our encounters with the competition? managers sometimes try to make sense of the unique phenomena before them. They surface and question their intuitive understandings; in order to test their new interpretations, they undertake on-the-spot experiments. Not infrequently, their experiments yield surprising results that cause them to reformulate their questions. They engage in reflective conversations with their situation.

The reflection-in-action of managers is distinctive in that they operate in an organizational context and deal with organizational phenomena. They draw on repertoires of cumulatively developed organizational knowledge which they transform in the context of some unique situation. And as they function as agents of organizational learning, they contribute to the store of organizational knowledge. *G*'s inquiry into production delays becomes a corporate exemplar for diagnosis of the troubles of the internal environment. In the consumer products firm, managers build up a corporate repertoire of cases, maxims, and methods which becomes accessible to new generations of managers.

But managers function as agents of organizational learning within an organizational learning system, within a system of games and norms which both guide and limit the directions of organizational inquiry. The case of *Product X* reveals a learning system that creates a pattern of corporate crises and at the same time prohibits public reflection-in-action on their causes.

As a consequence, the organizational learning system becomes immune to reflection-in-action. It is not publicly discussable; and because managers do not discuss it, they are often unable to describe it — although they may recognize the descriptions constructed by an outsider to the organization. Public discussion of the product development game would reveal the strategies by which general managers distance themselves from the uncertainties inherent in product development and the complementary strategies by which technical personnel protect themselves against the loss of corporate commitment. To reveal these strategies publicly, in an actual present instance where some action might be taken, would violate the norms of the product development game and would carry a perceived risk of vulnerability and loss of control.

Thus, organizational learning systems of the sort revealed by the case of *Product X* become diseases that prevent their own cure. Managers cannot extend the scope of reflection-in-action to their own learning systems without transforming the theories of action which they bring to their lives within the organization. And these, under the normal conditions of corporate life, are also immune to reflection-in-action.

The Art of Managing in Higher Education

Are phenomena such as these peculiar to the world of business management, or are they also to be found in the public sector and, especially, in the field of higher education? I think that managers in institutions of higher education frequently encounter opportunities for reflection-in-action, do sometimes reflect-in-action, and are frequently hemmed in by constraints similar to those I have just attributed to the corporate setting. A few examples will suggest the kinds of similarities I have in mind.

A doctoral student of mine conducted a longitudinal study of a department of civil engineering (Ehrmann 1978). He found that, over a period of some 30 years, the department had encountered a series of turning points. At each of these, the then department head and key faculty members reflected on the situation in which they found themselves and set in motion programs designed to solve the problem they had encountered.

But there was a fundamental dilemma which cut across these situations. In each new situation, the department confronted problems resulting from the "swing" they had taken at the previous turning point, and the managers appeared to be oblivious to their swings from one horn of the dilemma to the other. In the early sixties, the department responded to declining enrollments and reduced funding by redefining itself as a department of "systems management" in such fields as water resources and environmental conservation. With this shift of direction, they set themselves to bring in and develop new specialists in the relevant systems sciences. As they succeeded in building up these specialized competencies, they were increasingly subjected to a new challenge: in what sense were they one department? This issue arose most acutely in the students' demand for a "capping course" which would help them to synthesize the various bodies of special knowledge. The department attempted to offer such a course but they found, after repeated trials, that no member of the faculty was able to do the job successfully. After several years of such unsuccessful efforts at synthesis, the department lapsed into a more fragmented organization of specialized curricula. But after a while, this situation triggered new demands for synthesis, which gave rise to further dissatisfaction. At each new juncture, the managers of the department were able to reflect on the problematic situation and to design a response to it which relieved the immediate pressures. What they were unable to do was to take cognizance of their history of pendulum swings between the poles of specialized decentralization and synthesis, or to inquire deeply into the dilemma which underlay these swings.

In the sixties, Massachusetts Institute of Technology, like many other universities, engaged in a spate of innovations in curricula. Twenty years later, it is apparent that only one of these has had enduring effect on the institution. This one, known as "Undergraduate Research Opportunities," or UROP, grew out of the entrepreneurial resourcefulness of one faculty member, Margaret MacVicar, closely supported by a member of MIT's ruling triumvirate. The unfolding history of this innovation makes a case study of institutional reflection-in-action. MacVicar's original idea grew out of her reflections on the problematic nature of the organization of research and the quality of faculty-student interactions at MIT. In their early undergraduate years, students tended to encounter faculty only in large lecture halls or in the constraining context of the evaluation of problem sets. Students spoke of their undergraduate experience as "drinking from a fire hose." MacVicar guessed that both students and faculty would find it rewarding to experience other sorts of interactions, as coparticipants in research. For students, she thought, this would provide an opportunity to meet faculty in a new way and to test out career directions; for faculty, it would be a source of free research support and a more gratifying kind of relationship with students. Small amounts of MIT funds might be used to achieve substantial benefits for students and faculty alike.

In the actual working out of this idea, MacVicar and her colleagues developed a highly articulated sense of the way MIT actually works. Apparently trivial details were treated as signs of significant underlying issues — for example, the issues of "pay or credit" for student work — and changes in program design were taken seriously as institutional experiments. A great deal of attention was paid to the qualitative evaluation of student and faculty experience with the program. Working carefully, incrementally, and reflectively, taking advantage of opportunities that presented themselves over the years, MacVicar was able to build up a network of faculty members and administrators who supported the program, participated in it, and reflected with her on its adaptation to changing circumstance.

A large university is now in the midst of an assessment of its experience with affirmative action. As in many institutions of higher education, the experience has been of mixed quality. Far more success has been gained in the hiring, promotion, and tenure of women than of blacks. Institutional affirmative action procedures have tended to take the form of a central review of departmental plans which the departments often regard as a necessary annoyance and central administration often sees as ineffective. In spite of strong central commitment to the policy, experience with it has been disappointing. Now, an active equal opportunity committee is in the midst of an administration-supported effort to explore the sources of perceived ineffectiveness. A picture begins to emerge in which departments, faced with increasing frustrations in their efforts to compete for a small pool of highly qualified black faculty and unwilling to sacrifice their sense of academic standards, have tended to give lip-service to centralized plans and controls. Participants in the study are exploring a "distributed strategy" that would recognize the considerable diversity of interests, potentials, and constraints among departments and the extent to which departments are relatively autonomous controllers of their own destinies. Perhaps it would be possible to tap into local, departmental interests and ideas, allowing each department to define the affirmative action targets and strategies appropriate to it so as to achieve some experience of short-term success and to mobilize some of the entrepreneurial energies which enable departments to perform so brilliantly in other domains. There is an effort to convert a situation which is, at worst, a diplomatic battle between central administration and local faculty units into a cooperative central-local inquiry into new courses of action.

Examples such as these suggest something of the opportunities for reflection-in-action in institutions of higher education and suggest also how organizational systems may limit the scope and depth of reflection-in-action. In spite of the many important differences between the business world and the world of higher education, it seems to me very likely that there are important similarities both in the art of management and in the organizational impediments to its exercise.

Conclusion

We might begin to heal the split in the field of management if we were to recognize that the art of management includes something like science in action. When practicing managers display artistry, they reveal their capacity to construct models of unique and changing situations, to design and execute on-the-spot experiments. They also reveal a capacity to reflect on the meanings of situations and the goals of action. A more comprehensive, useful, and reflective management science could be built by extending and elaborating on what skillful managers actually do. Practitioners might then become not only the users but the developers of management science.

What would be the characteristics of a reflective management science, one in which practitioners could play a generative role? A full treatment of this question lies beyond the scope of this paper; nevertheless, I can suggest some of the directions for future inquiry. A reflective science of management practice would include these sorts of research:

Description and analysis of the ways in which practitioners frame their roles and the problematic situations in which they find themselves. Study of the framing process would include analysis of the types and sources of frames brought to management, and descriptions of the consequences of frame-selection for problem-solving.

Repertoire-building research. This would involve description of the category-schemes, the images, and the cases, precedents, and exemplars which skilled practitioners bring to the unique situations of their practice.

Description of the overarching theories of phenomena, and the associated methods of inquiry which some practitioners use to develop on-the-spot variations. By "overarching theories" I mean the highly general models which some managers use, in action, to determine what is an appropriate object of attention and what is an acceptable explanation.

Research on the process of reflection-in-action. How do individual practitioners design and conduct on-the-spot experiments? How do they tell when they are done? What are their norms for rigorous experiment? What are their patterns of reflective conversation with the situation?

How do these patterns of cognitive activity express themselves in individually varying styles? How are they linked to kinds of feelings and stance toward inquiry?

Research on the interactions between individual reflection-in-action and organizational learning systems. The scope and direction of individual reflection-in-action are shaped by the characteristics of organizational learning systems. Conversely, the organizational learning system may itself become an object of reflection-in-action. How, in actual practice, do these interactions work themselves out?

These types of research focus on actual management practice in particular organizational settings. They call for a variety of methods of case study through which investigators can explore what managers actually do in the situations of their practice and, what is equally important, how they think about what they do.

But when practitioners extend and deepen the scope of their reflection-in-action, they undertake self-study along these very lines. Reflective managers continually interrogate their ways of framing their roles and their problematic situations, the way in which they build and use their repertoires of images and exemplars, the models of the world which underlie their behavior, the processes by which they shape and interpret experiments, and the ways in which their private inquiries interact with the learning system of the organization of which they are members. Thus, what an outside researcher might regard as a contribution to research, a reflective manager would regard as a contribution to the development of his or her own capacity to perform. If we see matters in this way, we restructure the relationship between research and practice. Reflective managers become researchers into their own practice, and their private inquiries may be channeled into a growing body of reflective management science. Researchers who are not managers may come to see their primary mission as one of facilitating managers' reflection on their own practice, developing conceptual frameworks useful for it, and helping to document and synthesize the results of it.

Such a relationship between research and practice would have powerful implications for the roles and careers of managers and researchers, as well as for the institutional arrangements of research and practice.

REFERENCES

Alexander, Christopher M. (1968). *Notes toward a Synthesis of Form.* Cambridge, Mass.: Harvard University Press.

Barnard, Chester I. (1938). *The Functions of the Executive.* Cambridge, Mass.: Harvard University Press.

Ehrmann, Steven (1978). *Academic Adaptation: Historical Study of a Civil Engineering Department in a Research-oriented University.* Ph.D. thesis, Division for Study and Research in Education, Massachusetts Institute of Technology.

Mintzberg, Henry (1973). *The Nature of Managerial Work.* New York: Harper & Row.

Polanyi, Michael (1967). *The Tacit Dimension.* New York: Doubleday.

Taylor, Frederick (1911). *Principles of Scientific Management.* New York: Harper & Row.

Veblen, Thorsten (1904). *Theory of the Business Enterprise.* New York: Kelley.

Vickers, Geoffrey (1978). Unpublished memorandum.

CHAPTER 4

Transformative Power and Leadership

Warren Bennis

To understand "Transformative Power," the following question must be addressed: *what are the components of an organization that can translate intention into reality and sustain it?* The question itself contains a complexity and depth as well as a chronic elusiveness. The question, probably for the preceding reasons, tends to be avoided—though it is the essence of what is ordinarily meant to be organizational leadership. Even when it is obliquely touched on, the writer tends to avoid the orchestral richness which inheres in the question for the doctrinal, predictable, and prosaic clichés. Between the blur produced by trying to say too much at once and the banality produced by dismissing mysteries, there remains the possibility of articulating just what it is that causes some organizations to translate an intention into reality and sustain it. This is the starting point for an examination of what I am referring to as transformative power.

The Environment of Leadership in the 1980s

This much can be said about leadership for the '80s: those responsible for governing the enterprise will be spending more and more of their time managing external relations. All organizations are surrounded by an increasingly active, incessant environment—one that is becoming more and more influential—the senior partner, as it were, in all kinds of decisions which affect the institution.

Leadership, and its companion decision-making, will become an increasingly intricate process of multilateral brokerage including constituencies both within and without the organization. More and more decisions made will be public decisions; that is, they will affect people who insist on being heard. Leaders will have to reckon with the growing role of media as a "fourth arm" of government available for use by the people who oppose a particular decision as well as the people who support it. The idea of a relatively small group of "movers and shakers" who get things done is obsolete. Increasing numbers of citizens and stakeholders (and even those who are only indirectly involved in an issue) are interesting themselves in its outcome — and when the decision goes the "wrong way," very noisily so. This state of affairs has led one writer to describe the organization-of-today as a "jungle of closed decisions, openly arrived at."

The bigger the problem to be tackled, the more power is diffused and the more people have to be involved. Thus decisions become more complex and ill defined, affecting more different and sometimes conflicting constituencies.

Inevitably there will be frustration, not only among leaders but among followers who ask, "Who's in charge here?" as more and more people and groups have to be consulted. Leaders ask, "How do you get everybody in the act and still get some action?"

The name of the game is ambiguity and surprise, and leaders have to lead under uncertain, risky conditions where it's virtually impossible to get ready for *something* when you have to get ready for *anything.* Just as effective leaders know about and are becoming more competent in coping with the politicization of our institutions — by which I mean that institutions are becoming the focus for a new kind of politics, i.e., mobilizing public opinion or working more closely with legislative bodies at both the state and federal levels and other key constituencies — they are also learning more about an enlarged concept of the "management team."

No longer can "managing external relations" be left in the hands of the public relations department. Top leadership must be involved — directly. In short, the political role of the organization leadership's responsibility must be reconceived. These trends, these changing characteristics of the organizational and managerial environment that we are now living with, will become even more pronounced and problematic over the next ten or so years.

The Three Components of Transformative Power

The Leader

There are some important clues about the nature of effective leadership that have come out of a study I recently completed of 80 chief executive officers (CEOs) plus ten in-depth interviews conducted over the past few months with ten successful, "innovative" leaders (Bennis, 1983). These studies provide a basis for making some generalizations about those leaders who successfully achieve mastery over the noisy, incessant environment — rather than simply react, throw up their hands, and live in a perpetual state of "present shock." In short, the study which I am about to summarize was able to illuminate some of the darkness around the question earlier posed: how do organizations translate intention into reality and sustain it? Leadership is the first component, though as we shall see later on, leadership must be held within a context of other interacting factors.

What all these effective CEOs shared and embodied was directly related to how they *construed* the role of the CEO/chairperson. To use a popular distinction, they viewed themselves as *leaders* not *managers*, which is to say that they were concerned with their organization's basic purposes, why it exists and its general direction. They did not spend their time on the "how to. . . ," the proverbial "nuts and bolts," but with purpose and paradigms of action. In short, they were concerned not with "doing things right" (the overriding concern of managers) but with "doing the right thing." They were capable of transforming doubts into the psychological grounds of common purpose.

By responding to the question which guided my study — what common set of characteristics, if any, did those leaders possess who were capable of translating intention into reality — I can clarify the role of the effective leader. In varying degrees, it seemed that all of the CEOs possessed the following competencies:

Vision: the capacity to create and communicate a compelling vision of a desired state of affairs, a vision (or paradigm, context, frame — all those words serve) that clarifies the current situation and induces commitment to the future.

Communication and alignment: the capacity to communicate their vision in order to gain the support of their multiple constituencies.

Persistence, consistency, focus: the capacity to maintain the organization's direction, especially when the going gets rough.

Empowerment: the capacity to create environments — the appropriate social architecture — that can tap and harness the energies and abilities necessary to bring about the desired results.

Organizational learning: the capacity to find ways and means through which the organization can monitor its own performance, compare results with established objectives, have access to a continuously evolving data base against which to review past actions and base future ones, and decide how, if necessary, the organizational structure and key personnel must be abandoned or rearranged when faced with new conditions.

In short, nothing serves an organization better — especially during these times of agonizing doubts and paralyzing ambiguities — than leadership which knows what it wants, communicates those intentions successfully, empowers others, and knows when and how to stay on course and when to change.

The Intention

The second element of transformative power refers to the "compelling vision" mentioned earlier that will now be referred to as "the intention." The expression of an intention is the capacity to take an organization to a place it has never been before. The characteristics of the intentions that successful leaders employ include:

Simplicity: this characteristic is also known as or akin to Occam's Razor, the Law of Parsimony. This implies that each assumption or element is independent. The word "simple" derives from the notion of oneness or unity.

Completeness: this criterion requires that all the facts that are available are included. In most organizations the bulk of the major tasks that have to be accomplished are easily and readily incorporated within almost any kind of organizational structure. It is those few remaining tasks that test or prove the adequacy of the organization. Not only should the organization be capable of incorporating tasks that need to be performed at the time it is set up, it should also be capable of adjusting to and assimilating new tasks as they arise.

Workability: does it deliver the goods? Does the context achieve the organizational goals or contribute to them? William James, as usual, says it well: "By their fruits ye shall know them, not by their roots."

Communicability: this last criterion for judging contexts contains two components: the more obvious one relates to the ease in which the context is understood by the organization. The robustness of the organization, in terms of its empowerment, depends to a large extent on the degree to which the context is clear and understood. The other meaning of this criterion is alignment; not alignment, though, of organizational members, but alignment with other contexts indigenous to the particular organization. In other words, to understand organizational structure and its significance, it is important to keep in mind that its effectiveness is related to the mutual relatedness of its various contexts.

The problem with the above characteristics is betrayed by application of one of them, "completeness." The list is not complete. Originality, muting of ego, subtlety, and an aesthetic are all important which space limitations preclude anything but their mention now. The one exception to this is "an aesthetic," an exception based both on its significance and neglect. Indeed, I believe that the aesthetic of the intention plays an important, perhaps key, role in understanding how intention can lead to implementation, which is, after all, the whole point of leadership.

The Organization

Transformative power implies a transaction between the leader and the led, between the leadership and some sort of participative response.

If the leadership expresses the characteristics noted earlier and if the vehicle of this expression, the intention(s), are effectively expressed, the organization becomes a blending of each individual's uniqueness into collective action.

Such an organization is similar to something observed in healthy individuals; in fact, it is isomorphic to a healthy identity in an individual. More technically, we can assume that an organization possesses a healthy identity — organizational integrity — when it has a clear sense of what it is and what it is to do.

Achieving "organizational integrity" is easier said than done. Part of the problem is the lack of understanding of the various substructures that all organizations, no matter how small, contain. One block to our understanding is perpetuated by the myth of organization-as-monolith, a myth reinforced almost daily by the media and the temptation of simplicity. The myth is not only grossly inaccurate but dangerous as well. When the evening paper, for example, announces that the Defense Department or the University of California or IBM (or any corporate body for that matter) will pursue this or that course of action, the said action is typically consigned to a single, composite body, *the* administration. This administration, whose parts vibrate in harmony and whose acts, because we are denied a look at the human drama that leads up to them, take on an air of superhuman detachment, is as mythical as the griffin. Into every step taken by *the* administration goes a complicated pattern of meetings, disagreements, conversations, personalities, emotions, and missed connections. This very human process is bureaucratic politics. A parallel process is responsible for our foreign policy, the quality of our public schools, and the scope and treatment of the news that the media choose to deliver to us each day.

Our perceptions of organizational decision-making, based on such reports and other stimuli, tend to emphasize the *product* of decision-making, never (or rarely) the *process*. The result, of course, is false, at times destructively so. Those elements of chance, ignorance, stupidity, recklessness, and amiable confusion are simply not reckoned with; they are selectively ignored, it seems. Thus, the public rarely sees the hundreds of small tableaux, the little dramas, that result in a policy statement or a bit of strategy. It sees only the move or hears only the statement, and it not unreasonably assumes that such an action is the result of a dispassionate, almost mechanical process in which problems are perceived, alternative solutions weighed, and rational decisions made. Given human nature, that is almost never the case.

In order for an organization to have integrity, it must have an identity, a sense of what it is and what it is to do. Perhaps an analogy taken from personality theory will illustrate as well as foreshadow this point. Every person is a summation of various "selves." If those units of the person are not in communication, then the person cannot maintain valid communications with others. The problem of integrity, which is central to much of the contemporary literature in the mental health field, can in organizations be examined by understanding the various "organizational selves" or structures that exist.

Every organization incorporates four concepts of organization, often at odds with each other or existing in some strained coherence. There is the *manifest* organization, or the one which is seen on the "organization chart" and which is formally displayed. There is also the *assumed* organization, or the one that individuals perceive as the organization were they asked to draw their view of the way that things work, very much like the legendary New Yorker's view of the U.S. in which the Hudson River abuts Los Angeles. There is further the *extant* organization, or the situation as revealed through systematic investigation by, say, an outside consultant. Finally, there is the *requisite* organization, or the situation as it would be if it were in accord with the reality of the situation within which it exists.

The ideal, but never realized, situation is that in which the manifest, the assumed, the extant, and the requisite are aligned as closely as possible with each other. Wherever these four organizational concepts are in contradiction, the organizational climate is such that its identity is confused and its integrity difficult to achieve.

Another useful analogy to mental health shows up in this discussion. Many, if not all, psychotherapeutic schools base their notions of mental health on the degree to which the individual brings into harmony the various "selves" that make up his or her personality. The healthy person will be much the same person as he or she is known to others.

Virtually the same criterion can be used to establish organizational integrity, that is, the degree to which the organization maintains harmony—and knowledge—about and among the manifest, assumed, extant, and requisite concepts. It is not necessary that all four concepts be identical; rather, all four types should be recognized and allowance made for all the tensions created by imbalances. It is doubtful that an organization can or even should achieve total congruence. The important factor is recognition, a heighted consciousness of the confusions and contradictions.

To achieve openness, and through it integrity, in our organizations, each individual within the organization—particularly the leader—must strive to be open. From its embodiment in the individual, openness moves to the group level and, through individual and group interaction, infuses the organizational culture that sustains the characteristic of openness. The process is as slow as the building of a pyramid, and far more complex.

The Artform of Leadership

We have gone only partway in understanding leadership and transformative power by decomposing the three key elements at the political center of a complexly organized society, like an organization, into 1) a leader or governing elite or strategic core, 2) a set of symbolic forms expressing a tapestry of intentions, and 3) those constituent groups and individuals who make up the membership of the organization. The intention and its expression — crowns and coronations, limousines and conferences — give what goes on in organizations its aura of being not merely important but in some odd fashion connected with the way the world is built. The gravity of organizational leadership and the solemnity of high worship spring from liker impulses than might first appear.

The extent to which leadership is truly effective is based on the extent to which individuals place symbolic value on the intentions and their expression, the aesthetic referred to earlier. It is the relationship of the governed to the active centers of the social order that makes the difference between transformative power and other forms. Such centers have nothing to do with geometry and little with geography. Such centers have nothing to do with "humanizing the work place," Theory X or Theory Y, the "quality of worklife," or "participative management." What is important is that the organizations and their members are essentially concentrated on what appears to be *serious acts*. They exist at the point or points in a society where its leading ideas come together with its leading institutions to create an arena in which the events that most vitally affect members' lives take place. It is involvement, even oppositional involvement, with such arenas and with the momentous events that occur in them that "translates intention into reality and sustains it." *It is a sign, not of popular appeal or inventive craziness but of being near the heart of things.*

In sum, the transformative power of leadership stems less from ingeneously crafted organizational structures, carefully constructed management designs and controls, elegantly rationalized planning formats, or skillfully articulated leadership tactics. Rather, it is the ability of the leader to reach the souls of others in a fashion which raises human consciousness, builds meanings, and inspires human intent that is the source of power. Within transformative leadership, therefore, it is vision, purposes, beliefs, and other aspects of organizational culture that are of prime importance. Symbolic expression becomes the major tool of leadership, and leadership effectiveness is no longer defined as a "9–9 grid score" or a "system 4" position. Effectiveness is instead measured by the extent to which "compelling vision" empowers others to excell; the extent to which meanings are found in one's work; and the extent to which individual and organization are bonded together by common commitment in a mutually rewarding symbiotic relationship.

REFERENCE

Bennis, Warren, and Burt Nanus (1985). *Leaders: The Strategies for Taking Charge.* New York: Harper & Row.

Componaite of Trans Power

   1) The Leader
     - vision
     - communication power
     - persistone + focus
     - empowerment
     - org learning / monitor.)

   2) Intention - "Compelling Vision"

   3) The Org

CHAPTER 5

Leadership and Persistence

Barry M. Staw

Leadership research began as the study of personality and physical traits, evolved into an inquiry about behavioral styles in dealing with groups, and then turned into a label for nearly any strategy for increasing organizational effectiveness. As a concept, leadership has been used as independent and dependent variable, as structure and process, and as observable and metaphor. With such a track record it is understandable why leadership research has been as frustrating and noncumulative as to deserve the label "the La Brea Tar Pits" of organizational inquiry. Now located in Los Angeles, these asphalt pits house the remains of a long sequence of prehistoric animals that came to investigate but never leave the area.

With so little to show for our efforts, why do we keep coming back to leadership as an explanatory variable? One reason may be the "fundamental attribution error" frequently documented in psychological research on perception. Observers of an action tend to assign responsibility to personal characteristics or controllable actions whereas actors place greater causal weight on external circumstances and constraints. In the case of leadership, administrators may therefore not deserve all the blame or credit they get from an organization's fortunes. The administrator, as actor, is often acutely aware of the constraints under which he or she must operate, while we, as observers, tend to assign responsibility for events to the administrator's style of behavior, personality, or inventory of skills. When organizational actions either mesh or clash with environmental events we look for sources of wisdom and error, and we usually find something which satisfies our inquiry.

Given this rather pessimistic view of leadership research, where should

This paper is based, in part, upon an earlier article, "The Escalation of Commitment," *Academy of Management Journal*, October 1981, and the chapter "Counter-forces to Change: Escalation and Commitment as Sources of Administrative Inflexibility," in P. Goodman, ed., *Change in Organizations*, Jessey-Bass, 1982.

we go in the study of administrative behavior? One rather clear direction is to examine constraints on leader behavior since these have been underestimated in previous work. Pfeffer and Salancik (1978) have already staked out the boundaries of such an approach, but there are still few empirical studies using external control as the prevailing framework. A second approach is to examine leadership as an attributed rather than a substantive characteristic (Calder 1977; Staw and Ross 1980). From the attribution perspective, it is important to know how individuals are labeled as leaders rather than why their behavior may or may not affect organizational functioning. A third possibility is to treat leadership behavior just like any other set of actions and to explore those limitations in decision-making and judgement to which anyone may be subject. This alternative strips leadership of its mystical properties and treats leaders as mere mortals subject to all of the problems of perception, information processing, and choice. Thus, the only difference between a leader's mistakes and those committed by others in an organization is their potential consequences or impact. This paper will follow this third track, examining a problem in decision-making which may affect leaders, like others, in making important decisions.

The Problem of Persistence in a Course of Action

Many difficult decisions are not choices about what to do in an isolated instance but are choices about the fate of an entire course of action. This is especially true when the decision is whether to cease a questionable line of behavior or to commit more effort and resources into making that course of action pay off. Do individuals in such cases cut their losses or escalate their commitment to the course of action? Consider the following examples:

1. An individual has spent three years working on an advanced degree in a field with minimal job prospects, e.g., the humanities or social science Ph.D. The individual chooses to invest further time and effort to finish the degree rather than switching to an entirely new field of study. Having attained the degree, the individual is faced with the options of unemployment, working under dissatisfying conditions such as part-time or temporary status, or starting anew in a completely unrelated field.

2. An individual purchased a stock at $50 a share, but the price has gone down to $20. Because the individual is still convinced about the merit of the stock, he buys more shares at this lower price. Soon the price declines further and the individual is again faced with the decision to buy more, hold what he or she already has, or sell out entirely.

3. A city spends a large amount of money to improve the area's sewer and drainage system. The project is the largest public works project in

the nation and involves digging 131 miles of tunnel shafts, reservoirs and pumping stations. The excavation is only 10% completed and is useless until it is totally finished. The project will take the next 20 years to complete and will cost $11 billion. Unfortunately, the deeper the tunnels go, the more money they cost, and the greater are the questions about the wisdom of the entire venture (*Time* 1979).

4. A company overestimates its capability to build an airplane brake that will meet certain technical specifications at a given cost. Because it wins the government contract, it is forced to invest greater and greater effort into meeting the contract terms. As a result of increasing pressure to meet specifications and deadlines, records and tests of the brake are misrepresented to government officials. Corporate careers and credibility of the company are increasingly staked to the airbrake contract although many in the firm know the brake will not work effectively. At the conclusion of the construction period the government test pilot flies the plane; it skids off the runway and narrowly averts injuring the pilot (Vandiver 1972).

5. At an early stage of the U.S. involvement in the Vietnam war, George Ball, then undersecretary of state, wrote the following statement in a memo to Lyndon Johnson:

> The decision you face now is crucial. Once large numbers of U.S. troops are committed to direct combat, they will begin to take heavy casualties in a war they are ill-equipped to fight in a noncooperative if not downright hostile countryside. Once we suffer large casualties, we will have started a well-nigh irreversible process. Our involvement will be so great that we cannot — without national humiliation — stop short of achieving our complete objectives. Of the two possibilities I think humiliation would be more likely than the achievement of our objectives — even after we have paid terrible costs (*New York Times* 1971).

As evidenced in the above examples, many of the most injurious personal decisions and most glaring policy disasters can come in the shape of sequential and escalating commitments. From popular press accounts and the observation of everyday events it appears that individuals may have a tendency to become locked into a course of action, throwing good money after bad or commiting new resources to a losing course of action. The critical question from an analytical point of view, however, is whether these everyday examples denote a syndrome of decisional errors or are just a post hoc reconstruction of events. That is, do decisions about persistence to a course of action inherently lead individuals to errors of escalation or are we, as observers, simply labeling a subset of decisions whose outcomes turned out to be negative.

Understanding Escalation Decisions

If we posit an economically rational model of escalation decisions (Edwards 1954; Vroom 1964), resources should be allocated when future benefits exceed future costs. Such a rational perspective assumes that decision-makers function as good economists and that they make choices that maximize their own welfare. Of course, as many researchers have noted (Simon 1957; March and Olson 1976), individuals fall far short of the rational model in terms of information processing and choice. Errors in the perception and summarization of data are flagrant, as are mistakes in weighing and evaluating evidence when making decisions (Nisbett and Ross 1980).

Besides the shortcomings in information processing that accompany most decisions, choices about whether to persist in a course of action have some special properties that may lead to departures from rationality. In terms of economic rationality, losses or costs which may have been experienced in the past, but which are not expected to recur, should not enter into decision calculations. But, perhaps the crucial feature of escalation decisions is that an entire series of outcomes is determined by a given choice, the consequences of any single decision having implications for past as well as future outcomes. Thus, the sunk costs that economists exclude from decision calculations may not be sunk psychologically. To date, much of the research on persistence in escalation situations has attempted to show how sunk costs can affect resource allocation decisions and to specify a theoretical mechanism for their effect.

Research on the Escalation Effect

In an early study on what the authors called "entrapment" (Rubin and Brockner 1975), it was demonstrated that most individuals will wait for a valued resource beyond the point where benefits exceed costs. In performing an anagram task, subjects had to wait in line for a needed dictionary, but the longer they waited the lower was their overall reward. Results showed a generally high level of entrapment and also a heightening of entrapment when the value of the reward decreased slowly over time, when decline in the reward was not salient, and when subjects were led to believe that they were soon to receive the resource (the dictionary) necessary to attain the valued goal. Rubin and Brockner posited that escalation or entrapment decisions are the result of a field of forces that include the approach of goal accomplishment as well as the avoidance of past losses or wasted investment.

A related demonstration of the escalation effect was devised by Tegar (1980) using the dollar auction game. This game (Shubik 1971) involves bidding for a dollar sold at auction in which the highest bidder receives the dollar. The game proceeds as would a normal auction except for the rule that the second highest bidder must also pay his or her last bid, even if no prize is forthcoming. Thus, final bids are similar to irretrievable investments or sunk costs present in escalation situations. Tegar found that subjects frequently bid more than a dollar for a dollar, thereby demonstrating the basic escalation effect. As bidding escalated, individuals reported their motives as shifting from a desire to make money, to a desire to recoup prior losses, and finally to a competitive urge to defeat their opponents. Unfortunately, these reasons for escalation in the dollar auction game are difficult to interpret since the game is structured *both* as a situation of individual investment and interpersonal conflict.

In an investment simulation that more directly parallels administrative decision-making, Staw (1976) also demonstrated the escalation effect. In this study, business school students were asked to play the role of a corporate financial officer in allocating research and development funds. One-half of the subjects allocated R&D funds to one of two operating divisions of a company, were given feedback on their decisions, and were then asked to make a second allocation of R&D funds. The other half of the participants did not make the initial investment decision themselves, but were told that it was made by another financial officer of the firm. The results showed that subjects allocated significantly more money to the initially chosen division when they, rather than another financial officer, were responsible for the initial decision. These findings suggested that administrators seek to justify an ineffective course of action by escalating their commitment of resources to it.

Subsequent studies have replicated the effect of responsibility for negative consequences upon the escalation of commitment (Staw and Fox 1977; Fox 1981). It has also been found that escalation is associated with the perceived importance of the decision and disappointment with initial losses. These results support the proposition that at least some of the tendency to escalate may be explained by self-justification motives (Aronson 1976; Festinger 1957). By committing new resources, an individual may be attempting to turn the situation around so as to demonstrate the rationality of an original course of action. In short, when individuals escalate their commitment, they may be as motivated to rectify past losses as to seek future gain.

External vs. Internal Justification. While much research on the escalation effect has emphasized the role of justification, what has been tapped by these studies could be labeled an *internal justification* process. When justification is considered primarily as an intraindividual process, individuals are posited to attend to events and to act in ways to protect their own self-images (Aronson 1968, 1976). But within many social settings, justification may also be directed externally. When faced with an external threat or evaluation, individuals may be motivated to prove to others that they were not wrong in an earlier decision and the force for such *external justification* could well be stronger than the protection of individual self-esteem.

An empirical demonstration of the effect of external justification was conducted by Fox and Staw (1979). They hypothesized that administrators who have a strong need for external justification would be most likely to attempt to save a policy failure by committing more resources to it. To test this idea, an experimental simulation was conducted in which business students were asked to play the role of administrators under various conditions of job insecurity and policy resistance. Results showed that when a course of action led to negative results, the administrators who were both insecure in their jobs and who faced stiff policy resistance were most likely to escalate their commitment of resources and become locked into a losing course of action.

Also providing support for the external form of justification is a study by Caldwell and O'Reilly (1982). They showed that individuals can be made accountable for negative results even though they were not responsible for an original decision that went sour. They also showed that individuals will construct rationalizations of events if they are forced to present an accounting of events to external parties. Like companies which must explain poor results in their annual reports, individuals are highly selective in the information they pass to others, and thus biasing is significantly affected by responsibility for negative consequences.

Objective Forces. Cutting across these justification-predicted findings are studies that have shown more "objective" variables to affect escalation decisions. Some antecedents which have been explored are whether the cause of a setback is perceived to be endogenous or exogenous to a course of action (Staw and Ross 1978), whether resources allocated are perceived to be capable of turning the situation around (Staw and Fox 1977), and how escalation varies over time as repeated negative consequences are received (Staw and Ross 1978). These studies generally show that escalation can be increased or decreased by beliefs about a course of action and its likelihood of success. However, as Conlin and Wolfe (1980) have shown, individuals who follow a "calculating" decision strategy can still fall into the trap of escalation. Individuals can use calculations of expected value to justify a commitment decision as well as to see more clearly how withdrawal is the rational path. They can also mold the information used to reach a decision. As shown by Fox (1981), individuals have a strong preference for exonerating over implicating information, even when they may be sacrificing relevant data. Thus, although objective forces do affect escalation decisions, they are not so powerful as to reduce the escalation effect to a simple, rational calculus.

Norms for Consistency. In addition to justification and objective forces, a third factor has been identified as a possible contributor to the escalation effect. Recently, a number of popular press articles have argued that consistency is an essential aspect of political leadership, and national surveys on reactions to the presidency have shown that the perception of "indecisiveness" can be a major political liability (Gallup 1978). Thus, it is possible that a lay theory may exist in our society, or at least within many organizational settings, that administrators who are consistent in their actions are better leaders than those who switch from one line of behavior to another.

In order to empirically test the preference for consistency, Staw and Ross (1980) conducted an experiment on the reactions of individuals to selected forms of administrative behavior. Subjects included practicing managers, business school students, and undergraduates in psychology. Each subject was asked to study a case description of an administrator's behavior; manipulated in these case descriptions was consistency versus experimentation in the administrator's course of action as well as ultimate success versus failure of the administrator's efforts. In the consistency conditions, the administrator was portrayed as sticking to a single course of action through a series of negative results. In the experimenting conditions, the administrator was portrayed as trying one course of action and, when positive results did not appear, moving to a second and finally third alternative, as an administrator might behave within Campbell's (1969) "experimenting society." Ultimate success or failure of the administrator's actions was manipulated after two sets of negative results had been received by either the consistent or experimenting administrator.

Results showed that the administrator was rated highest when he or she followed a consistent course of action and was ultimately successful. There was also a significant interaction of consistency and success such that the consistent-successful administrator was rated more highly than would be predicted by the two main effects of these variables. This interaction supported a predicted "hero effect" for the administrator who remained committed through two apparent failures of a course of action, *only to succeed in the end.* Finally, the effect of consistency upon ratings of the administrator was shown to vary by subject group, being strongest among practicing administrators, next strong among business students, and weakest among psychology undergraduates. These results suggest not only that consistency in action is perceived to be part of effective leadership, but that this perception may be acquired through socialization for administrative roles.

Toward a Summary Model

In reviewing the research conducted to date it should be apparent that the escalation effect is complex, subject to multiple and sometimes con-

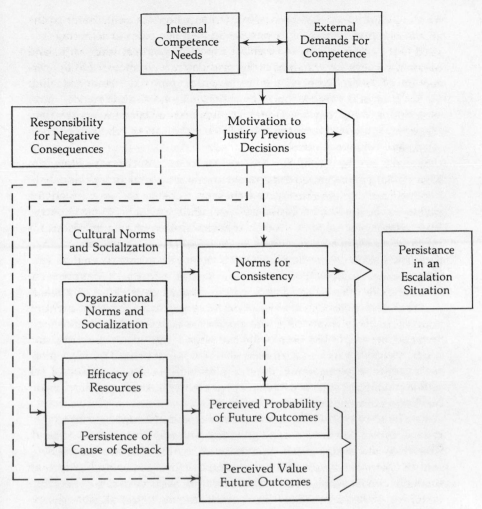

Figure 1. Determinants of persistance in an escalation situation.

flicting processes. Therefore, it may be helpful to consolidate in a single theoretical model the shape of forces now thought to affect persistence in escalation situations.

Figure 1 depicts four major determinants of persistence to a course of action: motivation to justify previous decisions, norms for consistency, probability of future outcomes, and value of future outcomes. Escalation research has concentrated upon the first two of these determinants, while the latter are obviously the two accepted determinants of economic and behavioral decision-making.

In examining Figure 1, motivation to justify decisions can be seen as a function of responsibility for negative consequences as well as both internal and external demands for competence. As depicted in the model, responsibility for negative consequences leads to a motivation to justify previous decisions if there is a need to demonstrate competence to oneself or others. As already noted, the traditional literature on dissonance and self-justification considers only the internal desire of individuals to be correct or accurate in decision making, whereas the need to demonstrate competence to external parties may also be a potent force. Such predictions may be culture-bound, but emphases on individual rationality and competence are so strong in Western societies that they are likely to foster concomitant needs for rationalizing one's actions (Wicklund and Brehm 1976). Likewise, because norms for rationality are so dominant in business and government organizations (Thompson 1967), role occupants in these settings may also find it necessary to justify their actions to constituents within and outside the organization.

Figure 1 also shows probabilities and values to be determinants of persistence in escalation situations. What adds to the complexity, however, is the possibility that individual perceptions of the likelihood and value of various outcomes can themselves be influenced by justification motives. Having been responsible for negative consequences may affect likelihood estimates via bias in information search and memory, while the value of future returns may increase as they may be needed to cover past losses. Hence, Figure 1 shows the interplay between some of the antecedents of justification with perceived probability and value of outcomes, the accepted elements of rational behavior.

In addition to the confluence of rationality and justification, norms for consistency are also shown to be of major importance in escalation decisions. Individuals may persist in a course of action simply because they believe consistency in action is an appropriate form of behavior, thereby modeling their own behavior on those they see as successful within organizations and/or society in general. Although modeling is usually viewed as a noncognitive process (Bandura 1971), the effect of norms could be integrated into an expectancy model of decision-making (Fishbein and Ajzen 1975) and be viewed as one element of an economically rational decision to commit resources. Likewise, norms for consistency could also be viewed as an outgrowth of individual needs for cognitive consistency (Festinger 1957) or socialization for consistency within the general society. The possible effect of justification upon norms for consistency is depicted by a dotted line in Figure 1, as is the possible effect of norms upon the perceived probability for future outcomes.

In summary, Figure 1 shows persistence in escalation situations as a complex process dependent upon justification and normative forces as well as on the standard properties of economic decision-making. Research has emphasized how escalation decisions are different from simple isolated choices and why constructs other than expectancy models can help explain persistence in such situations. Obviously, many of the variables we have explored must still be viewed as tentative determinants of persistence since they are based as much on theoretical deduction as empirical evidence. This is especially the case for the interactive effects shown in Figure 1.

Some Implications of the Escalation Effect

If we accept the conclusion that there is a tendency for persistence in escalation situations, what are its implications? Perhaps the most likely victims of an escalation effect will be behaviors that are perceptually associated as parts of a single course of action, because it is in these instances that both justification and consistency influences have been found to override more objective elements of the situation. Prime candidates for escalation therefore include resource allocation or investment decisions that are identified by an entering and exit value, life choices that are linked together by oneself or others with a label of a career, and policy decisions for which administrators are held accountable by others in an organization or by the general public. In these situations one must be especially wary of escalation tendencies and perhaps take counteractions to restore balance to decision-making.

In counterbalancing an escalation tendency, the variables outlined in Figure 1 may again be of use. For example, individuals should seek and follow the advice of outsiders who can assess the relevant issues of a decision situation without being responsible for previous losses nor subject to internal or external needs to justify past actions. Likewise, organizations that have experienced losses from a given investment or course of action should rotate or change those in charge of allocating resources. One applied instance of such a counterbalancing strategy was recently uncovered by Lewicki (1980). In a comparative case study, procedures were examined in two banks for coping with the problem of delinquent loans. The more financially aggressive bank, which had issued loans with greater risk, utilized separate departments for lending and "workout," the later department being in charge of efforts to recover the bank's investment from problem accounts. In contrast, the more conservative bank, which had fewer delinquent loans, had developed no formal procedure for separating responsibility for lending and workout, the original loan officer being charged with all phases of the loan relationship.

A second counterbalancing strategy might attempt to reduce the defensiveness often associated with decisional error. External sanctions for failure could be reduced and risk-taking encouraged. Likewise, responsibility for failure could be shared by superiors so that recognition of a failing course of action would not so adversely affect any single individual. Finally, efforts could be placed on evaluating the future potential of individuals without such heavy reliance on past performance. By deemphasizing the all-pervasive pressure to demonstrate past success, the defense of past policies might be replaced by greater efforts on improving performance in the future.

Leadership and Persistence

I began this paper by noting that it may be possible to say something of relevance to leadership by simply studying the behavior patterns of individuals. Given this posture, I have outlined a common syndrome of behavior in investment-type decisions and have discussed some of its determinants. By implication, leadership decisions should be subject to some of these same forces although they could be lessened or magnified in practice.

There are many reasons why an organizational leader would be subject to a tendency to become locked into a course of action. Few other individuals are assumed to have such free choice, given the opportunity to foresee the future, or probably possess the internal drive for competence as does the head of an organization. Few others' actions are so visible, consequential, or accountable as those of the leadership. As a result, both internal and external forces for justification should be quite high. Added to these forces for justification are probable efforts to appear consistent in a stream of action so that organizational policies appear logical and are accepted. Most leaders try to avoid the appearance of vacillation so that their constituents can have faith in a program or philosophy of management and can understand the direction that the organization is going. As we have seen, strong leaders are perceived to be consistent.

Cutting against these forces for persistence are the cruel realities of organizational life. Some leaders are acutely aware of how their organization must adapt to changing environmental conditions *and* how inappropriate their past actions may be to current situations. Thus some leaders may be especially aware of the prospectively rational aspects of decision-making, at least enough so as to blunt their own needs for justification and consistency.

In the tug of forces outlined here, some leaders may try to strike a balance. This may entail the rapid change of policy camouflaged by an overarching objective or stream of rhetoric. It may also entail the denial of responsibility for past decisions and the displacement of responsibility to others. Or, it may involve an admission of past errors as learning for future benefit. When Alfred Kahn, chief spokesman on inflation under President Carter, was questioned on why his new policies should be any more credible than those of the year before, he replied, "I am a much wiser person than I was a year ago!"

In a sense, much of the process of leadership could be viewed as the management of persistence. Leaders must bind or commit others to their policies, yet avoid becoming trapped in their own mistakes. There should be an illusion of consistency that is shown in one's actions, but such consistency should not preclude experimentation or organizational learning. Finally, as in most dictionary definitions of leadership, leadership often entails movement from one state or form to another. Because one has to be led somewhere for leadership to be detected, transformation or change may be emphasized by leaders — yet with the overtones of a persistent theme or objective.

These seemingly contradictory statements may underscore some of our difficulties in understanding leadership as an explanatory variable. The respected leader may exhibit a particular pattern of behavior *and* its opposite. He or she may undertake contrary actions or provide rhetoric where we expect substance and substance where we are looking for rhetoric. The issue of persistence is but one of the ways in which such contradictions can arise, but the interplay of forces affecting this variable may be central to the construct we call leadership.

REFERENCES

Aronson, E. (1968). "Dissonance Theory: Progress and Problems." In R. Abelson; E. Aronson, W. McGuire, T. Newcomb, M. Rosenberg, and P. Tannenbaum, eds. *Theories of Cognitive Consistency.* Chicago: Rand McNally.

_____. (1976). *The Social Animal.* San Francisco: Freeman.

Bandura, A. (1971). *Psychological Modeling: Conflicting Theories.* Chicago: Aldine-Atherton.

Calder, B. J. (1977). "An Attribution Theory of Leadership." In B. Staw, and G. Salancik, eds. *New Directions in Organizational Behavior.* Chicago: St. Clair Press.

Caldwell, D. F., and C. A. O'Reilly (1982). "Responses to Failure: The Effects of Choice and Responsibility on Impression Management." *Academy of Management Journal* 25(1), 121–36.

Campbell, D. T. (1969). "Reforms as Experiments." *American Psychologist* 24, 409–29.

Conlin, B. E., and G. Wolf (1980). "The Moderating Effects of Strategy Visibility, and Involvement on Allocation Behavior: An Extension of Staw's Escalation Paradigm." *Organizational Behavior and Human Performance* 26, 172–92.

Edwards, W. (1954). "The Theory of Decision Making." *Psychological Bulletin* 51, 380–417.

Festinger, L. (1957). *A Theory of Cognitive Dissonance.* Stanford: Stanford University Press.

Fishbein, M., and I. Ajzen (1975). *Belief, Attitude, Intention and Behavior: An Introduction to Theory and Research.* Reading, Mass.: Addison-Wesley.

Fox, F. V. (1980). "Persistence: Effects of Commitment and Justification Processes on Efforts to Succeed with a Course of Action." Unpublished Ph.D. dissertation, University of Illinois.

Fox, F. V. and B. M. Staw (1979). "The Trapped Administrator: The Effects of Job Insecurity and Policy Resistence Upon Commitment to a Course of Action." *Administrative Science Quarterly* 24, 449–71.

Gallup, G. (1978) *The Gallup Opinion Index.* Princeton, N.J.: American Institute of Public Opinion.

Lewicki, R. J. (1980). "Bad Loan Psychology: Entrapment and Commitment in Financial Lending." Working paper 80–25, Duke University: Graduate School of Business Administration.

March, J. G., and J. P. Olsen (1976). *Ambiguity and Choice in Organizations.* Bergen: Universitelsforlaget.

New York Times (1971). *Pentagon Papers* (based on investigative reporting of Neil Sheehan). New York: Bantam Books.

Nisbett, R., and L. Ross (1980). *Human Inference: Strategies and Shortcomings of Social Judgement.* Englewood Cliffs, N.J.: Prentice-Hall.

Pfeffer, J., and G. R. Salancik (1978). *The External Control of Organizations: A Resource Dependence Perspective.* New York: Harper & Row.

Rubin, J. Z., and J. Brockner (1975). "Factors Affecting Entrapments in Waiting Situations: The Rosencrantz and Guilderstern Effect." *Journal of Experimental Social Psychology* 31, 1054–63.

Shubik, M. (1971). "The Dollar Auction Game: A Paradox in Noncooperative Behavior and Escalation." *Journal of Conflict Resolution* 15, 109–11.

Simon, H. A. (1957). *Administrative Behavior.* New York: Macmillan.

Staw, B. M. (1976). "Knee-deep in the Big Muddy: A Study of Escalating Commitment to a Chosen Course of Action." *Organizational Behavior and Human Performance* 16, 27–44.

Staw, B. M., and F. V. Fox (1977). "Escalation: Some Determinants of Commitment to a Previously Chosen Course of Action." *Human Relations* 30, 431–50.

Staw, B. M., and J. Ross (1978). "Commitment to a Policy Decision: A Multitheoretical Perspective." *Administrative Science Quarterly* 23, 40–64.

———— (1980). "Commitment in an Experimenting Society: An Experiment on the Attribution of Leadership from Administrative Scenarios." *Journal of Applied Psychology* 65, 249–60.

Tegar, A. I. (1980). *Too Much Invested to Quit.* New York: Pergamon.

Thompson, J. D. (1967). *Organization in Action.* New York: McGraw-Hill.

Time (1979). "The State of Jimmy Carter." 5 February, 11.

Vandiver, K. (1972). "Why Should My Conscience Bother Me." In A. Heilbroner, ed. *In the Name of Profit.* Garden City, N.Y.: Doubleday.

Vroom, V. (1964). *Work and Motivation.* New York: Wiley.

Wicklund, R., and J. Brehm (1976). *Perspective on Cognitive Dissonance.* Hillside, N.J.: Lawrence Eribaum Association.

CHAPTER 6

*Time/Feeling/Focus
*Style unique

The Purposing of High-performing Systems

Peter B. Vaill

The thesis of this essay is that the definition and clarification of purposes is both a fundamental step in effective strategic management and is a prominent feature of every high-performing system I have ever investigated. Since the theory of leadership developed here derives from my studies of high-performing systems, it is necessary at the outset to describe what sort of systems I am talking about.[1] This section describes criteria by which I identify high-performing systems, while the next section states eight broad findings about high-performing system characteristics.

The data through which my ideas have developed since my original formulation of the idea of a high-performing system (Vaill 1978) comes from a variety of sources. In addition, I have had the benefit of a number of unpublished case studies passed along to me by friends and students. These include studies of a top college marching band; a Coast Guard cutter which went from a bottom to a top rating in six months; several studies of hospital emergency rooms and shock-trauma units; various accounts of military units both in battle and behind the lines; a highly successful drug rehabilitation agency; a study of one of Washington's most successful stock brokerages; various accounts of the formation of successful small businesses; plus a very large number of singular observations of excellence in one sort of human system or another.

An "excellent human system"—a high-performing system—presents one at the outset with a profound conceptual problem: how does one define excellent? Your "high-performing system" might be my "case of the compulsive pursuit of a socially useless objective,"[2] or vice versa. There is no real escape from this problem, for how we define "performance" and "excellence" depend on values. As working rules of thumb, I have treated as high-performing systems those organizations or groups which meet one or more of the following criteria:

(1) They are performing excellently against a known external standard. The cleanest example is a team which does more of something in a given time period, or does a set amount faster, than it is usually done, or than it is done by the team's competitors.

(2) They are performing excellently against what is assumed to be their potential level of performance.

(3) They are performing excellently relative to where they were at some earlier point in time, i.e., a developmental criterion.

(4) They are judged qualitatively by informed observers to be doing substantially better than other comparable systems.

(5) They are doing whatever they do with significantly fewer resources than it is assumed are needed to do what they do.

(6) They are perceived as exemplars of the *way* to do whatever they do, and thus become a source of ideas and inspiration for others, i.e., a style criterion.

(7) They are perceived to fulfill at a high level the ideas of the culture within which they exist, i.e., they have "nobility."

(8) They are the only organizations who have been able to do what they do *at all*, even though it might seem that what they do is not that difficult or mysterious a thing.

One of the delightful things about searching for high-performing systems is that one discovers a very large number of human systems which meet several of these criteria. Even though the behavioral sciences don't know it, excellence is alive and well. Some such organizations are famous, glamorous, "trendy," but others are very humble and insignificant, even drab. The criteria, though, lead one to discover many varieties of beauty in human relationships and many forms of striving which a "tighter" set of criteria would overlook. Whether doing serious social research, or just living in the world, these criteria will introduce one to extraordinary human phenomena.

The Characteristics of High-performing Systems

Here is what I have found out about high-performing systems:

(1) HPSs are clear on their broad purposes and on nearer-term objectives for fulfilling these purposes. They know why they exist and what they are trying to do. Members have pictures in their heads which are strikingly congruent.

(2) Commitment to these purposes is never perfunctory, although it is often expressed laconically. Motivation as usually conceived is always high. More important than energy level, however, is energy *focus*. Motivation is "peculiar" in the literal sense of that word: "Belonging exclusively to one person or group; special; distinctive; different." (Outsiders find

motivation peculiar too in the more usual sense of "weird, eccentric.") Energy is invested in particulars—in specific methods, tools, idea systems, arrangements, and styles.

In most HPSs, there will be some sense of its operation analogous to a feeling of rhythm. One of the "peculiarities" of motivation which is very important is the way members express their energy and commitment through getting into a "groove" of some kind.

(3) Teamwork in HPSs is focused on the task. Social psychology's favorite distinction between "task functions" and "group maintenance functions" tends to dissolve. Members will have discovered those aspects of system operations which require integrated actions and will have developed behaviors *and attitudes* which fulfill these requirements. Coupled with the previous proposition about the focus of motivation, this means that there is usually a strong conservatism evident in the HPS. There are firm beliefs in a "right organizational form," and a noticeable amount of effort is devoted to attaining and maintaining this form. Theoretically, "form follows function," but once members have found a form that works, they cling to it.

(4) Leadership in HPSs is strong and clear. It is unambivalent. There is no question of the need for initiative nor of its appropriate source although it may not always be the same person. Leader style varies widely from HPS to HPS but is remarkably consistent within a given HPS. Leader style is never conflicted: it does not swing between cool/warm, close/distant, demanding/laissez faire. Leaders are experienced as reliable and predictable.

(5) HPSs are fertile sources of inventions and new methods *within* the scope of the task they have defined and *within* the form they have chosen. HPSs are relatively conservative about new methods and inventions which take them outside the task boundaries and structural forms they have traditionally practiced. "They do not tamper with a good thing."

(6) HPSs are clearly bounded from their environments, and a considerable amount of energy, particularly on the part of leaders, is usually devoted to maintaining these boundaries. Bounding occurs in terms of firm, even if unofficial, membership rules; in terms of methods (technologies) employed; in terms of times and time durations in which the system is "on"; and in terms of the spaces the system occupies when it is operating. There will be a strong consciousness of "we are different" in the HPS, and these ongoing bounding efforts are one of the ways this consciousness displays itself most clearly.

(7) Proposition (6) leads to another consistent finding, that is that HPSs are often seen as "a problem" by entities in their environment, even entities which have a great deal of power over them. HPSs avoid external

* psychological rather than sociological bounding.

control. They scrounge resources from the environment nonapologetically. They produce what *they* want by *their* standards, not what someone else wants. Thus, they often frustrate environmental entities, especially in bureaucratic settings. One can note continual annoyance, even fury, with HPSs. People decide "they've got to be broken up." Especially when an HPS is a subunit of a larger organization, it is thus a paradox: it fulfills the larger system's desires for high performance, but the price is that it is relatively unmanageable.

(8) Above all, HPSs are systems which have "jelled," even though the phenomenon is very difficult to talk about. Neither mechanical nor organic metaphors are usually adequate for describing the "fit" of the various elements and practices of the system.

Frequently the elements of an HPS, when examined one at a time, do not seem to qualify it for membership; HPSs are often composed of cast-offs and rejects.

Beyond its concrete existence, the phenomenon of the HPS poses social science with a profound conceptual challenge, namely of learning to talk about intense human interdependency in terms more descriptively accurate than either physics or biology provide.

These propositions are what used to be called "clinical uniformities" based on the intensive study of individual cases. The propositions can be illustrated and certainly debated, but they are difficult to prove unequivocally. Each of these propositions, furthermore, could be discussed at much greater length. Each contains many unitary observations of great fascination. In the remainder of this essay, however, I am going to restrict myself to the implications of proposition 1 and proposition 4.

The Role of Clarity of Purposes

Many writers on large system leadership have stressed the importance of purposes. A fundamental remark is Chester Barnard's ". . . an objective purpose that can serve as the basis for a cooperative system is one that is *believed* by the contributors (or potential contributors) to it to be the determined purpose of the organization. The *inculcation of belief* in the real existence of a common purpose is an essential executive function [emphasis added]" (Barnard 1958, 87).

This observation captures, albeit awkwardly, the problematic character of purposes. They are not given; they do not exist independent of members' perceptions and values, or of the "pictures in their heads" as I called purposes above. Yet the implication of Barnard's remark is that the relativity of purposes — that they *do* depend on perception — is not something that should be prominent in members' minds as they go about the organization's work. "Why are we doing this? Why are we doing it this way?" are questions we would prefer not to have people asking whenever they feel like it. Can an organization act and at the same time be questioning the grounds of its action — doubting, as it were? Such a dual awareness is an attractive notion to those who philosophize about the consciousness of the truly civilized person, but one may question the idea's extension to the collective level. Systemic doubt is quite another matter.

The political scientist, Norton Long, put the matter of the leader's role with respect to doubts and second thoughts quite trenchantly in an extraordinary essay some years ago:

> In the everyday routine of life, the problematic nature of reality is made up of a multiplicity of potentially applicable norms cutting in different directions, a fragmentary state of information, an absence of any relevant substantial amount of scientific knowledge, and a pressure of time flooding by constraining decision on the most precarious definition of the situation. . . . The reduction of the political problem (i.e., of effective action) to a scientific problem is a natural result of the confusion of propositions of value and propositions of fact. It is also a result of the human desire to escape the sheer anguish of creative decision. *Leadership is concerned with the transformation of doubts into the psychological grounds of cooperative common action* [emphasis added] [1963, 4, 6].

Twenty-five years ago, Philip Selznick in his landmark *Leadership in Administration* proposed the "definition of institutional mission and role" and the "institutional embodiment of purpose" as being two essential functions of his "institutional leader" (Selznick 1957).

There is in these three sets of ideas stated above a quality of "ongoingness" which has often been overlooked. In my own experiences with management groups, I frequently encounter an impatience, even an exasperation, with discussions of basic purposes. It is as if leaders would rather believe either that these matters are understood once and for all by organization members, or that the ongoingness occurs by a kind of osmosis, but that in any case they, the leaders, have no creative responsibility to revivify purposes.

This impatience may be justified in a stable world. A pervasive sense of purpose in an organization endures, after all, in relation to other forces, and as long as these are stable and predictable, purposes will probably continue to mean what they have always meant. But these other forces are themselves in motion as has been widely remarked. Most important among the forces in my opinion are the following four categories:

(1) Environmental demands and opportunities: the more heterogeneous and dynamic these are, the more they present the organization with

an ongoing need to interpret and reinterpret what is going on. It can take nothing for granted. The changing equivocality of environmental signals must constantly be removed (Weick 1979).

(2) Organization members' needs, expectations, abilities, and values: these constitute the changing world brought into the organization. By the nature of organization itself, they must literally be "incorporated," and in the process it is frequently necessary to renegotiate the meaning of the organization's purposes.

(3) The technologies the organization employs in pursuit of its purposes entail learning time in order to exploit their productive and economic potential. If the organization is constantly "upgrading" its technologies, it may never reach a smooth flow of habituated actions, a flow on which the economics of efficiency and profitable action are based.

(4) The phenomenon of reorganization itself is less often noted than the previous three. Many more structural alternatives exist for the modern large system than existed twenty-five years ago, and many organizations are experimenting continually with new forms. The impact of these changes on role relationships, chains of command, felt senses of accountability, etc., is not as thoroughly discussed as it should be, particularly the impact of all this flux on purposes.

In other words, the extent to which members can come to share pictures in their heads about the organization's basic purposes depends on some degree of stability in environmental demands, members' own expectations and needs, the technologies they are operating, and the structures through which they are bound together. *Beyond some unknown threshold, too much change in this system of factors breaks down the shared sense of what the organization is, why it exists, and what its basic purposes are.*

This is the key implication of Emery and Trist's famous remark that in their Type IV-Turbulent Field "the ground itself is moving" (Emery and Trist 1965). The moving ground metaphor refers to the more basic paradigms and images we use to organize experience. It is one thing for the objectives and techniques which flow from a paradigm to be rapidly changing, but when the paradigm itself is undergoing substantial revision, there is no longer a firm basis for any proposal.

Emery and Trist are aware of the leadership problems this situation creates, but they did not deal with the question at any length. They suggest that McGregor's Theory Y seems to hold promise, which was a plausible expectation in the early '60s but which I think is considered to be quite insufficient today. They speculate quite prophetically about the ability of matrix structures to absorb large amounts of ambiguity. They are convinced that the articulation of overarching values is a crucial step. They seem to be saying that even if *things* cannot be stabilized, nevertheless consciousness might be through the development of broadly shared values. *Paradigm* leadership is needed; that is the apparent thrust of their argument.

Others of course were issuing similar calls in the 1960s when the first pains of the collapsing paradigm were felt ("This is the Age When Things Have Not Turned Out as We Thought They Would," said David Matthews on being sworn in as Secretary of H.E.W. in the early '70s.) Even now, I think the question of leadership under conditions of extreme turbulence is no nearer to a working solution than when first articulated twenty or thirty years ago. If the *need* is for paradigm leadership and through national policy we undertake to give decision-makers more freedom to act, it remains a kind of grand wager that these leaders will respond with forward-looking purposes for the 1990s and beyond.

So we must ask more urgently than ever, what becomes of the "inculcation of belief" (Barnard), the "embodiment of purpose" (Selznick), and the "transformation of doubts" (Long)? What does this behavior look like in the first place? Under increasingly turbulent conditions, how does it change? Who among leaders of the world's organizations of whatever kind is doing this work well?

First of all, the behavior we are talking about needs a name. I propose the word "purposing" to refer to *that continuous stream of actions by an organization's formal leadership which have the effect of inducing clarity, consensus, and commitment regarding the organization's basic purposes.* I decided on the term purposing as a result of investigating the etymology of the word "purpose" and discovering that it and the word "propose" derive from the same Latin root, "proponere." In other words, through the filters of Old and Middle French and English our thinking has come to divide an idea which was originally more unified: that there is *both* an ongoing stream of proposings and there are the results of the process—purposes. We need the new word purposing to remind ourselves that there is a special class of proposings that needs to occur in organizations—proposings which have to do with the establishment, clarification, and modification of purposes. This I "propose" we call "purposing."

The Functions of Purposing

With the idea of purposing in hand it is possible to begin to indicate some of the forms it takes in organizations. In general my argument is that high-performing systems are, among other things, systems where we can observe the phenomenon of purposing working well. People are not mixed up about why the system exists or about what their role in it is. Leaders, while they of course do not call what they do purposing, nevertheless can be seen inculcating belief, transforming doubts, and embodying purpose.

From high-performing systems as well as from other settings, I have identified the following seven functions of purposing:

(1) Purposing occurs in relation to expectations of those who own or charter the system. This does not mean that leaders merely preach conformity to these expectations, but rather that the content of what they talk about and do is seen to have these key outside forces as a referent.

(2) Purposing is seen in the articulation of the grounds for basic strategic decisions. These decisions may be of many different kinds — to add a particular person to the system; to change its posture toward systems with which it competes; to adopt new technology; to fundamentally alter its internal structure, etc. The point is that such decisions are not made or explained in isolation from basic purposes.

(3) Purposing is seen in leaders' accounts of the meaning of daily activity in the system. The hours people put in, the skills they practice to acquire, the sacrifices they make, the pains they take, and the pains they experience — all these can be interpreted in terms of the system's basic purposes, and in high-performing systems it is a very noticeable phenomenon.

(4) Purposing is evident in decisions NOT to do things, such as offer proposed new products, enter new territories, add available new technology, hire or retain particular people. "It's not us." "It wouldn't be right for us." These phrases are frequently heard in high-performing systems as Peters did in his study of America's best managed companies (Peters 1980). Attractive-options-foregone is one of the most powerful forms of purposing. It communicates and inculcates discipline.

(5) Purposing differentiates the organization from other superficially similar organizations. Members of every organization are conscious of what other systems somewhat like their own are doing. A key process by which they come to identify with their own organization is to be helped to see how it is not quite like any other. Bennis called this process "identity" several years ago. It is a phenomenon that needs to be much more widely understood (Bennis and Slater 1968).

(6) Purposing is the expression of what the leadership wants. In the social science literature preoccupation with what the boss wants is often treated as a kind of neurotic dependency reaction. But it is possible to be curious and concerned about what the boss wants in a healthy way.

It is important with this function to distinguish between wanting something for the system and wanting something for oneself. The leadership of many large systems today is "just passing through," "getting a ticket punched," "on a fast track." Self-aggrandizement and self-promotion are often these leaders' basic motives. The worst thing in the world, some of them seem to feel, is actually to become *entangled* in the system.

I have never found a high-performing system whose leadership was perceived by members as on a fast track to something else. To be perceived as wanting something for the system is crucial; it cannot be faked.

(7) Purposing in some sense entails the mythologizing of oneself and the organization. When Selznick speaks of the institutional embodiment of purpose, one aspect of the process is to let oneself come to embody the organization. People perhaps find it easier to identify with a personage than with a complex social system. This means the leadership becomes a kind of vessel or vehicle.

In the way leaders talk and act, in the preferences they express, in their passions and tantrums, meanings echo for members. Harrison Owen, a long-time observer of large system machinations in Washington, D.C., speaks of the leader needing to become the center of a "myth-modification process," an articulator of the new "likely stories," as Owen calls them, which can become the basis for future action.

To be willing to become a mythic figure is perhaps the true expression of the "loneliness of command." The loneliness derives from the felt discrepancy between what one is feeling and how one knows a contemplated action will be received by members and organization publics. The search, agonized as it may be, is for courses of action which are responsive to the ownership (#1, above), substantively sound (#2, above), not merely demagogic or exploitative (#3), consistent with the system's evolving identity (#'s 4 and 5), and honest expressions of one's own values (#6). No wonder it is so difficult; no wonder it is rare, although it is not as rare as some might think.

In high-performing systems, men and women are finding ways to conduct purposing in terms of the characteristics I have just discussed. This is why high-performing systems are such powerful and instructive exemplars. The final section of this essay is concerned with synthesizing many of these remarks into a simple statement of what it is leaders of high-performing systems do.

The Purposing of High-performing Systems

There are three characteristics of the actions of leaders of high-performing systems which I believe appear one hundred percent of the time. I think these three characteristics and their interrelationships have profound implications for the world of organizations and organizational leaders, not because they are such esoteric or mysterious factors, but because they are so well known and apparently easily overlooked.

1. Leaders of high-performing systems put in extraordinary amounts of *time.*

2. Leaders of high-performing systems have very strong *feelings* about the attainment of the system's purposes.

3. Leaders of high-performing systems *focus* on key issues and variables.

I have come to call this the Time-Feeling-Focus theory of high performing systems leadership. There are of course many nuances, subtleties, and local specialties connected with the leadership of any high-performing system, but over and over again, Time, Feeling, and Focus appear no matter what else appears. They may not be totally sufficient as conditions, but they are necessary. I now propose to say a few more words about each, following which I will describe what happens in human systems where one or two of the three are absent. The essay then closes with some comments about the interrelationships of leader development and system development, and some comments about the question of leader style.

Time

Leaders of high-performing systems work very hard; that is the basic thing to be said. They put in many hours. Their consciousness is dominated by issues and events in the system they are in charge of. They see the rest of life, often, in terms of the jargon, the technology, and the culture of their system. Their awareness of the system does not respect the clock and hence they can be seen scribbling notes to themselves or others, making phone calls, and replaying and debriefing system events at all kinds of odd times — evenings, weekends, vacation periods, the wee hours. Their consciousness does not respect place either: they work in the office, at home, in airport boarding areas, in the back seats of taxicabs, or anywhere else they happen to be. At halftimes and intermissions, they duck out to call the office. They are often seen by system members as well as others as living, eating, sleeping, and breathing the system.

The hours they put in are matters of frequent comment by those around them. Stories accumulate about the amounts of time they put in and about their nonstop work habits. Curiously, the *quality* of what they accomplish in all these hours is much less often commented on, not because the quality is thought to be mediocre or low but because it is apparently felt to be a natural result of the hours put in. What is noticed is the number of hours put in.

Of great importance is that these leaders put in large amounts of both micro-time and macro-time. Micro-time is the hour-to-hour, day-to-day kind of investment. Leaders of high-performing systems are always working, but less often noted is their macro-time involvement. Leaders of high-performing systems tend to stay in their jobs for numbers of years. They do not "pass through," as noted in the earlier discussion of purposing. They make not only a large commitment of micro-time but also a large commitment of macro-time.

Sometimes the high-performing system is a rather temporary system, i.e., it is not intended to last indefinitely. In this case, macro-time is the willingness to "commit for the duration."

Feeling

"An executive ought to want something," says my colleague, Professor David Brown. In this rather simple assertion growing from his own studies of large system leadership, he has neatly captured a second element which is always present in the attitudes and behaviors I see in leaders of high-performing systems. They care deeply about the system. This includes its purposes, its structure and conduct, its history, its future security and, although sometimes expressed in a way that would make a psychologist shudder, they care about the people in the system.

For the leader of a high-performing system, constant energetic purposing is a natural expression of Feeling, i.e., of his or her own deep values and beliefs. Purposing is not a style or function which is adopted for some occasion. Feeling furthermore sustains the person through the many hours of labor discussed under Time. Involvement with the system *is* the person's life which is why from his or her frame of reference the amount of Time put in is a natural thing to do.

Macro-time can often be seen to play a key role in the development and expression of Feeling. With many large systems it is not immediately clear what makes them special. A leader "cycling through" on an eighteen to twenty-four month assignment may never experience the system much more deeply than its immediate issues permit. Many, many executives bring high achievement motivation to their jobs. In macro-time this motivation becomes invested in the system's culture, and this culture comes to be seen as something valuable for its own sake rather than as a vehicle for the leader's ambition, development, and next assignment.

Motivation in high-performing systems has "peculiarity." In leaders this peculiarity can be seen in the way they have integrated their innate energies and ambitions with the needs and opportunities of the system. Selznick's "institutional embodiment of purpose," therefore, is not a one-way phenomenon. In high-performing systems there is a two-way embodiment in Feeling of leader-in-system and system-in-leader. When a person becomes "Mr. . . . (whatever the activity or industry is)" or "the First Lady of . . . (the activity or industry)," the two-way embodiment is complete.

Through Feeling, leaders of high performing systems tend to take themselves and their systems quite seriously. They often become the targets of worldly-wise cynics and satirists.[3] Their total absorption makes them vulnerable to interpretations of their behavior which are askant to the values and beliefs they hold.

More seriously, the very strength of Feeling can sometimes blind a leader to what the system needs as the environment changes. They sometimes cannot see that the meanings they have built up about the system may be becoming maladaptive, that they have to rethink what the system is and can be in the new conditions. All organizations go through this process and high-performing systems are not immune. The conservatism they manifest regarding new methods and bounding themselves from the environment exists in continuous tension with the dynamic environment. Where a system drifts into irrelevance over time, it is usually the result of a combination of very strong Feeling on the part of leaders and members and insufficient wisdom about the next element discussed — Focus.

Focus

The management literature has always contained much discussion of what it is the boss ought to be working on. Chester Barnard's original essay was devoted to this question. Situational theory has been answering this question in recent years by saying, "The boss ought to be working on whatever the system needs at the moment."

Leaders of high-performing systems have solved this problem. Behind the attention to detail which is possible because of Time, one can note persistent factors which they Focus on. In one system it may be recruitment, in another the securing of stable funding, in another the buffering of the system from the environment, and in another the hands-on involvement in the system's basic activity. There seems to be no fixed formula, no short list of variables which are always important. But with Focus there always is *some* short list which leaders have clearly in mind.

Furthermore, one can note leaders actively communicating their judgments about what is important to members. They help bring Focus to others' behavior as well as manifesting it in their own. This function is of extreme importance because in any organization, at any moment, there are many things that need attention. These factors do not exist as abstract impersonal matters but rather are actively voiced by various organization members. The organization is a texture of proposings, as I said earlier. Leaders of high-performing systems are not distracted by this cacophony. They know what few things are important, and in their statements and actions they make these priorities known. In macro-time members, too, learn what is important and, therefore, in high-performing systems the cacophony of proposings is less chaotic and centrifugal than in other systems, although it is rarely absent entirely. Focus is really

Focus*ing* in dynamic terms: it is an ongoing process of choosing what to emphasize and what to leave alone.

Strategic planning and strategic management as they are discussed in the literature are primarily the study of Focus. What are the key variables? In Peters's (1980) findings about America's best managed companies, excellent companies are shown to have "simultaneous loose-tight controls," i.e., they have picked out key variables and developed tight controls over these, and are willing to operate only relatively loose controls over the rest. Such an approach at one and the same time communicates what is important *and* a desire to allow as much freedom and latitude as possible.

Without Time and Feeling, strategic planning as discussed in the bulk of the current literature is an empty technical exercise. For example, one of the most common problems in strategic management is the length of view top managers take. It tends to be too short. Their term of office does not extend far enough into the future. They will not be around when the fruits (or poisons) of their decisions appear. This is why the concept of macro-time is so important. Focus constitutes the What of executive leadership, but it cannot carry by itself the Why or the When or the How. The Why resides primarily in what I am calling Feeling, the When in Time. The How, as I shall develop below, is not as important — in high-performing systems at least — as writers on leadership have made it.

Variations on Time-Feeling-Focus

I have said that these three elements are always present in the actions of leaders of high-performing systems. It is instructive to pause and comment on situations where one or two or all three are absent. Some very familiar patterns emerge.

1. *Time with no Feeling or Focus.* In this situation and the next are seen the phenomena associated with workaholism and Type A behavior. The investment of large chunks of Time without the positive Feeling that the activity is important and without Focus on key issues has the quality of compulsiveness. There are extreme forms which are indeed even neurotic, for with this pattern we are talking about a person who works very hard without knowing exactly what to work on or why. Attention to detail and the investment of Time alone is not found in leaders of high-performing systems.

2. *Time and Feeling without Focus.*[4] The leader who cares deeply and is willing to work very hard, but for whom everything seems to be of equal importance, is a somewhat tragic figure. In large and complex organizations this mix of factors can be an actual killer. Managers who speak of having to run harder and harder just to stay even may be stuck

in this pattern. The person who has Time and Feeling without Focus needs help understanding the system and in managing her or his own small "t" time. It is to this person that we say, "You need to step back and really think about what is important." Sadly, the person caught in the grip of this mix misinterprets the advice. He or she thinks the advice is, "Put in less Time; don't Feel so strongly." Of course the person can't do it — doesn't even want to do it. Time and Feeling are deep expressions of the person's history and character and are not easily modified. How such a person learns to Focus without cutting back on Time or Feeling is a major challenge to students of executive development.

3. *Time and Focus without Feeling.* Here I am afraid we have a large number of the young people we see in our professional schools of management today. I quickly add that the cultures of the schools themselves tend to reward this pattern lavishly, so even a young person not disposed toward this pattern at the outset will feel enormous pressure to adopt it.

Time and Focus without Feeling says, "Don't get too involved. Look at the facts. Make a decision and move on to the next thing. Be willing to work hard for there is no free lunch, but don't get your identity too wrapped up in what you are doing. Build your track record, get your tickets punched, do quality work at each milestone on the fast track. Somewhere out in your future — in your forties, perhaps — you'll have accumulated the 'clout' to do what you want to do and be the person you want to be" — you'll have earned the right to Feeling. Unfortunately for too many the forties do not bring this opportunity but instead a set of work habits and personal financial circumstances which seem to require continuation of the same patterns.

It is important to say with Time/Focus without Feeling that the pattern is not dysfunctional per se; it is just never found in leaders of high-performing systems. Some occupations, for example, require that Feeling be detached from the immediate system in favor of adherence to standards and procedures which are independent of the immediate system, i.e., which refer to another system the person is a member of. There is no question that this displacement of Feeling from an immediate system to some broader professional system is socially important; law, medicine, and auditing are examples. The possibility of a "high-performing relationship" with an immediate client is sometimes put second to professional standards.

4. *Feeling without Time or Focus.* Idealism and cynicism are the two labels by which this condition is more commonly described. It is possible to care very deeply about various organizations in society without actually putting in much Time on them or really understanding what is involved in operating them effectively (Focus). Without the commitment of energy expressed in Time and the thought and practicality expressed in

Focus, the Feeling-driven person issues calls to arms or fulminates. Again, this is a social role which history demonstrates to be of great importance, but it is not found in the leaders of high-performing systems.

5. *Feeling and Focus without Time.* Three very well known social roles frequently manifest this pattern. The staff person who does very good work but who goes home at five o'clock is one example. The astute social commentator is a second. Third is one of America's fastest growing industries: consulting. A good consultant has his or her efforts Focused on the right variables and cares that the client organization does better, but consultants are not continuously present. They phase in and out and are often not there when the system needs them most. Their function is not to sustain the system but to get it started, to get it pointed in the right direction. So once again, it is not that Feeling and Focus without Time are bad or dysfunctional per se, but rather that this mix is not found in the leaders of high-performing systems.

6. *Focus without Time or Feeling.* This describes a person who is working on the right things but who is not putting in more hours than required and for whom there is no very deep personal meaning in the activity. This mix is never found in the leadership of high-performing systems. Actually, this pattern describes an "employee" whose Focus actually derives from someone else having defined the task carefully. The person just works the expected hours at the expected energy level. Focus without Time or Feeling is . . . a job.

7. *Absence of Time, Feeling, and Focus.* So far I have described situations where one or two of the three elements are strongly present. What about where none of them is present to any significant degree? This essay is not concerned with diagnosing pervasive organizational or societal ills. My high-performing systems research, however, causes me constantly to wonder to what extent have we drifted into a broad social condition where one can be a member or even a leader of an organization without Time or Feeling or Focus as I have defined them? It is a very sobering exercise to reflect on all the social forces today which work against the investment of Time, the flowering of Feeling, and the attainment of Focus.

Relation of Time, Feeling, and Focus to System Development

The three factors seem to be interrelated and interdependent, although they do not exist in clean causal relationships one to another. In retrospect, however, one can see in the actions and attitudes of leaders of high-performing systems how investments of Time tend to deepen Feeling; how the development of Feeling leads to putting in more Time; how

Focus is both expressive *of* Time and Feeling and leads *to* further investments of Time and new patterns of Feeling. I emphasize that these relationships are noticed in retrospect. One cannot say, prospectively, that putting in Time, for example, will automatically deepen Feeling and make more likely the discovery of the key variables captured in the idea of Focus.

That strength in one of the factors does not automatically cause development in the other two suggests that there is some additional set of forces present in the development of leaders of high-performing systems which is relatively absent in the development of leaders of other systems. The obvious candidate forces lie in the system itself, for the system's developing strength and success somehow make more likely the discovery of the key things to Focus on, the willingness to put in Time, and the development of ever-stronger Feeling about the system and its purposes.

There is a good deal of anecdotal evidence to support this idea. One kind of evidence is the experience most of us have had at one time or another where success in some organizational effort seems to trigger a collection of improvements in the system in a sometimes startling fashion. Effort gets more efficient; morale jumps; members' confidence in each other increases strongly; leadership improves in a variety of ways, including the three factors I have been discussing. Sometimes such systems get on a "streak" where, for a period at least, they just seem to do everything right. A process like this, I am suggesting, little-understood as it is, could be a very significant influence on the development of the leadership of the system. As we say, nothing succeeds like success.

A second kind of evidence to suggest that the evolving success of the system has a powerful developmental effect on the leadership comes from the way members of high-performing systems talk about the early formative period of the system. There are consistent statements such as, "We had no idea things would turn out like this"; "In the early years, we hardly knew what we were doing"; "We were really groping"; "We just did what we thought we were supposed to do"; and so forth. I have never found a high-performing system member who claims that the high achievements of the system are merely the logical results of a preexisting plan, although the notion of "having a dream and seeking to realize it" is very common. Nor do I have data from members or leaders of high-performing systems to suggest that the leaders knew all along what they were doing. In a high-performing system, omniscient strategies are usually not attributed to the leadership.

So, in summary, my current thinking is that the grasp of Time, Feeling, and Focus by the leader develops and coexists with the life and achievements of the system. This, however, is not a particularly satisfying way to talk about leadership in high-performing systems. More tempting is the assertion that "leaders cause high-performing systems." That certainly is the thrust of much of the writing on management and leadership—that if the individual somehow does something to his or her attitude, knowledge, or style, major system improvements will occur. Social scientists have implicitly been promising this to practitioners for years. Marginal improvements do seem to occur in some cases, but I have no evidence that the breakthrough to a high-performing condition as I have defined it will occur.

I said earlier that high-performing systems have "jelled" in a way that is not easily discussable in the language system of mechanical and organic metaphors that we have. That finding is relevant to this question of the relation between the leader's attitude and behavior, and the development of the system. One reason I think the Time-Feeling-Focus model has promise is because it is simple. It does not overcategorize and overspecify what it is we are trying to understand. Similarly, the eight broad generalizations about high-performing systems given at the beginning of this essay are deliberately phrased in as commonsense a way as possible. I am trying to keep our attention on the experience of members and leaders in these settings.

I have discussed the Time-Feeling-Focus approach to this point as a way of understanding leaders' behavior. The scheme is also very useful for understanding members' behavior and for understanding the system as a whole. With due regard for the different roles they play and scopes of responsibility they carry, Time-Feeling-Focus can be used for looking at anyone in the high-performing system. It is not just the leader but the system as a whole which can be seen functioning at all sorts of odd times and in odd places. Members come in on evenings and weekends. The culture of the system blends into the cultures of their families. These are manifestations of the Time factor. Congruence of Feeling as I have said several times is a distinguishing characteristic of a high-performing system. What I called the peculiarity of motivation is *shared* and intensely valued among members. Focus as an intermember phenomenon is one of the most striking features of a high-performing system as contrasted with other human systems. In a high-performing system, people actually agree, without having to go through tortuous processes of negotiation and conflict management, what the key factors are!

For perhaps a high-performing system is not an objective entity at all. The criteria by which its success is asserted are subjective. The meanings it has to members and to observers in its environment are intensely personal and subjective. It is full of all kinds of events and processes which social science has tended to ignore (Vaill 1978). Statements like these, of course, could be made about all social systems. They are all objects of consciousness in the first instance and as such should not be reduced to

simple machine models, cause-effect models, or other superficially attractive metaphors. I think Phenomenology has the most interesting
things to say about these issues, but an exploration of these things is
beyond the scope of this essay (cf., Keen 1975; Zaner 1970). Suffice it to
say, for the moment, that I regard a high-performing system as a frame
on which members' consciousnesses interact. The interesting thing about
leaders' consciousnesses is that they seem to be described by the Time-
Feeling-Focus scheme.

The Question of Style

One final observation about the Time-Feeling-Focus idea is that the
style with which the leader expresses herself or himself in the system
seems *not* to be a determining factor. My learnings about high-performing systems are therefore at variance with the tremendous amount of emphasis managerial style and leader style have received in the literature
over the last twenty-five years. Most of our research has been done in
low-performing systems. We have concluded rather frequently that the
way a leader/manager was working — style — was having a significant
negative effect. We have extrapolated from this conclusion to the idea
that a change in style will repair the damage that is being done to motivation, morale, communication, trust, and problem-solving. I need not further review the thousands of pages there are on the subject of warm vs.
cool, participative vs. autocratic, demanding vs. accepting, etc. My
main point is that for the most part, all this interest in style is beside the
point *in high-performing systems* (Harvey 1975).

I have seen every style I can conceive of in the leadership of high-performing systems. There are tyrants whose almost maniacal commitment
to achieving the system's purposes makes one think that they'd be locked
up if they were not in charge of an organization that was the best of its
kind. There are warm, laid-back parent figures who hardly seem to be
doing anything at all, until one looks a little more closely. There are tech-
nocrats devoted to computerized representations of the system and
dreamers who seem to care nothing about the operational data. Some of
these leaders are educated to the highest levels, and others never finished
high school. Owing to the Focus factor, they all possess expertise in what
the system does, but some express this expertise constantly and others
don't. Some seem clearly to be "Type A's" on the way to exhaustion or an
early grave, but most are in good health and of noticeably strong consti-
tution. Some are rah-rah optimists and others are dour critics who express their love for the system by enumerating its imperfections. Leaders
of high-performing systems are all over the style map.

What the theory described in this essay says to the would-be leader is,

"Seek constantly to do what is right and what is needed in the system (Focus). Do it *all out* in terms of your energy (Time). Put your whole psyche into it (Feeling)." This is the normative lesson I derive from studying leaders of high-performing systems. It is a very simple prescription, and in its simplicity is somewhat at variance with the fine and precise distinctions in the literature. But it is these three factors, always understood as a mix rather than one at a time, which my results suggest.

Conclusion

In high-performing systems as I have defined them one can note their constant purposing by the system leadership. Purposing occurs through the investment of large amounts of micro- and macro-Time, through the experience and expression of very strong Feeling about the attainment of purposes and the importance of the system, and through the attainment of understanding of the key variables in system success (Focus). All leaders of high-performing systems have integrated these three factors at a very high level of intensity and clarity.

The number of social scientists who are trying to understand excellence in human systems is very small. Pathology is more accessible and, for some, more fun. The question of what it takes to govern and lead a high-performing system, and the question of how we are going to develop more men and women who are equipped to do it awaits the increased attention which I believe high-performing systems deserve. This essay has been an effort to stimulate such attention.

NOTES

1. Many, many people have contributed over the years to my understanding of high-performing systems, but no one has been more important than my colleague at George Washington University, Professor Jerry B. Harvey. His intellect and wit and continuous support, and his unfeigned delight in the ideas which fall out of the HPS focus are of simply incalculable value to me. "This is not yet *the* paper on high-performing systems, Jerry, but on the other hand, it's not not-the-paper, either."

2. I once asked a student, who was insisting on an exact definition before she could write her term paper, "If this were a course in Botany, and the assignment was to describe a beautiful flower, would you find that impossible?" This rhetorical question she did not find too helpful, although I was pleased with it.

3. Some years ago in the *Harvard Business Review*, Seymour Tilles compared the strategy the founder of Lestoil used to beat Proctor & Gamble to the strategy Hadrian used. *The New Yorker* quoted a key paragraph in one of its famous column footings with the editorial remark: "Every age has its heroes."

4. In retrospect, this is the pattern which I think best describes my five-year deanship of George Washington University's School of Government and Business Administration.

REFERENCES

Barnard, Chester (1958). *The Functions of the Executive.* Boston: Harvard University Press (first published 1938).

Bennis, Warren G., and Philip E. Slater (1968). *The Temporary Society.* New York: Harper & Row.

Berger, Peter L., and Thomas Luckmann (1967). *The Social Construction of Reality.* New York: Doubleday Anchor Books.

Emery, F. E., and E. L. Trist (1965). "The Causal Texture of Organizational Environments." *Human Relations* 18(1), 21–32.

Harvey, Jerry B. (1975). "Eight Myths OD Consultants Believe In . . . And Die By!" *OD Practitioner* 7(1), 19–22.

Keen, Ernest (1975). *A Primer in Phenomenological Psychology.* New York: Holt, Rinehart, & Winston.

Long, Norton E. (1963). "The Political Act as an Act of Will." *Sociology* 69(1), 126–38.

Peters, Thomas J. (1980). "Putting Excellence into Management." *Business Week* 21, 196–205.

Selznick, Philip (1957). *Leadership in Administration.* New York: Harper & Row.

Vaill, Peter B. (1978). "Toward a Behavioral Description of High Performing Systems." In McCall, Morgan, and Michael Lombardo, eds. *Leadership: Where Else Can We Go?* Durham, N.C.: Duke University Press, pp. 103–25.

Weick, Karl E. (1979). *The Social Psychology of Organizing.* 2nd ed. Reading, Mass.: Addison-Wesley.

Zaner, Richard M. (1970). *The Way of Phenomenology.* New York: Bobbs-Merrill Co., Pegasus Books.

CHAPTER 7

Leadership as Cultural Expression

Thomas J. Sergiovanni

How often it seems in leadership that battles are won but wars are lost; that progress is made event by event with no qualitative organizational effect; that administrative energies are expended and routine competence is maintained with no commensurate hint of excellence or greatness. Thanks to sound management, research centers increase the number of research contracts won but decline in reputation; courses are revised according to logical principles of curriculum development, but programs do not excell; new resources are obtained by rational administrative efforts but excellence escapes; and technically superb plans are developed to redistribute existing resources with declines in morale and overall productivity. These apparent contradictions in part can be explained by differentiating between tactical and strategic leadership. Tactical leadership involves analyses which lead to administrative action and means of minor magnitude, which are of small scale, and which serve larger purposes. Strategic leadership, by contrast, is the art and science of enlisting support for broader policies and purposes and for devising longer-range plans.

It seems trite to note that quality leadership requires balanced attention to both tactical and strategic requirements. Despite this common knowledge, leadership research and practice reflect a bias in favor of the tactical. At best, attention to the tactical at the expense of the strategic maintains day-by-day organizational competence, but excellence remains out of reach. In part, the emphasis on tactical requirements of leadership reflects the broader management culture of Western society. Such values as efficiency, specificity, rationality, measurability, and objectivity combined with the belief that good management is tough-minded are part of this culture. Results-oriented management is the slogan; the bottom line is worshiped; and the direct, in-control manager is admired. Leadership is broadly defined as achieving objectives effectively and efficiently. Leadership theory puts the emphasis on the leader's behavior and on results. The metaphors of the battlefield are often used to remind us that one must be hard-nosed, and that the going is tough. Evaluation is quick and to the point and success is determined on the basis of short-term accomplishments. Key to this management culture is the assumption that ambiguity is an organizational ill to be rooted out by rational management techniques. Good administrators manage with certainty, are decisive, and can back up action with rational and logical arguments. Given these cultural demands no wonder that the tactical requirements of leadership are emphasized. Missing from these tactical issues are holistic values of purpose, goodness, and importance. Missing is an emphasis on long-term quality.

In recent years conventional views of management and leadership have been called to question. Theorists, for example, are coming to realize that uncertainty and ambiguity are not only natural but desirable (March 1980; Pascale 1978). Further, cultural aspects of organization are being offered as better able to account for the artificial, purposive, and practical aspects of organizational life.

There is more to leadership than meets the tactical eye. The real value of leadership rests with the meanings which actions import to others than in the actions themselves. A complete rendering of leadership requires that we move beyond the obvious to the subtle, beyond the immediate to the long range, beyond actions to meanings, beyond viewing organizations and groups within social systems to cultural entities. These are the strategic issues which will be discussed in this chapter.

Let's take as an example the important tactical skill of mastering a contingency approach to leadership, characterized by careful reading of situations and by applying the right doses of the correct mix of leadership styles. Combine this tactical skill with a leader who has certain purposes, beliefs, and commitment to what the school or university is and can be and who can communicate these in a fashion which rallies others to the cause, and we are achieving proper balance. One would not want to choose between the tactical and strategic in this case, but if I had to make such a choice, my vote would be with the latter. What a leader stands for is more important than what he or she does. The meanings a leader communicates to others is more important than his or her specific leadership style. Critical to understanding this relationship is a view that humans, beyond rudimentary animalistic tendencies, do not behave but act. Actions differ from behavior in that they are born of preconceptions, assumptions, and motives, and these are imbedded with meanings. Leadership acts are expressions of culture. Leadership as cultural expression seeks to build unity and order within an organization by giving attention to purposes, historical and philosophical tradition, and ideals and norms which define the way of life within the organization and which provide the bases for socializing members and obtaining their compliance.

Developing and nurturing organizational value patterns and norms represent a response to felt needs of individuals and groups for order, stability, and meaning. The concept of "center" is used by Shils (1961) to describe this need. Organizational centers represent the focus of values, sentiments, and beliefs which provide the cultural cement needed to hold people together in groups and groups into an organizational federation. Lacking an official center, "wild" centers emerge within the organization as a natural response to felt needs. Wild centers are only accidentally compatible with the official, thus the "domestication" of wild centers is important to leadership as cultural expression.

Recognizing that organizations often resemble multicultural societies and that subgroups must of necessity maintain individual and cherished identities, the domestication process seeks *minimally* to build a cultural federation of compatibility which provides enough common identity, enough common meanings, and enough of a basis for committed action for the organization to function in spirited concert.

Leadership as cultural expression results from the complex interplay of several dimensions, prime among which are leadership skills, antecedents, and meanings. Leadership skills have been traditionally emphasized in the management literature, are considered important in the complex interplay of dimensions, and represent tactical requirements. Less considered have been antecedents and meanings—dimensions which comprise strategic requirements. From leadership skills, meanings, antecedents, and culture can be extracted ten principles of quality leadership. These principles are depicted in Table 1. There is always a risk in reducing the subtle and complex to a handful of abbreviated and specific principles. I accept this risk in order to provide busy professionals with a useful and easily remembered framework. The risk will be reduced if we agree that the ten principles are not meant to be recited as one would a litany, but are offered to bring to one's consciousness a cognitive map of the requirements for quality in leadership. A careful reading of other chapters in this section will reveal that most of the principles have already been considered, either directly or indirectly. This rendering, therefore, should be viewed in part as a summary and in part as an extension and synthesis which seeks an integrated image of quality dimensions in leadership (Sergiovanni 1981, 1982).

The first principle to be considered is that of *prerequisites.* Prerequisites refer to the various leadership skills needed to develop and maintain basic leadership competence. Such skills as mastering and using various contingency leadership theories, conflict management tactics, team management principles, shared decision-making models, and group process

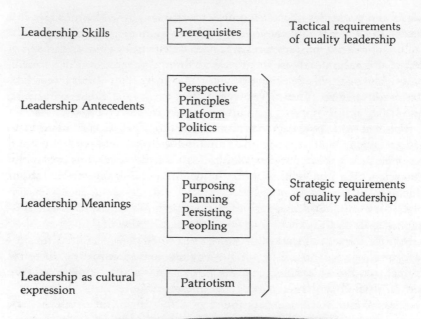

Table 1. The 10-P Model of Leadership

techniques are examples of basic leadership requirements. Leadership skills are tactical in the sense that they are situationally specific, of short duration, and focused on specific objectives or outcomes. Successful leadership is not likely to be within the reach of those who are not competent in the basic leadership skills, but competence and excellence are different. To move beyond routine competence one must shift attention from the tactical to the strategic. The remaining principles are strategic in nature. They give meaning and direction to the leadership skills.

The next group of four principles are leadership antecedents in the sense that they represent conditions, feelings, assumptions, cognitive maps, and attitudes of the leader which determine his or her reality and which guide his or her decisions, actions, and behavior. As antecedents vary among leaders, so does leadership quality and meaning.

Perspective refers to the ability of the leader to be able to differentiate between the tactical and strategic and to understand how they are related. One with perspective brings a broader, patient, more long-range view to his or her leadership responsibilities which enables the sorting of trivial from important events and outcomes and the determining of worth. What the leader stands for and believes about schooling, the place of education in society, how schools should be organized and operated, and how people should be treated comprise the guiding *principles* which bring integrity and meaning to leadership. Leaders stand for certain ideals and principles which become cornerstones of their very being. In a recent *Wall Street Journal*-Gallup poll, for example, integrity was the factor considered most important for advancement by chief executives of 282 of the nation's largest firms in describing characteristics of subordinates. The number one failing of weak managers, by contrast, was limited point of view. Integrity suggests that the leader values something important and is able to communicate this value to others.

Platform refers to the articulation of one's principles into an operational framework. Platforms are governing in the sense that they represent a set of criteria and an implicit standard from which decisions are made. One's teaching platform governs the decisions he or she makes about teaching and provides a set of ideals which make teaching decisions sensible to a person. Educational and management platforms, so essential to quality in leadership, operate in much the same fashion.

Politics is the final leadership antecedent to be considered. At its simplest level, leadership can be defined as the ability of an individual to influence another individual or group in a fashion which helps to achieve certain desired goals. In schools and universities political behavior is a key ingredient in successful leadership. Schools and universities, like other arenas of public administration, are political organizations characterized by multiple interest groups, unclear and competing goals, diffuse sources of power, and ambiguous lines of authority. Unlike the simple business firm or owner-operated store, the educational administrator typically cannot exercise direct authority to obtain compliance or cooperation from others. Often, groups to be influenced are outside the organization itself, or are outside of the administrator's authority. Typically, the administrator must obtain voluntary cooperation, support, and good will from others to get things done. Sensitivity to *politics* and knowledge that the leader is typically dependent upon the good wishes and voluntary compliance of others if he or she is to be effective in the long haul is thus a necessary leadership antecedent.

The next group of leadership principles reflects the *meanings* theme. Key to quality in leadership and quality in educational organizations is that academics and others find their work to be interesting, satisfying, and meaningful. Meaning suggests as well that people believe in what they are doing and appreciate its importance to the organization, to society, and to themselves. Leadership meanings can be summed in the four principles: purposing, planning, persisting, and peopling.

Purposing breathes life and meaning into the day-to-day activities of people at work. It helps people to interpret their contributions, their successes and failures, their efforts and energies in light of the organization's purposes. Through this process, seemingly ordinary events become meaningful with subsequent motivational benefits to the organization. In addition, purposing is the means by which leaders articulate the antecedents of principle and platform. It represents as well the rallying point for bringing together all human resources into a common cause.

Planning is the articulation of purpose into concrete but long-term operational programs. Planning sketches out the major structures and design to be implemented, the major steps to be taken, and the major milestones to be achieved. The time frame is long-range and planning as a strategic requirement of leadership should not be confused with such tactical requirements as management by objectives, the specification of short-term outcomes or results, or the various scheduling devices such as Gantt or PERT (Program Evaluation Review Technique). Despite the usefulness of such tactics in the short range, they can mislead if they are not part of a more long-range plan.

Tactical planning responses by universities to shifting marketplace demands on educational programs is a case in point. Such responses typically include reallocating existing resources from low to high demand areas. The tactical logic of such reallocation rests in changes in the ratios of FTEs (Full Time Equivalents) to instructional units. Thus, such areas as fine arts, social science, education, and the humanities are today's losers to such high-demand areas as science, engineering, and business administration. The domination of tactical logic and short-term planning responses to marketplace demands gives attention to the "body" of the university at the expense of its "soul." A strategic view of planning would seek to balance marketplace demands against images of what constitutes the concept university and would seek to protect the integrity of these images. Further, as demands once again shift in favor of today's losers, as they most surely will, undue commitments to short-range planning will result in the university being in a strategically poor position to face newer pressures and to maintain long-term quality.

Persisting refers to the attention leaders give to important principles, issues, goals, and outcomes. Symbolically how an administrator uses time is a form of administrative attention which communicates meanings to others in the school. It is assumed by most that an administrator gives attention to the events and activities he or she values. As others learn the value of this activity to the leader, they are also likely to give it attention. Administrative attention, then, can be considered as a form of modeling for others who work in the school. Through administrative attention, the leader contributes to setting the tone or climate of the school and communicates to others the goals and activities which should enjoy high priority.

The social-psychological effects of administrative attention tend to occur whether or not they are intended. An elementary school principal might, for example, espouse an educational platform which suggests a deep commitment to building a strong educational program sensitive to individual needs of students, taught by a happy committed faculty, and supported by his or her school community. But this platform is likely to be ignored in favor of the one which students, teachers, and parents infer on the basis of administrative attention. Protestations to the contrary, if most of the principal's time is spent on the many trivial activities associated with routine administrative maintenance, observers will learn that "running a smooth ship" is the goal of real value to the principal and the school.

Peopling recognizes that little can be accomplished by the leader without the good wishes of others. More than mere compliance from others is necessary if excellence is sought. Instead, the leader seeks to fine tune and match more closely the goals, objectives, and desires of people with those of the organization. Growth and development of the human organization enjoys equal status, as a tactical objective, with increased organizational outputs. Indeed, lower levels of organizational achievement might well be appropriate in the short term if human values would otherwise be endangered. When considered in the long term, an undisputed link exists between the satisfaction and development of the human organization and increased organizational performance, both in quantity and quality. Peopling is a key strategic requirement of quality leadership. Accepting short-term gains which compromise the quality of life which people enjoy in schools and universities simply does not make strategic sense.

When leadership skills, antecedents, and meanings are successfully articulated into practice, we come to see leadership as less a behavioral style or managment technique and as more a cultural expression. Here, a set of norms, beliefs, and principles emerge to which organizational members give allegiance. These represent a strong bond which brings people together to work on behalf of the organization. Indeed a culture emerges which details what is important and provides guidelines that govern behavior. The principle of *patriotism* is key to viewing leadership as cultural expression. In highly effective organizations workers share a set of common beliefs, and reach a set of common agreements which govern what will be done and how it will be done. Members express loyalty or patriotism to this way of life. Organizational patriots are committed to purposes, they work hard, believe in what they are doing, feel a sense of excitement for the organization and its work, and find their own contributions to the organization meaningful if not inspirational.

In sum, organizational patriotism can be defined as commitment and loyalty to the characteristics which give an organization or organizational subunits unique meaning. This meaning is part of the unit's culture and is implicit in its governing platforms. Goals, sense of mission, philosophy, expected ways of operating, and images of excellence are examples. The more explicit these are and the more patriotic are members, the more likely that excellence can be attained.

Symbolic Aspects of Leadership

Studies of leadership give too much attention to the instrumental and behavioral aspects and not enough to symbolic and cultural. The principles presented here, by contrast, give attention to the more informal, subtle, and symbolic aspects of leadership. Symbols evoke and bring to the forefront one's history. Meanings are raised to one's consciousness and through these meanings one is able to link on to some aspect of his or her world. But evoked meanings from any given object are never quite the same for everyone and thus need to be tied together into persistent cultural strands which define the organization's mission and activities. Answers to such questions as what is this organization about, what is of value here, what do we believe in, why do we function the way we do, and how are we unique come from such a definition. Persistent cultural strands introduce an orderliness to one's organizational life, provide one with a sense of purpose, and enrich existing meanings.

But symbols are more than superficial images tossed around for public effect. As Ricoeur (1974, 299) suggests, "I am convinced that we must think not *behind* the symbols, but starting from symbols, according to symbols, that their substance is indestructible, that they constitute the *revealing* substrata of speech which lives among men. In short, the symbol gives *rise* to the thought." He cautions against glib responses or even reading between the lines in attempting to figure out the meaning of symbols, preferring that the symbols themselves do the work. Symbols should be allowed to raise one's consciousness and unravel one's history.

Some have argued that most aspects of the school's culture are unrealistic and unattainable. Indeed, the word symbol suggests that aspirations and beliefs may be more shadow than real. Should this matter? Probably not. What is important is that the group's cultural imperatives represent a common rallying cry and provide a standard to which the group strives. Some point out that the domestication of organizational cultures is either autocratic (for example, merely a rephrasing of the center-periphery struggle described by Schön, 1971) or unrealistic given the strength of wild centers which exist in multicultural societies. Though an enriched, domesticated center would be ideal from an administrative perspective, the likely domesticated center is a federated one whereby enough common values are articulated to give people common purpose and common meanings but where cherished local values are protected.

~~Over time, compatibility increases as center and periphery values each take on characteristics of each other~~.

Our Tacit Understanding of Excellence

Many of the leadership principles articulated here are given credibility by other authors who wrote chapters for this section. The current popular interest of management theorists implicit in Japanese management practices reveals as well insights and prescriptions which resemble the ten principles (Ouchi 1981; Pascale and Athos 1981). These principles have been historically espoused in the writings of the human resources theorists (Arygris, Bennis, Likert, Maslow, and McGregor, for example) though perhaps not in an integrated and systematic leadership model. But perhaps the most convincing evidence comes from our own tacit understanding of excellence in organizations.

In his presentations on high-performing systems, Peter Vaill often asks listeners to engage in an exercise designed to raise to consciousness tacit understanding of high-performing systems. Adopting his strategy here, take a moment to recall in your life experiences that one group, team, unit or organization which, when compared with all others from your personal experience, was the most high-performing. You might go back to your teen years and recall a childhood or high school group, or perhaps to your experiences as a family member, or as a member of some social group or fraternity, or perhaps your military years, or to your experiences on a sports or sandlot team. Perhaps your attention will focus more on the world of work and you might recall some job you had, either recent or past, which included membership in a particularly high-performing group. Whatever the case, recall how the system operated. How did you feel about membership in the group? What made you work so hard? What accounted for your enthusiasm? Why did you enjoy being associated with the group? What was the system trying to accomplish? How loyal were you and why? How meaningful was your membership and why? Chances are that your analysis of this system highlights many of the quality leadership "P's" proposed here. Repeat this exercise, limiting yourself to schools or universities and work groups within these institutions with which you are familiar even though you may not have been a member. Recall the one most effective, most excellent, most high-performing from among all your experiences with these groups. Describe the system, what it valued, and how it worked. Take the time to sketch out some ideas on a sheet of paper. Again, compare your analysis with the quality leadership "P's." You should find a remarkable resemblance between the two.

Debates over such issues as skills versus meanings or tactics versus strategy can be misleading. This chapter, for example, is not a plea to substitute the heroic for the technocratic; to abandon sound management principles for the symbolic; to replace administrators with poets and artists. The issues of concern should be ones of balance and integration. It is clear that presently, in educational administration, the leadership emphasis is not balanced but tilts too much in the direction of leadership skills and the prerequisite management techniques they suggest.

The function of such skills is not to stand alone or even to be "added in" but to be integrated into a larger focus. This integration is suggested in the following quality leadership equation:

$$QL = LS (LA + LM + LCE)$$

Quality leadership (QL) results from the compounding effects of leadership skills (LS) *interacting with* leadership antecedents (LA), meanings (LM), and cultural expression (LCE). In sum, the 10-P model of leadership is offered as an interdependent and interlocking network. Though conveniently sorted into four categories of skills, antecedents, meanings, and cultural expression, the art of leadership is celebrated in their integration in practice.

REFERENCES

March, James G. (1980). "How We Talk and How We Act: Administrative Theory and Administrative Life." David D. Henry Lecture, University of Illinois, Urbana-Champaign.

Ouchi, William (1981). *Theory Z: How American Business Can Meet the Japanese Challenge.* Reading, Mass.: Addison-Wesley.

Pascale, Richard T. (1978). "Zen and the Art of Management." *Harvard Business Review* 56(2), 153–62.

Pascale, Richard T., and Anthony G. Athos (1981). *The Art of Japanese Management.* New York: Simon and Schuster.

Ricoeur, Paul (1974). "The Hermeneutics of Symbols and Philosophical Reflections." Translated by Charles Freilich. In Don Ihde, ed. *The Conflict of Interpretations: Essays in Hermeneutics.* Evanston, Ill.: Northwestern University Press.

Schön, Donald A. (1971). *Beyond the Stable State.* New York: Random House.

Sergiovanni, Thomas J. (1981). "Symbolism in Leadership (What Great Leaders Know That Ordinary Ones Do Not)." Occasional paper, Institute of Educational Administration, Melbourne.

———— (1982). "Quality Leadership: Requirements and Principles." *Educational Leadership* 39(5), 330–36.

Shils, Edward (1961). "Centre and Periphery." In *The Logic of Personal Knowledge: Essays Presented to Michael Polanyi.* London: Routledge & Kegan Paul, pp. 117–31.

PART II

Organizations as Cultural Systems

Leadership and its organizational context are inseparable and thus it is difficult to understand one without the other. This problem is even more complex since the destiny of any organization rests with environmental interactions. In Part II, organizations are viewed as cultural entities and as part of a broader cultural system. Understanding organizational life, within this view, requires that one go beyond descriptions of organizational reality to interpretations of reality, from beyond phenomenon as is to reconstructed phenomenon. It is often noted, for example, that organizations are irrational; that the management of organizations is similar to the management of organized anarchies; and that structural looseness confounds rational attempts to bring order and control to organizational life. Revolutionary just a few years ago, these images of organizational structure and life are now common, but accepting these images and understanding them are different. Understanding can be facilitated by adopting a more cultural perspective.

Consider the difference between how leaders act and talk and between how organizations are formally structured and actually operate. To understand the nature of these differences, one needs to consider that such terms as irrationality and ambiguity may well be misleading. Organizations structure themselves in response to their internal and external environments. By accepting certain structural and figurative imperatives from these environments (such as goals, formal hierarchy, rational norms, and other considerations), organizations become legitimate. As Meyer states in his chapter, "organizations celebrate their own existence by manipulating environmental symbols of legitimacy." In action, behavior rarely matches the substance of this celebration. Frequently organizational structures cannot fit both the myth of rationality required for legitimacy and the internal tasks which must be undertaken and completed. This dilemma is real, purposive, and, in a curious sense, very rational.

Traditionally, organizations have been defined as purposive aggregates of individuals who exert a concerted effort toward some common goal (Blau and Scott 1962). Modern definitions acknowledge that goal consensus in organizations is often more myth than real, and thus they focus on the stable patterns of interaction which exist among individuals who comprise the aggregate. Ouchi (1980), for example, characterizes organizations as markets, bureaucracies, or clans, depending upon the nature of this interaction. How this interaction is studied varies depending upon whether one views organizational life as expressed or reconstructed reality (Silverman 1971).

One's view of organizational reality and subsequent mode of analysis also depends on one's interpretations of social system complexity. Consider Boulding's (1968) attempt to create a general theory of systems by categorizing systems into a hierarchy of complexity. He proposes nine categories of increasing complexity as follows: (1) frameworks, (2) clockworks, (3) controlled systems, (4) open systems, (5) blueprinted-growth systems (6) internal image systems, (7) symbol processing systems, (8) multicephalous systems, and a ninth level to accommodate images not yet fully developed or invented. If organizations are viewed as falling into one or another of these categories, then certain modes of analysis will dominate inquiry. Modes of analysis are predetermining in the sense that how one looks determines what one sees. It follows that whoever investigates organizational phenomenon determines what will be found.

Organizational theorists typically study organizations as if they belonged in levels 3, 4, or 5. Levels 6, 7, and 8, by contrast, provide an image of organization more complex, social, and human where individual perceptions, interpretations, meanings, and common understandings provide an uncertainty, depth, and richness more difficult to harness into a uniform framework. The chapters in Part 2 provide examples of analyses which stem from views of organizational life as higher forms of complexity than that which is now common in organizational theory.

In Chapter 8, William Taylor begins his analysis of organizational cultures in universities by noting that culture stands among the most complex words in the English language. Unlike structural-functional analysis which studies universities as social forms — as objects "out there" — cultural analysis is more psychic in character and reflects a tension between tangible examination of parts and holistic perceptions. He acknowledges the controversy between scholars who value what theory has to say about goals, systems, and structures and those who focus more on meanings attached to different expressions of social action. Taylor cautions both camps that "to argue for the primacy of meaning over form, iconography as against morphology, is a sterile exercise. Both are 'real.' " Using universities as an example, he then tackles the problem of reconciling meaning and form in the pursuit of a unified comprehensiveness. "Both symbolic and material cultures have their place in any rounded consideration of how universities are organized and the place of administrative leadership within them."

Having examined these epistemological issues Taylor turns his attention to studying universities as "sacred" organizations. Noting that "to examine the culture of a sacred organization is to threaten that culture," he suggests that the greater the emphasis of analysis is on interpretation, evaluation, and understanding, the more likely that inquiry will be resisted. Descriptive analyses, by contrast, study the university as a theoretical object suspended into a space of form and function. This impersonal, indeed antiseptic approach to inquiry into its affairs is more likely to be tolerated, if not accepted, by universities.

In attempting to reconcile meaning and form, Taylor turns to the work of George Kubler on the history of art. Kubler relies on the concept of formal sequence as "a historical network of gradually altered repetitions of the same trait" as a frame for studying and interpreting phenomena. Within this frame the notions of "prime object" and "replication" become important. Prime objects refer to principle inventions which produce historically valid and unique entities. Replicas are the entire system of reproductions, copies, and transfers derived from a prime object. Prime objects are culturally rich with generative capabilities which result in cultural dissemination; replicas are manifestations of this dissemination.

In examining universities as prime objects Taylor notes that several unique prototypes within the United Kingdom come to mind: Oxford and Cambridge, civic universities, and polytechnics are examples. (Australian and United States examples would be universities and advanced colleges of education; elite multiuniversities, state colleges, and universities; liberal arts colleges; and community colleges.) Within any type certain institutions stand out as models (prime objects) to be imitated by others (replicas). But not all prime objects across types enjoy equal status and thus frequently institutions of one type seek to mimic the prime objects of another. For example, "emerging" universities often link their destinies to imitating higher status prime objects of another type with uneven success. A more promising future might be for these universities to achieve excellence within a prime object frame or to create an entirely new frame.

The emergence of some prime objects as more powerful than others has important cultural implications. In illustrating this point, Taylor examines the academic pedigrees of higher education leaders in Great Britain and Northern Ireland, noting that most not associated with polytechnics attended Oxford or Cambridge. Polytechnic leaders, by contrast, emerged from the technical service tradition. In each case biographies of leaders indicate that they have shared in certain common experiences which later represent "cultural baggage" that helps determine their organizational realities as leaders. Taylor concludes that the cultures of institutions of higher education are strongly influenced by a modest (perhaps too few) number of prime objects.

In Chapter 9, Thomas B. Greenfield proposes that elementary and secondary schools and other organizations can be better understood as cultural entities and presents a theory of leadership more appropriate to this understanding. Reason, logic, predictability, and order are the leadership canons which those who live and study organizations find reassuring. It is assumed that a natural order of events exists which characterizes humankind and this order should therefore guide organizational functioning. A vast literature exists which blends together leadership reasoning and organizational rationality into a convincing and popular statement of organizational life. Doubt as to the accuracy of this representation matters little in sustaining its popularity and longevity. After all, could leadership be successfully described as willfulness and organizational life successfully described as following a nonnatural order even if these descriptions were accurate?

It is against these odds that Greenfield proposes a theory of leadership as willfullness expressed within organizations better understood as cultural entities than theoretical and operational systems. Starting with the premise that organizations are as different as the people who give them life and that they therefore should be studied in context, he notes that inductive inquiry is preferred to inquiry guided by abstract principles and general laws. Abstract inquiry obliterates the very essence of what really matters. Thus in studying leadership the emphasis should be on the leaders themselves as actors on the stage in a human drama known as organization life. It is the character of leaders and not leadership characteristics which should be the focus of inquiry.

When organizations are understood as human creations and nonnatural, they are regarded as cultural "artifacts" within which activities are considered to be products of individual actions, intentions, and will. Cultural views of organizations, maintains Greenfield, do not preclude the possibility of an organizational science. At issue is not scientific inquiry guided by a theoretical framework, but the kind of inquiry and the nature of this framework. Greenfield suggests that two kinds of scientific inquiry would be appropriate within the cultural framework: the first would "characterize the moral order that prevails in organizations and describe what happens within them"; the second would seek to establish which kind of moral order is best, recognizing, of course, that the question can never be finally answered.

In pursuit of characterizations of this moral order, Greenfield believes that "artistic and other nonrational modes of representation of reality might convey the meaning of social organizations as well, or better than, the linear, concise, and highly quantified abstractions that now usually count as science." With respect to the second kind of inquiry, arguments seeking to establish the relative worth of a particular moral order and consequences of that order on organizational life and society returns science to the realm of philosophy. Recent developments in critical theory as applied to organizational life would be helpful in building scientific capability in this area. (Chapters 13 and 14, by William Foster and Richard Bates, pick up this challenge by examining critical theory and practice within the context of educational administration in more detail.)

When describing organizational reality Greenfield has in mind the meaning as well as the configuration of leadership and life; both *brute* and *sense* data and events are important. Returning to his theory of willfulness, he notes that organizations are essentially façades designed to cover and legitimize individual intention and will.

What is the task of leaders in organizations conceived as cultural entities? To this question Greenfield responds, "The task of leaders is to create the moral order that binds them and the people around them." He notes further that leadership acts are moral and, while it is important to understand how an act is accomplished, we ultimately must judge the act itself.

Following the work of Geertz and relying on case studies by Wolcott and Metz, Greenfield then provides an analysis of what we might see if we were to look at leaders rather than leadership in schools. One might, for example, quibble with the adequacy of expressed leadership (personal style, management techniques, stated objectives, and subsequent efforts) of the principals studied by Wolcott and Metz, but each, nonetheless, had a clear cultural concept of his or her school which required nurturance and protection. *These principals were less managers of an enterprise in pursuit of stated objectives and more priests charged with the responsibility of maintaining and extending an existing social order and set of accompanying moral precepts.* The schools in question were more sacred organizations, protective of a set of values and dedicated to socializing others to these values, than instrumental organizations, designed to effectively and efficiently pursue certain academic objectives. Thus as leaders in sacred cultures the principals received higher marks than they might if all that was important was the accomplishment of objectives. "The practical implication of this notion of organizations and their leaders is simply that leaders will try to commit others to the values they themselves believe as good. Organizations are built on the unification of people around values. The business of being a leader is therefore the business of being an entrepreneur for values. Those who cannot readily be recruited into the moral structure for which the leader stands must be sold into it by persuasion, calculation, guile, persistence, threat, or sheer force."

In Chapter 10, Paul Hirsch and John A. Y. Andrews examine the use of symbols by administrators, pointing out the importance of knowing which set of symbols to evoke at different points in time. Emphasizing the importance of administrative responses to forces in the environment, they note that theories of organization and administration have traditionally examined variations within a stability frame. Environmental concerns are internal and goals, objectives, and missions are assumed to be givens. Thus attention is focused on the theoretical and operational development of administrative and organizational means by which aspirations might be effectively and efficiently pursued.

Within the stability frame the locus of active authority is at the managerial and technical levels. Challenges to authority arise from internal concerns such as one department versus another or line versus staff. Top administrators give attention to legitimizing routines and emphasizing the symbolic value of structures and procedures. Standard operating procedures and organizational charts become the operative symbols. Departments and units are loosely structured, delegation is employed, and unobtrusive controls are exercised.

But what happens when stability is threatened? How does the organization respond? What symbols emerge to thwart the threat and what roles do administrators at various levels assume? Hirsch and Andrews examine two such challenges, performance and value, and chart organizational responses. Performance and value challenges present conditions of change to the organization. "Performance challenges occur when organizations are perceived by relevant actors as having failed to execute the purposes for which they are charted and that claim support." Performance challenges are not challenges of the organization's basic values, but only the extent to which values are being expressed in the form of achievement.

When the basic purposes of an organization are called into question, the challenge stakes are escalated considerably. "Value challenges place the organization's mission and legitimacy for existence at issue, regardless of how well it has fulfilled its agreed-upon goals and functions." Public organizations and particularly educational organizations are susceptible to performance and value challenges. As tax dollars become scarce and enrollments continue to decline outright or shift from one curriculum to another or one school site to another, governing boards and school boards put pressure on the organization to reorganize in pursuit of efficiency. Top administrators respond similarly by putting pressure on definable subunits within the organization.

Hirsch and Andrews point out that both performance and value challenges "entail fundamental challenges to the legitimacy of an organization's continued existence." What is at first a performance challenge, for example, can readily become a value challenge. Performance challenges to schools and universities as a whole can become value challenges to suborganizations or units. In response to pressures to become more efficient and demands that educational organizations demonstrate they are achieving given costs, a series of quality studies of subunits might be launched. Low achievers, as defined by the particular organizational culture, can be identified and dealt with. But increasing the performance of subunits may not be enough to allow the organization to escape from outside threats. Soon some units (within the university, perhaps the agricultural extension program, off-campus public administration program, vocational-technical education department, geology department, or some other unfortunate area) are targeted for harassment and perhaps extinction. The ground rules now change from how well the victims are doing to how well do they *fit into* the larger university culture. Effectiveness and efficiency arguments by the harassed units fall on deaf ears. The closing of public schools and elimination or restriction of programs within schools follow a similar pattern.

Hirsch and Andrews suggest that when organizations are faced with a performance challenge, the locus of administrative activities is at the top echelon. Attention is focused on the organization's delivery system and performance record. Administrators respond by displaying symbols which demonstrate that performance is actually better than apparent indicators (yes, enrollments are down but student quality is up; yes, FTEs [Full Time Equivalents] in proportion to IUs [Instructional Units] are up but the faculty is nationally recognized; yes, faculty are teaching less but researching more), and arguments are made that measurement and evaluation techniques being applied are not appropriate to the units being evaluated (qualitative, not quantitative, information is needed).

By contrast, the key actors in value challenges are outside people and top administrators (governing boards and chancellors, academic vice-presidents and deans, deans and chairpersons, communities and school boards, school boards and superintendents, superintendents and principals). Here the organization's very existence is threatened and top administrators seek an active redefinition of purpose and structure. The process is often accompanied by budget-cutting attempts. Sometimes the organization (or subunit within) is destroyed and resurrected in the same breath but in a "new" image (a recent fate of many colleges of education). The victimized units fight back by redefining purposes and repackaging programs in order to survive. Some beat their oppressors to the gun by taking the lead, like the phoenix, in their own destruction, hopefully reemerging as a stronger part of the broader culture.

Characterizing administrators as "hucksters of the symbol," Hirsch and Andrews provide an analysis of symbol management under stable, performance, and challenge situations based on the following premises: the type of leader behavior appropriate for a given situation varies with the legitimizing context of the organization; contexts are subject to change; and a key aspect of leadership is knowing what symbols to evoke and what authority type to exercise given changes. In their language "organizations embody efforts to maintain and adapt to external, institutional value complexes and, in turn, convey corresponding cultural symbols to their members and the world at large." When faced with performance and value challenges, leadership behavior resembles "symbol wars" and leadership success depends upon a certain deftness in symbol management and situational sensitivity.

"Organizations as Ideological Systems" is the title of Chapter 11 by John W. Meyer. In the face of evidence which indicates that little relationship exists between how organizations are organized and how they operate; between norms of rationality and order which govern what administrators say and what they actually do; between official planning and decision-making protocols and day-by-day operational decisions, Meyer asks the question, why bother with formal procedures and stated theories at all? In his words, "A great deal of trouble and expense go into building and changing formal structures in modern organizations. If all this is epiphenomenal to the real activities of organizational work and life, why the charade?"

He notes the growing literature on the symbolic aspects of organizational life, the symbolic origin and consequence of structure and structure-sustaining myths, stories, and sagas. Believing that this route of inquiry does not dig deep enough, he argues that the structure of an organization *itself* is a symbolic system. It is the role itself, not the nuances expressed by the role incumbent and the rules themselves, not the idiosyncracies of rule talk, which represent the substance of symbolism. He develops this theme by examining the origins and effects of structure as symbolism and implications of the symbolic aspects of structure on role performance.

Beginning with an analysis of existing theoretical work, Meyer concludes that "formal organizational structures of schools and universities are rationalized myths of the organization's functioning; these structures serve to legitimize the organization in the eyes of internal and external constituencies by providing a rational account of this functioning; the

importance of seeking legitimacy by appearing rational overrides considerations of whether the formal structure is indeed consistent with the
work which needs to be done or the characteristics of workers; and, in
educational organizations characteristics of loose-structuring and ill-
defined and competing outcomes make the presentation of rational structures in pursuit of legitimacy even more important." If organizations cannot prove that they are responsible and effective, they must at least
"look" responsible and effective. Conversely, the more concrete the evidence that an organization is performing responsibly and effectively, the
less conventional it need appear. The proof is either in the pudding itself
or in the logic of the recipe.

Schools and universities, for example, conform closely to accreditation rules as testimony to their competency. They develop elaborate
managerial rituals and quality-control procedures as testimony to their
responsibility. They develop standardized degree-graduation requirements and a tightly linked, highly reliable curriculum as testimony to
their integrity. Accreditation rules, however, emphasize clock hours of
study, amounts of library space, and course titles as surrogates for quality and excellence but rarely assess the real thing. Teacher-evaluation procedures in the public schools are time-consuming and important rituals,
but research suggests they have doubtful effect on school quality. Academics in every discipline can recount tales of Ph.D.s who managed to
properly jump all of the hurdles and graduate despite tacit reservations
of faculty. But who can imagine hiring a graduate of a professional
school or soliciting the services of a professional (architect, dentist,
teacher, engineer) from a nonaccredited school which does not have a
formally detailed quality-control system and where course and graduation requirements are ambiguous and informal? In the absence of these
stamps of legitimacy, arguments about quality of graduates would not be
very convincing.

Formal structures, according to Meyer, are ideologies which reflect the
key cultural strands of our technically oriented Western society. For example, to be considered legitimate, organizations in this society must be
rationally structured and logically operated. The structures need to be
linked to purposes. A control mechanism must exist to harness and coordinate efforts of workers in some systematic form in pursuit of these purposes. Outputs need to be standardized and provide testimony that the
job is being accomplished. And every organization must work within a
boundary which clarifies for internal and external audiences what the organization can and cannot do. These ideas are so ingrained that even
scholars who disclaim them intellectually and ignore them operationally
espouse them personally. An example that comes to mind is the professor who after giving a convincing lecture on the theories of James G.

March and Karl Weick, races off to a faculty meeting to give an impassioned speech on how important it is for the college to develop clear goals, articulate them into some set of standardized procedures, and link them to a rational decision-making mechanism. This professor then hurries to the office to finish an overdue research article. The data analysis and conclusion sections are complete and now it is time for the purposes of the study to be decided upon, in light of the findings, and that section prepared.

Using many examples, Meyer then provides us with an account of structure as ideology considering such topics as the structuring of uncertainty, actually using structure as an ideological account and maintaining the appearance of rationality. He provides a detailed discussion of how one can manage the formal structure to make or reinforce an ideological statement. Administration need not be a passive reflection of existing ideology but can shape ideology by manipulating structure. Meyer points out that within the concept of structure as ideology, the administrator is a symbolic entity and administrative actions represent key symbolic elements.

REFERENCES

Blau, Peter M., and W. Richard Scott (1962). *Formal Organizations*. San Francisco: Chandler Publishing Company.

Boulding, Kenneth (1968). "General Systems Theory — the Skeleton of Science." In Walter Buckley, ed. *Modern Systems Research for the Behavioral Scientist*. Chicago: Aldine.

Ouchi, William G. (1980). "Markets, Bureaucracies and Clans." *Administrative Science Quarterly* 25(1), 129–41.

Silverman, David (1971). *The Theory of Organizations*. New York: Basic Books.

CHAPTER 8

Organizational Culture and Administrative Leadership in Universities

William Taylor

Raymond Williams maintains that culture is "one of the two or three most complicated words in the English language." He argues that this is so because of the way in which the use of the term has developed historically, not only in English but in other European languages, and because of the part that it plays in a number of intellectual disciplines and "distinct and incompatible systems of thought" (Williams 1976, 77).

Arguments about the meaning of culture and attempts to pin it down by means of conceptual analysis and clarification reflect not so much confusion as the essential complexity of the phenomena to which it relates, and the recognition of the interrelations between phenomena that the choice of this particular term implies. "Culture" has a holistic character. We can successfully isolate elements of social structure, concede them to be the property of disciplinary subspecialisms, subject them to minute analysis, and manipulate them statistically, all without suffering too much intellectual angst or feeling that we are acting in a way that denies the imperatives of academic inquiry. On the contrary, the analysis and disaggregation involved in such processes are entirely consistent with forms of inquiry commonly recognized as "scientific."

When it comes to culture, the position is rather different. We can, and do, pick out particular features of cultural life, such as language, mythology, belief systems, conventional understandings, and so on for study and interpretation. But the reification that makes us comfortable with the methodologies and outcomes of structural analysis, the treating of social forms as objects, "out there" in the external world, created by man but possessing a superordinate reality and power of constraint, is more difficult to achieve in relation to cultural phenomena.

In studying culture we are constantly aware of its psychic character. Such study involves a tension between analysis and holistic perception that is not so evident in, for example, the literature of social structure and process. Thus to wrench a single element from the unity of cultural experience is inevitably to distort it, to deprive it of the framework of history and action necessary to its meaning and significance.

It follows from all this that to study the culture of an organization is a very different matter from analyzing its structure and social process. The disaggregation and discontextualisation that are possible and even essential in the latter case are illegitimate and unhelpful in the former. Deprived of these opportunities for reductionism, we look for the smallest identifiable human group to which we can apply comprehensive interpretative principles, in relation to which we can realistically and sensibly typify a coherent set of cultural values and understandings. To make study of the concept manageable we identify subcultures and sub-subcultures; we isolate groups to the whole life of which particular interpretative schema can be applied, rather than isolating elements of behavior and response, aspects of institutional structure and process, which can be analyzed and subjected to conceptual and statistical manipulation. The study of cultures is always, therefore, a study of wholes, whether these be of a society, a region, a university, or a department.

This does not entail any very far-reaching assumptions about value consensus between groups at these different levels. The projection upon the external world of our holistic interpretation of self, which as Dilthey (1976) and others have shown is a reflection both of time and the structure of individual consciousness, produces a strain toward unity that distorts the complex realities of cultural organization. A highly unified culture would either have to be associated with a very low rate of social change, with socialization of traditional values going largely unquestioned, or it would have to be enforced by totalitarian control over thought and the transmission of ideas. Organizations differ according to their history, purposes, and structure, in the scope of their moral and cultural integration, and in the extent to which commitment to core values and exemplary behavior is required or enforced.

Such requirements are of greater significance to sacred rather than utilitarian organizations and vary according to the position that individuals occupy in the organizational hierarchy. A junior instructor can align with student viewpoints in a clash with the administration and avoid lasting penalty, not so a departmental chairperson or dean. The duty of the full-time salaried administrators—the secretaries and registrars and finance officers—is clear. They must follow the decisions of the responsible academic bodies, making common cause with the duly elected or appointed academic heads, or suffer the consequences. Although the imperative is clear, its implementation, given the pluralism of some university communities and the divisions of views that exist among senior academics, is by no means easy. Universities are engaged in sacred rather than utilitarian activities, yet the diversity of these activities does not make for high levels of moral integration. This can give rise to particular difficulties when they attempt to act corporately in the face of external threat.

Meaning and Form

In view of the stress being placed at this conference on alternative approaches to the study of organizations and of leadership, something needs to be said at this stage about the controversy between those who value what organization theory has to say about goals, systems, structures, and constraints, and those who focus more on the meanings that participants attach to different kinds of social action. To argue for the primacy of meaning over form, iconography as against morphology, is a sterile exercise. Both are "real." One of the dangers of a stress on meanings and symbols, and one from which sociology has by no means been immune, is a descent into a crude solipsism which extends the important sense in which reality *is* "socially constructed" to deny the existence of any reality other than individual mental representations.

Another risk in stressing meaning is that of according primacy to "common sense." Greenfield has argued that "the logic of the researcher's analysis can have no force in the every day world unless it conforms to the logic that people use in every day situations. Unless there is a close match between the world as researchers construct it and the world as people perceive it and act on it, the researcher's efforts to establish social truths will be a self-contained and ultimately self-deluding pastime" (1978, 13). That one social construction of reality has achieved paradigmatic status, while others are still emergent and struggling for an audience, carries no *necessary* entailments as to truth. The logic of common-sense reality has no ontological or epistemological priority over the logics of disciplinary analysis. *Both* are social constructions. Research workers are in the business of offering alternative meanings, of trying to enhance our understanding of a phenomenon by looking at it in ways that are *not* those of everyday common sense. For everyone to accommodate themselves to the requirements of the latter is a recipe not for radical change but for the reinforcement of a highly conservative and uniform set of meanings.

Forms are real. Meanings are real. Universities, colleges, and departments have a material culture located in space and time. The elements of such culture include buildings, tools, equipment, furniture, books, and tapes. They also have a symbolic culture of language, ritual, ideology, myth, and belief. Every element of symbolic culture requires a vehicle for its transmission. Spatial organization and orientation, committee procedures, rules for the distribution of resources, academic robes, regulations governing the submission of theses, all these are the signifiers that convey what is signified by organizational culture. An emphasis on the socially constructed nature of reality appeals to the radical. Attributing primacy to the symbolic undermines the "hardness" and constraining reality of the material culture, and suggests that what people have made they can now proceed to undo and to reconstruct.

The problem of reconciling iconographic and morphological forms of analysis and making whole the criteria that might guide action based on such a unified comprehension is not, unfortunately, resolved by adopting the varieties of symbolic interactionism, in the tradition of G. H. Mead and his followers, that have become fashionable over the past decade. What we face here are the age-old problems of reconciling self and world that crop up in philosophical distinctions between subject and object, in researcher's choices of quantitative or qualitative methodologies, and in organizational analysts' preferences for positivist or humanistic orientations. In a manner that often does little justice to the complexity and rigor of philosophical and sociological discourse concerning these matters, students of organizations contrast different approaches to structure, process, culture, and change. Convoluted and wordy conceptual systems are erected on the basis of a very limited range of firsthand study and observation. I share many of Greenfield's criticisms of such writing about organizations, but on somewhat different grounds.

For the student of organizations who knows the literature of his or her field, the citation of a particular author at once casts an interpretative network over current thoughts and perceptions, serving to organize these in relation to rule-bound schema of greater or lesser rigor, according to the established scope and standing of the source. Thus much of what is written about organizations comprises not accounts of new descriptive and analytical work on multinational corporations, pigeon clubs, universities, political parties, schools, and the like, but the review and reworking of existing "texts." Consider, for example, the complexity of the interpretations called for by a passage such as the following: "Kahn's prescription for research and the ideas of these organizational theorists most frequently cited with approval by organization development practitioners, 'March and Simon, Blake and Mouton, Coch and French, Lawrence and Lorsch, Morse and Reiner, Trist and Banforth, Katz and Kahn, Drucker and James Thompson' (Weisbord, 1974), reveal that many have forgotten that they are dealing with human organizations . . ." (Mangham 1978, 66). Here Taylor quotes Mangham who quotes Weisbord quoting March and Simon, etc., etc. According to our familiarity or otherwise with the names quoted, interpretive schema are invoked, by means of which the intentions and meanings of the author of the text who makes the citations are better grasped and understood.

This is merely to describe a process common to all academic endeavor. The esoteric language in which we indulge serves many purposes, some of them instrumental to achieving more accurate description, greater rigor, and fruitful theoretical elaboration, some directed more to boundary definition, to appropriating intellectual assets. The possibility of self-regarding motives and outcomes taking precedence over those of scholarship and the improvement of practice are greater when more attention is devoted to the reworking of texts than to the collection and interpretation of data. The current literature of organizations does not encourage me to believe that we are doing enough to avert this danger.

It would be a pity if, in laying stress on the symbolic aspects of organizational culture, we neglected the still important tasks of field work, observation, documentary analysis, and data collection, the absence of which has marred the quality of contemporary radical scholarship. Lorenz is right to urge that for ". . . the scientist aiming to objectivate the phenomenal world it is a duty to take into account the achievements as well as the limitations of our culturally determined 'world view apparatus,' in exactly the same way as he treats the inherited *a priori* mechanisms of our cognition" (Lorenz 1977, 175). Both symbolic and material culture have their place in any rounded consideration of how universities are organized and the place of administrative leadership within them.

Studying the Cultures of Higher Education

To examine the culture of a sacred organization is to threaten that culture. The significance of this threat mounts as one moves from description through analysis, comparison, interpretation, evaluation, and explanation. Most members have long since been coerced or socialized into accepting a limited range of descriptive categories and labels as being appropriate to the public accounts that legitimate the existence and activities of their organizations. The processes of selective attention and classification sedimented in these accounts have been rendered invisible by socialization, habit, and ideology. Refusal to be bound by these categories is, of course, a very obvious threat to organizational integrity and is likely to be resisted. Official descriptions are, in formal doctrine, isomorphic with the organization itself. Description is tolerated within limits. Analysis, comparison, interpretation, evaluation, and explanation are more threatening. Mapping features of the organization onto other systems deprives it of uniqueness. The reductionism involved in analysis robs it of dignity. Potentially at least, comparison and evaluation can undermine the authority and status of its leaders. The alternative accounts offered by interpretation and explanation weaken the power of official ideology. If these accounts acquire credibility, those providing them will be accorded untoward respect and attention.

Little has in fact been written about the organizational cultures of universities, polytechnics, and colleges in the United Kingdom. Nor does the general literature on organizational culture, English and American, offer many handles with which to grasp the realities of the British scene. Bob Clark, with his work on student subcultures has done more than most to explore the notion of culture in the context of the university (Clark 1970). In his most recent work he identifies four types of academic culture, those of *discipline, profession, enterprise,* and *system,* and accommodates within this framework some of the valuable ideas from his earlier studies of distinctive colleges and student peer groups (Clark 1980).

In the United Kingdom, Pettigrew (1979) has looked at development and change in organizational cultures in a school, structuring his account around a series of "dramas" in which the entrepreneurial activities of individual headmasters played a prominent part. Halsey and Trow (1971) reported a seven-year study of the attitudes, beliefs, and orientations of university staff in the United Kingdom, and Halsey (1978, 1979, 1981) has undertaken a further survey of staff, this time including those working in polytechnics. The culture of the former colleges of education, recently reconstituted as a third sector of degree-granting higher education institutions, has been examined by Taylor (1964, 1969) and Bell (1981).

Harrison and Handy identify four types of organizational culture, centering around *power, role, task,* and *person.* It is argued that each of these terms encompasses aspects of the material and symbolic culture of organizations in a sufficiently distinctive way to enable the whole organization to be designated as power-, role-, task-, or person-oriented. Researchers with positivist leanings would no doubt wish to challenge the empirical basis for such typologies. To what extent are the diverse elements of the material and symbolic culture distributed in such a way as to permit classification by this means? Perhaps this is the wrong question to ask. Handy argues that a culture cannot be defined with precision, "for it is something that is perceived, something felt" (Handy 1976, 185). Possibly more seriously, while Harrison's original framework offers a valuable basis for discussion and comparison of individual impressions, it has not served to generate a substantial body of empirical work such as might validate and refine the categories employed.

It is not difficult to fit academic institutions within the analytical framework proposed by Harrison. He identifies three personal and three organizational "interests" which are the subject of ideological tension and struggle within institutions and shows how the response to these varies between power, role, task, and person ideologies. We could, I imagine, have a lively exchange of views about the extent to which current political and economic pressures and constraints upon universities are forcing a move from a person-oriented to a role- and power-oriented culture. Handy's elaboration of Harrison's framework is especially useful here in that it takes in trait, style, contingency, and "best fit" theories of leadership.

Reconciling Meaning and Form

At this stage, one begins to wonder about the utility of "culture," a term so broad and amorphous in character, depicting an orientation of some kind or another reflected in, and lending analytical coherence to, so many diverse features of organizational life. In fact, "culture" does all too often function as a residual category, an all-purpose term that encompasses everything but specifies nothing with precision, a way of complementing and correcting for clashes between analytical disaggregation and the unity of moment to moment experience. Are these weaknesses intrinsic to the concept of culture, or is there some way in which the potentialities of the idea of culture in relation to organizations can be exploited, without falling into the vague usages so characteristic of writing in this field?

A possibly fruitful approach to be found is the work of George Kubler (1962) on the history of art. I am not here proposing to employ this particular area of study as a metaphor for organizational life, in the way that Mangham (1978) and Lyman and Scott (1976) have employed theater, and Beer (1967) has mapped organizational structures and processes onto the conceptual models offered by acoustics, biology, cybernetics, demography, engineering, fluid dynamics, and genetics (giving up at "g" only through lack of space). Rather, I wish to employ the conceptual framework offered by Kubler as a way of classing objects without sole recourse to the separation involved in analyses of meaning and of form (iconography and morphology).

As we have seen, one of the difficulties about an economical depiction of organizations in terms of cultural "types" is the absence of empirical tests whereby the *primacy* of the characteristics that feature in the typology can be established. Frequently, of course, the terms we choose to symbolize the whole are consistent with our hortatory and pedagogic purposes. All such efforts serve a more or less explicit normative intention. Although authors and researchers may vigorously oppose efforts to pick out one feature or another as "more desirable," this is the almost inevitable fate of their work. Whether it is MacGregor's (1960) Theory X or Theory Y, or Bennett's (1976) formal and informal modes of teaching, or the cosmopolitans and locals of Merton (1957), the process of interpreting the meaning of "neutral" findings soon involves ranking preferences and sharpening normative differences.

Weak morphologies, apparent formlessness, the need to impose meanings on many events of short duration, all of which are characteristic of social phenomena, influence the way in which taxonomies originate and develop, and are disseminated, validated, and evaluated. In the field of art history, Kubler suggests that the iconological diminutions implied by most classifications of "style" run the risk of reducing the plentitude of *things* to a very limited range of skeletal *meanings*. The interpretative texts generated by each new picture (events, research findings) impose, to a greater or lesser degree according to their authority and influence, new meanings on all that has gone before. In the study of organizations, the elaboration and reworking of theory (texts) has become a more central activity than the collection of data about the process and events (pictures) that these theories purport to describe and explain. But what criteria determine the authoritativeness or influence of a particular text or interpretation?

A key consideration here is the relationship of an interpretative text to the formal *sequence* of which the phenomena interpreted forms part. A formal sequence is defined by Kubler as a historical network of gradually altered repetitions of the same trait. As such, it possesses principles of internal coherence, but no "necessity" of appearance is implied — "the presence of the conditions for an event does not guarantee the occurrence of that event in a domain where Man can contemplate an action without committing it" (Kubler 1962, 36). In the process of establishing a formal sequence, the related notions of *prime objects* and *replications* assume considerable importance. "Prime objects and replications denote principal inventions, and the entire system of replicas, reproductions, copies, reductions, transfers and derivations, floating in the wake of an important work of art" (Kubler 1962, 39). Kubler calls this system the "replica-mass." If we were engaged in mapping the culture of universities onto biological systems, we would no doubt talk about the need to identify the phenotypes from which the originating genotypes would be deduced.

The point about using the notion of the prime object in this context is that it is quite unquestionably *there;* it exists and has a reality that influences perceptions and constrains behavior. What we make of it is inevitably a mental construct; for one person, an Oxford or Cambridge evokes resonances of all that is important and valuable in the world of scholarship; for another, it is a symbol of the way in which capitalist elites use the force of tradition to maintain social inequalities. But for neither person is the place to be confused with a butcher's shop or a soap factory or a means for organizing egg distribution.

Libraries and lecture rooms and laboratories and studies and academic robes constitute the elements of a material culture that facilitate some kinds of symbolic representation and inhibit others. So when Greenfield says that it is the placing of meaning upon experience "which shapes what we call our organizations and it is this process which should be the focus of the organization theorist's work" (Greenfield 1975, 169) we are still left with the problem of how such "experience" is presented and constrained by the material culture.

The individual standing on a curb and wanting to cross the road has at that moment an almost infinite number of sensations to which attention might be given and a choice of many meanings to attach to those sensations — but unless this individual has learned to single out the movements of traffic from left and right for particular attention, he or she is unlikely to reach the other side alive. The untutored viewer may have difficulty in interpreting a picture, in placing it within its historic and social context, in judging it in relation to criteria that reflect many years of attention from competent scholars — but it is still a picture, a two dimensional creation in oil or some other medium, which evokes responses (like/dislike, beautiful/ugly) appropriate to pictures rather than to, say, omelettes or screwdrivers.

The prime object is *of* both the material *and* the symbolic culture. As such, it must clearly be distinguished from apparently related notions such as the Weberian "ideal type" which is an exclusively mental construct. By relating contemporary cultural forms to prime objects, we introduce a historical dimension lacking in many approaches to organizational culture. The importance of this historical dimension is particularly great in the case of universities. The final report of the 1980 Carnegie Council on Policy Studies in Higher Education states that there are some sixty-six institutions in the Western world which existed in the year 1530 and which are still present in recognizable forms. These are the Lutheran Church, the Catholic Church, the parliaments of the Isle of Man and of Iceland — and sixty-two universities. The commission goes on to say: "Universities in the past have been remarkable for their historic continuity, and we may expect this same characteristic in the future. They have experienced wars, revolutions, depressions, and industrial transformations, and have come out less changed than almost any other segment of their societies" (Carnegie Annual 1980, 9).

During the late sixties and early seventies in many Western countries, the very fact of this continuity was an affront and a challenge to those who wished to overturn and remake social and educational institutions. Awareness of the sheer weight of historical experience embodied in the structures and processes of universities lends support to Kubler's remarks about the relationships between the possible and the achieved in the world of art.

Perhaps all the fundamental technical, formal, and expressive combinations have already been marked out at one time or another, permitting a total diagram of the natural resources of art, . . . should
that ratio between discovered positions and undiscovered ones in
human affairs greatly favour the former, then the relation of the
future to the past would alter radically. Instead of regarding the past
as a microscopic annexe to a future of astronomical magnitudes, we
would have to envisage a future with limited room for changes, and
these of types to which the past already yield the key. The history of
things would assume an importance now assigned only to the strategy of profitable inventions [Kubler 1962, 125–26].

The force of these remarks becomes clear when we explore the range of
words available to designate levels of organization in universities below
that of the whole institution. In current usage I have discovered the
following: area, center, college, chair, department, division, faculty,
group, institute, school, team, and unit. There may be others. The prime
object within this list is an organization of knowledge, usually defined in
terms of a discipline or professional specialism. Differences exist *within*
institutions in the kinds of teaching and research bases designated by
these terms. In university X, centers are not the same as departments, or
faculties, divisions, etc. The meaning and significance of these differences are well understood by those who work within the institution. In
university Y, the same word designates entirely different sets of relationships, specific to the university.

The University as Prime Object

In most countries, higher education is carried on in a variety of institutions. Baldridge and Deal (1978) have identified eight institutional types
in the United States – private and public multiversities, elite liberal arts
colleges, public comprehensives, public colleges, private liberal arts colleges, community colleges, and private junior colleges.[1] In the United
Kingdom, distinctions may usefully be made between Oxford and Cambridge; London (a federation of largely autonomous colleges, several of
them as large as independent universities elsewhere in the country); civic
universities established prior to World War II (initially, in some cases, as
University Colleges awarding London degrees); the new postwar foundations that were established *ab initio*; the technological universities that
developed from postwar colleges of advanced technology, sometimes
based upon technical colleges founded at a much earlier period; polytechnics, again upgraded from technical college status, but without independent charters and still maintained by local education authorities; and
finally, the colleges and institutes of higher education which were created

following the diversification and merger of the former monotechnic colleges of education. The Open University, founded directly by the central government, and the independent University College of Buckingham, which does not receive state support, stand outside these categories.

The universities of Oxford and Cambridge, and the commitments they are seen to embody to the highest standards of scholarship and research, to a particular form of relationship between senior and junior members, to academic self-government, and to freedom of inquiry and expression, have furnished prime objects of which many social and educational processes at other universities and colleges have been more or less clear-cut replications. The Oxbridge tradition is visible not so much in the material culture and organization of the civic universities and the newer postwar foundations (although some, e.g. York, Lancaster, and Kent have consciously chosen a collegiate framework for both teaching and residence) but in the rituals, beliefs and attitudes, and ways of acting, thinking, and believing that make up the symbolic culture.

Oxford and Cambridge are not, however, the only prime objects. The technical college tradition—regional and local, utilitarian, vocational, and service-oriented—can also be found replicated in many universities and particularly in the polytechnics. Burgess (1977) distinguishes between academic and service traditions which permeate the tradition of higher education in the United Kingdom today. Expanding on this notion, we can say that universities differ from polytechnics and some other public sector colleges in that their activities are rooted in public traditions of scholarship for which they are regarded as the appointed guardians; that their work is free from the application of strict criteria of utility; that almost equal amounts of time and efforts are expended on research and teaching; that greater independence from government is enjoyed; that students and staff are both better qualified; that per capita expenditure is higher; and that universities, particularly Oxford and Cambridge, educate a larger proportion of those who occupy influential positions in public life, industry, and commerce.

It is in such valuations that the seeds of what in the United Kingdom is called "academic drift" are to be found. Allegations that the polytechnics have sought, contrary to the intentions of their founders, to emulate the academic models provided by the universities is a recurring theme in the recent literature of higher education. This is hotly denied by spokespersons for the polytechnics, who spell out ways in which their institutions constitute a new "prime object," not a mere replication (Lindop 1981). Such efforts to underline distinctiveness, without at the same time slipping into admission of some kind of inferiority, are a major task for leaders of new categories of institutions.

The same problem faced the secondary modern schools during the two decades following the Education Act of 1944 (Taylor 1963). Today, comprehensive school leaders frequently have to argue for the distinctiveness of their own approach to secondary education as opposed to that of the former grammar schools. To achieve prime object status is not easy, especially when aspects of the material culture — buildings and equipment — are inherited from earlier periods.

The reductionism inherent in the nature of science,[2] and the need to secure rigor within the accepted paradigms of a public tradition, exert powerful countervailing force against attempts to draw new maps of knowledge, to construct new interdisciplinary fields and to break down the barriers of established disciplines. The more specialized a subject, the more rigorous its methodology and techniques, the easier it is *in principle* to create new prime objects, to offer theories and formulations of such precision, elegance, and power that they provide the basis for many subsequent replications and feature prominently in the index of citation. "Easy" in this sense must not be misunderstood. Such theories and formulations are rare, even in the so-called hard sciences. Elsewhere, the complexity and the value-laden nature of the variables involved mean that new formulations seldom achieve any general acceptance and are often as ephemeral as they are conceptually and theoretically insignificant.

The Administrative Leaders

I have argued that the organizational culture of British higher education is powerfully influenced by the "prime objects" furnished by the ancient foundations, by the institutions that embody the traditions of technical education, and by disciplinary paradigms which give the appearance of "hardness" and which serve current interpretations of social and economic relevance. If this is the case, we would expect the backgrounds and experience of the heads of academic institutions to reflect the core values of this culture. The individuals concerned are the vice-chancellors and principals of the forty-four universities and of the colleges that make up the federal universities of London and Wales; the directors of the thirty officially designated polytechnics; and the college heads at Oxford and Cambridge, together constituting a group of about 150 persons.

Data relating to the vice-chancellors and principals of all the universities of Great Britain and Northern Ireland, the multifaculty schools of the University of London, the colleges of Oxford and Cambridge, and the English and Welsh polytechnics were obtained from *Who's Who*, and from other publicly available sources. For the purposes of the analysis reported in this section, the vice-chancellors of Oxford and Cambridge (who are also heads of colleges) and of provincial universities were grouped with those from Scotland, Wales, and Northern Ireland as well as with the heads of the London colleges which are often equivalent in size to a university elsewhere.

In their study of British academics, Halsey and Trow stated that "there can be no clearer evidence of the continued pre-eminence of Oxford and Cambridge than the recruitment of Vice-Chancellors and Principals to other universities" (1971, 164). They cited a study by Collison and Millen (1969) showing that in 1935 two-thirds of the vice-chancellors and principals in Great Britain had received their own university education at the ancient foundations, but by 1967 this proportion had fallen to 59 percent, while the numbers educated at provincial universities had doubled from 3 to 10 percent. On the basis of an analysis carried out in 1981, it appears that 60 percent of vice-chancellors and principals still come from Oxford and Cambridge, but that the share of the provincial universities has grown very substantially.[3]

But if the institutional origins of academic and administrative heads have remained constant, their subject specialites have not. Collison and Millen showed that between 1935 and 1967 the proportion of vice-chancellors and principals who had read arts subjects fell from 68 to 48 percent, and the proportion of scientists rose from 19 to 41 percent. By 1981, these trends had become even more marked. No fewer than 67 percent of vice-chancellors and principals had specialized in scientific subjects, including medicine. A further 13 percent had been specialists in the social sciences, and the proportion of the arts-trained had fallen to less than 20 percent.

The career prescription for everyone who would scale the commanding heights of British academe is fairly straight forward. Attend an independent or direct grant school (44 percent of current vice-chancellors have done so). Read physics or chemistry as a scholar or exhibitioner at Cambridge or, alternatively, at Oxford (nearly a third of vice-chancellors have specialized in these two subjects). Obtain a fellowship at an Oxford or Cambridge college, a chair in Scotland or at one of the larger and more prestigious London colleges, or if all else fails, at a provincial university. Avoid precipitate movements between institutions — two-thirds of present vice-chancellors had held three posts or fewer prior to appointment — and stay in the most senior position achieved for more than a decade as, again, some two-thirds of present incumbents have done. Establish by your mid-forties a claim to a fellowship of the Royal Society or a fellowship of the British Academy through the excellence and originality of your research and publications. Undertake public service on national commissions and committees dealing with important topics. If at all possible, fit in a period as a visiting professor at prestigious American universities. Secure some experience on major decision-making bodies within your own university, preferably as chairperson of those dealing with the allocation of resources.

All this done, by the time your half-century is reached, you have a reasonable claim for consideration. Many vice-chancellorships are now publicly advertised, but the vast majority of those actually appointed are picked out in the course of a search process that is often as lengthy as it is thorough. Mistakes can be costly. Most appointments to vice-chancellorships, polytechnic directorships, and headships of Oxbridge colleges are still made without term. Few people, however, obtain such an appointment until their early fifties, and with a retiring age of sixty-five from universities and polytechnics this means that average tenure is on the order of ten or twelve years. The heads of Oxford and Cambridge colleges can serve until they are a good deal older.

From the mid-seventies, universities and polytechnics have been under considerable financial pressure and have experienced great uncertainty concerning their future funding. A majority of present heads have never held office outside this period; for them, uncertainty and cuts are in a sense part of the natural order of things. They have had no choice but to operate within a culture of contraction rather than one of growth (Taylor 1980a, 1980b).

A high proportion of vice-chancellors and Cambridge college heads have held chairs in universities at some time in their careers. Oxford tends to recruit more of its heads from among the fellows of its own colleges, or from such other sources as the diplomatic service or the world of industry and commerce. A few of the polytechnic directors have previously been professors, but the majority are taken from within the nonuniversity higher education system or from industry. Experience in polytechnic work among university and college heads is virtually nonexistent, and the amount of regular contact between university and nonuniversity academic leaders is in practice very limited. They are members of separate organizations (the Committee of Vice-Chancellors and Principals for the Universities, and the Committee of Polytechnic Directors), are remunerated on separate principles, and have somewhat different educational and occupational backgrounds.

Conclusion

I have tried in this paper to suggest that we can obtain a better grasp of the relations between organizational culture and administrative leadership in institutions of higher education if we avoid the oppositional rhetoric that has characterized some discussions about the relative merits of, on the one hand, studying institutional *forms* (goals, roles, tasks, etc. in terms of positivist methodology) and, on the other, the structure of

meanings given symbolic embodiment in individual and group constructions of reality. The symbolic cultures of universities interact with their
material endowment and technologies and are considerably indebted to
the history and traditions of the institutions concerned.

Adapting the terminology suggested by George Kubler (1962), I have
argued that the culture of universities is strongly influenced by a modest
number of "prime objects," the "meaning" of which is bounded by historical and material characteristics but is not invariant. Within the English
tradition, the universities of Oxford and Cambridge, the work of technical colleges during the nineteenth and early twentieth century, an emphasis on scientific scholarship consistent with the needs and aspirations of
an advanced technological society, and a number of core values that are
sedimented in the governance of many different kinds of higher education institutions, provide the bases for the (to use Kubler's term) "replica-
mass" which embodies the morphological and iconographic substance of
the culture of higher education.

If, as is argued here, the prime task of administrative leaders in universities is to represent the core values already identified, we would expect
to find many of these replicated in their individual biographies. An examination of the educational histories and experiences of vice-chancellors and college heads suggests that this is indeed the case. There is in the
United Kingdom a visible split between the role played by such "prime
objects" as Oxford and Cambridge on the one side, 60 percent of vice-
chancellors having studied in these two universities, and the technical
service tradition on the other, from which nearly all polytechnic directors come.

NOTES

1. See also *A Classification of Institutions of Higher Education* (1976),
Carnegie Council on Policy Studies in Higher Education, Berkeley, California.

2. ". . . it is an article of faith with many, if not most biologists, that their science is really not biological at all but is only physics and chemistry writ large.
And when they get the writing small and precise enough, they say it *will* be
physics and chemistry" (Grene 1966, 206).

3. The basis of comparison is not exact, since the published sources used in the
1981 survey show some vice-chancellors as having been educated at more than
one university.

REFERENCES

Baldridge, J. V., and Terrence Deal (1978). *Policy Making and Effective Leadership.* San Francisco: Jossey-Bass.

Bell, A. (1981). "Structure, Knowledge and Social Relationships in Teacher Education." *British Journal of the Sociology of Education* 2(1), 3-23.

Bennett, N. (1976). *Teaching Styles and Pupil Progress.* London: Open Books.

Beer, S. (1967). *Management Science: The Use of Operations Research.* London: Aldus.

Burgess, T. (1967). "Excellence or Equality — A Dilemma in Higher Education?" *Higher Education Review* 10(1), 26-39.

Carnegie Annual on Policy Studies in Higher Education (1980). *Three Thousand Futures: The Next Twenty Years in Higher Education.* San Francisco: Jossey-Bass.

Clark, B. R. (1966). "The Organizational Context." In T. M. Newcombe and E. K. Wilson, eds. *College Peer Groups.* Chicago: Aldine.

_____ (1970). *The Distinctive College.* Chicago: Aldine.

_____ (1980). *Academic Culture.* Working Paper 42, Yale Higher Education Research Group.

Collison, P. and J. Millen (1969). "University Chancellors, Vice Chancellors and College Principals: A Social Profile." *Sociology* 3(1), 77-109.

Dilthey, W. (1976). *Descriptive Psychology and Historical Understanding.* Translated by Richard Zaner and Kenneth Heiges. The Hague: Martinus Nijhoff.

Greenfield, T. B. (1975). "Theory about Organization: A New Perspective and Its Implications for Schools." In M. Hughes, ed. *Administering Education: International Perspectives.* London: Athlone.

_____ (1978). "Reflections on Organization Theory and the Truths of Irreconcilable Realities." *Educational Administration Quarterly* 14(2), 1-23.

Grene, M. (1961). *The Knower and the Known.* London: Faber and Faber.

Halsey, A. H. (1979). "A Tale of Two Systems." *Times Higher Education Supplement,* 16 November.

_____ (1979). "Are the British Universities Capable of Change? *New Universities Quarterly* 33(3), 402-16.

_____ (1981). *The Senior Common Room: A Study of British Universities and Polytechnics After Expansion.* Oxford: Clarendon Press.

Halsey, A. H., and M. Trow (1971). *The British Academics.* London: Faber and Faber.

Handy, C. (1976). *Understanding Organizations.* London: Penguin.

Harrison, R. (1972). "Understanding Your Organization's Character." *Harvard Business Review* 50(3), 119-28.

Kubler, G. (1962). *The Shape of Time.* New Haven: Yale University Press.

Lindop, N. (1981). "Poly Perceptions." *Education* 15 (May), 441-49.

Lorenz, K. (1977). *Behind the Mirror.* London: Methuen.

Lyman, S. M., and M. B. Scott (1976). *The Drama of Social Reality.* London: Oxford University Press.

MacGregor, D. (1960). *The Human Side of Enterprise.* New York: McGraw-Hill.

Mangham, I. L. (1978). *Interactions and Interventions in Organizations.* Chichester: John Wiley.

Merton, R. K., ed. (1957). *Social Theory and Social Structure.* New York: Free Press.

Pettigrew, A. M. (1979). "On Studying Organizational Cultures." *Administrative Science Quarterly* 24(4), 570-81.

Pugh, D. et al. (1969). "The Context of Organizations and Structures." *Administrative Science Quarterly* 14, 91-114.

Ranson, S., B. Hinings, and R. Greenwood (1980). "The Stucturing of Organizational Structure." *Administrative Science Quarterly* 25(1), 1–17.

Taylor, W. (1963). *The Secondary Modern School.* London: Faber and Faber.

_____ (1964). "The Training College Principal." *Sociological Review* 12(2), 19–26.

_____ (1969). *Society and the Education of Teachers.* London: Faber and Faber.

_____ (1980a). "The Teaching Function." In *Australian Universities to the Year 2000.* Canberra: Australian Committee of Vice-Chancellors and Principals.

_____ (1980b). "Managing Contraction." In R. Farquher and I. Housego, *Canadian and Comparative Educational Administration.* Vancouver, B.C.: University of British Columbia.

Williams, R. (1976). *Keywords.* London: Fontana.

1) Examiy "Sacced Fust." is Threateniy

CHAPTER 9

Leaders and Schools: Willfulness and Nonnatural Order in Organizations

Thomas B. Greenfield

There exist only three beings worthy of respect: the priest, the
soldier, the poet. To know, to kill, to create.
Charles Baudelaire
Mon Coeur Mis à Nu, XXII

To be just, that is to say, to justify its existence, criticism
should be partial, passionate and political, that is to say, written from an exclusive point of view.
Charles Baudelaire

The secret of leadership is to keep the six guys who hate your
guts from talking to the six guys who haven't made up their
minds about you.
Casey Stengel

The epigraphs above may appear incongruous or irrelevent in a discussion of what social science knows about leadership. Nevertheless their
presentation is consistent with a certain view of social reality, the view
that sees reality as woven by human will from stuff created from our
imagination and colored by our personal interests. The crux of this argument is that we can do nothing to validate our perceptions of reality
other than to describe it as we see it and argue for the truth of our description. This writing will therefore argue for the validity of its point of
view as an attorney might argue a case and hope thereby to convince a
judge and jury of its truth.

These are the themes of the argument. First, leadership is a willful act
where one person attempts to construct the social world for others. Second, an observation on what is happening in the world is a point of view.
Both the critic and the scientist must strive, therefore, to make clear what

their points of view are, because the observer and the observation are in some sense one. Third, we cannot escape ourselves as we make our world and as we try to understand the world others have made around us. The critic and the scientist must wonder at the artifice that inevitably goes into the making of social reality and into our interpretation of it.

These themes are explored by raising questions about the nature of organizations and in particular about schools as organizations. Are schools, in common with organizations generally, a manifestation of a natural order or are they rather products of diverse human invention that renders them not only different from other organizations but different as well among themselves? Are schools everywhere essentially the same or are they so varied in quality, meaning, and event that we must think of them as different as the people within them who give them life?

I have chosen to speak of schools as cultural entities to emphasize their humanness (if not their humaneness), to emphasize their differences rather than their similarities. The gist of this argument, therefore, is that schools, and also organizations in general, are best understood in context, from a sense of the concrete events and personalities within them rather than from a set of abstractions or general laws. The implication of this argument is that we should speak about leaders rather than leadership and about the character of leaders rather than their characteristics.

Before elaborating the main themes of this paper, I would like to offer what might be called a theoretical background note. Consider, for example, the historical evolution of science in Western thought. It may be argued that science began with logic and mathematics in ancient times. This basic knowledge found its application first in astronomy, the science that deals with matters most remote from people and their lives. Later thinkers such as Galileo and Newton, Boyle and Lavoisier established physics and chemistry by extending experimental reasoning and empirical inquiry into new fields. Biology and zoology are much later sciences but they are generally recognized as having extended again the now well established methods of the older sciences in the quest for objective knowledge about the world that lives.

When science came finally to look at individuals and the relationships among them, the nature of the knowledge gained and the method for achieving it were held still to be extensions of the now long line of the earlier sciences. Viewing the sciences in this historical and logical perspective, Comte proclaimed the "hierarchy of the sciences" (Giddens 1977, 12). This conception of scientific knowledge is one that sees only successive, successful applications of *the* scientific method — first to the physical, then to the biological, and finally to the social features of our environment. This view of the world and of human efforts to explain and control it leaves us with what Bauman calls "the French-Cartesian legacy of rationalism," (1978, 19) where reality is a billiard-ball world of cause and effect in Euclidean space and where law-like statements such as those of physics are regarded as being the only reliable knowledge and the highest form of explanation of the world around us. Scientific knowledge takes us in a direction that no other knowledge leads: toward control of our environment, first in the physical realm, then in the biological, and ultimately in the social and personal.

The point to be made here is that this slow emerging and development of the sciences may lead us to believe in the complementarity of the sciences or, with Comte, in the uniformity of them as well. That is, we may see not the sciences, but Science, and assume in our deference to this capitalized, god-like entity that its achievements flow from the application of a single powerful method that is equally applicable to all fields of human enquiry, whatever the subject of investigation or whatever the scientist's own interest in it. On the contrary, there are enormous differences and qualitative leaps between the realities studied in the sciences. The physical sciences deal only with the world that has no life, the biological sciences with the world that lives, the social sciences with the world of conscious life — the world that lives and reflects. Social science alone deals with the reality of individuals who know and know they know. In elaborating the differences among these realities, Schumacher (1977) shows that we have no reason for thinking that a single method and a uniform logic are appropriate for understanding them. He denies the common assumption that, because one invented logic has been eminently successful in understanding and controlling the physical world, it must therefore apply with equal force in realms that are inherently different and infinitely more complex than physical reality. Moreover, as Giddens points out, we cannot in social science find the same "sensational illumination and explanatory power" as science has yielded in our search to understand and control nature (1977, 13). Indeed, if we look for the same explanatory power that comes from the "seeming certainties" and "precise laws" of classical mechanics, we must by this token, says Giddens, reckon social science to be a failure.

Now is not the time to argue why I believe that the failure of organizational studies can be explained as a misplaced faith in Science; I have argued that point elsewhere (Greenfield 1980). Instead, I have several other things in mind now and would like to explore them with you. That is to say, I have intentions with respect to you and myself. The notion of intentionality as a key to explaining social reality is a theme that will recur throughout this paper. More formally, however, the paper serves four purposes. Actually, the paper has no purposes, but the kind of talk that says it does is an example of how we disguise human action behind a façade that appears to exist without human support. I shall therefore follow Mary-Claire van Leunen's (1978) advice and try to avoid the devices of academic writing that hide the self as it constructs the façade of opinion it hopes will be regarded as objective fact. I will assert and take responsibility for the following ideas: first, organizational studies should be seen as inquiry into nonnatural orders. Second, there exists a theory of willfulness that may help us to understand organizations. Third, organizations are manifestations of culture and we may understand them with only as much ease or difficulty as we can understand the culture in which they are embedded. Finally, I will describe by example some things that happen in schools that speak meaningfully to me about leaders.

Before I begin to explicate these ideas, let me ease into them by giving you two artistic metaphors that represent in some way the meaning of my intentions. The reasons for doing so are not frivolous. I am coming to believe that the science of organizations can better express its truths as metaphors than it can through the sophistry of complex quantification or through the grey images of reality that the limitations of Cartesian thought present to us (Schumacher 1977).

The first metaphor is from William Wordsworth, who tells us something about what science and technology do to living things:

> Sweet is the lore which Nature brings;
> Our meddling intellect
> Mis-shapes the beauteous forms of things: —
> We murder to dissect.

The justification for dissection is, of course, that it brings us knowledge we can gain in no other way. And so it does in some cases — those drawn from the objective, physical world, from the world that is not human, that is not ourselves and that we may experience only by observation. When we wish to understand the beauteous forms of things human, when we want to understand social realities, we should take care not to kill them before we try to come to know them and to understand them. For with their death there dies also the possibility of understanding those forms as they understand themselves.

The other metaphor is from V. S. Naipaul, the writer whom *The Times* calls "the new Dickens." In his novel, *A House for Mr. Biswas*, Naipaul (1961) describes a Trinidadian family that "fate had brought from India to the sugar-estate" to live in a "crumbling mud hut in the swamplands." In telling what happens to these people and what they do to each other, Naipaul deals only in the concrete and the specific. The events of the story and its impact are carried by talk. The talk never stops. It pours on relentlessly like a river. Naipaul seldom describes the setting and he never pauses to generalize or to point a moral. People are central in Naipaul's method. Ultimately they talk themselves into the reader's reality. They seem to exist apart from the pages and the words on them. But the novel is also about ideas. It is about education and development. It lets us see a life that moves from poverty and tradition-bound ignorance to the brink of the deepest insights that education and literate understanding can offer. The transition is not easy. It is in fact searingly painful and we recognize in the end that intellectual freedom and insight are won at an appalling personal cost.

The novel follows the youngest son of the family who becomes a journalist and whose life is seen in retrospect. Shortly before his death, Mr. Biswas is sacked by the *Trinidad Sentinel*, since "in less than a year he had spent more than nine weeks at the Colonial Hospital and convalesced at home for even longer." So his employer had seen no other choice but to give him three months' notice, though it "continued, up to the time of his death, to supply him every morning with a free copy of the paper."

Naipaul describes the early education of Mr. Biswas at the hands of Lal, who was "converted to Presbyterianism from a low Hindu caste" and taught in the Canadian Mission School. Lal held all unconverted Hindus in contempt and "as part of that contempt spoke to them in broken English." We join Mr. Biswas as he and his companions are learning *arithmetic*.

> *Ought oughts are ought,*
> *Ought twos are ought.*

The chanting of the children pleased Lal. He believed in thoroughness, discipline and what he delighted to call stick-to-it-iveness, virtues he felt unconverted Hindus particularly lacked.

"Stop!" Lal cried, waving his tamarind rod. "Biswas, ought twos are how much?"

"Two."

"Come up here. You Ramguli, ought twos are how much?"

"Ought."

"Come up. That boy with a shirt that looks like one of his mother bodice. How much?"

"Four."

"Come up." He held the rod at both ends and bent it back and forth quickly. The sleeves of his jacket fell down past dirty cuffs and thin wrists black with hair. The jacket was brown but had turned saffron where it had been soaked by Lal's sweat. For all the time he went to school, Mr. Biswas never saw Lal wearing any other jacket.

"Ramguli, go back to your desk. All right, the two of you. All-you decide now how much ought twos is?"

"Ought," they whimpered together.

"Yes, ought twos are ought. You did tell me two." He caught hold of Mr. Biswas, pulled his trousers tight across his bottom, and began to apply the tamarind rod, saying as he beat, "Ought twos are ought. Ought oughts are ought. *One* twos are two" (44–45).

This image from Naipaul should remind us that education is a moral enterprise that inculcates values. The values come in forms that are inextricably bound up with facts and knowledge. Schools are places that distribute values in the form of information and they do so by force, a force that is expressed through figures of authority called leaders who may resort to physical violence when the violence of authority alone does not suffice to do the job.

The inevitable combination of fact and value can be extraordinarily subtle. For Bertrand Russell (1973), $1 + 1 = 2$ was not only a proposition of symbolic logic and mathematics, but also a declaration of intent meaning "*Know that*" or "*Know that I am aware that*" $1 + 1 = 2$. There is therefore also an intentionality in logic, mathematics, and, apparently, objective science (Greenfield 1982). For Wittgenstein, it is we who are inexorable, not mathematics. And he says, "That is why it is inexorably insisted that we shall all say 'two' after 'one,' 'three' after 'two' and so on" (1975, 130). Thus it is that Lal, drilling arithmetic into reluctant heads in the Canadian Mission School in Trinidad, is not just teaching facts. He is a teacher and also a leader. He does what he thinks he has to do. He acts not only out of a sense that he is intellectually right, but also out of the conviction that what he says and does is *morally* right. So it is and must be with leaders. To those who see social reality as manufactured out of language and culture there is an ironic double meaning in Lal's words as he beats knowledge into Biswas. "Ought oughts are ought," he chants. Indeed they are, as anyone who has been to school ought to know.

Organizations as Nonnatural Order

The metaphors of traditional theory see organizations as ordered structures that exist spontaneously as a part of nature. Organizations are therefore a natural order in the social relationships among people. The framework, the catalogue, the clock, the thermostat, the candle flame, the guided missile, the living body in an environment, the balanced aquarium, and *the controlled system* are the predominating images that theory offers us as models for understanding organizations (Boulding 1968). The predominating feature of these images is order with accompanying intimations of rationality and goodness. These visions of organization are also depersonalized in the sense they presume that the order exists without human action or intention. The implication of looking at organizations in this way is that they may be studied as any other naturally occurring phenomenon may be studied. That is to say that organizations may be studied scientifically and objectively without engaging the interests, passions, and biases of the observer. Organizations are one thing and those who observe and study them are something else. With these notions about organizations, it would be possible for observers to establish universally validated truths about organizations free from the personalities of the scientists. Bauman shows how such ideas have given us a faith in the incontrovertible truths of science:

> However important the role of individual genius, insight, lucky accident or flash of inspiration in *articulating* the new idea, there must be a set of universal rules (which specifically did not hinge on unique, personal factors) employed in *validating* the claim of the idea to the status of truth. Science was seen as an utterly legal-rational, therefore impersonal and democratic, activity. Discovery was a matter of genius or talent, but validation was founded on rules which could be applied by everybody who mastered the publicly accessible skills, and which therefore avoided the differences arising from the personalities of scientists [1978, 13].

They have equally led us to believe in the truths of an incontrovertible, depersonalized, and objective science of organizations.

Habermas (1963) has pointed out how from at least the time of Hobbes there has been a school of social philosophy that rests upon the notion of a natural order in society and a natural law that governs it. In this thinking, the governance of civil society and its organizations becomes a scientific study just as the laws of physical motion that govern the movement of the planets can be discovered. Using "the Cartesian demand for a method . . . Hobbes for the first time develops a physics of sociation. As soon as insight into the mechanics of the societal state has been gained, the technically required arrangements can be fashioned to produce the correct social and political order" (72). What Hobbes offered, therefore, was a "social philosophy constructed after the model of modern physics" (74). From this position it is but a small step to see the sovereign as guardian of the natural order—that is, of the natural social order—and of the general will of the public. Such a general will would not, of course, be synonymous with notions of majority rule or democracy. The general will would rather be interpreted by the sovereign (whatever form this power might take) assisted only by technicians skilled in applying the impersonal and objective science of social organization.

The Hobbesian rationale for a physics of social organization has been extended in modern times by adherents of the organic metaphor in organization theory. Such theorists include systems analysts and systems theorists whose fundamental view of organizations regards them as either highly complex machines or organisms. To those who complain that the purely rational and machine models of organization are too simplistic, the organicists reply by endowing the machine with life. Organizations in this view retain many machine-like properties, but their internal processes and their relationships with their environments now become "dynamic." As living entities, organizations not only have bodies but sense and response systems as well. Like all organisms, they must learn to adapt themselves to increasingly complex and changing environments or face the penalty that nature exacts from any species ill adapted to its environment — extinction.

The organic metaphor is seen in the view that speaks of the "health" of organizations, of "organizational personality," and of "organizational climate." It is endemic in the organization development movement (OD) and in much of the planned change literature. In a chapter entitled "Toward a 'Truly' Scientific Management: Organization Health," Bennis, for example, speaks of organizations as individuals. He and other theorists require the organization to "meet reality" and to "do work" in order to "maintain themselves in existence." One of his chief concerns is for the mental health of organizations and presumably for their minds as well. Since the organization *is* a person, the methods of organizational diagnosis and those of psychotherapy become virtually identical for Bennis. "Both the norms of science and the methodology of psychotherapeutic work have the same goal and methodology: to perceive reality, both internal and external, and to examine unflinchingly the positions of these realities in order to act intelligently. . . . For an organization to develop adaptability, it needs to know who it is and what it is to do; that is, it has to have some clearly defined identity" (1966, 50).

I have examined the flaws in this kind of thinking elsewhere (Greenfield 1973, 1979). John Macmurray has pointed out the philosophical implications of the organic metaphor and its relationship to social structure and individual freedom in his commentary on Kant:

Kant's scepticism . . . is a prophetic warning of the peril of freedom which lurks in the romantic outlook, the danger that the form of the organic will be used to plan and construct the good society on earth. . . . Totalitarianism is the result of determining the good as an object in the spatio-temporal world, and planning its achievement by the use of scientific techniques within a heuristic framework of organic concepts. Kant's condemnation of the attempt is this, that though it intends a free and self-determining society, it must necessarily result in destroying freedom, and with freedom morality and religion, so bringing human personality under the bondage of a total determination [1957, 83].

Those who think we should plan to make organizations good, those who write prescriptions to restore organizations to health, and those who think we should train leaders to create organizations in the image of the happy, healthy, productive organism should ponder this warning from the philosophers. The alternative appears to lead to organizational tyranny in greater or lesser measure.

If we are to oppose a belief in organizations as manifestations of a natural order that is subject to universal and impersonal scientific laws, we must regard them as nonnatural, as orders that are man-made and therefore arbitrary in some sense, ephemeral, and certainly not universal. To speak of organizations as nonnatural entities is to speak of them as cultural artifacts and to regard what goes on in them as products of individual action, intention, and will. The notion of a sovereign who rules by virtue of laws of social action that are as immutable as the laws of physics is replaced by notions that see specific people acting for reasons that seem adequate to them. The ontological justification for their actions is now gone, however, and the conflicts so visible within organizations are no longer seen as contests of individuals against a general will but as struggles among knowing contestants. Social relations are to be understood as the application of will or as submission to it. Organizational life is reduced to bending others to your will — or of submitting and being bent by their wills.

What can be done scientifically within this conception of organizations? Is science possible at all within it? I believe that scientific inquiry into organizations is still possible within such a theoretical framework, but the kind of science that results may be rather different from the kind we have been accustomed to in the past. I would suggest that two kinds of general inquiry are open to us. We may first characterize the moral order that prevails in organizations and describe what happens within them. Secondly, we may argue about which kind of moral order is best, though we should not expect to find final answers to such questions. The first of these alternatives — description — opens up the possibility that artistic and other nonrational modes of representation of reality might convey the meaning of social organizations as well as, or better than, the linear, concise, and highly quantified abstractions that now usually count as science. The second alternative — argument — opens up science, or rather returns it, to the realm of philosophy in which certainty comes only from values that lie beyond any proof that science can offer.

The idea of organizations as nonnatural realities means that they are founded in meanings, in human intentions, actions, and experience. Organizations are therefore cultural artifacts: they are systems of meaning that can be understood only through the interpretation of meaning. In this way of thinking, we cannot look to find what have been called "the brute data" of organizations. Brute data are those facts that press themselves upon our understanding so forcibly that no one can question their existence. It is brute data, for example, to say that a living body fell from the fifth floor of the police station in a northern Italian city and was dead after its impact upon the ground. But as anyone knows who has seen Dario Fo's bitterly humorous play, "The Accidental Death of an Anarchist," the explanations of who that body was, why it came to fall from the window, and indeed whether it fell or was pushed and whether the person was a criminal or a hero, are matters that lie far beyond brute data. Such "facts," if we can call them such, are part of organizational reality; they rest upon human meaning and action and upon the interpretation of social reality. So the important facts of organizational life call non-brute data into play. They rest upon the interpretation and upon the interpretation of interpretations in a process that continues without end and without ever reaching the definitive statement, the final judgement, or the ultimate social truth.

As Taylor points out, the non-brute facts of organization are not just subjective states of mind and values that somehow interact with an objective social reality. Rather, it is non-brute facts themselves that define and constitute social reality.

These meanings do not fit into the grid; they are not subjective beliefs or values, but are constitutive of social reality. In order to get at them we have to drop the basic premise that social reality is made up of brute data alone. For any characterization of the meanings underlying [organizational] practices is open to question by someone offering an alternative interpretation. The negation of this is what was meant by brute data. We have to admit . . . that meanings as subjective are not just in causal interaction with a social reality made up of brute data, but that as intersubjective they are constitutive of this reality [1971, 25].

There is therefore no ultimate reality in the understanding of organizations and those who would apply science to gain such understanding so that we may "control" organizations in the same way that physical science enables us in some circumstances to control nature are moving on a path that leads either to disappointment and defeat or else to self-delusion. In this way of thinking, understanding leads not to technique and technique to control; understanding leads only to greater understanding and (if we follow the insights of Eastern religions) to escape through insight, art, suspension of the will, and ultimately to oblivion.

A Theory of Willfulness in Organizational Life[1]

I said at the outset that I would speak of a theory of willfullness that might help us to understand organizations. Such a theory denies a natural order in organizations and rejects brute data as offering any comprehensive or satisfactory explanation of what goes on in them. It rests instead upon will and imagination. We will our desires into realities and in doing so encounter opposing wills. The organization arises from a web of cross-connected wills as active agents live their lives and strive to make the world as they know it is or as they want it to be.[2] But as Schopenhauer says, we sense our will only when we feel opposition to it. "Just as a brook forms no eddy so long as it meets with no obstructions, so human nature . . . is such that we do not really notice and perceive all that goes on in accordance with our will. . . . On the other hand, everything that obstructs, crosses, or opposes our will, and thus everything unpleasant and painful, is felt by us immediately, at once, and very plainly" (1974, 291). What most often opposes our will in organizations is, of course, other people.

Organizations are the façade that covers individual intention and will; they are the marionette show that dazzles and deceives an audience — an audience of people who will themselves to believe the performance. But behind the façade are human actors who do what they want to do. As spectators we can choose to be enchanted or duped by the show or we can ask to see behind the façade and to discover who pulls the strings. Human effort creates organizations, but we usually choose to forget the effort and to focus on its outcome. We admire the achievement and deal with it as a detached, objective reality that is independent of the individuals who created it.

Organizations are abstractions. They are symbolic (Meyer and Rowan 1977), but they are also important. They hold the power of life and death over us as, for example, in the questions of whether the foetus has a right to life and whether a person whose unconscious life depends on an artificial life-support system has a right to die. But these questions and all that lie between them are answered not by abstractions, but by other people. As Sartre said, hell has no need of brimstone and turning on the spit. Hell is other people. It exists here and now. We ourselves make it. Once made, we call the resulting order organization.

A theory of organizations as will and imagination may be summed up in two statements: first, a statement that rejects group mind and rejects an overarching social reality thought to lie beyond human control and outside the will, intention, and action of the individual; second, a statement that acknowledges the tumult and irrationality of thought itself. Acting, willing, passionate, fearful, hoping, mortal, fallible individuals and the events that join them are therefore always more complex, interesting, and real than the ideas we use, forever vainly, to explain them. Let me offer several short observations that may illuminate and helpfully elaborate this outline of the basic theory.

1. It is the individual that lives and acts, not the organization. It is therefore the experience of individuals that we must seek to understand.

Huxley says it clearly: "We live together . . . , but always in all circumstances we are by ourselves. The martyrs go hand in hand into the arena; they are crucified alone" (1977, 11).

2. Clearly, there is something "out there" that contains forces man does not control. The individual does not give birth to himself or herself; nor can the individual by will withstand death. But, within these limits, the individual has enormous creative scope. As Wittgenstein (Kenny 1973) makes us see, the ideas in our heads are not so much models of the world as models for the world. We believe in the ideas in our heads. We trust our models for the world so deeply that we make them true. We will them to be true.

3. We live in separate realities. What is true for one person is not for another. In that sense, we live in different worlds. Each of us, as Huxley says, is an island universe. There is no action — however terrible or appalling it may appear to some of us — that is not sensible and rational to others.

4. Facts and values are closely interwoven. Positivistic science insists on splitting them and disregarding the values. It thus ignores the most important part of our lives and falls into the error of thinking that values can be derived from facts. Facts decide nothing. It is we who decide about the facts.

5. Modern science and ancient philosophy have taught us to think that a universal logic and rationality governs the world. We are taught to hope as well that those who master the logic and the rationality may also govern the world.

6. Individuals are responsible for what they do. Organizations and our habit of thinking in categories ease this sense of responsibility. As Hodgkinson (1978) points out, the required allegiance to the organization removes notions of right and wrong. The organization is not only reified but also deified. The individual is thereby no longer author of his act but agent for a larger reality. Absolutist Christians often speak — usually through clenched teeth — of loving the sinner and hating the sin. This schizophrenia of thought serves both to sanctify the Christians and to justify what they are about to do to the sinner.

7. The question is whose will is to predominate. Or, as Hodgkinson says, "We are all either administered or administering" (1978, 208), while William Blake says, "I must Create a System, or be enslav'd by another Man's." And G. B. Shaw's Don Juan argues that it is better "to be able to choose the line of greatest advantage instead of yielding in the direction of the least resistance. . . . To be in Hell is to drift; to be in Heaven is to steer." This leads us to think that it is better to run organizations than to be run by them.

8. The alternative to action and probable evil is disengagement. Or-

well (1957) uses the metaphor of Jonah inside the whale to express the individual's best approach to forces that are totally beyond his control. The image here is of security attained by personal detachment from the maelstrom that swirls around the individual. But detachment from events does not mean nonawareness of them. As Orwell says, we should think of the whale as transparent. In this circumstance, Jonah becomes an observer who can see what others locked in the struggle are oblivious to.

9. History and law should be our models for studying organizations, for these branches of knowledge know of no completion and recognize the interests of the writer and the advocate as crucial to what is declared to be true and right.

10. Language is power. It literally makes reality appear and disappear. Those who control language control thought, and thereby themselves and others. In the words of Thomas Szasz, "The less a person understands another, the greater is his urge to classify him — in terms of nationality, religion, occupation or psychiatric status. . . . In short, classifying another person renders intimate acquaintance with him quite unnecessary — and impossible" (1976, 46). And he adds, ". . . the human larynx and tongue are actually used as claws and fangs, and words as venom" (42). Organizations are sets of categories arrayed for the linguistic and other wars that people wage among themselves. Or we may think here of the quip that runs: a language is a dialect that has its own army and navy. So an organization is a set of meanings that people act out, talk out, and back up with their own armamentarium of forces — psychological, moral and physical.

Organizations as Cultural Artifacts

The cultural world is one of man-made reality and its creation is like a conjuror's trick. When we reach out to touch such reality, to measure it, to study it, or to explain it, or to reduce it to its elements, it slips away from us and eludes our grasp. So we may say with Prospero:

> . . . These our actors,
> As I foretold you, were all spirits and
> Are melted into air, into thin air;
> And, like the baseless fabric of this vision,
> The cloud-capped towers, the gorgeous palaces,
> The solemn temples, the great globe itself,
> Yea, all which it inherit, shall dissolve
> And, like this insubstantial pageant faded,
> Leave not a rack behind.   We are such stuff
> As dreams are made on. . . .

Thus Shakespeare has anticipated modern interpretive social scientists by several centuries. They put the matter more formally, but without adding a great deal to Shakespeare's poetic insight. Rabinow and Sullivan, for example, argue that human life cannot be studied in a vacuum or a scientifically controlled environment and therefore

> the exactitude that is open to the human sciences is quite different from that available to the natural sciences. Our capacity to understand is rooted in our own self-definitions hence in what we are. What we are is a self-interpreting and self-defining animal. We are always in a cultural world, amidst a "web of signification we ourselves have spun." There is no outside detached standpoint from which to gather and present brute data. When we try to understand the cultural world, we are dealing with interpretations and interpretations of interpretations [1979, 6].

I would like now to underscore this understanding of culture and organization with an example from the anthropological studies of Clifford Geertz. In a piece of writing that is lucid, convincing, and powerful (qualities not usually found in scholarly writing in the social sciences), he provides what he calls "Notes on a Balinese Cockfight" (1979). His notes are first of all descriptive but at the same time reflective. He not only lets us understand a distant culture and its organization, he also shows how it is possible to obtain such understanding and why obtaining it is always fraught with difficulties whether the culture to be understood is close to us or distant.

The thing to understand about cockfighting in Bali is that it is banned there as it is in most other countries of the world. It should be understood, too, that the cocks are armed with steel spurs "sharp enough to cut off a finger or run a hole through a foot." The mounting of the spurs on the animals is "an obsessively deliberate affair." The spur blades that have been "kept out of the sight of women" and sharpened only "at eclipses and the dark of the moon" are carefully bound around the leg of the cock. The confrontation between the two cocks is carefully managed and timed. A gong is sounded and a coconut shell with a hole in it is placed in a pail of water where it will take about twenty-one seconds to sink. A gong sounds again and the round is over. Sometimes the cocks do not fight. In this case, they are picked up at the end of the round and "fluffed, pulled, prodded and otherwise insulted, and put back in the centre of the ring and the process begins again."

Geertz describes what happens then:

> Most of the time, in any case, the cocks fly almost immediately at one another in a wing-beating, head-thrusting, leg-kicking explosion

of animal fury so pure, so absolute, and in its way so beautiful, as to be almost abstract, a Platonic concept of hate. Within moments one or the other drives home a solid blow with his spur. The handler whose cock has delivered the blow immediately picks it up so that it will not get a return blow, for if he does not the match is likely to end in a mutually mortal tie as the two birds wildly hack each other to pieces. This is particularly true if, as often happens, the spur sticks in its victim's body, for then the aggressor is at the mercy of his wounded foe [192].

There follows then an interval in which the handler tries to revive the wounded cock. He blows in its mouth, puts its whole head in his mouth, binds up its wounds with medication, and tries by whatever means to bring the wounded cock back into fighting trim by arousing "the last ounce of spirit which may be hidden somewhere within it." Oftentimes the wounded cock expires in the trainer's hands or is soon dispatched when it is replaced in the ring. But as Geertz notes, this is not always the case. "For if a cock can walk, he can fight, and if he can fight, he can kill, and what counts is which cock expires first. If the wounded one can get a stab in and stagger on until the other drops, he is the official winner, even if he himself topples over an instant later" (192).

What explains why men cause such things to happen? "Men" here is the right word, for cockfighting in Bali is, of course, a man's sport and Geertz entitles his notes "Deep Play" to give us a clue to what is going on here. The cockfight is a symbol of Balinese society and of the individual's place in it. It is a play about social organization in which everything is risked but nothing is changed. As Geertz explains, "The Balinese see in fighting cocks themselves, their social order, abstract hatred, masculinity, demonic power" and the archetypal image of their culture — "the arrogant, resolute, honor-mad player with real fire" whom legend made their king (211).

How did Geertz come to understand these things? Does he understand them aright? There are no easy answers to these questions. They face anyone who observes and tries to understand any cultural setting. The task of choosing images, metaphors, statements to represent the organization as a cultural artifact is not easy. There are no rules for such representation, for the explication and interpretation of reality.

A recently released film by Louis Malle is called "Phantom India." Through six hours we see a kaleidoscope of images about a culture we scarcely know or understand. Malle claims that his images are "accidental" but no consciously constructed representation of reality rests solely on chance. There is always a dialogue of some sort between the observer and the observed. Whose view of the event is to prevail? Again we return to choice and to will. Malle wonders what he is filming. We see dancers transfixed in the ultimate gesture, where the line between dance and dancer disappears. We see tea-pickers in an idyllic landscape, delicate, like figures in Eastern art, but we know that these young women bending over the tea plants are virtually indentured to landowners as they work to save the sum for their necessary dowries. How shall we understand these images? Malle wonders whether they show more than those he photographed watching him as he watched them (Scott 1980).

Geertz engages his readers in similar questions as he describes Balinese culture and the significance of cockfights within it. He points out that his first problem as he attempted to work in a Balinese village was to make it across "some moral or metaphysical shadow line" so that he and his wife might be regarded as real and be taken as "human beings rather than a cloud or a gust of wind" (182). There movement across this line is accomplished suddenly following a cockfight that was raided by police as they were in attendance. The police, who were Javanese rather than Balinese, roared up to the fight in trucks and jumped out waving guns while Geertz and his wife took flight with the other villagers. Finding themselves running in the wrong direction, they followed a man into his courtyard where his wife, apparently used to such scenes, "whipped out a table, a tablecloth, and three chairs, and three cups of tea." Composing themselves as the police arrive and demand an explanation for the presence of "White Men" in the yard, their host of five minutes gave an elaborate and impassioned explanation of who and what they were. "We had a perfect right to be there, he said, looking the Javanese upstart in the eye. We were American professors; the government had cleared us; we were there to study culture; we were going to write a book to tell Americans about Bali. And we had all been there drinking tea and talking about cultural matters all afternoon and did not know anything about any cockfight" (184). This explanation came despite the fact that Geertz had been able to speak to almost no one in the village up to that time. These events provided the entrée and acceptance that was needed to get to understand the happenings they were witnessing before the police arrived.

He begins to understand and explain the cockfight as the Balinese themselves do. He finds that the identification of Balinese men with their cocks is "unmistakeable" and the double entendre is also. "It works," he says, "in exactly the same way in Balinese as it does in English, even to producing the same tired jokes, strained puns, and uninventive obscenities." The place of cocks in the household is a special one. They are kept in wicker cages and given the best spots to receive sun and shade. They are fed special diets and receive extraordinary time and attention from their owners. "Maize is offered to the animal kernel by kernel. Red pepper is stuffed down their beaks and up their anuses to give them spirit. They are bathed in the same ceremonial preparations of tepid water, medicinal herbs, flowers, and onions in which infants are bathed, and for a prize cock, just about as often" (186).

The cock is a symbolic expression of the owner's self and "the narcissistic male ego." The cock also symbolizes, according to Geertz, the Balinese aversion for animals and any behavior regarded as animal-like. The demons that the Balinese see about them are represented in animal forms that recur throughout their sculpture, dance, ritual, and myth. The cock is therefore the thing that the Balinese male identifies with most closely and the thing he fears most. For him the cock is his ideal self, his penis, but it is also "what he most fears, hates, and ambivalence being what it is, is fascinated by — The Powers of Darkness' " (189).

I have dwelt at some length on these descriptions and explanations from Geertz because they make plain that culture is, as Weber said, "a web of meaning we ourselves have spun." Though we ourselves make the web, we are usually unaware of it, even as we find the meaning of self within it. It gives us being even as it creates our powers and our weaknesses. The web creates statuses and relationships among people; it deals with life and the order of the social world. Geertz interprets the meanings he found in one culture and shows how he arrived at them. His method is descriptive and expository. He leaves us with powerful images of a culture and insight into what social order means within that culture. The very foreignness and oddity of the images and the intensity of them help us to understand the dynamics that are at work in our own organizations. His method of portrayal appears deceptively simple, but it points a way through a host of problems and offers means that are not widely employed in trying to understand cultural entities that are closer to us and that shape us even as we shape them.

Leaders and the Administrative Act

This paper has perhaps failed to say very much about "leadership in educational settings." If this lack is indeed a failure, then it is because I have been trying to avoid such phrases as "leadership in educational settings" and to justify why it is right to do so. I am not convinced we know very much about leadership as a general phenomenon, whether it occurs in schools or other places. I have argued instead for a theory that moves us away from the abstract toward the concrete and I have tried to show that it is individual human effort, intention, and will that make the entities, the social reality, we call organization. When we understand something of what is going on around us in our organizations we must therefore end by talking about individuals and about the meanings that surround them. To talk of leadership, therefore, we must talk about leaders and about those who follow them or who fail to follow them. We must talk too about the meanings that bind leaders, followers, and all participants together in the social setting. Such a setting we may call the organization or just life. As we come to understand it, we will see schools and organizations generally as cultural artifacts, as products of human imagination bearing the imprint of individual men and women. We will see how it is that Prospero's actors and his cloud-capped towers, gorgeous palaces, solemn temples, and the great globe itself can be made out of air, out of thin air.

What do we see if we turn our attention to leaders and the social order of schools? In this section I will suggest that the task of leaders is to create the moral order that binds them and the people around them. They weave the social fabric that allows us to be, to exist. The following internal monologue was collected from a teacher who was asked how he establishes order and control in his classroom. The dynamics he speaks of well illustrate the process by which leaders control themselves and achieve as well the social order that controls others. The statement speaks of the work of the leader as a performance given by a skillful actor before an audience that dares not disbelieve, or chooses not to disbelieve, what it sees.

A Teacher is More Than a Person

"When I get up in front of a class, I am someone in addition to Ken the person—I am Ken, the teacher. A teacher has authority—or he should have it in the classroom, and while it does no one good if that authority is continuously overt, it is useful to exercise it under certain circumstances. At the beginning of each class, it is like the start of a new day. For each student, it will be his or her first class with me, so the student is beginning the process of interaction with me for that day and that class. I suppose that my standing up there symbolizes something. It symbolizes my authority in the classroom, for only when students acknowledge my presence there do I begin. It's a role—that's what it is. A teacher engaged in activity like that is acting. He is putting on a performance and the acting has to be good enough to convince the students—of the teacher's authority, that is. I don't mean to sound like Machiavelli or something, but I do feel that to begin the class by focusing on the teacher provides ultimately a better atmosphere for teaching and learning. My role up there is essentially giving the message to the kids that—well—okay, we have to have some kind of control before we can learn anything—and after the initial noise and everything, my standing there says I am ready. The kids eventually respond and then we can get something done. They know that when I stand there that it's time to begin. If they forget, I usually give them a gentle nudge—you know, like 'shut up'." Ken laughed when he said this [Ramsoomain 1980].

It is odd that the study of leadership is limited to a rather narrow band of human endeavour. Others who stand aside for a time to observe the passing human parade are not likely to speak of it in terms of leadership at all but in terms of concrete events and specific people. It is not usual to talk of kingness, queenness, popeness, and presidentness when we talk of those who in the minds of most of us are acknowledged as leaders. We speak instead about kings, queens, popes, and presidents and we talk about what they do and do not do and of the reasons for their actions. But in the study of organizations, we are apt to remove the personal element and to speak of faceless ciphers who "perform a leadership function" and "manage the human resources of the enterprise." What happens in organizations and what leaders in fact do can thereby be reduced to fit the assumptions of a science that removes the eccentricity and fullness of individual action to reduce it to a grey universality. While such generality is not without its own truth and while such truth can also be useful, it is now time to redress a balance and take more care for the individual and the concrete. In studies of educational organizations and their leaders, such a change will mean speaking not as we have been prone to do of the leadership of the principal or superintendent but of superintendents and principals as leaders.

When leaders act, when they decide or choose, we may speak of the administrative act. Such acts are acts of intention and will. In any setting that brings people together, there will be many wills, intentions, and meanings at play and many of these will be incongruent or even in conflict with each other. The leader is the person who decides what will be and who acts to make it so. Leaders are therefore arbiters and constructors of social reality even as Prospero was. Their acts are moral acts and to know them we must surely understand how the act is accomplished; ultimately we must also judge the act itself. To conclude that leadership is a moral activity is perhaps to belabor the obvious or to state a platitude. But it is strange how often the obvious and the platitudinous are overlooked in studies of leaders in school and strange, too, how frequently such truths are ignored.

What do we in fact see if we look at leaders rather than at leadership in schools? The answer to this question is that we see very little because there are few studies that examine schools in the way that Geertz examined Balinese culture. There is, of course, the great sociological tradition that goes back to Willard Waller (1932) who looked at schools in intense, long-term, and fine-grained detail. And there is the small band of those who follow the Waller tradition in its modern ethnographic manifestation. The work of Smith (1971), Rist (1973), and Willis (1978) among others gives us detailed close-ups of what goes on in school. But for the most part these studies are concerned chiefly with relations among teachers or between teachers and students. They are concerned for the replication of society in students and with the maintenance of the social institution called school. It is not so much that leaders are absent from the picture of schools presented in these studies, but rather that the question of what leaders do is not brought sharply into focus.

Two major studies do focus upon school principals as leaders. Wolcott (1973) gives us a picture of an elementary school principal and Metz (1978) provides an unusually valuable insight into the lives of two secondary school principals. Wolcott's study lets us see Ed Bell, a man whose life is filled every day with little things, with many little things. While none of these things is of any great moment, yet each act is necessary, unavoidable, and filled with meaning. He chases a dog off the school grounds, he takes school time to pick up his wife's car from the garage, he traces down a lost cupcake from a second grader's lunch box, he explains to three fifth grade girls who "teamed up" and came to school in pedal pushers why they must "dress like ladies," he fills in for a teacher who is late, he discusses a "problem boy" with a guidance committee, and he explains and demonstrates new lunchroom procedures to the first and second graders. His day goes from early to late and includes, on the one day we follow him closely, a principals' meeting where he listens to a police officer explain how to interview children who are suspected of "crimes." He also listens to a report on salary negotiations with the school district and asks the obligatory questions to let his colleagues know that he is actively defending his status in the ranks of principals.

When I present this picture of Ed Bell's life to students who are themselves principals and teachers, they are virtually unanimous in criticizing him for his "inefficiency." When asked if they think the statement of Ed Bell's life presents a fair picture of what they see going on in elementary schools, they agree that it is accurate but often complain that it is "too negative." I have come to conclude that a "positive" picture of the elementary principal would show only a person who is super-efficient and organized: that is, it would portray a decision-maker who never agonized over a decision, who communicated decisions rapidly to those affected by them, and whose actions were never challenged or questioned by those around him. Such a principal would arrive at school shortly before it opened, move from tidy desk to orderly meetings and depart early for home in the confidence that everything in the organization was humming along smoothly and as it should. The wish in this case to see a "positive" picture of the school overwhelms our experience of what we know goes on in schools and casts doubt on what we know about the ways principals act in them.

The urge to judge Ed Bell also obscures what he does as a leader. Indeed, if leadership has to do at all with achieving a purpose well and in permitting no challenge of that purpose, then Ed succeeds in important ways. His job is to keep things as they are, to maintain life in the school as he knows it should be. This is his task: to maintain a way of living and being in the school, to ensure people behave as they should, personally and collectively. Some might consider Ed's day and say that nothing happens in it — at least, nothing of major consequence. But nothing never happens in social reality. Something is always going on and that something must be attained, achieved. This is what Ed does as a leader. He achieves what appears to be nothing, but is in fact everything. As a leader, Ed Bell acts through his thousand varied activities to ensure that things do not change, that the unexpected never occurs. If the unexpected or unusual does occur in the social reality around him, Ed sets out to set it right — that is, to eliminate it or make it routine. Boys must be made to realize that it is wrong to steal cupcakes, that it is wrong to shove others in the cafeteria line, to wear a torn or soiled T-shirt in the reading teacher's class, or to eat meals at home that he regards as unwholesome or nutritionally unbalanced. Girls, of course, must not band together to threaten the sacred but unwritten school dress code and must come to see why they should want to "dress like ladies." Indeed, nothing *never* happens in Ed Bell's school. The social order there is achieved, it is of great importance, and Ed is its leader.

Metz (1978) presents a detailed comparison between two secondary-school principals who stand in sharp contrast to each other as leaders. Mr. Brant is a leader who believes in and acts according to the dictum that says, "Sooner or later you'll do it my way and be glad you did." His rhetoric is one thing, his action another. Order for him is everything and he never doubts that the order he demands and speaks for is the larger social good — the general will that justifies the imposition of his will upon others. All of this is accomplished, of course, within an unwavering good humor, with a smile and firm handshake always at the ready to soothe any troubled situation. Mr. Brant's "managerial style" is resolutely democratic as long as democracy makes the decisions that he would make in any case. He runs the school in such a way that his vision of human relationships comes to be seen as "inherent in the inevitable character of public schools" and if anyone balks at his decisions, his technique is "to kill them with enthusiasm." Nothing is left to chance, however. He appoints the committees, places their reports late on the agenda of faculty meetings if he disagrees with them, or simply overrules them at a later date.

He makes his organizational world in his image but never acknowledges his part in its creation. He simply does what he knows has to be done. He makes his school the way it ought to be, the way that larger forces want it to be. And he is the instrument of those larger forces; he is the instrument of society. As he sets out to get his way, he denies the existence of conflict with those who oppose him. He says: "I see your point of view," and then with regret but firmness finds that this view is unfortunately contrary to "the law," to the bulky ambiguity of the school handbook, or to "district policy." While he sees himself as representing the general will and the good of society, those who oppose him are seen as individuals. While *he* stands for society, *they* are individuals acting only in pursuit of their own personal ends. What Brant sees is not conflict but the maladjustment of the individual to the social order. As individuals bent upon their own purposes, they are therefore responsible themselves for whatever trouble he, the doer of social good, may put in their way as they pursue their aims. Few of those who oppose him have the wit, time, or opportunity to notice, let alone challenge, the fact that only Brant's reading of the law, the handbook, or district policy counts as the valid interpretation of them. Only what Brant says constitutes a sound guide for action, and only Brant's action can therefore be legitimate.

The other principal, Mr. Henley, used few of the devices practiced by Mr. Brant, though their positions in schools that had been recently desegregated were in many ways similar. Instead of masking differences of value and opinion, Mr. Henley let those who held different points of view feel the conflicts among them in hopes that their ultimate resolution would be sounder and more generally accepted. When the pledge of allegiance and a flag-raising ceremony became an issue in Mr. Brant's school, he buried the problem in committees, consultations, and reports, while the pledges and ceremonies went on as before. In Mr. Henley's school the same issues were raised, dealt with openly, but not resolved. Instead they boiled over from the school into the community. On the occasion of the assassination of Martin Luther King, there was a crisis in both schools. Mr. Brant handled it by underlining the need for order and by defusing the emotion felt by students. Both of the schools held an assembly, but in his school Mr. Brant ensured that the students attended no mass assembly but rather came in small groups to ceremonies that were adult- and teacher-dominated. His aim was to get through the crisis, not to find new and disturbing meanings in it. Mr. Henley held a single large assembly in which students participated actively and in which they gained understanding of the meaning of the event for themselves as individuals and for the wider community.

It is worth noting that Mr. Henley was fired at the end of the year in which these events occurred while Mr. Brant sailed smoothly onward and presumably upward in his career.

The Antileadership Position

These arguments suggest what might be called the antileadership position. The basic question here is what allegiance people owe to the collective, to the organization of which they are part. It is also a question of what allegiance they owe to the representatives of the collective—that is, to its leaders. Taylor (1971) points out that the study of politics has been concerned at least from the time of Plato with the question of the legitimacy of the social order. Some orders appear to command the allegiance of their members out of a "spontaneous cohesion" and to permit freedom within structure, while other social systems appear to be constricting and to rest largely upon the use of force. In coercive organizations, those who are in power—the leaders—seek to maintain their positions and to exclude those against whom they use their power from access to it.

The desirable social order is one in which the values and commitments of the group find expression through the leader. Two intractable difficulties stand in the way of attempts to realize this desirable order. The first is the simple consideration that all people are not committed to the same values. And even if they were so committed, a general agreement on values in a group does not make them right, especially when they are used against dissident members of the group or against other, less-powerful groups. The second difficulty arises from the consideration that the very existence of groups depends on an external purpose that the leader embodies. Instead of representing the values of the group, the leader is more frequently the instrument who determines what the group values are.

Therefore, in deciding what to do on behalf of a group, the leader faces Arrow's General Impossibility Theorem which states that we must either believe in group mind or recognize that decisions in groups are made by the imposition of one person's judgement on another's, whether by persuasion, reason, coercion, or guile.[3] Chester Barnard (1938) recognized this dilemma for the leader as well. He spoke of the leader as an *embodiment of the central purpose of the organization* and he described the leader's task as being that which commits others to that purpose. In other words, the leader cannot escape deciding, even if the decision is only to decide not to decide. And in deciding the leader moves inevitably into the process of committing others to that decision. The leader therefore is the person who *is* the group or who can make it appear so. Bound up with that identification of the leader with the group is a mystery and often an awesome power as well.

In practical, if not Machiavellian, terms the effective social order is therefore the one in which leaders can claim that their actions rest not upon their own preferences and intentions but upon a general will that is larger and more deserving of respect and obedience than any individual's interest or desire. In this alchemy, leadership is transmuted from personal desire into selfless action on behalf of the larger polity. We move from the case where leaders act out of preference, uncertainty, and choice to the notion of leadership as a general will that expresses itself through a chosen vessel — the leader. The justification for social order — for any social order — is therefore that it "provides men freedom, that it emanates from their will, that it secures them order, the rule of law, or that it is founded on tradition, or commands obedience by its superior qualities" (Taylor 1971, 31).

Since we are all against coercion and in favor of freedom within order, it is but a short step from talk about leadership to the new organizational Sermon on the Mount that proclaims: "Blessed are leaders whose work is legitimated or who can make it appear so, for they shall wield power and feel good about it." And this beatitude might be extended into its corollary that states: "Cursed are those without power, for they lack leadership potential and are doomed to an uphill struggle against those who have it." Leadership is therefore by definition on the side of society and legitimation, and those who challenge these verities do so at their own risk.

I have called the opposing view the antileadership position. It is one that recognizes a plurality of values in human society and that denies ultimate legitimacy to any action. What we are left with, therefore, is contention among values or, more accurately, among those who espouse different values. In this view we are all leaders in some degree. We all have legitimacy in the degree to which we act out of our own values and can involve others in them. This view rejects the idea of a simple, unitary value structure as the foundation for any large, complex social order. In this view all social orders are pluralistic and there will always be struggle and contention among those who represent the conflicting values within the structure. Those who represent the contending values are the leaders and they are in all respects human, fallible, self-interested, perverse, dogged, changeable, and (fortunately) ephemeral. In social possibility, we are all leaders. Certainly none of us can claim the ultimate right to leadership, to an ontological justification that is denied to others.

What happens in Balinese cockfights evokes this notion of antileadership. Everything within the order — no matter how stable and unchanging it appears — rests upon struggle and personal contention among individuals. The war is never over. No victory is ever decisive; no defeat, however devastating, is ever final. No matter what happens in today's battle, no matter how satisfying the victory or how humiliating the defeat, there will be another round tomorrow. Leaders are never secure in their positions. In the cockpit everyone is potentially equal; the outcome of the struggle is never sure, and yesterday's triumph fades in the face of the present challenger.

Organizations in the antileadership view are contexts for the expression of individual willfulness. They are the moral order — however complex, conflicted, or ambiguous it be — made apparent in action. If this conception of organizations and leaders is accepted, there are two implications — one of theoretical, the other of practical significance — that we may note. As far as theory is concerned, this conception of the organization and its leaders limits us to describing the moral structure within which personal action occurs. Beyond this we might argue about the rightness of the moral order we depict, but there appears to me to be no possibility that we can control the moral order by science, by finding and proving the fundamental, unalterable laws of the mechanics upon which it operates. There are no such mechanics in an objective, ontological sense; there is only the world of will: people acting out of whatever reasons seem good and sufficient to them.

The practical implication of this notion of organizations and their leaders is simply that leaders will try to commit others to the values that they themselves believe are good. Organizations are built on the unification of people around values. The business of being a leader is therefore the business of being an entrepreneur for values. Those who cannot readily be recruited to the moral structure for which the leader stands must be sold into it by persuasion, calculation, guile, persistence, threat, or sheer force. The appeal of values — especially if they are sold as ultimate values — can be powerful indeed. A recent recruitment advertisement for the British Army took up two pages in the *Sunday Times* and was headed: "A Tough Act to Follow." It showed the marble pillars of the chapel at Sandhurst inscribed with the names of former cadets whose "careers ended in the Great War." (It is perhaps significant that the text speaks of careers ending when it was surely the lives of the cadets that came to an end.) The text with the picture asks those who are considering a career as an army officer to examine their intentions. It comes quickly to the point: "The question isn't how deeply you're moved. [Though if you're not please don't apply.] It's whether you're prepared to do what they did." It goes on to say that applicants must be prepared to die, "to accept the possibility of being killed or wounded. And as an officer, you must lead your men to accept it, too." Now that is an up-front and honest appeal to higher values. Nor does the text invoke the usual inducements: money, travel, women, the good life. While one may argue with its values, the point to be made here is simply that this statement recognizes what an army does and makes no bones about the fact that those who are to be leaders within it have to be committed to certain values and have the task of committing others to those same values as well.

We may think of leaders and followers in another sense too. The image here comes from Buddhist thought that sees knowledge and spiritual enlightenment as a personal bond between guru and disciple. Through the rope of time, the learner is seen as linked to a more insightful and experienced teacher by a slender line dangling in the abyss of existence. The chain of knowledge and experience thus continues from generation to generation. We are all so linked and, if we extend the metaphor, we may see the personal linkage as that between climbers struggling through a storm to advance up the side of a difficult mountain. The way is uncertain, the links between the climbers frail. Crampons, ropes, trust, skill, their own hands and bodies, and their steadfastness are all these climbers have to make their way up the slope of some isolated and mysterious peak — Annapurna, F-6, or the north face of Everest. What does it mean to be a leader or follower in a situation such as this? Without having answered this question, it is nevertheless appropriate to conclude this discussion that has, I hope, at least showed why this question is worth raising. Education is a deeply mysterious process and so is the business of being a leader.

NOTES

1. Parts of this section are adapted and abridged from Greenfield, "Against Group Mind." The anarchism metaphor in that discussion is changed here into an assertion about the willfulness of individuals in organizations.

2. The text here uses "will and imagination" and "active agent" to evoke Arthur Schopenhauer's *The World as Will and Idea* (1819) and John Macmurray's *The Self as Agent* (1957).

3. The force of Arrow's theorem in administrative action is seen in Christopher Hodgkinson's (1973) "Why Democracy Won't Work," *Phi Delta Kappan* 54(5), 316; and "The Failure of Organizational and Administrative Theory" (1978), *McGill Journal of Education* 13(3), 272.

REFERENCES

Barnard, Chester I. (1938). *The Functions of the Executive.* Cambridge, Mass.: Harvard University Press.

Bauman, Zygmunt (1978). *Hermeneutics and Social Science: Approaches to Understanding.* London: Hutchinson.

Bennis, Warren G. (1966). *Changing Organization: Essays on the Development and Evolution of Human Organization.* New York: McGraw-Hill.

Boulding, Kenneth E. (1968). "General Systems Theory — The Skeleton of Science." In Walter Buckley, ed. *Modern Systems Research for the Behavioral Scientist.* Chicago: Aldine.

Geertz, Clifford (1979). "Deep Play: Notes on a Balinese Cockfight." In Paul Robinson and William Sullivan, eds. *Interpretive Social Science: A Reader*. Berkeley: University of California Press.

Giddens, Anthony (1977). *New Rules of Sociological Method: A Positive Critique of Interpretive Sociologies*. London: Hutchinson.

Greenfield, Thomas B. (1973). "Organizations as Social Inventions: Rethinking Assumptions about Change." *Journal of Applied Behavioral Science* 9(5), 551–74.

_____ (1979). "Organizational Theory as Ideology." *Curriculum Inquiry*, 9(2), 97–112.

_____ (1980). "The Man Who Comes Back through the Door in the Wall: Discovering Truth, Discovering Self, Discovering Organizations." *Educational Administration Quarterly* 16(3), 26–59.

_____ (1982). "Against Group Mind: An Anarchistic Theory of Organization." *McGill Journal of Education* 17(1), 3–11.

Habermas, Jürgen (1963). *Theory and Practice*. Boston: Beacon Press.

Hodgkinson, Christopher (1978). *Towards a Philosophy of Administration*. Oxford: Basil Blackwell.

Huxley, Aldous (1977). *The Doors of Perception/Heaven and Hell*. Frogmore, England: Triad/Panther.

Kenny, Anthony (1973). *Wittgenstein*. Harmondsworth, England: Penguin.

Macmurray, John (1957). *The Self as Agent*. London: Faber and Faber.

Metz, Mary Haywood (1978). *Classrooms and Corridors: The Crisis of Authority in Desegregated Schools*. Berkeley: University of California Press.

Meyer, John W., and Brian Rowan (1977). "Institutionalized Organizations: Formal Structure as Myth and Ceremony." *American Journal of Sociology* 83(2), 340–63.

Naipaul, V. S. (1961). *A House for Mr. Biswas*. Harmondsworth, England: Penguin.

Orwell, George (1957). *Inside the Whale and Other Essays*. Harmondsworth, England: Penguin.

Rabinow, Paul, and William Sullivan, eds. (1979). *Interpretive Social Science: A Reader*. Berkeley: University of California Press.

Ramsoomain, Franklin (1980). Field Notes. Toronto, Ontario: Institute for Studies in Education.

Rist, Ray C. (1973). *The Urban School: A Factory for Failure*. Cambridge, Mass.: MIT Press.

Russell, Bertrand (1973). *An Inquiry into Meaning and Truth*. London: Penguin University Books.

Schopenhauer, Arthur (1974). *Parerga and Paralipomena*, vol. 2. Translated by E. F. J. Payne. Oxford: Clarendon Press.

Schumacher, E. F. (1977). *A Guide for the Perplexed*. New York: Harper.

Scott, Jay (1980). "Malle Captures Sights but not Soul of India." *Globe and Mail* (Toronto), 20 June.

Smith, Louis M. (1971). *Anatomy of an Educational Innovation: An Organizational Analysis of an Elementary School*. New York: Wiley.

Szasz, Thomas (1976). *Heresies*. Garden City, N. Y.: Anchor.

Taylor, Charles (1971). "Interpretation and the Sciences of Man." In *The Review of Metaphysics* 25(1), 3–51.

Van Leunen, Mary-Claire (1978). "Scholarship: A Singular Notion." *Atlantic Monthly* 241(5), 88–90.

Waller, Willard (1932). *The Sociology of Teaching.* New York: Wiley.

Willis, Paul E. (1978). *Learning to Labour: How Working Class Kids Get Working Class Jobs.* Westmead, England: Saxon House.

Wittgenstein, Ludwig, quoted by Michael F. D. Young (1975). "Curriculum Change: Limits and Possibilities." *Educational Studies* 1(2), 130.

Wolcott, Harry F. (1973). *The Man in the Principal's Office: An Ethnography.* New York: Holt, Rinehart & Winston.

* Failure of Org Studies is due to faith in Science
  - should study Org as "Nonnatural"
- orgs are artifacts of society
  - facades of individual wilfulness

CHAPTER 10

Administrators' Response to Performance and Value Challenges: Stance, Symbols, and Behavior

Paul Hirsch and John A. Y. Andrews

This chapter explores some ramifications of the following observation: *an important aspect of administrative leadership consists of knowing which set of symbols to invoke at different points in time.*

This modest proposition highlights the importance of change over time and a corollary variation in organizational stances — two issues largely neglected in the corpus of literature on organization, but widely identified by social scientists and administrators as potentially critical to the definition and survival of firms, educational institutions, and virtually all other organizations. It calls to mind the old Chinese curse — "May you live in interesting times —" for despite the litany of positive connotations accorded the word "change" by administrators, they resemble people in general by not meaning it very seriously. As March and Simon (1958) and many others have noted, few of us like surprises and nearly all of us like the rules of the game to be clear: seldom do we look forward to changes which would drastically transform organizational worlds with which we are already familiar.

Our proposition, in short, sets the stage for a serious dialogue about theories of organization and administration, for the preponderance of this scholarship examines variations within what we shall call here a "stability frame."[1] Indeed, so far as such fundamental issues as survival, legitimacy, and institutional functions are concerned, most research and theories about organization per se have little to offer. This is a deliberate and self-conscious consequence of our building a body of knowledge within a stability frame, for its main concepts and premises assume that these problems *already have been solved.*

The historical basis for this formulation is, of course, Weber's concept and definition of bureaucracy as an efficient tool or instrument for *implementation*. With such institutional questions as goals, mission, and support levels taken as *givens*, the primary function accorded administrators was to execute policies decided elsewhere and to develop increasingly efficient means for their implementation. In this pure form, for example, a charismatic leader has no place, and the organizing idea for this volume on "administrative leadership" borders on a contradiction in terms. Within the stable frame produced as a *consequence* of the consolidation of the fruits of earlier, less disciplined, activist leadership, charismatic and dramatic turns of behavior are ideally and deliberately designed out of an organization; these should be unnecessary and can easily disrupt such a smooth-running machine. Organization and administrative theory thus thrives and informs us within this conceptual framework of stability (or dull times). Its major focus and contribution center on questions of technique and efficiency — comparing the relative performance of similar organizations to each other, or seeking comparisons of established criteria across different types of organizations (Etzioni 1961; Hirsch 1975, 1979). The degree of environmental variation permitted by the framework in which these studies are designed is comfortable, convenient, and restrictive. Outliers on the distribution of success and failure are seldom considered or accounted for. Because extreme scores on such an extended continuum seldom can be explained within the stability frame, we suggest broadening organizational analysis to incorporate them better and, to this end, will shortly set out (1) the exploratory concepts of value- and performance-challenges, and (2) some corresponding implications for administrators' definitions, behavior, and use of language and symbols.

The Impact of Changing Values and Ideology

At a higher level of aggregation, functionalist and ecological models have long informed us that organizations may be sorted within the dichotomy of success and collapse: those which survive and do best are seen as most central to the niches they occupy — providing models of successful adaptation for those who impute intentionality to top executives, or examples of dumb luck for those who relax or doubt such an imputation. From our standpoint, this perspective (Aldrich 1979; Pfeffer and Salancik 1978) has advanced organization theory by focusing attention on the importance of external environments and directing interest to extreme scores on the continuum of success and failure in performance. However it, too, is limited by what it chooses not to address. The population ecology perspective, for example, is self-consciously indifferent to what types of products or services arrive at the societal marketplace, as well as to how or why certain of their providers are found to perform better than others. It also encourages the observation that any "output" (cars, sermons, students, or patients) may be viewed as a commodity, whose value is gauged, post hoc, by its concrete place in society at any fixed point in time.[2]

But, over time, the valuations (social and economic prices) on many such "products" go through major changes, and to understand the processes involved requires a shift in the levels and types of organizational analysis employed. It is at this point that concepts like culture, ideology, politics, symbols, and value complexes reenter conventional models to insist that they are more than composite residuals, epiphenomena, and random error terms. Indeed, in times of social change — when the institutional niches in which we place organizations are themselves being renegotiated — the comfortable assumption that values, culture, and symbols can be pushed aside or held constant (after the cursory acknowledgement provided at the start of most treatments of organization theory) begins to disintegrate. Whereas traditional theories of administration stressed greater efficiencies in implementing policies set elsewhere, the ecological framework takes organizational survival as primary, irrespective of the goals and policies of any particular organization. *Both* exhibit a shared indifference to organizational purpose. Whether leadership and charisma are seen as routinized or irrelevant, respectively, both of these theories about organization exhibit a distinct preference for downplaying the sacred aspects of these social creations (purpose and goals) in favor of the mundane: matters of value are conceptually eliminated in the search to locate commonalities across organizations; whatever may be distinctive about any, or otherwise serve to distinguish it from the others, is ignored. Despite a clear difference in the level of analysis employed by each, both perspectives are uncomfortable with the process of leadership in unstable times given their respective orientations to routinized maintenance, on the one hand, or to cross-sectional and post hoc counting of dichotomous (i.e., success or failure) outcomes, on the other.

Consider the recent history of the National Science Foundation in terms of two organizational "states" and one telling experience between 1980 and 1982. For well over twenty years, the congressional appropriation to NSF both increased annually and provided the agency's top administrators substantial discretion concerning the allocation of its funds to programs and units within the organization. This first condition — allowing for year-to-year variations in the size of the increment awarded and the amount of debate preceding the award — (a) falls well within the purview of the stability frame associated with traditional approaches in organization theory, and (b) fits the definition by population ecologists of a successful organization occupying a functional niche.

This state was altered somewhat in 1981, when President Reagan's budget message specified cutbacks for the agency's division of social and economic sciences. Here, the discretion of the agency's top administrators to treat allocations to divisions as an internal matter was reduced, although the overall budget proposed for the agency as a whole was still above the previous year's. Further, the basis for the agency's funding of research by this division was questioned in the president's encompassing conclusion that the results of research in behavioral science simply had "not contributed to furthering the well-being of society." Taken together, the specified cut for this division and the president's statement of doubt concerning its mission suggest a less stable frame and convey less optimistic signals about NSF's success than the agency and its staff had experienced in previous years.

A particularly critical "event," from our standpoint, occurred later in the spring of 1981, when the entire allocation for the National Science Foundation was omitted altogether in the proposed federal budget submitted by the Office of Management and Budget to, and approved by, the U.S. Senate. According to the *Washington Post*, several days passed before NSF staff members checked with OMB to find that the omission was no accident: the story reports that these staff members, viewing the event as inconceivable, were aware of the absence, assumed that it was simply a clerical error, and had assumed further that it would be automatically and routinely rectified.

Performance and Value Challenges

The two conditions and one event described in the above example illustrate a distinction we propose between a stable framework for organizational analysis, and two conditions of change we term "performance" and "value" challenges. Within the stability frame, organizations falling between the extremes on the continuum of success and failure are easily, and often interestingly, compared. During the years of incrementally rising appropriations to most government agencies, for example, the recipients could be compared in terms of their efficiency and effectiveness in relation to the relative increases obtained by each. Similarly, studies like Lawrence and Lorsch's (1967) examination of which types of organization structure corresponded to the relative profitability of the firms in their sample from three industries is a prototype of conceptualizations within the stability frame. By this, we mean none of the sample firms verged on bankruptcy; apparently all were "successful" but differed by matters of degree, as measured by the percentage difference of annual increases in profitability.

Peformance challenges occur when organizations are perceived by relevant actors as having failed to execute the purpose for which they are chartered and claim support. The values they serve are not at issue, but rather their performance in "delivering the goods" and meeting the goals of their mission are called into serious question. Examples include Chrysler's hard-won campaign to obtain federal loan guarantees; journalists' efforts to maintain public confidence in their objectivity and unbiased reporting or analysis of news events; and poverty agencies' efforts to demonstrate that their programs indeed serve the "truly needy." In each of these instances of a "performance challenge," the affected organization or profession undertakes to demonstrate that it is innocent of serious charges of poor management or errors in judgment, that it does indeed honorably strive to fulfill its purpose, deserves continued public (or market) confidence, and retains its right to social legitimacy and financial support. The *purpose* each claims to embody is not called into question in these instances.

Value challenges place the organization's mission and legitimacy for existence at issue, regardless of how well it has fulfilled its agreed-upon goals or function. The effectiveness or efficiency with which it has performed these is not taken as problematic, though inadequate performance may bring on the crisis of a value challenge. Campaigns leading to Prohibition and the elimination of broadcast advertising for cigarettes questioned the social value of liquor and tobacco, irrespective of the financial performance of firms manufacturing them. Similarly, government cutbacks for Amtrak and the national endowments for the arts and humanities hinge primarily around the social value of public funding for these functions rather than on the performance or managerial efficiency of these organizations.

Performance and value challenges both entail fundamental challenges to the legitimacy of an organization's continued existence. Each places the target in an inherently more unstable situation than is addressed in comparative or longitudinal examinations of administrative efficiency. Because organizational failure is a far more distinct possible outcome in each of these conditions, the population ecology perspective becomes more relevant — after the fact — than more traditional approaches to organizations within the stability frame.

In the face of such challenges; however, the executives and staffs of the target organizations strive mightily to fend off organizational failure and to bring about a return to conditions more closely approximating a stable environment. In the Weberian sense, such "interesting times" necessarily call for "administrators" to act more like "leaders," and require of them different styles of decision-making and utilization of new sets of symbols. In James Thompson's terms, their critical task at this point is to develop methods which convert these constraints on their action into contingencies, and contingencies into variables amenable to control. While in his classic *Organizations in Action* (1967) Thompson counseled organizations and their administrators to master environmental uncertainties, he wrote explicitly within the bounds of rationality norms which largely *presuppose* that such fundamental questions as survival, legitimate reasons for existence, and functions performed for society at large have *already* been resolved. Circumstances in which these cannot be taken as given are exceedingly disruptive to any organization's sphere of action, he warns, making it unusually difficult to plan, cope, and design structures which add incrementally to conventional measures of efficiency and effectiveness.

In pointing administrators toward strategies for "coaligning" the internal structures of their organizations with environmental demands and contingencies, Thompson articulated the strain toward stability and control presupposed in much of the literature on organizations. But he also cut off from consideration such problematic extremes as the possibility of an environment *itself* radically changing, being unpatterned, unpredictable, irrational, or mandating types of adaptation where an organization can be rewarded for inefficiency or punished for attempting to improve its performance. Each of these possibilities brings us closer to conditions during which legitimacy and symbols increase in salience, the times in which concepts like performance and value challenges come to supplement organizational analyses, which assume a more stable environment.

Legitimacy Contexts and the Exercise of Authority

The contrast between times of stability and times of change underlies the overall theme of this volume, and can facilitate the integration of several longstanding perspectives that often ignore both each other and the need to distinguish stable from changing contexts for organizational legitimacy. As suggested above, organizational analysis is most highly developed for the stable context in which legitimacy is not a serious issue — a condition also assumed throughout most literature about administration and regarded as an ideal state by administrators as well. How do, or should, administrators respond, however, when major environmental changes like those addressed by the concepts of performance and value challenges enter the picture?

In his recent essay on symbols and social change, Marshall Sahlins notes that leadership often implies accurately interpreting and responding to the surrounding culture in times of change. Where legitimacy must be negotiated rather than assumed, this suggests that changes will be called for in administrative styles as well as through the invocation of different symbols. The reasons for such changes in emphasis and rhetoric are developed in his implication that effective leaders must also be adept "hucksters of the symbol":

. . . the interest taken in such conceptual correspondences as work-er/capitalist: youth/adult is in no way an idealism. Their recogni-tion by the anthropologist or economist, like their existence in the society, reflects a real experience of that society — if always the only kind of real social experience, namely, that mediated symbolically. The anthropologist did not put them there, any more than the peo-ple just made them up and thereupon decided to live by them. They are the true armature of the cultural order, and the anthropologist in arranging them in a way faithful to experience does no more than discover that order. In doing so — and this is the second implication — he acts in something of the same way as a market researcher, an advertising agent, or a fashion designer, unflattering as the compari-son might be. For these hucksters of the symbol do not create de novo. In the nervous system of the American economy, theirs is a synaptic function. It is their role to be sensitive to the latent corre-spondence in the cultural order whose conjunction in a product-symbol may spell mercantile success.

Or perhaps, more frequently, theirs is to respond to the ceaseless reformulation of symbolic relations within the national life [1976, 217].

Sahlins's insight can be expanded to suggest that performance and value challenges require the leaders of organizations confronting such crises to invoke different symbols and behave differently than even the same leaders/administrators might behave in a more stable legitimacy context. Before explaining which types of organization structures, sym-bols, and decision-making styles seem most appropriate for each of these three conditions, it may be useful to distinguish briefly between two types of authority utilized at different times in nearly all organizations. Each tends to appear in particular institutional climates and contexts for legitimation, and we shall call them: (1) authority as effective power, and (2) authority as negotiated by legitimate use.

When viewed as effective power, authority is the position-based con-trol, by someone holding an appropriate title, over resources and subordi-nates. At single points in time, this may appear absolute and overwhelm-ing, and is communicated in the form of operational commands. Here, the authority symbols are built in, and the messages transmitted are specific, literal, and relatively "hard." They occur most often in communications in-ternal to the organization, and seem most appropriate to all parties con-cerned when the organization is in a *stable* institutional environment pos-ing few issues of legitimacy for its leaders and administrators.

In the second instance, where the exercise of authority hinges on its legitimate use, we enter a longitudinal dimension suggesting that both leaders and their organizations are vulnerable to the judgments of others concerning how satisfactorily they have pursued the institutionally defined values from which their power derives and in whose name their actions were taken. In this sense, top administrators must frame their actions with an eye toward maintaining (rather than squandering) the legitimacy of organizational authority as it is continually exercised and justifying or accounting for their use of that authority in terms of their own organization's history and the broader social and cultural values it claims to serve. This is particularly the case when these values are ambiguous, subject to change, or in flux. Communications in this mode tend to be unspecific and symbolic, directed primarily toward actors and institutions external to the organization itself.

While each of these authority types gives rise to communications that, on the one hand, link command formats with internal order from the top down and, on the other, link legitimacy concerns with an outward focus, we know these brushstrokes are broad and that predicting when each mode should appear is a far more complex matter. These sets of characteristics are more typologically than empirically distinct, for both aspects of authority are found jointly in almost any form of organizational communication, though in varying proportions. The normative assertion that "what is good for General Motors is good for America" is an example of a command format directed *outward*, while virtually the entire movement called "organizational development" is predicated on directing symbolic communications to and among members *within* the boundaries of the organization. The utilization and mix of these authority types nevertheless have some bearing on variations in the behavior of administrators and organizations under different conditions and legitimacy contexts as we shall elaborate shortly.

Following from the preceding discussion and Sahlins's image of "hucksters of the symbol" — and going beyond the limited variability envisioned in the stability frame's assumption of organizational legitimacy — four summary statements are:

(1) The type of leadership behavior appropriate for given situations varies with the legitimacy context in which an organization is located.

(2) These contexts are subject to change.

(3) An important aspect of administrative leadership consists of knowing which set of symbols to invoke and which type of authority to exercise at different points in time. As environments have become more complex, some organizations have formally divided authority over internal operations and external relations between different top executives. Corporate chief executives as well as university presidents expend an increasing amount of time outside their own organizations — addressing stock analysts, governmental bodies, alumni, donors, etc. These leadership functions entail greater resort to our second type of authority (as "nego-

tiated") than the more internally directed vocabulary of command. The use of symbols and vocabularies associated with this negotiated mode takes on even greater importance under conditions of performance and value challenges. Administrators who may be superb in one authority mode but not both may well be unprepared or maladapted when greater reliance on its alternative is called for. Leadership thus often demands that the same individual knows *when* to act like a fox and when to act like a lion.

(4) Organizations embody efforts to maintain and adapt to external, institutional value complexes and, in turn, convey corresponding cultural symbols to their members and the world at large. The most successful adaptation to one set of such external conditions may itself stand in the way of responding effectively to significant changes in an organization's symbolic environment; for over time, as Robert Merton and others have noted, many members and administrators come to treat these symbols as tangible, even immutable, and they take on a life of their own.

Types of Legitimacy Contexts and Organizational Response. Table 1 derives, very roughly, from several ideal types relating organizational structures and those legitimacy contexts laid out above. In our discussion, we will also point to some implications for the styles and types of administrative decision-making most characteristic of and appropriate for each of these conditions, as well as for their relation to the type of authoritative communication employed.

In the first column, designated the "stable" condition, organizations face no serious challenge to their legitimacy claims. Here, when communications take the form of operational commands, organization members are least likely to be surprised, for the content of these communications is also unlikely to contain surprises of great moment or departures from past policy. Prior expectations can be met and standard operating procedures adhered to. Absenting external challenges and setbacks, top administrators' exercise of authority as effective power is considered a reasonable prerogative of their positions in the organizational hierarchy. Organizational life here is predictable and relatively comfortable.

The "stable" condition contains organizational entries close to the ideal typical closed system model, but can only approximate it at best since a large number of contingencies and constraints may still arise which have nothing to do with legitimacy issues. An organization like the Internal Revenue Service exemplifies this condition: it is generally considered to be reasonably efficient, it is believed to perform an indispensable service of social value in a basically satisfactory manner, and incidentally its success depends upon the willing acquiescence of the public, however grudgingly given. Interestingly, its top administrators acted swiftly to maintain this stable condition by moving to minimize the symbolic im-

Table 1: Types of Legitimacy Contexts and Organizational Responses

	Legitimacy Contexts		
Organizational Attributes	*Stable*	*Performance Challenge*	*Value Challenge*
Locus of Active Authority	managerial and lower echelon	top echelon	outside actors and top echelon
Target of Challenge	internal positional authority (e.g., line vs. staff)	organizational delivery or performance	organizational and institutional existence
Role of Top Managers	passive legitimation of routines; symbolic value of structures and procedures	active symbolic role; attempts to show performance is better than apparent indicators	active redefinition, with specific operational action — budget-cutting, etc.
	routine — no redefinition	metric or evaluative redefinition	operational redefinition fighting back
Operative Symbols	SOPs; organization charts	indicator repertoires; proliferation of structures without operational power	budgets
Coupling	variable	moderate to tight	tight
Administrative Style and Range of Authority Exercised	delegated command and unobtrusive control	enforcement of strategic rituals; intrusive control	recentralized operational command
Typical Studies	Cross-sectional organization studies; Blau & Schoenherr	Meyer and Rowan; (strategies for neutralizing environmental demands)	Biggart, Amtrack, public education, universities

pact of Richard Nixon's large "tax break" on the sale of his presidential papers. While the need to reclaim its legitimacy as an impartial enforcer seldom arises, the IRS was widely described during Nixon's term as leaking to the press information about efforts to use the agency politically which, if unchecked, could have damaged its credibility and forced it out of our "stable condition" column.

In stable organizations one may anticipate that the locus of active authority is at lower echelons: major policy pronouncements by the top management are rarely called for, either externally or internally. Authority is delegated along clearly delineated avenues; organizational routines and standard operating procedures smooth and steer organizational actions along established channels, and supervision can be fairly relaxed. Such challenges as may rise frequently involve internal "turf" disputes, which may be seen chiefly as disputes over the distribution of legitimate authority among positions. With respect to such disputes, the top officials may serve as a court of arbitration between the two sides, rationalizing their decision typically as a logical extension of policies and procedures already in place within the organization. Organizations in this condition are not necessarily static, but their growth is typically incremental rather than discontinuous.

The second condition, performance challenge, arises when an organization's legitimacy is questioned on the ground that it is failing to serve the values on which its authority claims are based, though the legitimacy of these values themselves is not questioned. Meyer and Rowan's (1978) analysis of elementary schools illustrates what we mean here: they found that school administrations are under relatively constant external pressure to show that education is in fact being provided and have responded by producing a large amount of documentation on everything but what actually occurs in the classroom. Attendance records are kept assiduously, formal qualifications of teachers are diligently scrutinized, and dollar-to-pupil ratios are zealously calculated. Almost nonexistent, however, are any operational measures of whether teachers are actually teaching well and whether students are actually learning what they are supposed to be learning. Meyer and Rowan suggest that this seeming "negligence" is in fact a very logical organizational adaptation: via the "loose coupling" of school systems (Weick 1976), administrators — with the acquiescence of their assessors — have traditionally and symbolically defined school performance in terms of attendance, dollar-to-pupil ratios, and the like in order to forestall serious examination of the "technical core" of the school itself. Such scrutiny would be both difficult to design and administer and disruptive to the organizations themselves.[3]

What Meyer and Rowan show to be routine in elementary schools occurs also in nonroutine ways in other types of challenges to organizations. Chrysler is perhaps the clearest case in point. None of the values which the corporation is chartered to serve have come under serious attack (e.g., no one questioned the legitimacy of the company's purpose of manufacturing cars), but Chrysler's performance in carrying out these goals was slipshod at best. In the face of performance challenges we expect the top echelons of an organization to become very active as symbolic mediators to the institutional environment. As part of this mediation, we expect them to try to use a repertoire of alternative measures of performance, "explanations" for apparent failure, searches for "silver linings" or "lights at the end of the tunnel," and lastly, to introduce new structures and positions without much effective power as a "facelifting" device. Lower-level personnel cannot play this role with respect to the outside without the explicit and public support of the top leadership, inasmuch as their authority is delegated from those in high positions and is readily revocable by the latter. Top leaders are hence responsible for conveying to outside audiences an image of the activities of the organization, and if these audiences acquiesce, the symbols which the leaders employ will be those which are least disruptive of those activities. In most cases organizations have a repertoire of performance indicators which will serve this purpose very nicely. If both these and insignificant structural "facelifts" do not suffice, the challenge may move on into the third condition.

Value challenges are the most serious type because it is here that (1) the organization's purpose for existing is called into direct question; (2) its leaders can no longer assume agreement with their challengers as to which types of changes in their organization's performance (e.g., higher profits or test scores) would lead to calling off the attack. Unlike the performance challenge, in which these shared understandings still exist, the value challenge places the target organization in the world of somebody else's "frame." Value challenges may arise for a number of reasons and through a number of different processes. They all entail a downgrading of the values served by the organization, irrespective of the organization's success in serving those values. In some cases bad performances by one or a number of organizations serving a particular institutional value may give rise to the questioning of the value itself, but many other factors may produce the same result. The Legal Services Corporation, the Public Broadcasting System, abortion aid clinics, and Amtrak exemplify organizations which experienced challenges not because they fail to serve the purpose for which they are chartered but rather because those values are themselves under attack. In this third condition, the role of the top leaders is active, including operational redefinition of the organization. Symbolically the organization head has three major avenues of response: first, to aggressively defend the values embodied by his or her organization and hope to ride out or defuse the strength of the attacking parties; second, to attach the organization to values which are *not* under attack (e.g., "Legal Services is an effective and inexpensive deterrent to crime . . . "); and third, to conduct a major restructuring of the organization, specifically by anticipating, participating in, or proposing a menu of budget cuts and program reductions or terminations. Within the third strategy, and to some extent in the second, organizational coupling necessarily becomes very tight and the top leaders become most significantly intrusive upon the actions of their subordinates.

Conclusion

Organizations are rife with symbols and inhabit a cultural space. Crises erupt when they are deprived of the legitimacy associated with the institutional niches and value complexes they claim to represent and embody. Organizational leadership entails the mediation of internal and external environments through the utilization of the appropriate symbols, stances, and behaviors called for by particular conditions and surroundings. A central point in this chapter has been that the appropriateness of the symbols invoked, examples set, and type of authority employed is *variable*, depending on the environmental signals and conditions to which these must respond: what is adaptive administrative leadership in a stability frame may be entirely unsuited to the demands imposed by performance and value challenges, and vice versa. During the 1960s and 1970s, we suspect the frequency of external challenges to organizations' assumptions of a stable environment and legitimacy context increased significantly. The ethics of lawyers, doctors, journalists, and other professionals were cast into doubt; public confidence in virtually all institutions showed a steep decline; and the Reagan administration undertook significant cutbacks or outright elimination of many government programs and agencies previously accustomed to overall growth and support.

We have emphasized the external and institutional dimensions of legitimacy contexts in which organizations operate because it is here that the most influential theories of organization and administration have made the smallest contribution. Although Parsons (1960) noted that organizations are most tightly coupled at their lower levels and that the importance of symbolic language and its articulation of values increases at higher levels in the hierarchy, neither his interest in symbolic stance nor its further implications have been seriously examined or explored in most literature on organization and administration. Nor with few exceptions, such as Gouldner (1954) and Etzioni (1961) has Weber's strong concern for legitimacy and the exercise and different types of authority been considered.

In pointing to this gap in the literature, this paper has merely scratched the surface of the symbolic aspect of leadership at the top levels of organization. We did not address the ways in which internal coordination is effected by the use of symbols, for example, or explore the symbolic meaning to organizational clients or consumers conveyed by procedures and standard practices commonly employed. Recent contributions by Ouchi (1981), Ouchi and Johnson (1978), Wilkins and Martin (1979), and Pondy (1977) offer significant strides in the former direction; Schwartz's (1974) analysis of how waiting time and queuing procedures adopted by organizations replicate and respond to social stratification in general addresses the latter. While popular interest in the use of symbols in organizations also has increased in the last decade, much of what we see has been embedded in discussions of specific issues surrounding lower-level compliance, job satisfaction, employee newsletters, and the watches or tie clips accompanying forced retirements. Much more systematic work is needed on how images of what is going on are created at the top by means of symbols, and on how these symbolic images are then articulated with each other as policy and procedure within the organization.

To a degree, there is some virtue in top leaders and boards of directors or trustees retaining an aura of ambiguity surrounding their exercise of authority and utilization of symbols. By holding their power in reserve, they also retain a freer hand for action in situations where a basic redefinition of the organization may become necessary. Even though critics of current corporate governance find boards to be largely passive, ornamental, and honorific bodies, a more useful indicator of their effectiveness than their failure to act under stable conditions is whether they capitalize on the flexibility thus provided to (a) take on a more activist role in the face of performance challenges and (b) respond to value challenges by redefining organizational purpose, mounting the organization's defense, or forcing adherence to the pressures thereby brought to bear on the organization.[4] A failure to alter the stance taken and symbols invoked under these latter conditions reduces the likelihood of an orderly return to the stability frame to which all parties concerned are more accustomed and strive to maintain.

Our analysis of, and concern for, the conditions which characterize more "interesting" times is in recognition of the facts that (1) stability is not a permanent condition; (2) organization theory needs to better incorporate and address circumstances where its objects of study are buffeted by crises and environmental shifts. In short, organizational sociologists have been slow to explore a number of the implications of challenges to legitimacy in the past. Cross-sectional and structural analyses of organizations, while major contributions, have tended tacitly to assume institutional stability, whether for purposes of analytic tidyness or because most organizations most of the time exhibit at least some of the characteristics of stability. While a number of case studies have been made of organizations in less stable conditions, we have not reached the point of a cumulative and thorough theoretical treatment, and systematic treatments of institutional value contexts have yet to be carried out.

NOTES

1. We are grateful to John Meyer for comments on the original draft of this presentation, and to Yale University's Program on Non-Profit Organizations and the University of Chicago Searle Fellowship Program for funds to support some of the research on which this paper is based.

2. In this, it is similar to economics and accounting, though these latter fields have more highly developed models; employ fewer variables; assume preferences are fixed; do not take as problematic variations in organizational purpose and history; do not seek to address a wide variety of decisions made by the managements of single organizations.

3. The increased reliance on nationwide test scores by external authorities thus created a short-term crisis for this system of shared and implicit understandings about the performance of schools. Prior to this external change, for example, receipt of a high school diploma was more of a dichotomous (yes-no) event, with less concern for the ranges in quality across schools over how much learning it represents. Recent drops in the support levels for public schools go beyond this type of performance question, however, for they seem far more rooted in a cultural shift, posing a value challenge concerning the allocation of more public funds to educate society's youth, regardless of the quality of teaching and learning delivered.

4. The resignation of board members is widely believed to contribute to this last outcome. A recent example is J. P. Stevens Co., whose board members' resignations helped to bring about the firm's long-resisted recognition of its employees' right to join unions and form collective bargaining units. By resigning, key board members acceded to external pressures and strengthened the value challenge confronted by the corporation.

REFERENCES

Aldrich, H. E. (1979). *Organizations and Environments.* Englewood Cliffs, N. J.: Prentice-Hall.

Biggart, N. W. (1977). "The Creative-Destructive Process of Change: The Case of the U.S. Post Office." *Administrative Science Quarterly* 22, 410–26.

Blau, P. M., and R. A. Schoenherr (1971). *The Structure of Organizations.* New York: Basic Books.

Etzioni, A. (1961). *A Comparative Analysis of Complex Organizations.* New York: Free Press.

Gouldner, A. W. (1954). *Patterns of Industrial Bureaucracy.* New York: Free Press.

Hirsch, P. M. (1975). "Organizational Analysis and Industrial Sociology: An Instance of Cultural Lag." *American Sociologist* 10, 3–12.

———— (1979). "Expanding the Horizons of Organizational Research." In W. M. Eva, ed. *Frontiers in Organization and Management.* New York: Praeger.

Lawrence, P. R., and J. W. Lorsch (1967). *Organization and Environment.* Boston: Harvard University Graduate School of Business Administration.

March, J. G., and H. A. Simon (1958). *Organizations.* New York: Wiley.

Meyer, J. W., and B. Rowan (1977). "Institutionalized Organizations: Formal Structure as Myth and Ceremony." *American Journal of Sociology* 83, 440–63.

_____ (1978). "The Structure of Educational Organizations." In M. Meyer and Associates, *Environments and Organizations.* San Francisco: Jossey-Bass.

Ouchi, W. (1981). *Theory Z: How American Business Can Meet the Japanese Challenge.* Reading, Mass.: Addison-Wesley.

Ouchi, W., and J. Johnson (1978). "Types of Organizational Control and Their Relationship to Emotional Well Being." *Administrative Science Quarterly* 23, 293–317.

Parsons, T. (1960). "The Analysis of Formal Organizations." In T. Parsons, *Structure and Process in Modern Societies.* New York: Free Press.

Pfeffer, J., and G. R. Salancik (1978). *The External Control of Organizations: A Resource Dependence Perspective.* New York: Harper & Row.

Pondy, L. R. (1977). "Leadership is a Language Game." In M. McCall and M. Lombardo, eds. *Leadership: Where Else Can We Go?* Durham, N. C.: Duke University Press.

Sahlins, M. (1976). *Culture and Practical Reason.* Chicago: University of Chicago Press.

Schwartz, B. (1974). "Waiting, Exchange, and Power: The Distribution of Time in Social Systems." *American Journal of Sociology* 79, 841–70.

Thompson, J. D. (1967). *Organizations in Action.* New York: McGraw-Hill.

Weick, K. (1976). "Educational Organizations as Loosely Coupled Systems." *Administrative Science Quarterly* 21, 1–19.

Wilkins, A., and J. Martin (1979). "Organizational Legends." Research Paper No. 521, Graduate School of Business, Stanford University.

CHAPTER 11

Organizations as Ideological Systems

John W. Meyer

Formal organizations depict themselves, and are depicted in modern society, as bounded, rational, purposive systems. Social scientific analysts of them have for decades been trapped in the net of this deeply institutionalized ideological depiction — struggling to escape, but continually enmeshed. This is reinforced, not only by the fact that social science is deeply imbued with this modern understanding, but also by the fact that the academic field of organizations theory is closely linked to the managerial role: managers, too, are to be rational and active and purposive.

Many strands of organizational theory celebrate rationality: technical theories of organizational structure and, in a more complex way, political theories; decision theories; contingency theories; and theories of organizational control. Other lines of theory are primarily *reactive* to the institutionalized line; they are theories that assert less about what happens than that *rationality doesn't happen*. Thus a long tradition in sociology (at least since Barnard) discusses the gaps between rational formal structure and "informal organization," or what really happens. Recently this has been relabeled as "loose coupling" — that idea that means and ends are little related in reality, that formal structures are little implemented, and that distinct organizational subunits and programs are poorly connected (March and Olsen 1976; Weick 1976; Meyer and Rowan 1977). A branch of decision theory, since Cyert and March (1963), discusses the formal irrationalities of decision-making. Whole sets of natural and open systems theories treat organizations as in fact entirely interdependent with their environments (e.g., Pfeffer and Salancik 1978).

In one sense, all this is kibitzing or muckraking commentary on the established myth of rationality. The line is, "Yes, the formal structures of organizations give the appearance of rationality, but it is not so in reality."

I am indebted to my colleague Richard Scott for his assistance in developing this chapter.

This evades causal questions about the formal structure itself: Why is it there? What effects does it have? A great deal of trouble and expense go into building and changing formal structure in modern organizations. If all this is epiphenomenal to the real activities of organizational work and life, why the charade? Alternatively, if there is some reason for all the effort — some causal consequence — why have we so little theory and research about such effects?

A recent line of discussion focuses on symbolic aspects of organizational life: the symbolic origins of structure and their symbolic consequences. Starting especially with Clark (1972), organizations are seen to carry in their structures myths, stories, sagas, and legitimating accounts. A whole literature has developed around this theme.

The basic idea is a good one, but it has not been carried far enough. Research has focused on the idiosyncratic and "cute" aspects of organizational life — the symbolic functions of stories about the charisma of the "old man," of peculiar organizational accounting tricks, of myths and stories that flow through organizations relatively informally, and of advertising and publicity gimmicks. Odd things a sales manager might do are seen as "symbolic." The whole line of thought in the literature concentrates on such peripheral matters.

This paper goes to an extreme in the other direction. Organizational structure itself is viewed as a symbolic system. The sales-manager role, not the incumbent's idiosyncrasies, is a symbolic element; the formal rules, not the casual talk, are a symbolic structure. Two issues are approached from this perspective: (1) the origins and effects of structure as symbolic, and (2) the implications of the symbolic aspects of structure for managerial role performance.

Theoretical Background

Some central beginning ideas have been elaborated elsewhere (Meyer and Rowan 1977, 1978; Meyer, Scott, and Deal 1981).

1. Formal organizational structures are rationalized myths of the organization's functioning. They are sometimes constructed internally, but are more often taken over from legitimated rules in the environment.

Thus the table of organization of a university, with its definitions of departments, schools, teachers, students, administrators, and curricula, is mostly drawn directly from the environment. Parts are taken from the basic accreditational rules. Many other parts are drawn from institutionalized and widely practiced custom which often takes on binding power. A university, for instance, has an economics department less because of any internal decision that economics instruction is needed than because everyone — both outsiders and such inside groups as students — knows that a good university has teaching and research in economics, and that such instruction is generally seen as advantageous for a variety of career and social goals. Established practice and binding rules mingle in the environment, creating an established depiction of rational structure for a university. Particular universities find it advantageous to conform to this depiction.

2. These structures aid the organization by legitimating it to internal and external constituencies. They provide a rational account of the organization's functioning.

Thus, a university with the standard structure will be accredited both formally and informally. Few questions will be raised, in contrast to the many questions likely to be raised about an idiosyncratically structured school, no matter how effective. Similarly, a firm with the standard structure is more likely to seem sound to external investors and regulators. Internal constituencies, too, come to see the more standardized forms as legitimate.

3. The effort to maintain a structure that meets the criteria of externally defined rationality may make it necessary or wise to leave that structure inconsistent with the work that needs to get done. Decoupling results, buffering the formal structure from ongoing activity.

Thus, a formal structure that provides a clear depiction of conformity to externally defined rationalities may not in fact meet coordination requirements, deal with uncertainties, or respond to inconsistencies in the work process. And one designed to deal with the latter problems may not appear rational in terms of externally defined criteria. A solution is to maintain both systems simultaneously and to buffer them from each other.

The simplest situation here is one in which, for external reasons, an appearance of standardization is required that may be difficult to implement in reality. Thus, a university psychology department will find it wise to have a course called introductory psychology. Many versions of this course, taught by very different people with very different ideas, may be found in practice, but a kind of ritual standardization is achieved by concealing this variability. All the courses will have the same formal description, give the same credit, entitle the students to enroll in the same further courses, and be taught by people who are all formally defined as proper faculty members. The unity of introductory psychology as a standard structural element is maintained by some concealment of what actually goes on, by the myths of the standardized professionalism of psychologists, and thus by the buffering of classroom reality from the unified structural element.

4. In organizations especially dependent on environmental legitimation and weakly dependent on technical outcomes, structure especially

reflects legitimating considerations and is especially decoupled from activity.

Thus, universities and other schools conform especially closely to custom and accreditational rules and tend to have little *organizational* control over instructional processes or outcomes, which are often concealed. These organizations display with much pride the numbers and types of their graduates but ordinarily avoid reporting standardized achievement scores which might better reflect the actual instructional work. Because their environments evaluate them structurally rather than in terms of outcomes, they tend to conform to external definitions of structural rationality. Similarly, hospitals as organizations attend in detail to formal environmental requirements about structure, but pay little attention to the details of work process or outcome. These are clear cases: schools are paid by attendance and credit unit, not by outcomes; hospitals are paid for treatment in the right structural form, regardless of its success.

5. In social domains with unclear technologies and outcome definitions, elaborate formal organizations arise only as the environment provides legitimating definitions of rational formal structure.

Universities and other schools are created as formal organizations and expand in number, size, and structural complexity in response to environmental definitions more than to the coordinative requirements of work activity. It is a mistake to think of such organizations as expanding into complex structures on their own, and only then searching for external legitimations. The external legitimating apparatus of higher education — the whole structure of degrees and departments, certificated teachers and clearly defined students — makes possible the expanded modern university. It is slowly created in the environment by historical processes, and each university gains in complexity through conformity to it.

The theoretical problem is that once the points are made that much formal structure is legitimating ideology, that it is often derived from the environment, and that it may often be decoupled from inconsistent and disorderly realities, many problems of explanation still remain. Whether environmental in origin or not, what are the criteria of adequacy of formal structures as ideologies? What kinds of legitimating needs do they serve? Clearly it is not enough for an organization to blindly copy rationalized elements from the environment. Each organization must put these together in a convincing and adequate way. The discussion below considers formal structures as adequate ideologies, and then goes on to consider implications for management.

Formal Structures as Ideologies

In this discussion, constraints imposed on organizational structure by the real world of work activity and technology are ignored. Formal organizational structures — explicit rules, roles, and other organizational units — are seen as dramatic appearances; as legitimated and legitimating depictions to insiders and outsiders of what the organization is about. What criteria must such a structure, as an ideological account, meet?

In an odd way, the traditional literature from Weber on provides much help with this issue. Its focus is on organizations as rational and rationalized structures. And while this literature takes the rationality in question as going on in the real world of work activity, that assumption can here be ignored. A useful starting point is, therefore, the idea that *formal organizational structures are depictions of rational or rationalized activity.*

This idea makes much sense. Almost all observers see the distinctive feature of modern formal organization, in contrast to social units like communities, societies, associations, or families, as lying in its explicitly rationalized character. This property justifies and legitimates it and brings it into existence and into its presently dominating role. In modern society even education, medical care, and recreational activity are organized in such structures.

If rationality is a centrally legitimating feature of formal organization, it is reasonable to expect depictions of rationality to be prominent in explicit formal structures. It may be anticipated that organizations display the main dimensions of rationalization formally. These are discussed extensively in the classic literature on the subject (see, e.g., March and Simon 1958). The only step away from this discussion taken here is the idea that organizational structure depicts rationality quite independently from whether or not these depictions are implemented in work activity.

1. Organizations must have *purposes:* without clearly defined purposes, formal organizations make less sense than other social forms. Organizations thus formalize and define the outputs related to their main purposes — standardize them, count them, and measure them. This is obvious with many kinds of organizations involved in technical productions but other organizations must do this too. Organizations built around purposes that are unclear and ambiguous thus tend to organize special output definitions which simplify and standardize; this is often, in the literature, considered goal displacement accomplished to effectively confront environmental requirements. It is more than that — a necessary step in constructing a clear ideological account that will permit formal organizations. Thus schools can organize stably around the production of graduates but not learning; hospitals can organize around accounted patient treatment but not health; and government bureaus count formal procedures but not effects. In modern societies that extend the principles of formal organization to highly ambiguous domains, ritualized and

standardized goal depictions are necessary. In all cases, exogenous definitions of purposes help a good deal.

Universities, for instance, do some purpose-work of their own, documenting their special missions or purposes. But much of this is already managed by rationalized environmental definitions: the notions of university graduates of various kinds are standardized in the culture and often in legal requirements, as are definitions of various types of fields. The whole conception of university education is built around a good deal of cultural consensus — much of it is now world-wide. A particular university needs only to connect itself to these more widely legitimating ideas through clear documentation (e.g., the procedures of a registrar's office, departmental definitions of courses, and degree requirements).

2. Organizations must be *rational:* structures must give an ideological account of the means-ends chains by which purposes are to be accomplished. Sometimes, these accounts make up the main depicted division of labor of an organization. Thus, some companies organize explicitly around the steps of the production function: departments that purchase, that produce, and that sell — with collateral departments depicting subroutines (research, finance, personnel, labor relations, and maintenance). The main structure of the elementary school depicts the production process, with functionaries carefully arrayed from kindergarten teacher to sixth-grade teacher. In other organizations, the symbolizations of the rationalized technology occur at a lower level, with the main differentiation following other criteria: thus a hospital organizes medical services around a number of different kinds of input problems, with each service internally managing many steps of the production process.

Rationality, of course, is mainly contextual in character: what is rational by way of a depiction of means and ends depends on cultural agreements. Sometimes these are embedded in socially agreed-upon technologies, as with typical production firms. Sometimes, however, the technology is almost completely social in its construction and meaning, as when institutional and legal rules define what steps are required in an accredited education, or accredited and fundable medical treatment, or a properly accomplished social welfare service. In such instances, organizations are especially likely to build the socially required steps explicitly into their structures. If the cultural environment defines "sociology" as a legitimate academic field, most universities will incorporate departments of sociology in their explicit formal structure; if proper environmental impact reports are required as part of production processes, organizations will be likely to create specialized formal units paralleling this requirement.

Universities, at least in America, depict rationality in a number of different ways. Increasingly, formal structures depict the flow of students:

an admissions office, deans of students and of undergraduate studies, record-keeping offices, alumni offices. Some rationalized subroutines appear: health care departments, recreation programs, and residential advising systems. But much, especially at the graduate level, is delegated to a set of parallel departments, each of which organize a more primitive structure along the same lines but with more curricular emphasis than the university as a whole. Departments delight in giving the appearance that courses occur in rationalized categories and sequences, and that students are being processed in a rational way.

There are striking examples here of the contextual character of rationality. American universities, in a society which emphasizes *technical* rationality, depict themselves much more in this way than do universities in other countries; there are many more finely differentiated administrative structures, more curricular rationalization in departments, and many more committees handling specially recognized problems. All this develops in the American context as a whole and is copied by each university.

3. Organizations must *structurally depict* their control over their socially recognized domains. In the modern cultural world, with its detailed recognition of the specifics of the physical and social, this involves extended myths of control. An organization cannot define itself simply as diffusely controlling a mass of peasants: each peasant is now a citizen, a worker, a member, a client, and so on. Thus the organizational structure as a formal depiction must contain elements accounting for the entry, motivation, status, and career progress of each individual, though in highly standardized ways. Thus a modern company will organizationally "know" many things about each worker, so also with the material world, and the inventories and technologies the organization incorporates from it.

The simplest depiction of control is hierarchy, and modern organizations are filled with organizational charts describing simple hierarchies, no matter how unrealistic these depictions may be. Universities and school districts depict elaborate hierarchies, though these are not known in practice to effectively control work.

Integration of the depiction of control with the depiction of rationality and purpose is often problematic. Organizations that primarily embody the will of a single sovereign defining purpose and technology ordinarily elaborate structurally on the control dimension; thus the classic political bureaucracies organize around hierarchy. Organizations built around complex technologies or markets emphasize rationality in their structures, with main elements depicting steps in rationalized technology. Organizations under both pressures embody them at different structural levels.

4. Rationalizations require the *standardization* of inputs and input

values. Here, the monetarization of modern societies provides a general yardstick. But for some types of organizations, major inputs are not entirely monetarized. Schools and universities, for instance, take in students of great variability, and instruct them with teachers whose labor capacity is also very variable. Here historical processes have introduced the needed standardizations. The infinite student variability is reduced through the social standardization of the earlier steps of the education system. Universities take in *high school graduates*, whose variation is reduced to managable grades and test scores. Teachers are similarly standardized through professional credential systems. All these social changes make large-scale educational organization possible, despite the actual uncertainty in work and product.

5. Rationality requires fixed units with *boundaries.* To depict itself as rational, an organization must clearly distinguish itself from its environment. In materials-processing organizations, this may be easier, and still more so with modern notions of property and of monetarization. People-processing organizations, like universities, require clear demarcations of admission, expulsion, and graduation, as well as clear definitions of faculty and staff membership.

In summary, organizational structures are depictions of themselves as bounded entities exercising control over their domains and as taking in standardized inputs and through standardized processing generating clear products of general use. Sometimes these structures arise through the exigencies of work coordination. More often, as in the case of universities or schools, they arise only when the environment has developed institutionally standard definitions of inputs, technologies, or outputs. The forms organizations take are dependent on the environment, both on what it demands and on what it provides. Structural elaboration occurs along lines where the environment demands accountability and on which it provides rationalized definitions.

Thus American organizations, operating in an environment in which technical rationalization is both required and highly developed, create elaborate depictions of technical flows in their formal structures. American universities, for instance, are well known for their extraordinarily differentiated formal structures depicting student flows or services. In America, central authoritative sovereignty is relatively weak, so typical organizations make much less display of hierarchy than do organizations elsewhere. In continental Europe, with much legitimation of centralization, organizations attend in their structures to the elaboration of hierarchy and much less to the display of lateral technical differentiation.

There is little evidence, of course, that all these variations in depicted formal structure make much difference in the way work is actually conducted. Indeed, in actuality, work processes—for instance, in university life — are probably more similar around the world than are formal structures. They may even pose constraints on the possible variability of formal structures in response to environmental pressures.

Structuring Uncertainty

Organizations often — and increasingly in the modern world — encompass domains or activities filled with ambiguity. But rational and stable formal organization requires certainty and clarity. The ideas above provide some suggestions on how this inconsistency is resolved. First, organizations arise in highly ambiguous domains only when the environment has developed more certainly defined structural categories. At the input side, university formalization is stabilized by environmental historical processes which define a congeries of eighteen-year-olds as high school graduates with formal properties that make them eligible for college. The formal structuring of uncertain instructional work as well as research is facilitated by clear environmental definitions of the various categories of legitimated fields and curricula. And the whole system is made more stable by environmental processes that define university products — whatever their substantive properties or competences — as socially licensed graduates.

Second, the argument above has it that the environmentally conferred structural stability is aided by decoupling processes that conceal the real variabilities in work and competence allowing the formal classification system to retain its legitimating clarity. Much of this work is done in the environment, too — the definition of teachers in terms of certificates rather than competencies, the similar definitions of students, and the legitimation of the existence of academic fields independent of demonstrable social utility.

Any given organization has these environmental resources available; assembling a rational structure is therefore made much easier. But the same principles can be used by a particular organization itself to resolve difficult problems. The organization itself can create structures to answer problems — this is less useful than when the environment provides prefabricated and prelegitimated ones, but still answers some problems of justification. And any given organization can try to decouple such structures from the actual work and outcomes at hand.

Thus, at the level of a particular organization itself, an interesting argument on the conditions of the creation of formal structure can be added to those obtaining in the literature. Classically, much organization theory is built around the simple notion that the more complex the tasks assigned to an organization, the more complex and differentiated will be that organization's formal structure.

There is no reason to quarrel with this basic notion that technical complexity affects structural complexity. But the arguments above provide an additional idea: the more invisible or undoable the tasks assigned to an organization, the more complex and differentiated will be that organization's formal structure.

To stabilize and give meaning to unclear or ambiguous work or goals, structure, and structure decoupled from actual activity, is especially useful. One may have to create a new committee in order to get some organizational work done, but it may be even more necessary to create a committee if tasks exist for which there is no known work to do. How else can it be demonstrated — if no substantive demonstration is possible — that the organization is carrying out its assigned responsibilities?

These ideas can be illustrated by considering universities — a form of organization in a classically ambiguous domain (Cohen and March 1974; March and Olsen 1976). Faced with pressures to take on various responsibilities that are difficult to manage, universities have a number of solutions.

First, the same environmental pressures that define new tasks often provide recipes for their solutions which can be structurally incorporated. If various pressures make it necessary to undertake instructional work in business management, these pressures also come with the already legitimated definition of a business school. The university does not have to decide what to teach: the structure can simply be incorporated.

Second, professionalization is available as an all-purpose solution to many problems. The university does not have to decide what to do about needed instruction in operations research if a professionalized category of persons called operations researchers is already extant. Many new professions in the student services area are available to provide automatically legitimated solutions to problems.

Third, new administrative structures can be created by the organization itself. A new office can be created to deal, say, with energy costs; or an extant department can be split in two to give the impression of more coverage of the relevant responsibilities; or a new committee can be set up to manage a problem.

Fourth, in the absence of better solutions, the organization can set up a *planning* structure which can be claimed to provide solutions in the future. Plans as symbolic structures are important devices for controlling both future uncertainties and present ones. A problem can often be postponed indefinitely by rational planning for it.

Fifth, in the absence of better devices, a "crisis" can be created. That is, an event or task can be defined as anomalous, and a variety of ad hoc structural solutions can then be employed.

In an uncertain world, all the solutions above may work better if a good deal of decoupling work goes on. Detailed inspection of the actual work activities and outcomes of the structures created to solve problems may reveal anomalies and inconsistencies and failures. All the structural devices listed above are ways of maintaining a rational and formally controlling symbolic structure by cleaning the "real world" out of organizational life. Obviously, costs are involved in this, but there are many benefits, too. An organizational structure is a way of providing an adequate legitimating account to a variety of constituencies about the organization's functioning. It maintains an orderly and rational appearance to the world, and maintaining appearances — especially in domains in which activity is in reality rather unclearly structured or structurable — may be extremely important.

The Uses of Organizational Structure as an Adequate Ideological Account

An organizational structure that provides an adequate account has many uses. First, it provides an answer to environmental forces about the organization's functioning that legitimates the organization. In extreme cases, an adequate formal structure and only such a structure will legitimate the organization. No school or university can be accredited on the grounds that students learn a great deal; the school must by law have the appropriate formal structure: administrators, spaces, curricular topics, credentialed teachers, properly defined students, and so on. And if a school has these proper elements, it will be accredited regardless of evidence on student learning. Similarly, hospital accreditation depends on structural conformity to externally defined standards.

These are extreme cases. But even a business firm is more likely to satisfy creditors, investors, regulators, and, often, even consumers, if it has the standardized structures. One way, for instance, that a firm can show that it is trying to conform to affirmative action rules is to structurally incorporate the appropriate office. So also with safety or environmental regulations. But it is more likely to satisfy investors if it has the appropriate controlling financial officers, too.

Second, the various internal constituencies of an organization are more likely to see the structure as legitimate if it incorporates an adequate account. For any problem, there should be an appropriate office and telephone number: this clarifies responsibility, enabling actors to get rid of their problems and to maintain at least a superficial faith in their rational solvability.

Third, particular internal actors are more likely to function better if their function is structurally symbolized and clarified. Even if neither rationality nor control are in fact built into the structure, subordinate actors in a clearly symbolized structure are more likely to act as if order and rationality are present: they may do their best to construct something ad hoc. In the absence of a symbolizing structure, they are less likely to know, or have confidence in, their place. It is often thought, for instance, that actors function better if their units are highly placed in the symbolic structure of the firm than if they are not. It may be more important to have a clearly defined sales manager than to have someone actually managing sales work.

The Appearance of Rationality

The larger point here is that the modern world discovered not only the principle of rationality as an organizing device but the principle of rationality as a collective normative one. It is unimportant whether the structuring of modern society around this principle arose from its own cultural sources or simply developed out of extended experience with successful rationalized structures in domains such as business firms or the state. In either case, the principle of rationality has taken on a legitimating moral force quite external to life in a particular given organization. A particular university does not discover this principle: every environmental force requires it to articulate and justify its purposes and structure in rational terms. Acting out this faith in the real world requires action that is in a sense unrealistic. To act realistically would be to sacrifice all the legitimating benefits that conformity to the wider principle of rationality can give. A main solution is to build organizational appearances — what are here called structures — around the wider faith but to decouple them sufficiently from practical action as to permit more realistic adaptation in practice.

By constructing gigantic rationalized and controlling symbolic structures, actors are brought much more into line with the wider faith than would be possible through any assembly of individual experiences and beliefs. Organizations, thus, are liturgical structures, celebrating wider principles in part by ignoring many aspects of experiential reality. To fill this function — giving rational appearances — they must make more sense as dramatic structures than could reasonably be justified in any other way.

Some conclusions follow from this. First, formal structures tend to contain more hierarchical and lateral differentiation than can be justified by their actual coordinative and controlling capabilities. This is especially true with organizations managing uncertain or chaotic domains. And second, faced with uncertainties, organizations will tend to elaborate structures or to conceal uncertainty. This effect, too, will result especially in situations in which technologies are weak.

Managing Formal Structure as Ideology

Formal organizational structures are ideological in character, at least in part. They are symbolic structures conforming to dictates of rationality, order, and purpose. In filling this role, they meet requirements quite different from the problems of actually controlling technical work activity and outputs, and thus are often disconnected from such local realities. Formal structures, that is, need to give the proper appearances.

The conception that formal structures must keep up organizational appearances has some implications for management and managerial strategy. There are two distinct issues here: (1) the problem of managing symbolic formal structure, and (2) the problem of carrying out the role of manager as an element in symbolic structure. In both these areas, it turns out that reasonable managers may well act very differently out of consideration of symbolic requirements than they might in simply attempting to manage work.

Managing Formal Structure

Issues here have received considerable discussion in the literature, though often with a tone of disrespect. It is well known, for instance, that managers faced with uncertainties may *create ritual formal structure* without much intention that effects in actual activity will ensue. Thus, managers may create committees, rules, offices, consultantships, and organizational units as a way of getting rid of a problem, without any intention that something will actually be done. Some classics include the ancient safety departments, and the blossoming "no smoking" rules and signs — these little formal structures help legitimate the organization in the eyes of external regulators, at little cost.

Most discussions of the managerial pattern of ritual structure-creation denigrate it. This is a mistake. For many purposes, it is extremely important to create properly legitimating formal solutions to problems that cannot be solved. The discussion above covers some of the important legitimating functions of formal structure: as new uncertainties arise, it may be more important to give the appearance of effectively dealing with them than to deal with them.

Consider three types of problems managers may face. First, there are problems the manager must appear to solve, but that may not need to be solved. In a university, vague faculty discontents about the curriculum are often situations of this kind. Second, there are problems that both need to be solved and must be solved with the proper appearances. A university example might have to do with the allocation of secretarial time or of space. Third, there are problems that must actually be solved, but that it is unwise to appear to take solution responsibility for. University examples might include personal conflicts between a student and a

faculty member, conflicts between individual faculty members, or budgetary problems that require the concealed reallocation of funds.

Appearing to solve problems. Often problems arise, and come to be
recognized in an organization or its context, for which there are no
known and useful solutions — yet the organization, to be rational and in
control, must recognize them. Clearly, ritual structure-creation helps
here. Faced with the modern recognition of the rights of the handicapped, for instance, schools create structures with almost no clear associated activities: they hire special teachers with credentials in something
called "special education." Faced with this demand, universities also create structures — courses, programs, and certificates in "special education."
Nothing may actually go on differently than in the past, but the organization gives the appearance of rational responsibility.

Similarly, a business manager who must project the unprojectable
clearly needs a professional expert — perhaps an economist or an operations researcher or a management accountant. And in any organization,
the creation of a committee to work on a problem, or a new structural
unit, is a mark of good faith.

Under many conditions, the manager involved might not want the created unit to do much: action might be a waste of time and money, or
might interfere with vested present interests or programs. A standard
problem for modern organizations lies in the fact that sometimes structures created only for appearances spring into life, consuming resources,
expanding staffs, and altering activities in unnecessary ways. Managers,
to be effective, must often work out ways to make sure that created
structures will not take on lives of their own. Budgetary restrictions may
help, as may restrictions in the allocation of staff time. Artificially paced
reporting deadlines can also limit institution-building — for instance, a
committee faced with a large-scale problem is asked to report in six
weeks. Or managers may be careful to assign "responsible" (or lazy) staff
members to the created structure; in universities, some faculty members
are known to be usefully ineffective at administrative or problem-solving
work. Still another solution here is to assign the problems being ritualized to units which are powerless before stronger ones that actually have
jurisdiction. In universities, curriculum reform committees that do not
overlap with the real curriculum-decision structure help in avoiding unnecessary implementation.

Both solving and appearing to solve problems. Problems often arise
which must be confronted on both legitimation and practicality grounds.
There are conditions under which it makes sense both to create a formal
element in the organization and to use this element to deal with the problem. Thus a business may have a problem controlling inventory and creates a unit both to control inventory and to appear to do so. This may

seem like a routine organizational situation, although it has a few elements not ordinarily discussed: as a manager wishes to create the legitimating appearance of problem-solving as well as to problem-solve, more elaborate structure-creation and more publicity may be required. These have the function of letting internal and external constituents know about and have confidence in the problem-solution.

In universities, for instance, minor problems are sometimes confronted in very major ways with the involvement of important functionaries, much attention and discussion, and great publicity. In this way, central rationality and responsibility can be displayed, and the organization's jurisdiction over the domain in question made clear to everyone.

A second situation is more complex: it may be that problem-solution and appearances require *different* decisions and actions. For instance, a manager may decide to solve a problem by delegating some decisions to a particular subordinate functionary, but if this does not meet legitimacy requirements, the manager may also create an ostensibly important committee as window dressing. These situations can arise in many ways: when the real solution is deviant or illegal or disreputable; when the problem of legitimating decisions is substantial and requires vastly more dramatic displays than actions; when the real solution does not meet all the appearance requirements; or when the solutions required for appearances are unwieldy in practice. In universities, for instance, committees which are supposed to decide on space allocation — an important internal legitimacy problem — often play little role, or certain decisions are ostensibly made by central functionaries who merely sign off on subordinate decisions. Thus graduate and undergraduate degrees are often formally signed by a major dean, with actual decision power left in the hands of functionaries many levels down the hierarchy.

Solving problems without appearing to do so. Administrative time is often spent on covert problem-solution. There are many reasons for this. First, the acknowledgement of certain kinds of problems would be organizationally embarrassing — personnel difficulties are illustrations. Second, public confrontation with a problem might give it too much standing or importance, as with issues about which person or groups are entitled to use a particular rest room. Third, appearing to solve a problem might create annoying precedents which could not be raised if the problem-solution is covert: a situation whose easiest solution is to give special privileges to a faculty member or student might be a good example. Fourth, a problem that is unsolved, at least to public appearance, may be more valuable to a manager than a solved one. Academic departments often solve space problems covertly while continuing to press the university administration for the no-longer-needed space. Or an administrator who has solved in practice a budgetary shortfall problem may usefully continue to pretend that it exists in order to maintain disciplinary control over subordinate units.

In general, the appearance of powerlessness is often of some use in administration. It has costs in terms of wider legitimation, but benefits in created freedom or flexibility. Much depends on whether it is more important for a manager to maintain a public status or a more concealed resource and decision capacity. For managers of technically productive organizational units, the latter capacity is probably more important. For managers of institutionally legitimated structures, the former may be, in which case a "high profile" may often be the best strategy. Empirical studies could investigate the types of managers within universities who display the most elaborate appearances as compared with those who play quieter public roles and concentrate more on the accumulation of resources. The impression is often created that the main-line academic administrators — those whose authority is most highly symbolic and institutionally legitimated — concentrate most on displays of plumage in public, while staff administrators with nonacademic functions often concentrate on a low-key style.

Context and appearances. Managers in differing domains give differential attention to public appearances and private decision capacity. There may be national differences here, too. It is possible that American managers — operating in a context in which the ceremonial aspects of life are denigrated — are less sensitive to symbolic requirements than managers in other countries. The easiest way to study this would be to compare formal organizational charts — the most public residue of structure creation — for similar organizations in different countries. A subject population (e.g., business school students) could be asked to rate charts from different countries for their "rationality" or for various specific dimensions of rationality. It may be that American organizations would *look* less rational than, say, French organizations: charts would probably display sprawling differentiation with limited controlling hierarchies. Following such a research strategy could also help in understanding the criteria, apart from their effectiveness, by which formal structures are evaluated.

The Manager as a Symbolic Entity

The discussion above parallels other ideas in the literature. Less often considered than the management of symbolic systems is the role of the manager as a symbolic element of the organization as ideology (but see Thompson 1961). Managers, to be effective — especially in highly institutionalized contexts — must attend to the celebration of their own existence. They must properly dramatize their own role. This is a difficult point to understand in American culture, with its exaggerated emphasis on *action and decision* and its inattention to constitutive existence. The manager is supposed to *do* something. But the point here is that the manager is supposed to *be*. This is not only a matter of private interest, as is sometimes thought, but is a necessary ingredient in the organization as an ideological system. "They also serve who only stand and wait."

Much is known, but also misinterpreted, here. Managerial attention to status is recognized but treated as a private interest rather than as a corporate one — it is seen as a kind of corruption similar to managerial self-dramatization, managerial inclinations to pretend to do something without actually doing anything, and managerial tendencies to create meetings and occasions where "nothing happens." All this makes much more organizational sense than is commonly recognized. Thus:

1. Managers celebrate the *purposes* embedded in their roles. They emit statements of goals, plans, targets — whether or not these have practical meaning.

2. Managers celebrate the organizational *rationality* embedded in their roles. They dramatically enact what Weber called "the authority of expertise," engaging in practically meaningless demonstrations of competence and relevance.

3. Managers celebrate *control* (Weber's "authority of office") with little rituals of hierarchy and authority, of symbolic inspection, of responsibility. They collect *data*. Much of this has no practical function beyond celebration.

In such ways, managers maintain the existence of their roles, of the units they supervise, and maintain the importance of these for the organization as a whole. By earlier arguments, much of this activity has importance for the maintenance of the organization as a coherent ideology.

According to the arguments made earlier, managerial symbolic self-dramatization should be most important and common in the least technical and most institutional settings. In business firms, it should be least common in production management. It should in general be more common in universities than in business firms. And it seems likely that such behavior would systematically vary across countries, being somewhat less common in American organizations.

Various constituencies are involved in a managerial display of existence — any drama has one or more audiences. First, there is the external audience. External constituencies are to be impressed by the clarity of purpose, the displays of competence, and the symbols of authority the manager flaunts. From such forms of evidence, external groups will see that the organizational structure is real and alive and responsible. Thus a personnel manager demonstrates the rationality of the organization by attending professional meetings, displaying a Ph.D., showing data on the personnel system of the organization, and revealing knowledge of particular examples, instances, or problems. Not all this is useful in any practical sense: the manager exists partly to report, but also reports part-ly to exist—and this is an important way in which the organization legitimates itself to its external environment.

Second, the manager dramatizes existence before other sectors of the organization. A sales manager must attend meetings and "show the flag" even though nothing will happen; must emit rules and statements and re-ports that may have little content or relevance; must insist on the proper representation of the unit in organizational decision-making, whether or not this is relevant to practical action.

Third, the manager dramatizes existence before subordinate roles. Meetings are called with no practical import. Rules and policies appear, unrelated to practical action. Data and documents are assembled. Even if nothing relevant is going on by way of practical coordinating, every-thing will work better if the manager can persuade subordinates that the unit exists, has purposes, and is rationally located vis-a-vis the larger or-ganization.

Inconsistencies. Problems arise in that the activities required to prop-erly celebrate existence are often inconsistent with those required to actu-ally control and coordinate work. Time spent attending "meaningless" meetings to show the flag is time taken away from attempts to "work." Occasions structured to dramatize symbolic matters may be ineffective in accomplishing coordination in fact. Dramatizations of purpose, ra-tionality, and authority that are effective symbolically may be destruc-tive of accomplishment. Solutions are not easy to find.

Many such problems seem to be at least partly resolved through de-coupling behavior. In all sorts of ways, managers draw a line in social reality between the things that "really count" and public appearance mat-ters. Meetings scheduled for appearances have a subtly different charac-ter than the meetings at which the "real decisions" are supposed to be made. There are different participants, and they carry themselves differ-ently in speech and dress and physical posture. Procedures and agendas seem differently structured, too.

So also with organizational documents. A university transcript—de-scribing the output that "counts"—looks quite different from a diploma. Working and decision documents seem different from public-appearance ones.

Finally, there seems a considerable tendency to separate sharply be-tween the ritualistic control systems linked to public appearances and those by which day-to-day controls of some kind are made, as if to con-fuse the two might be problematic. Symbolic inspections and evaluations and accountings are often sharply differentiated from those that are to be taken seriously in everyday work.

In all these areas, the simple separation of the two aspects of organizational life, analogous to the public and the private, may be a device that lowers the costs and confusions involved in inconsistencies between the two. If the dramatic distinction between front-stage and back-stage is clearly maintained, participants may find it easier to structure their activity.

Conclusion

Formal organizational structures function as legitimating ideologies as well as structured work activities. In meeting ideological requirements, general environmental demands or the requirements of the appearances of rationality, structures may commonly assume forms quite inconsistent with the requirements of work life. Legitimating considerations have a logic of their own. Understanding this makes it clear what apparently useless or irrelevant formal structures are created and continue to exist, and why formal structures are so poorly linked to what may otherwise appear to be reality.

Given this situation, formal structures are often *alternatives* to, rather than means of, organizational technical action. They are highly elaborated in organizations and organizational situations in which technical activity may be little differentiated or require little coordination. If, in the classic literature, structures arise in response to complex tasks, the proposition can be added that structure-creation is especially common when an organization is faced with an undoable or invisible task.

Managers must attest to both types of considerations — to control and coordination, and to the proper appearances of control and coordination. The importance of the two aspects varies according to the dependence of the organization on technical or institutional considerations. When this is understood, such managerial action that might otherwise appear self-interested or irrational comes to be understood as behavior maintaining the organization as a pageant. In the modern cultural system, rationality is not only a value, but also an institutionalized value: a manager must adapt to both aspects of it, and must often do so in different ways. The proper *celebration* of rationality may often be inconsistent with local rationality.

REFERENCES

Clark, Burton. (1972). "The Occupational Sage in Higher Education." *Administrative Science Quarterly* 17, 178–84.

Cohen, Michael, and James March. (1974). *Leadership and Ambiguity*. New York: McGraw-Hill.

Cyert, R. M., and James G. March. (1963). *A Behavioral Theory of the Firm.* New York: Prentice-Hall.

March, James G., and Johann P. Olsen. (1976). *Ambiguity and Choice in Organizations.* Bergen: Universitetsforlaget.

March, James G., and Herbert Simon. (1958). *Organizations.* New York: Wiley.

Meyer, John W., and Brian Rowan. (1977). "Institutionalized Organizations: Formal Structure as Myth and Ceremony." *American Journal of Sociology* 83 (September), 340–63.

_____ (1978). "The Structure of Educational Organizations." In M. W. Meyer, ed., *Environments and Organizations.* San Francisco: Jossey-Bass.

Meyer, John W., W. Richard Scott, and Terrence E. Deal. (1981). "Institutional and Technical Sources of Organizational Structure." In Herman Stein, ed. *Organization and the Human Services.* Philadelphia: Temple University Press.

Pfeffer, Jeffrey, and Gerald Salancik. (1978). *The External Control of Organizations.* New York: Harper and Row.

Thompson, Victor. (1961). *Modern Organizations.* New York: Knopf.

Weick, Karl E. (1976). "Educational Organizations as Loosely Coupled Systems." *Administrative Science Quarterly* 21 (March), 1–19.

PART III

Theory of Practice
in Educational Administration and
Organizational Analysis

The appearance of Thomas Kuhn's book *The Structure of Scientific Revolutions* (1962) sparked a series of controversies on the nature of knowledge and its development that continue today. Kuhn argued that scientific progress emerges from a history of paradigm succession. Paradigms might be thought of as lenses through which scientists view the world. At one point in time a particular lens dominates to be subsequently replaced by a different lens. The physics of Newton and Einstein are often cited as examples. As lenses vary, so does one's view of reality.

Normal science, according to this view, is defined as the dominant paradigm at the time and other views of science are considered to be competing. The idea of the replacement of one paradigm with another seems to fit better the natural than the social sciences. The social sciences might be thought of as multiple paradigm fields (Ritzer 1975) where a number of views of reality exist side by side, each able to highlight some features of this reality better than others.

Presently, the dominant paradigms governing administrative thought and organizational analysis are aligned with the philosophy of logical positivism (see for example Chapter 1 where efficiency, person, and political perspectives on administrative theory and practice are described). The cultural perspective is proposed in this book as an additional view. The chapters in Part III seek to examine some of the philosophical and theoretical underpinnings of the cultural perspective in an effort to point the way toward a more useful theory of administrative leadership and organizational life.

Part III begins with Graham Allison's analysis (Chapter 12) of similarities and differences in public and private management. Allison writes in response to Wallace Sayre's aphorism, "Public and private management are fundamentally alike in all unimportant respects." Focusing first on similarities he offers the following as functions of general management: establishing general strategy by identifying objectives and priorities; devising operational plans and making operational decisions; organizing, staffing, and motivating; directing and controlling performance; and managing external constituencies by dealing with related organizations, the press, and the public. This analysis leads him to conclude that there is a level of generality where management is management whether public or private.

Operationally and substantively, however, important differences exist. Allison first examines these differences by reviewing some better-known comparative lists. This review reveals differences in time perspectives (shorter in public), length of service in office (shorter in public), measurement of performance (more ambiguous in public), personnel constraints (civil service and tenure system in public), equity and efficiency (equity emphasized over efficiency in public), openness to public scrutiny (more so in public), legislative and judicial impact (greater in public), scrutiny by the press and media (more influential in public), and ability to convince others of one's effectiveness (more difficult in public).

Citing lists of differences and disclosing their impact on leaders and leadership are quite different tasks. Not content with only the first, Allison then operationally examines these differences by comparing the jobs and responsibilities of two leaders: Doug Costle, the director of the Environmental Protection Agency in 1977, and Roy Chapin, the president of American Motors in 1967. The case studies he provides give life and meaning to how each of the leaders deals with strategy and the management of internal and external constituencies. It is clear from this analysis that lists of management functions and activities and the content and substance of these functions and activities differ. Thus while public and private management may look similar, they differ considerably in operation.

Allison then turns his attention to implications of this comparative analysis for research and training in public administration, cautioning that widespread use of general frameworks from the social and management sciences are inappropriate. Indeed, he suggests that unique situations, contexts, and cases should be emphasized. Criticizing the wholesale borrowing of skills and understandings from other areas, he calls for the development of public administration as a unique field of inquiry and practice.

In Chapter 13 William P. Foster examines critical theory as a framework for understanding educational administration. Critical theory is concerned with the nature of practice informed by theory and emerges from Hegelian and Marxian dialectic thought regarding the political and economic structure of our society. When applied to problems of administration and organization, critical theory shifts from providing a forum for radical political thought to a process for understanding and evaluating administrative decisions and the quality of organizational life. Critical theory seeks to bring together the logic of scientific explanation and the tradition of cultural understanding into an evaluative framework which aspires to the good life and just society.

Foster begins by providing a brief historical sketch of the critical theory movement emphasizing its characterization as a critique of positivism. Relying on the seminal work of Habermas, three basic cognitive interests to humankind and organization are described: the technical, the practical, and the emancipatory. The technical interest is a manifestation of empirical science and represents a desire to exert control based on the logic and authority of science. The practical interest represents a cultural concern for establishing a sense of community based on intersubjective understanding. The emancipatory interest is manifested in normative discourse which seeks to establish the ideal situation. The three interests are critical to organizational understanding and administrative decision-making. Administrative decisions, for example, should reflect sound and verifiable descriptions of the real world and how it works; be sensitive to the unique cultural understandings and meanings of the situation; and strive to better the human condition. Critical theory provides the forum for bringing the three interests to bear on administrative and organizational problems.

Foster argues for the integration of the three cognitive interests of Habermas as follows: "The objective methods of the natural sciences, the hermeneutic methods of the cultural sciences, and the reflective methods of the critical sciences must stand in a close and compelling relationship." He concludes that critical theory seeks an integration which is oriented toward "discovering the possibilities of increased personal and interpersonal freedom; toward avoiding an institutional dominance so severe that it perverts rationality in the name of rationality."

Turning his attention to the practice of educational administration, Foster calls for a greater emphasis on disciplined critique of existing institutions and practices and on the development of informed practices built from a unique understanding of particular organizations and particular environments. Traditional social science inquiry has a role to play within this shift of emphasis: "It does a disservice to critical theory to suggest that such reflections must remain limited to subjectivistic impressions; empirical verification is required; data are necessary."

Foster then provides a number of examples of research efforts in the areas of classroom and school effects and of external social structures which he views as being on the right track but incomplete because of neglect of important value issues. A critical theory of educational administration would not only allow value questions to become important considerations but would use them as compass settings to steer research in certain directions now neglected (i.e., the hidden curriculum, the latent ideological content of school structures and management decisions).

Foster argues that the dominant modes of inquiry in administrative and organization behavior give too much attention to such social psychological concepts as leading, motivating, role, climate, and communication systems as *descriptive* concepts. A critical theory perspective would seek to ferret out and understand the ideological content of such concepts in action. What do they mean to people involved and what values do they represent? Are they, for example, disguises for an ideology of change and progress committed to structural domination? What implications do they have for such values as self-determination, human dignity, and freedom? In his words, "The reliance on social-psychological indicators of human performance, without a concommitant consideration of the ethical issues of manipulation possible to organization leaders, is in itself disturbing." He continues, "As long as the literature here concentrates on providing sets of techniques to allow administrators to increase employee morale, without allowing the critical evaluation of the nature of the institution itself, it will remain inadequate for the purposes of critical theory."

Foster concludes his exploration into the possibility of building a critical theory of educational administration by providing an analysis of biases in our present thinking and by suggesting what needs to be done to increase receptivity to changing our views.

Chapter 14, by Richard J. Bates, explores further the development of a critical practice of educational administration. His analysis begins with a critique of the theory movement of the '60s and its continuance today in the form of a quest for developing a behavioral science of administration. Claiming that those who aspire to this quest are "blissfully" unaware of recent thinking in science, philosophy, and social theory (i.e., the new sociology, the new educational administration), he criticizes the movement as being noticeably lacking in its attention to unique characteristics of educational organizations and other contextual matters such as educational values and issues.

Bates argues that "organizations are cultures rather than structures, and it is the maintenance and contestation of what it is to constitute the culture of organizational life that provides the dynamic of rationality, legitimation, and motivation in organizations." The practice of educational administration is conceived within this dynamic. Culture, he maintains, is the "prime resource of educational practice. Thus, a theory of educational administration that ignores this central preoccupation can hardly be counted as a theory of educational administration in any very serious sense."

Aspects of organizational culture to be understood include beliefs, language systems, usages, rituals, knowledge, conventions, and other artifacts of human life. These constitute the cultural "baggage" of an organization which determines what is thought and how and which governs acceptable behavior. Part of this baggage is factual and lends itself to inquiry and exploration characterized as empirical, descriptive, and objective. But another part of this cultural baggage is mythical and more concerned with meanings and perceptions than facts and objective reality. Sometimes myths are omnipresent, owning the allegiance of most organizational members and constituents. But often myths are in competition with each other and thus schools and universities become "battle grounds in which contending mythologies compete for the holy grail — control of the future." An adequate theory of educational administration would therefore be concerned with the myths which guide organizational life and the meanings by which myths are perpetuated and negotiated.

Bates proposes that attention be given to three aspects of cultural events: metaphors, rituals, and the language of negotiation. Metaphors, he maintains, allow individuals to structure and create meanings out of experience. They translate objective facts into subjective reality. So powerful are metaphors that they serve as well as "fly bottles, to keep us trapped in invisible prisons." They consciously and unconsciously determine one's attitudes and frames of reference to the world, its events and actions.

Bates then provides an analysis of the use of metaphors to define relationships and establish power structures within schools. He notes that metaphors are often used by administrators to obscure actual intents and to maintain existing power relationships. Such organizational metaphors of the school as clinic and factory are explored, as are metaphors used to characterize students. He reviews studies, for example, which suggest that metaphors applied to students differ depending upon their social class and, as symbolic labels, the metaphors signal and justify quite different approaches to teaching and schooling for different groups.

Rituals, Bates maintains, are mechanisms of control in organizations: they revivify the relationships that constitute and define forms of order and sets of expectations in given social situations. School rituals, for example, are means to maintain order and to win unquestioned compliance. "Rituals can often be so powerful as to take on a life of their own. Conformity to rituals may be so complete as to govern movement, place, time, language, sequence of activities, participants' response, and the use of artifacts." Using the examples of curriculum innovation and school restructuring Bates illustrates the capacity of schools to maintain their own rituals in the face of change.

Language is the means by which administrators intervene in the metaphorical and ritualistic aspects of school life. Thus the language of negotiations becomes another critical aspect of cultural understanding. Language is power and whoever controls its framing determines meaning. Administrators who seek to increase power by centralizing decision-making in the face of opposition can win the battle against aspirants to power equalization by framing centralization as a means to increase accountability and to bring about a more coherent statement of organizational purposes and quality. Those who oppose centralization, once the concept is framed in this manner, oppose as well accountability, coherence of purpose, and quality. Language, then, is "a mechanism of control in negotiation over action."

Metaphor, ritual, and the language of negotiation are the cultural currency for understanding organizational life. Critical theory inquiries into the effects of cultural currency exchanges. This inquiry is particularly important in educational organizations where members are unequal in power and where, despite subcultural differences (students, faculty), dominant cultures articulated by powerful organizational elites (teachers, administrators) count in the end.

Bates concludes by noting that school cultures are products of conflict and negotiations over definitions of situation. Through language, metaphor, myth, and ritual administrators contribute to determining culture which is "reproduced in the consciousness of teachers and pupils." A critical theory of practice would be "reflective concerning such negotiations, placing them within the context of a critique of domination and a commitment to struggle in the interest of a better world."

In Chapter 15, Thomas J. Sergiovanni provides a summary to Part III by outlining criteria necessary for developing a relevant science of administration. He proposes the concept "Theory of Practice" as being more appropriate to educational administration than traditional scientific theory or models of applied science.

Traditional scientific inquiry, for example, seeks to "establish truth and refute conjecture; to bring about hegemony of thought through systematic experiental research; to find the right answer, the correct explanation, and the best way." In applied science a direct correspondence is assumed between knowledge verified as true by a particular discipline and professional practice. Applied sciences seek to "establish the one best analysis of a problem, the one best way to practice given existing scientific knowledge." Conceptions of science and applied science have great appeal in our Western society since they reflect a broader commitment to technical-rational values. In addition they provide administrators with a secure footing, albeit intellectual, as they work and inquire in a complex and ambiguous world.

Sergiovanni points out that administrative theory and practice are distinct enterprises characterized by both applications of scientific knowledge and human activity. As human sciences they are not only concerned with efficient means and instrumental ends but with appropriate means and better ends. In his view, "educational administration is a science of designing courses of action aimed at changing existing structures into preferred ones." This normative quality of the human sciences brings a certain artificiality to inquiry and practice. As Simon (1969) argues, the natural sciences are more concerned with how things are; the sciences of the artificial are concerned with how things ought to be and with designs which help to attain these goals.

The human sciences, Sergiovanni notes, "are artificial in phenomenological and cultural senses as well. Despite the fact that objective reality exists and is worth pursuing, reality is also a state of mind whose validity and meaning are determined by the private worlds within which each of us lives. Reality is also created and validated in our interaction with others and this interaction network constitutes a cultural web of which we are a part."

Concluding that traditional conceptions of theory have not been able to capture the complexity and sensitivity needed to accommodate the purposeful, practical, and human qualities of administrative life, Sergiovanni notes that a theoretical framework, systematic analyses, and informed practice are necessary nonetheless. The issue, therefore, is not theory but the adequacy of its conception. He provides some critical assumptions and features he believes are necessary in developing a theory of administration with relevance to practice. Such a theory, for example, would be concerned with four critical questions: what is reality in a given situation; what ought to be; what do these events mean; and given these conditions, what should one do? The questions represent the bringing together of descriptive, normative, and interpretive sciences to bear on problems and issues and to inform administrative decision-making. Further, they comprise the building blocks of a theory of practice.

REFERENCES

Kuhn, Thomas (1962). *The Structure of Scientific Revolutions*. Chicago: University of Chicago Press.

Ritzer, Goerge (1975). "Sociology: A Multiple Paradigm Science." *American Sociologist* 10, 156–67.

Simon, Herbert A. (1969). *The Sciences of the Artificial*. Cambridge, Mass.: MIT Press.

CHAPTER 12

Public and Private Administrative Leadership:
Are They Fundamentally Alike
in All Unimportant Respects?

Graham T. Allison

> Scholars are of all men those least fitted for politics and its ways. The reason for this is that they are accustomed to intellectual speculation, the search for concepts and their abstraction from sense-data . . . they do not, in general, seek to make their thoughts conform to external reality, but rather deduce what ought to exist outside from what goes on in their minds.
>
> Now those who engage in politics must pay great attention to what goes on outside, and to all the circumstances that accompany and succeed an event. Hence men of learning, who are accustomed to generalizations and the extensive use of analogy, tend, when dealing with political affairs, to impose their own frame of concepts and deductions on things, thus falling into error.
>
> Ibn Khaldun
> *The Muqaddimah*

My subtitle puts Wallace Sayre's oft quoted "law" as a question. Sayre had spent some years in Ithaca helping plan Cornell's new school of business and public administration. He left for Columbia with this aphorism: public and private management are fundamentally alike in all unimportant respects.

Sayre based his conclusion on years of personal observation of governments, a keen ear for what his colleagues at Cornell (and earlier at the office of personnel administration) said about business, and a careful review of the literature and data comparing public and private management. Of the latter there was virtually none. Hence, Sayre's provocative "law" was actually an open invitation to research.

Unfortunately, in the fifty years since Sayre's pronouncement, the data base for systematic comparison of public and private management has improved little. This paper takes up Sayre's invitation to speculate about similarities and differences among public and private management in ways that suggest significant opportunities for systematic investigation.

To reiterate: this paper is not a report of a major research project or systematic study; rather, it provides a brief summary of reflections of a dean of a school of government who now spends his time doing a form of public management — managing what James March has labeled an "organized anarchy" — rather than thinking, much less writing.[1] My primary aim is not to be definitive but rather to stimulate a discussion which could lead to more systematic research efforts.

Framing the Issue: What Is Administrative Leadership?

What is the meaning of "administrative leadership"? Is "administrative leadership" different from "management"? Is it broader or narrower than "administration"? Should we distinguish between leadership, management, entrepreneurship, institution-building, administration, policy making, and implementation?

Who are "administrative leaders" or "public managers"? Mayors, governors, and presidents? City managers, secretaries, and commissioners? Bureau chiefs? Office directors? Educators? Legislators? Judges?

To judge from some recent discussions of leadership, one might conclude that "administrative leadership" is, in fact, an oxymoron — a contradiction in terms. James MacGregory Burns's massive study, *Leadership* (1978), is a case in point. Defining bureaucracy as "the simple application of authority from the top down," (1978, 298) he declares leadership an impossibility in bureaucratic settings. In Burns's administrative world, leaders are not required for managers have sufficient authority to get their own way without exerting qualities beyond the mere exercise of bureaucratic power.

This and many other such discussions tend to invest the concept of leadership with connotations of particular interest to an author and then to discover this special interest as the essence of the concept. Still, it is possible to review the literature on leadership, distill from it common leadership qualities, and then search for these qualities in administrative settings. Among the concepts compared in such an exercise would be:

Machiavelli and Pareto: Lions and Foxes. Combining strength with craftiness, Machiavelli's prince-leader maintains his position by knowing "not to keep faith when by doing so it would be against his interest," (Machiavelli 1950, 64) or, as Burns concludes about Franklin Roosevelt and what seemed to many his obsession with power, "by using the tricks of the fox to serve the purposes of the lion" (quoted in Safire 1978, 379). Pareto's wrinkle on the lions and foxes concept is found in his discussion of the "circulation of elites" (Pareto 1935). Here, "foxes and lions" are terms used to describe two distinct leadership styles. Innovators, or "foxes," are important at early stages of societies as architects of new programs and methods. Once these innovations have been institutionalized, it is time for the "lions" to take control — to cut back in order to assure survival. When new conditions arise and societies need to readapt, the foxes return.

Lao Tse: Invisible Leadership. Judging leadership as the ability to lead without seeming to lead, Lao Tse's classic aphorism:

> A leader is best
> When people barely know he exists.
> Not so good when people obey and acclaim him,
> Worse when they despise him.
> "Fail to honor people,
> They fail to honor you";
> But of a good leader, who talks little,
> When his work is done, his aim fulfilled,
> They will say, "We did this ourselves"
> (cited in Seldes 1966, 398).

This has been a point of departure of students and practitioners for centuries — and remains so to this day.

Max Weber: The Routinization of Leadership. In Weber's classic essay on bureaucracy, bureaucratic organization is seen as a technical device designed to routinize the ability to achieve objectives in a rational, efficient manner — without the necessity of charismatic leadership. Funneling purpose through set channels, it performs activities that would otherwise not take place. For Weber, leadership in such a world consists of the ability to point bureaucratic entities in particular directions, setting policy and defining organizational mission.

Philip Selznick: Institutional Leadership. Seeking to shift the focus of study from political leaders to institutional managers, Selznick draws attention to the character of organizations and the men and women who run them (Selznick 1957). Leadership, he says, is not merely officeholding or the authority to make decisions. It is, rather, a function *first* of the manager's recognition that his or her organization (defined, presumably after Weber, as a "rational instrument to do a job") is, in fact, an institution with its own history and external milieu, and its own internal social world; second, the decisions he or she makes which define the institution's mission and role build these purposes into its structure.

John Gardner: Disaggregated Leadership. Such is the nature of society's current problems that leadership "in the storybook sense" is no longer a valid concept. Instead, countless initiatives must be taken by individuals at all levels of society if leadership, measured as "purposeful social change," is to be achieved. For Gardner, these individuals, or leaders, fall into three basic categories: *clarifiers and definers*, who help explain issues, set priorities, and judge performance; *implementers and problem solvers*, who build support and activate or redesign existing institutions (inventing new ones if needed); and *mobilizers*, who create a climate conducive to achieving the level of effort necessary to obtain results.[2]

Peter Drucker: The Society of Organizations. In Drucker's view, ours has become a society of organizations. "Every major societal task," he writes, "is being performed in and through large, managed institutions" (1974, 807). Commanding both the organizational resources and the competence to use them in an efficient, socially purposive manner, it is not surprising that those who manage these institutions have emerged as society's principal leadership group. Their responsibilities? To make their organizations function — a task involving management for results as measured by traditional yardsticks of performance — and to make them live up to their newer, larger societal mission — a task involving the integration of the needs and interests of contending groups in a pluralistic society.

While insightful and illuminating, I find the claims of these authors to have isolated the "real thing" ultimately unpersuasive. Certainly the evaluative aspects of the term leadership encourage "persuasive" definitions. Unfortunately, such terminological tangles seriously hamper the development of knowledge about leadership. In our efforts to discuss the public management curriculum at Harvard, I have been struck by how differently people use these terms, how strongly many individuals feel about some distinction they believe is marked by a difference between one word and another, and consequently, how large a barrier terminology is to convergent discussion. These verbal obstacles virtually prohibit conversation that is both brief and constructive among individuals who have not developed a common language or a mutual understanding of each others' use of terms.

This terminological thicket reflects a more fundamental conceptual confusion. There exists no overarching framework that orders the domain. In an effort to get a grip on the phenomena — the buzzing, blooming confusion of people in jobs performing tasks that produce results — both practitioners and observers have strained to find distinctions that facilitate their work. The attempts in the early decades of this century to draw a sharp line between "policy" and "administration," like more recent efforts to mark a similar divide between "policy-making" and "implementation," reflect a common search for a simplification that allows one to put the value-laden issues of politics to one side (who gets what, when, and how), and focus on the more limited issue of how to perform tasks more efficiently. But can anyone really deny that the "how" substantially affects the "who," the "what," and the "when"? The basic categories now prevalent in discussions of administrative leadership in public settings — strategy, personnel management, financial management, and control — are mostly derived from a business context in which executives manage hierarchies. While relevant to the problems that confront public managers, these terms do not map the territory directly.

Finally, there exist little ready data on what public managers do. Instead, the academic literature, such as it is, mostly consists of speculation tied to bits and pieces of evidence about the tail or the trunk or other manifestation of the proverbial elephant. In contrast to the literally thousands of cases describing problems faced by private managers and their practice in solving these problems, case research from the perspective of a public manager is just beginning. This paucity of data on the phenomena inhibits systematic empirical research on similarities and differences between public and private management, leaving the field to a mixture of reflection on personal experience and speculation.

For the purpose of this discussion, I cannot hope to surmount these formidable obstacles. Thus, this paper will attempt to circumvent them by taking a less abstract, more simplistically empirical path: focusing on people playing lead roles in administrative settings and asking what they do and how their functions differ between public and private organizations. Following Webster I will use the term "lead" to mean "to show the way by going in advance; to conduct, escort, or direct." Those who lead in administrative settings, I will call managers. Again, following Webster, I will use the term "management" to mean the "purposive organization and direction of resources to achieve a desired outcome." I will focus on general managers, that is, individuals charged with managing a whole organization or multifunctional subunit. I will be interested in the general manager's full responsibilities: *inside* his or her organization in combining the diverse contributions of specialized subunits; *outside* his or her organization in mobilizing the necessary participation and support for the organization and its program; and *among* the multiple dimensions of his or her task in integrating competing activities to achieve results.

I will begin with the simplifying assumption that managers of traditional government organizations are public managers, and managers of traditional private businesses, private managers.[3] Lest the discussion fall victim to the fallacy of misplaced abstraction, I will take the Director of EPA and the Chief Executive Officer of American Motors as, respectively, public and private managers. Thus our central question can be put concretely: in what ways are the jobs and responsibilities of Doug Costle as director of EPA similar to and different from those of Roy Chapin as chief executive officer of American Motors?

Similarities between Public and Private Managers

At one level of abstraction, it is possible to identify a set of general management functions. The most famous such list appeared in Gulick and Urwick's classic *Papers in the Science of Administration* (1937). Gulick summarized the work of the chief executive in the acronym POSDCORB. The letters stand for:

Planning
Organizing
Staffing
Directing
Coordinating
Reporting
Budgeting

With various additions, amendments, and refinements, similar lists of general management functions can be found through the management literature from Barnard to Drucker.

I shall resist here my natural academic instinct to join the intramural debate among proponents of various lists and distinctions. Instead, I simply offer one composite list (see Table 1) that attempts to incorporate the major functions that have been identified for general managers, whether public or private.

Differences between Public and Private Managers

While there is a level of generality at which management is management, whether public or private, functions that bear identical labels take on rather different meaning in public and private settings. As Larry Lynn has pointed out, one powerful piece of evidence in the debate between those who emphasize "similarities" and those who underline "differences" is the near unanimity on this issue among individuals who have been general managers in both business and government.[4]

My review of these recollections, as well as the thoughts of academics, has identified three interesting orthogonal lists that summarize the current state of the field: one by John Dunlop; one major *Public Administration Review* survey of the literature comparing public and private organizations by Hal Rainey, Robert Backoff, and Charles Levine; and one by Richard E. Neustadt prepared for the National Academy of Public Administration's panel on presidential management.[5]

Table 1. Functions of General Management

Strategy

1. *Establishing general strategy, objectives and priorities* for the organization (on the basis of forecasts of the external environment, the organization's capacities, and the fit between the two). This function includes not only selection of strategy, objectives, and priorities but also the institutionalization of these values.
2. *Devising operational plans and making operational decisions* to achieve these objectives.

Managing Internal Components

3. *Organizing, staffing and motivating:* in organizing the manager establishes structure (units and positions with assigned authority and responsibilities) and procedures (for coordinating activity and taking action); in staffing the manager tries to enlist the right persons in the key jobs.*
4. *Directing personnel and the personnel management system:* the capacity of the organization is embodied primarily in its members and their skills and knowledge; the personnel management system recruits, selects, socializes, trains, rewards, punishes, and exits the organization's human capital, which constitutes the organization's capacity to act to achieve its goals and to respond to specific directions from management.
5. *Controlling performance:* various management information systems—including operating and capital budgets, accounts, reports and statistical systems, performance appraisals, and product evaluation—assist management in motivating performance, making decisions, and measuring progress toward objectives.

Managing External Constituencies

6. *Dealing with "external" units* of the organization subject to some common authority: most general managers must secure some level of participation or support from general managers of other units within the larger organization—above, laterally, and below—to achieve their unit's objectives.
7. *Dealing with independent organizations:* agencies from other branches or levels of government, interest groups, and private enterprises that can importantly affect the organization's ability to achieve its objectives.
8. *Dealing with the press and public* whose action or approval or acquiescence is required.

---

*Organization and staffing are frequently separated in such lists, but because of the interaction between the two, they are combined here. See Allison and Szanton (1976, 14).

John T. Dunlop's "impressionistic comparison of government management and private business" is summarized in Table 2.

The Public Administration Review's major review article comparing public and private organizations attempts to summarize the major points of consensus in the literature on similarities and differences among public and private organizations (Rainey, Backoff, and Levine 1976). Table 3 presents that summary.

Table 2. Government Management and Private Management:
A Comparison by John T. Dunlop*

	Government Management	Private Management
1. Time perspective	Relatively short, dictated by political necessities.	Longer; oriented toward market developments, technological innovation, and organization building.
2. Duration of service	Averages no more than eighteen months; successor is not trained by outgoing manager.	Longer, both in same position and in same enterprise; successor is trained.
3. Measurement of performance	Little if any agreement on standards.	Various tests: financial return, market share, performance measures for executive compensation.
4. Personnel constraints	Two layers of sometimes hostile officials: civil servants and political appointees; organized under unions or government regulations; lines of responsibility are diffused.	Even when unionized, greater latitude, more authority to direct personnel; direct lines of responsibility.
5. Equity and efficiency	Great emphasis on equity among constituencies.	Greater emphasis on efficiency and competitive performance.
6. Openness to public inspection	Very exposed and open to public scrutiny.	Less public review, more private review.
7. Roll of press & media	Consistently under review by media which has impact on decision-making.	Less open to media inspection.
8. Persuasion & direction	Often seeks to form alliances and coalitions; authority comes from various directions.	Structure of authority clearly from top to bottom.
9. Legislative & judicial impact	Subject to close scrutiny; constrains freedom to act.	Little impact.
10. Bottom line	Usually unclear.	Profit, market performance, survival.

*John T. Dunlop, "Public Management," draft of unpublished paper, 1979.

Table 3. Public Administration Review Research Developments

Summary of Literature on Differences Between Public and Private Organizations.
Main Points of Consensus

The following table presents a summary of the points of consensus by stating
them as propositions regarding the attributes of a public organization, relative to
those of a private organization.

Topic   Proposition

I. Environmental Factors

I.1 Degree of market exposure (reliance on appropriations)	I.1.a Less market exposure results in less incentive to cost reduction, operating efficiency, effective performance.
	I.1.b Less market exposure results in lower allocational efficiency (reflection of consumer preferences, proportioning supply to demand, etc.).
	I.1.c Less market exposure means lower availability of market indicators and information (prices, profits, etc.).
I.2 Legal, formal constraints (courts, legislature, hierarchy)	I.2.a More constraints on procedures, spheres of operations (less autonomy of managers in making such choices).
	I.2.b Greater tendency to proliferation of formal specifications and controls.
	I.2.c More external sources of formal influence, and greater fragmentation of those sources.
I.3 Political influences	I.3.a Greater diversity of intensity of external informal influences on decisions (bargaining, public opinion, interest group reactions).
	I.3.b Greater need for support of "constituencies": client groups, sympathetic formal authorities, etc.

II. Organization-Environment Transactions

II.1 Coerciveness ("coercive" "monopolistic," unavoidable nature of many governmental activities)	II.1.a More likely that participation in consumption and financing of services will be unavoidable or mandatory (government has unique sanctions and coercive powers).

Table 3. Public Administration Review Developments — cont'd

Topic	Proposition
II.2 Breadth of impact	II.2.a Broader impact, greater symbolic significance of actions of public administrators (wider scope of concern, such as "public interest").
II.3 Public scrutiny	II.3.a Greater public scrutiny of public officials and their actions.
II.4 Unique public expectations	II.4.a Greater public expectations that public officials act with more fairness, responsiveness, accountability, and honesty.

III. Internal Structures and Processes

III.1 Complexity of objectives, evaluation and decision criteria.	III.1.a Greater multiplicity and diversity of objectives and criteria.
	III.1.b Greater vagueness and intangibility of objectives and criteria.
	III.1.c Greater tendency of goals to be conflicting (more "trade-offs").
III.2 Authority relations and the role of the administrator	III.2.a Less decision-making autonomy and flexibility on the part of the public administrators.
	III.2.b Weaker, more fragmented authority over subordinates and lower levels. (1, subordinates can bypass, appeal to alternative authorities; 2, merit system constraints).
	III.2.c Greater reluctance to delegate, more levels of review, and greater use of formal regulations (due to difficulties in supervision and delegation, resulting from III.1.b).
	III.2.d More political, expository role for top managers.
III.3 Organizational performance	III.3.a Greater cautiousness, rigidity; less innovativeness.
	III.3.b More frequent turnover of top leaders due to elections and political appointments results in greater disruption of implementation of plans.

continued

Table 3. Public Administration Review Developments — cont'd

Topic	Proposition
III.4 Incentives and incentive structures	III.4.a Greater difficulty in devising incentives for effective and efficient performance.
	III.4.b Lower valuation of pecuniary incentives by employees.
III.5 Personal characteristics of employees	III.5.a Variations in personality traits and needs, such as higher dominance and flexibility, higher need for achievement on part of government managers.
	III.5.b Lower work satisfaction and lower organizational commitment.

(III.5.a and III.5.b represent results of individual empirical studies, rather than points of agreement among authors.)

Source: *Public Administration Review*, March/April, 1976, p. 236–237.

Third, Richard E. Neustadt, in a fashion close to Dunlop's, notes six major differences between presidents of the United States and chief executive officers of major corporations (see Table 4).

Underlying these lists' sharp distinctions between public and private management is a fundamental *constitutional* difference. In business, the functions of general management are centralized in a single individual, the chief executive officer. The goal is authority commensurate with responsibility. In contrast, in the U.S. government, the functions of general management are constitutionally spread among competing institutions — the executive, two houses of Congress, and the courts. The constitutional goal was "not to promote efficiency but to preclude the exercise of arbitrary power," as Justice Brandeis observed. Indeed, as *The Federalist Papers* make starkly clear, the aim was to create incentives to compete: "The great security against a gradual concentration of the several powers in the same branch, consists in giving those who administer each branch the constitutional means and personal motives to resist encroachment of the others. Ambition must be made to counteract ambition."[6] Thus, the general management functions concentrated in the CEO of a private business are, by constitutional design, spread in the public sector among a number of competing institutions and thus shared by a number of individuals whose ambitions are set against one another. For most areas of public policy today, these individuals include at the federal level the chief elected official, the chief appointed executive, the chief career official,

Table 4. U.S. Presidents and Chief Executive Officers of Corporations:
A Comparison by Richard E. Neustadt*

	U.S. Presidents	Chief Executive Officers
1. Time horizon	Four years, with the fourth and, now, the the third dominated by campaigning for reelection.	On the average, about a decade.
2. Authority over the enterprise	Shared with well-placed members of Congress, who do no necessarily reflect the president's views and goals.	Sets goals and organizational structures, monitors results, reviews key decisions, and deals with outsiders. Subject only to board of directors which generally shares same views and goals.
3. Career system	Generally little experience working in Washington; often unfamiliar with appointees or their roles.	Often lifetime experience. A model corporation is a true career system — executives are chosen from within or from other firms of same industry.
4. Media relations	Routinely in public eye; the press is part of and necessary to daily business.	Represents firm and, in exceptional cases, speaks for it publicly. Otherwise, gives press little access to internal operations.
5. Performance measurement	Judged often by very subjective measures: public perceptions and press interpretations. Congress and interest groups judge according to how well *their* best interests are being served.	Is judged by and judges subordinates by profitability, a criterion which is generally accepted by business community.

continued

Table 4. U.S. Presidents and Chief Executive Officers of Corporations:
A Comparison by Richard E. Neustadt* — cont'd

	U.S. Presidents	Chief Executive Officers
6. Implementation	Responsible for budgetary proposals but poorly placed to monitor the actions of states, cities, corporations, unions, or foreign governments — often the executants of the president's policies; limited ability to change personnel in charge of actual policy implementation.	Oversees policy implementation, monitoring through the information system and taking corrective action through the personnel system.

*Richard E. Neustadt, "American Presidents & Corporate Executives," a paper prepared for the Panel on Presidential Management of the National Academy of Public Administration, 1979.

and several congressional chieftains. Since most public services are actually delivered by state and local governments, with independent sources of authority, this means a further array of individuals at these levels.

An Operational Perspective

If organizations could be separated neatly into two homogeneous groups, one public and one private, the task of identifying similarities and differences between managers of these enterprises would be relatively easy. In fact, as Dunlop has pointed out, "the real world of management is composed of distributions, rather than single undifferentiated forms, and there is an increasing variety of hybrids." Thus for each major attribute of organizations, specific entities can be located on a spectrum. On most dimensions, organizations classified as "predominantly public" and those as "predominantly private" overlap. Private business organizations vary enormously among themselves in size, in management structure and philosophy, and in the constraints under which they operate. For example, forms of ownership and types of managerial control may be somewhat unrelated. Compare a family-held enterprise, for instance, with a public utility and a decentralized conglomerate, a Bechtel with ATT and Textron. Similarly, there are vast differences in management of governmental organizations. Compare the Government Printing Office or the TVA or the police department of a small town with the Department of Energy or the Department of Health and Human Services. These distributions and varieties should encourage penetrating comparisons within both business and governmental organizations, as well as contrasts and comparisons across these broad categories, a point to which we shall return in considering directions for research.

Without a major research effort, it may nonetheless be worthwhile to examine the jobs and responsibilities of two specific managers, neither polar extremes, but one clearly public, the other private. For this purpose, and primarily because of the availability of cases that describe the problems and opportunities each confronted, consider Doug Costle, Administrator of EPA, and Roy Chapin, CEO of American Motors.[7]

Doug Costle, Administrator of EPA, January 1977

The mission of EPA is prescribed by laws creating the agency and authorizing its major programs. That mission is "to control and abate pollution in the areas of air, water, solid wastes, noise, radiation, and toxic substances. EPA's mandate is to mount an integrated, coordinated attack on environmental pollution in cooperation with state and local governments" (U.S. Govt. Manual 1978/79, 507).

EPA's organizational structure follows from its legislative mandates to control particular pollutants in specific environments: air and water, solid wastes, noise, radiation, pesticides, and chemicals. As the new administrator, Costle inherited the Ford administration's proposed budget for EPA of $802 million for fiscal 1978 with a ceiling of 9,698 agency positions.

The setting into which Costle stepped is difficult to summarize briefly. As Costle characterized it:

> Outside there is a confusion on the part of the public in terms of what this agency is all about: what it is doing, where it is going.

> The most serious constraint on EPA is the inherent complexity in the state of our knowledge, which is constantly changing.

> Too often, acting under extreme deadlines mandated by Congress, EPA has announced regulations, only to find out that they knew very little about the problem. The central problem is the inherent complexity of the job that the agency has been asked to do and the fact that what it is asked to do changes from day to day.

> There are very difficult internal management issues not amenable to a quick solution: the skills-mix problem within the agency; a research program with laboratory facilities scattered all over the country and cemented in place, largely by political alliances on the Hill that would frustrate efforts to pull together a coherent research program.

In terms of EPA's original mandate in the bulk pollutants we may be hitting the asymptotic part of the curve in terms of incremental clean-up costs. You have clearly conflicting national goals: energy and environment, for example.

Costle judged his six major tasks at the outset to be:

assembling a top management team (six assistant administrators and some 25 office heads);

addressing EPA's legislative agenda (EPA's basic legislative charter — the Clean Air Act and the Clean Water Act — was being rewritten as he took office; the pesticides program was also up for reauthorization in 1977);

establishing EPA's role in the Carter administration (aware that the administration would face hard trade-offs between the environment and energy, energy regulations and the economy, EPA regulations of toxic substances and the regulations of FDA, CSPS, and OSHA. Costle identified the need to build relations with the other key players and to enhance EPA's standing);

building ties to constituent groups (both because of their role in legislating the agency's mandate and in successful implementation of EPA's programs);

making specific policy decisions (for example, whether to grant or deny a permit for the Seabrook nuclear generating plant cooling system or deciding how the Toxic Substance Control Act, enacted in October 1976, would be implemented. This act gave EPA new responsibilities for regulating the manufacture, distribution, and use of chemical substances so as to prevent unreasonable risks to health and the environment. Whether EPA would require chemical manufacturers to provide some minimum information on various substances, or require much stricter reporting requirements for the 1,000 chemical substances already known to be hazardous, or require companies to report all chemicals, and on what timetable, had to be decided and the regulations issued);

rationalizing the internal organization of the agency (EPA's extreme decentralization to the regions and its limited technical expertise).

No easy job.

Roy Chapin and American Motors, January 1967

In January 1967, in an atmosphere of crisis, Roy Chapin was appointed chairman and chief executive officer of American Motors (and William Luneburg, president and chief operating officer). In the four previous years, AMC unit sales had fallen 37 percent and market share from over 6 percent to under 3 percent. Dollar volume in 1967 was off 42 percent from the all-time high in 1963, and earnings showed a net loss of $76 million on sales of $656 million. Columnists began writing obituaries for AMC. *Newsweek* characterized AMC as a "flabby dispirited company, a product solid enough but styled with about as much flair as corrective shoes, and a public image that melted down to one unshakeable label: loser." Said Chapin, "We were driving with one foot on the accelerator and one foot on the brake. We didn't know where the hell we were."

Chapin announced to his stockholders at the outset that "we plan to direct ourselves most specifically to those areas of the market where we can be fully effective. We are not going to attempt to be all things to all people, but to concentrate on those areas of consumer needs we can meet better than anyone else." As he recalled, "There were problems early in 1967 which demanded immediate attention, and which accounted for much of our time for several months. Nevertheless, we began planning beyond them, establishing objectives, programs and timetables through 1972. Whatever happened in the short run, we had to prove ourselves in the marketplace in the long run."

Chapin's immediate problems were five:

1. The company was virtually out of cash and an immediate supplemental bank loan of $20 million was essential.

2. Car inventories — company-owned and dealer-owned — had reached unprecedented levels. The solution to this glut took five months and could be accomplished only by a series of plant shutdowns in January 1967.

3. Sales of the Rambler American series had stagnated and inventories were accumulating; a dramatic merchandising move was concocted and implemented in February, dropping the price tag on the American to a position midway between the VW and competitive smaller U.S. compacts, by both cutting the price to dealers and trimming dealer discounts from 21 percent to 17 percent.

4. Administrative and commercial expenses were judged too high and thus a vigorous cost-reduction program was initiated that trimmed $15 million during the first year. Manufacturing and purchasing costs were also trimmed significantly to approach the most effective levels in the industry.

5. The company's public image had deteriorated; the press was pessimistic and much of the financial community had written it off. To counteract this, numerous formal and informal meetings were held with bankers, investment firms, government officials, and the press.

As Chapin recalls, "With the immediate fires put out, we could put in place the pieces of a corporate growth plan — a definition of a way of life in the auto industry for American Motors. We felt that our reason for being, which would enable us not just to survive but to grow, lay in bringing a different approach to the auto market — in picking our spots and then being innovative and aggressive." The new corporate growth plan included a dramatic change in the approach to the market to establish a "youthful image" for the company by bringing out new sporty models like the Javelin and by entering the racing field, by "changing the product line from one end to the other" by 1972, and by acquiring Kaiser Jeep, all of which meant selling the company's nontransportation assets and concentrating on specialized transportation, including Jeep, a company that had lost money in each of the preceding five years, but one that Chapin believed could be turned around by substantial cost reductions and economies of scale in manufacturing, purchasing, and administration.

Chapin succeeded. For the year ending 30 September 1971, AMC earned $10.2 million on sales of $1.2 billion.

Recalling the list of general management functions in Table 1, which similarities and differences appear salient and important?

Strategy. Both Chapin and Costle had to establish objectives and priorities and to devise operational plans. In business, "corporate strategy is the pattern of major objectives, purposes, or goals, and essential policies and plans for achieving these goals, stated in such a way as to define what business the company is in or is to be in and the kind of company it is or is to be" (Andrews 1971, 28). In reshaping the strategy of AMC and concentrating on particular segments of the transportation market, Chapin had to consult his board and had to arrange financing, but the control was substantially his.

How much choice did Costle have at EPA as to the "business it is or is to be in" or the kind of agency "it is or is to be"? These major strategic choices emerged from the legislative process which mandated whether he should be in the business of controlling pesticides or toxic substances and if so on what timetable, and occasionally even what level of particulate per million units he was required to control. The relative roles of the president, other members of the administration (including White House staff, congressional relations, and other agency heads), the EPA administrator, congressional committee chairpersons, and external groups in establishing the broad strategy of the agency constitutes an interesting question. While Costle had a wider range of strategic options than he in fact recognized, they were, when compared with Chapin's, more subtle and more constrained.

Managing internal components. For both Costle and Chapin, staffing was key. As Donald Rumsfeld has observed, "The single, most important task of the chief executive is to select the right people. I've seen terrible organization charts in both government and business that were made to work well by good people. I've seen beautifully charted organizations that didn't work very well because they had the wrong people" (1979, 92).

The leeway of the two executives in organizing and staffing were considerably different, however. Chapin closed down plants, moved key managers, hired and fired, all virtually at will. For Costle, the basic structure of the agency was set by law. The labs, their location, and most of their personnel were fixed. Though he could recruit his key subordinates, again restrictions like the conflict of interest law and the prospect of a Senate confirmation fight led him to drop his first choice for the assistant administrator for research and development since he had worked for a major chemical company. While Costle could resort to changes in the process for developing policy or regulations in order to circumvent key office directors whose views he did not share, for example Eric Stork, the deputy assistant administrator in charge of the mobile source air program, such maneuvers took considerable time, provoked extensive infighting, and delayed significantly the development of Costle's program. As Michael Blumenthal has written about the Treasury Department,

> If you wish to make substantive changes, policy changes, and the Department's employees don't like what you're doing, they have ways of frustrating you or stopping you that do not exist in private industry. The main method they have is Congress. If I say I want to shut down a particular unit or transfer the function of one area to another, there are ways of going to Congress and in fact using friends in the Congress to block the move. They can also use the press to try to stop you. If I at Bendix wished to transfer a division from Ann Arbor to Detroit because I figured out that we could save money that way, as long as I could do it decently and carefully, it's of no lasting interest to the press. The press can't stop me. They may write about it in the local paper, but that's about it [1979, 39].

In the direction of personnel and management of the personnel system, Chapin exercised considerable authority. While the United Auto Workers limited his authority over workers, at the management level he assigned people and reassigned responsibility consistent with his general plan. While others may have felt that his decisions to close down particular plants or to drop a particular product were mistaken, they complied. As George Shultz has observed, "One of the first lessons I learned in moving from government to business is that in business you must be very careful when you tell someone who is working for you to do something because the probability is high that he or she will do it" (1979, 95).

Costle faced a civil service system designed to prevent spoils as much as to promote productivity. The Civil Service Commission exercised much of the responsibility for the personnel function in his agency. Civil service rules severely restricted his discretion, took a long period to exhaust, and often required complex maneuvering in a specific case to achieve any results. Equal opportunity rules and their administration provided yet another network of procedural and substantive inhibitions. In retrospect, Costle found the civil service system a much larger constraint on his actions and demand on his time than he had anticipated.

In controlling performance, Chapin was able to use measures like profit and market share to reduce those objectives to subobjectives for lower levels of the organization and to measure the performance of managers of particular models, areas, and divisions. Cost accounting rules permitted him to compare plants within AMC and to compare AMC's purchases, production, and even administration with the best practice in the industry.

Managing external constituencies. As chief executive officer, Chapin had to deal only with the board. For Costle, within the executive branch but beyond his agency lay many actors critical to the achievement of his agency's objectives: the president and the White House, the departments of Energy and the Interior, the Council on Environmental Quality, and OMB. Actions each could take, either independently or after a process of consultation in which they disagreed with him, could frustrate his agency's achievement of its assigned mission. Consequently, he spent considerable time building his agency's reputation and capital for interagency disputes.

Dealing with independent external organizations was a necessary and even larger part of Costle's job. Since his agency's mission, strategy, authorizations, and appropriations emerged from the process of legislation, attention to congressional committees, members of Congress and their staffs, and people who affect congressional activities rose to the top of Costle's agenda. In the first year, top level EPA officials appeared over 140 times before some 60 different committees and subcommittees.

Chapin's ability to achieve AMC's objectives could also be affected by independent external organizations: competitors, government (the Clean Air Act that was passed in 1970), consumer groups (recall Ralph Nader), and even suppliers of oil. More than most private managers, Chapin had to deal with the press in attempting to change the image of AMC. Such occasions were primarily at Chapin's initiative, and around events that Chapin's public affairs office orchestrated, for example the announcement of a new racing car. Chapin also managed a marketing effort to persuade consumers that their tastes could best be satisfied by AMC products.

Costle's work, in contrast, was suffused by the press: in the daily working of the organization, in the perception by key publics of the agency and thus the agency's influence with relevant parties, and even in the setting of the agenda of issues to which the agency had to respond.

And finally, what of the bottom line? For Chapin, the bottom line was profit, market share, and the long-term competitive position of AMC.

For Costle, what were the equivalent performance measures? Blumenthal answers by exaggerating the difference between appearance and reality: "At Bendix, it was the reality of the situation that in the end determined whether we succeeded or not. In the crudest sense, this meant the bottom line. You can dress up profits only for so long—if you're not successful, it's going to be clear. In government there is no bottom line, and that is why you can be successful if you appear to be successful—though, of course, appearance is not the only ingredient of success" (1979, 36). Rumsfeld says: "In business, you're pretty much judged by results. I don't think the American people judge government officials this way . . . in government, too often you're measured by how much you seem to care, how hard you seem to try—things that do not necessarily improve the human condition. . . . It's a lot easier for a President to get into something and end up with a few days of good public reaction than it is to follow through, to pursue policies to a point where they have a beneficial effect on human lives" (1979, 90). As George Shultz says: "In government and politics, recognition and therefore incentives go to those who formulate policy and maneuver legislative compromise. By sharp contrast, the kudos and incentives in business go to the persons who can get something done. It is execution that counts. Who can get the plant built, who can bring home the sales contract, who can carry out the financing, and so on" (1979, 95).

This casual comparison of one public and one private manager suggests what could be done—if the issue of comparisons were pursued systematically, horizontally across organizations, and at various levels within organizations. While much can be learned by examining the chief executive officers of organizations, still more promising should be comparisons among the much larger numbers of middle managers. If one compared, for example, a regional administrator of EPA and an AMC division chief, or two comptrollers, or equivalent plant managers, some functions would appear more similar, and other differences would stand out. The major barrier to such comparisons is the lack of cases describing problems and practices of middle-level managers.[8] This should be a high priority in further research.

The differences noted in this comparison, for example, in the personnel area, have already changed with the Civil Service Reform Act of 1978 and the creation of the senior executive service. Significant changes have also occurred in the automobile industry: under current circumstances, the CEO of Chrysler may seem much more like the administrator of EPA. More precise comparison of different levels of management in both organizations, for example, accounting procedures used by Chapin to cut costs significantly as compared to equivalent procedures for judging the costs of EPA-mandated pollution control devices, would be instructive.

Implications for Research and Instruction on Public Management

The debate between the assimilators and the differentiators reminds me of the old argument about whether the glass is half-full or half-empty. I conclude that public and private management are at least as different as they are similar, and that the differences are at least as important as the similarities. From this review of the "state of the art" and instruction, such as it is, let me draw a number of implications for research on public management. I will try to state them in a way that is both succinct and provocative.

First, a predominant feature of life in advanced industrial society is the conduct of most productive activity in and through large managed organizations — private and public. The emergence of a professional management class as a key actor in society is a recent phenomenon whose implications are still being discovered.

Second, while economics and leadership in the private sector have spurred businesses and schools of business to develop systematic learning about effective business management practice, American society has not built capacity for *organized learning* about what effective public managers know and do. President Derek Bok of Harvard has identified the gap as "the principal missing link in American higher education today."[9]

Third, in management capacity, and performance in management positions, human beings differ as markedly as they do in most other realms of capacity and performance. As in tennis or logic, some individuals perform ten times as effectively as others. Individual effectiveness is a function of endowment, motivation, experience, and knowledge.

Fourth, the demand for higher performance from public managers is both realistic and right. The perception that public managers' performance lags behind private business performance is also correct. While every effort should be made to borrow transferrable lessons and skills from the private sector, and while much can be transferred in special arenas, the hope that the focal issues of public management can be resolved by direct transfer of private management practices and skills is misguided.

Fifth, performance in many public management positions can be improved substantially, perhaps by an order of magnitude. That improvement will come not, however, from massive borrowing of specific private management skills and understandings. Instead, it should come, as it did in the history of private management, from an articulation of the general management function and a self-consciousness about the general public management point of view. The single lesson of private management most instructive to public management is the prospect of substantial improvement through recognition of and consciousness about the public management function.

Alfred Chandler's prize winning study, *The Visible Hand: The Managerial Revolution in American Business* which describes the emergence of professional management in business is particularly valuable in this regard. Through the nineteenth century most American businesses were run by individuals who performed management functions but had no self-consciousness about their management responsibilities. With the articulation of the general management perspective, the refinement of general management practices, and the emergence of specialized schools of business, by the 1920s these businesses had become competitive in the management function. Individuals capable of management and self-conscious about their management tasks—setting objectives, establishing priorities, and driving the organization to results—entered firms and industries previously run by family entrepreneurs or ordinary employees and brought about dramatic increases in productivity. (Analogously, at a lower level, the articulation of the salesperson's role and task, together with sales skills and values made it possible for individuals with moderate talents at sales to increase their level of sales tenfold.)

The routes by which people reach general management positions in government, however, do not assure that they will have consciousness or competence in management. As a wise observer of government managers has written, "One of the difficult problems of schools of public affairs is to overcome the old-fashioned belief—still held by many otherwise sophisticated people—that the skills of management are simply the application of 'common sense' by any intelligent and broadly educated person to the management problems which are presented to him. It is demonstrable that many intelligent and broadly educated people who are generally credited with a good deal of 'common sense' make very poor managers. The skills of effective management require a good deal of uncommon sense and uncommon knowledge" (Miles 1967).

The challenge presented by the federal government's creation of the senior executive service—a corps of individuals explicitly identified as general managers in government—is to assist people who occupy general management positions to actually become general managers.

Sixth, careful review of private management rules of thumb that can be adapted to public management contexts will pay off. The 80–20 rule—80 percent of the benefits of most production processes come from the first 20 percent of effort—does have wide application, for example, in EPA efforts to reduce bulk pollutants.

Seventh, Chandler documents the proposition that the categories and criteria for identifying costs, or calculating present value, or measuring the value added to intermediate products are not "natural." They are invented, creations of intelligence harnessed to operational tasks. While there are some particular accounting categories and rules, for example, for costing intermediate products, that may be directly transferable to public sector problems, the larger lesson is that dedicated attention to specific management functions can, as in the history of business, create for public sector managers accounting categories, rules, and measures that cannot now be imagined (1977, 227–79).

Eighth, it is possible to learn from experience. What skills, attributes, and practices do competent managers exhibit and less successful managers lacks? This is an empirical question that can be investigated in a straightforward manner. As Yogi Berra noted, "You can observe a lot just by watching."

Ninth, the effort to develop public management as a field of knowledge should start from problems faced by practicing public managers. The preferences of professors for theorizing reflects deep-seated incentives of the academy that can be overcome only by careful institutional design.

In the light of these lessons, I believe one strategy for the development of public management should include:

Developing a significant number of cases on public management problems and practices. Cases should describe typical problems faced by public managers. Cases should attend not only to top-level managers but to middle and lower-level managers. The dearth of cases at this level makes this a high priority for development. Cases should examine both general functions of management and specific organizational tasks, for example hiring and firing. Public management cases should concentrate on the job of the manager running his or her unit.

Analyzing cases to identify better and worse practice. Scientists search for "critical experiments." Students of public management should seek to identify "critical experiences" that new public managers could live through vicariously and learn from. Because of the availability of information, academics tend to focus on failures, but teaching people what not to do is not necessarily the best way to help them learn to be doers. By analyzing relative successes, it will be possible to extract rules of thumb, crutches, and concepts, for example Chase's "law": wherever the product of a public organization has not been monitored in a way that ties performance to reward, the introduction of an effective monitoring system will yield a 50 percent improvement in that product in the short run. GAO's handbooks on evaluation techniques and summaries suggest what can be done.

Promoting systematic comparative research: management positions in a single agency over time; similar management positions among several public agencies; public management levels within a single agency; similar management functions—for example, budgeting or management information systems among agencies; managers across public and private organizations, and even crossnationally. The data for this comparative research would be produced by the case development effort and would complement the large-scale development of cases on private management that is ongoing.

Linking to the training of public managers. Intellectual development of the field of public management should be tightly linked to the training of public managers, including individuals already in positions of significant responsibility. Successful practice will appear in government, not in the university. University-based documentation of better and worse practice, and refinement of that practice, should start from problems of managers on the line. The intellectual effort required to develop the field of public management and the resources required to support this level of effort are most likely to be assembled if research and training are vitally linked.

The strategy outlined here is certainly not the only strategy for research in public management. Given the needs for effective public management, I believe that a major research effort should be mounted and that it should pursue a number of complementary strategies. Given where we start, I see no danger of overattention to, or overinvestment in, the effort required in the immediate future. But I believe that this constitutes one viable strategy for building a capacity for *organized learning* about what effective public managers know and do.

NOTES

1. This paper is, in effect, a revised draft of a paper delivered at the Public Management Research Conference, 19–20 November 1979, in Washington, D.C., cosponsored by the General Accounting Office, the General Services Administration, the Office of Management and the Budget, and the Office of Personnel Management. I am indebted to several colleagues at Harvard involved in an ongoing discussion about the development of the field of public management, especially Joseph Bower, Hale Champion, Gordon Chase, Charles Christenson, Richard Darman, John Dunlop, Philip Heymann, Laurence Lynn, Mark Moore, Richard Neustadt, Roger Porter, and Don Price. The author also wishes to acknowledge the assistance of Paul Zigman.

2. Correspondence from John Gardner to Joseph Slater, 23 March 1978.

3. The management of educational institutions tends to be more closely related to public management than to private management. The university or college president finds himself or herself responsible to a complex array of power and influence, from a board of trustees or a state legislature to increasingly active and aware students. According to Donald Walker, this interplay of competing forces is best perceived and managed as a political institution: ". . . the most effective administrators perceive the university as operating, to a considerable degree, like a political, democratic community." In the discussion which follows, educational management will therefore be assumed to be a natural ally of public management, even though there will always be cases in which this shoe does not fit. See Donald E. Walker, *The Effective Administrator* (Jossey-Bass, 1979).

4. See, for example, "A Businessman in a Political Jungle," *Fortune* (9 April 1964); "Candid Reflections of a Businessman in Washington," *Fortune* (29 January 1979); "A Politician-Turned-Executive," *Fortune* (10 September 1979); and "The Abrasive Interface," *Harvard Business Review* (November-December, 1979).

5. A fourth and equally interesting list specifically contrasting schools, as one type of public organization, with private organizations is presented in Thomas J. Sergiovanni and Fred D. Carver, *The New School Executive*, 2nd. ed. (Harper & Row, 1980), p. 69.

6. *The Federalist Papers*, No. 51. The word "department" has been changed to "branch," which was its meaning in the original papers.

7. These examples are taken from Bruce Scott, "American Motors Corporation" (Intercollegiate Case Clearing House #9-364-001); Charles B. Weigle with the collaboration of C. Roland Christensen, "American Motors Corporation II" (Intercollegiate Case Clearing House #6-372-350); Thomas R. Hitchner and Jacob Lew under the supervision of Philip B. Heymann and Stephen B. Hitchner, "Douglas Costle and the EPA (A)" (Kennedy School of Government Case #C94-78-216); and Jacob Lew and Stephen B. Hitchner, "Douglas Costle and the EPA (B)" (Kennedy School of Government Case #C96-78-217). For an earlier exploration of a similar comparison, see Joseph Bower, "Effective Public Management," *Harvard Business Review* (March-April, 1977).

8. The cases developed by Boston University's public management program offer a promising start in this direction.

9. At the dedication of the school of government's new home, President Bok put his argument succinctly: "These truths I do believe to be self-evident: our government has assumed a critical role in the resolution of virtually every significant problem facing our society today. The problems that public leaders confront in discharging these responsibilities are among the most difficult and intricate of any issues that any leadership group is called upon to face in this society. The agencies that government leaders must administer to carry out the nation's policies are among the largest and most unwieldy of any organizations known to man. And yet, despite the difficulty of the issues our leadership face, despite the difficulty of managing our public institutions, we have had no tradition of serious, careful preparation for positions of public leadership comparable to the preparation provided for those entering our great private professions. That is the principal missing link in American higher education today. And supplying that vital link represents the special contribution that Harvard's School of Government can make to improve the quality of government and build those bridges between the world of affairs and the world of knowledge that President Kennedy spoke of so often."

REFERENCES

Allison, Graham, and Peter Szanton (1976). *Remaking Foreign Policy*. New York: Basic Books.

Andrews, Kenneth R. (1971). *The Concept of Corporate Strategy*. New York: Dow Jones-Irwin.

Blumenthal, Michael (1979). "Candid Reflection of a Businessman in Washington." *Fortune*, 99(2), 36-49.

Burns, James MacGregor (1978). *Leadership*. New York: Harper & Row.

Chandler, Alfred (1977). *The Visible Hand: The Managerial Revolution in America*. Cambridge, Mass.: Belnap Press.

Drucker, Peter (1974). *Management: Tasks, Responsibilities, Practices.* New York: Harper & Row.

Dunlop, John T. (1979). "Public Management." Unpublished paper.

Gulick, Luther, and Al Urwick, eds. (1937). *Papers in the Science of Public Administration.* New York: Institute of Public Administration.

Lynn, Lawrence E., Jr. (1981). *Managing the Public's Business.* New York: Basic Books.

Machiavelli, Niccolo (1950). *The Prince.* Modern College Library Edition. New York: Random House.

Miles, Ryfus (1967). "The Search for Identify of Graduate Schools of Public Affairs." *Public Administration Review,* 27(4), 343-56.

Neustadt, Richard E. (1979). "American Presidents and Corporate Executives." Panel on presidential management of the National Academy of Public Administration, Washington, D.C.

Pareto, Vilfredo (1935). *Mind and Society.* Arthur Livingston, ed. New York: Harcourt Brace.

Rainey, Hal G., Robert W. Backoff, and Charles N. Levine (1976). "Comparing Public and Private Organizations." *Public Administration Review,* 36(2), 233-44.

Rumsfeld, Donald (1979). "A Politician-Turned-Executive." *Fortune,* 100(5), 88-94.

Safire, William (1978). *Safire's Political Dictionary.* New York: Random House.

Seldes, George (1966). *The Great Quotations.* London: Lyle Stuart.

Selznick, Philip (1957). *Leadership in Administration.* New York: Harper & Row.

Shultz, George (1979). "The Abrasive Interface." *Harvard Business Review,* 57(6), 93-97.

U.S. Government Manual (1978-1979). *Environmental Protection Agency.* Washington, D.C.: Superintendent of Public Documents.

CHAPTER 13

Toward a Critical Theory
of Educational Administration

William P. Foster

There is a certain arrogance which underlies the appropriation of the term Critical Theory, for this is a historically situated project of the most complex scope and ambition. Associated with the members of the Frankfurt school, Critical Theory took as its subjects the positivism of philosophy and science, the rethinking of Marxian constructs, and the exposure of systems of political, economic, and legal domination. Critical Theory, however, was always concerned with the nature of practice informed by theory, and it is this that encourages us to begin the consideration of a critical theory which may serve in the examination of such a practical field as the administration of schooling. This critical theory indeed receives its inspiration and method from the rigorous formulations of Critical Theory, yet really only represents an attempt to inject critique into the spirit of psychologism which dominates American administrative thinking. That said, the background of Critical Theory requires some explanation.

The origins of Critical Theory lie in the continuation of Hegelian and Marxian dialectical thought and in its application to the political and economic organization of capitalistic society. The nature of Critical Theory is such that its concern lies with the critique of modern rationality which underlies both scientific and industrial projects which subjugate the individuality of the person. As Bernstein says, "Critical theory aspires to bring the subjects themselves to full self-consciousness of the contradictions implicit in their material existence, to penetrate the ideological mystifications and forms of false consciousness that distort the meaning of existing social conditions" (1976, 182).

This chapter is based on a paper presented at the annual meeting of the American Educational Research Association, New York, March 1982.

In the first part of this paper, I would like to expand on these "aspirations" of Critical Theory by examining its commentary on a) instrumental rationality and scientific and philosophical positivism, and b) the relationship between theory and practice. A detailed analysis of the foundations of Critical Theory (as the various ideas — both complementary and contradictory — are developed by Horkheimer, Adorno, Marcuse, and other members of the Frankfurt School) is beyond the scope of this paper; the interested reader is referred to Bernstein (1976), Held (1980), Schroyer (1973), McCarthy (1978), Jay (1973), and Arato and Gebhardt (1978).

Positivism and Rationality

According to Sewart (1980, 324), "The leitmotif of the work of the Frankfurt School as a whole can be characterized as a critique of positivism." For Horkheimer and Adorno, positivism was evident when philosophy agreed in some of the following:

All (synthetic) knowledge is founded in sensory experience. Meaning is grounded in observation. Concepts and generalizations only represent the particulars from which they have been abstracted. Conceptual entities don't exist in themselves — they are mere names; positivism is (normally) associated with nominalism.
Sciences are unified according to the methodology of the natural sciences. The ideal pursued is knowledge "in the form of a mathematically formulated universal science deducible from the smallest possible number of axioms, a system which assures the calculation of the probable occurrence of all events."
Values are not facts and hence values cannot be given as such in sense-experience. Since all knowledge is based on sensory experience, value judgments cannot be accorded the status of knowledge claims [Held 1980, 163–64, quoting in part Horkheimer 1972, 138].

The claim against the positivist attitude is that it is essentially a conservative one which, by removing reflective and dialectical thought from the province of meaningful expression, allows the perpetuation of the extant social order. Human rationality becomes only mathematical reason; the calculation of the instruments needed to achieve ends which are preordained by the nature of the productive system. Thus, a false objectivism results, harmless perhaps when it is limited to the individual communities of natural scientists but "dangerous when it is extended to all the areas of the various sciences, and is no longer acknowledged as a fiction" (Wellmer 1974, 14). Social processes themselves are objectified and the roles of various groups in the community, including the role of domination, are seen as a natural historical development.

In this way, the scientific control over nature is extended to people-as-part-of-nature. Having become a "fact" in the arsenal of scientific discourse, the possibility of value-laden discussion over the meaningfulness of ends is removed from the performance of science itself; yet science has become an irresistible force in the shaping of human history.

The foundation of this positivistic approach to the world lay in the transformation of the concept of reason. A critique of the primacy of instrumental reason was to become a major project of members of the Frankfurt School. Horkheimer, in particular, devoted considerable attention to what he termed the "eclipse of reason" in the modern world and the attendant emphasis on a positivistic social science. Horkheimer distinguished between what he termed "subjective" reason and "objective" reason. Subjective reason is that which inheres in the subject and is oriented toward the discovery of the most "reasonable" means to achieve essentially established ends. Objective reason, however, may be thought of as theology without gods: it refers to the practical search for ends which are true and right. Objective reason ". . . aimed at evolving a comprehensive system, or hierarchy, of all beings, including man and his aims. The degree of reasonableness of a man's life could be determined according to its harmony with this totality. Its objective structure, and not just man and his purposes, was to be the measuring rod for individual thoughts and actions" (Horkheimer 1974, 4).

Subjective reason was incorporated as part of this grand design, but remained subordinate to the dialogue in the just state. With the coming of the age of Enlightenment and the destruction of religio-mythical beliefs, subjective reason became the dominant force in social relations. While lip service was paid to the traditional ideals, in reality there was no agency which could relate these ideals to objective social conditions (Horkheimer 1974, 23). Science, with no concern for the ideal, became the new religion: "According to the philosophy of the average modern intellectual, there is only one authority, namely, science, conceived as the classification of facts and the calculation of probabilities. The statement that justice and freedom are better in themselves than injustice and oppression is scientifically unverifiable and useless. It has come to sound as meaningless in itself as would the statement that red is more beautiful than blue, or that an egg is better than milk" (Horkheimer 1974, 24).

This concern with logic of the social sciences is continued in the work of Habermas (1970a, 1970b, 1971, 1974, 1975, 1979) who, beginning with a critique of positivism gradually turned toward, I think it could be claimed, a more positive approach to Critical Theory. Habermas engages in his own critique of subjective, or, as he terms it, instrumental and strategic, rationality by distinguishing, first, between two types of human activity: symbolic and communicative, and purposive-rational (1970a, 93). Traditionally, he claims, purposive or goal-seeking rationality was, as Horkheimer implied, imbedded within an institutional or communicative framework of social action. Given changing social structures, however, purposive-rational action separated from its context. "The threshold of the modern period would then be characterized by that process of rationalization which commenced with loss of the 'superiority' of the institutional framework to the sub-systems of purposive-rational action. Traditional legitimations could now be criticized against the standards of rationality of means-ends relations" (Habermas 1970a, 114).

Purposive-rationality served the needs of one of what Habermas defines as three basic cognitive "interests" (1971), the technical, the practical and the emancipatory, and "each of these cognitive interests is grounded in one dimension of human social existence: work, interaction, or power" (Bernstein 1976, 193). The technical interest is reflected in empirical science — the desire to exert control. The practical interest, however, reflects the need to establish senses of community, shared communication, and intersubjective understanding while the emancipatory interest looks to the identification of the ideal human situation. In a sense, the emancipatory interest remains imbedded within the other two: it serves to provide purpose for the development of law-like statements within the context of open institutions.

Against the position that social science can only be concerned with technical interests, Habermas has begun the reconstruction of Critical Theory, adding to its negative thrust a positive dimension. Thus, in discussing the modern-day rationality problem (a central focus for current philosophers, Bernstein 1976, 208), Habermas provides for the development of a "critical" science which can serve the needs of our emancipatory interest and which goes beyond pure formalism. Sewart finds that for Habermas "a critical theory of society must not only be capable of identifying coercive power relations hidden in cultural meanings (as the critique of ideology), it must also provide for the dissolution of such relations in the very process of interpretation. In this way a critical theory of society must address coercion and unequal social relations with an eye to providing for emancipation from these relations" (1980, 339).

A critical theory, then, not only identifies ideological relationships, such as the application of an instrumental rationality to social intercourse for the purpose of industrial advancement, but attempts to cross the gap between theory and practice, indeed identifying this dichotomy, like the fact-value one, as essentially a false categorization. A social or political science which claims as its foundation the development of knowledge isolated from practice (discovering, for example, the "facts" without regard to the "values") is in the position of allowing itself to be used by dominant interest groups, regardless of the other significant questions of self-delusion. Theory, as developed by such a science, and practice, as reflected in the critique and development of social forms, are intimately related. Thus, as McCarthy (1978) discusses, the value-neutrality of positivism was able to expose the pseudoscientific character of world views which legitimated certain political systems; yet this scientific neutrality was itself ideological and allowed only the application of instrumental reason to human projects. The ultimate result of this application of instrumental reason to human affairs is that public discourse on political agendas is nullified; either "decisionistic" or "technocratic" models come to replace rational discussion of developmental ends. The decisionistic model is that wherein the political action and consciousness of the public at large is limited to voting in or out of office certain politically elite groups without the possibility of discoursing on the aims of the society. The technocratic model is one where political discourse is eliminated in favor of rational administration; that is, the procedural development of administrative systems which steer the social system in order to provide optimum economic growth and stable administration. In general, the technocratic model has become the dominant driving force behind systemic decisions: "the objective necessity disclosed by experts seems to predominate over the decisions of leaders" (McCarthy 1978, 9). At their heart, though, the positivistic models are incapable of dealing with the practical problems of human existence. Habermas says:

> But such a rational administration of the world is not simply identical with the solution of the practical problems posed by history. There is no reason for assuming that a continuum of rationality exists extending from the capacity for technical control over objectified processes to the practical mastery of historical processes. The root of the irrationality of history is that we "make" it without, however, having been able until now to make it consciously. A rationalization of history cannot therefore be furthered by an extended power of control on the part of manipulative human beings, but only by a higher stage of reflection, a consciousness of acting human beings moving forward in the direction of emancipation [quoted in McCarthy, 1978, 11].

The forward thrust, then, of Habermas's argument lies in the possibility of movement toward emancipatory relations, economic and social. The ideal situation which would result would be when a society permits and endorses the reality of truly rational discourse and, accordingly, one function of Critical Theory becomes both exposing the conditions preventing such discourse and outlining the conditions underlying the possibility of such discourse. This is where, as McCarthy and others have noted, the argument takes a "linguistic turn" with distinctly Freudian overtones. Simply stated, one might claim that the aim here is the reembedding of systems of purposive-rational action within systems of communicative interaction. This project would require the application of empirical, hermeneutic, and critical approaches to social analysis. Some dimensions of the problems of distorted communication will be discussed in a later section.

The Empirico-Hermeneutic Tension

In part, Critical Theory can be seen as an analytical and reflective process which stands adjacent to the search for 1) empirical verification of the reality of the world and 2) understanding of meaning-systems. In this sense, a critical theory must rely on objective and subjective knowledge and on both technical and practical interests. The relationship between these areas is well illustrated by Apel's (1967) analysis of the possibility of a unified science based on the identification of "true" sentences of science. The British school of philosophical positivism was to claim that "any knowledge obtained in the Geisteswissenschaften [cultural/understanding science] must be translatable into sentences of the one, intersubjective language of science, i.e. into the objective language about things and facts" (Apel 1967, 5). What Apel is able to do is to show that such an "objective" language is premised on some assumptions which destroy it, notably that such sentences must be "understood," and such an understanding implies a preunderstanding of concepts embodied in a community, even a community of scientists. However, "objective explanation of facts and intersubjective communication about what is to be explained are . . . complementary aspects of human knowledge—in the sense in which N. Bohr used the word" (Apel 1967, 23). He goes on to say, "They exclude each other and they presuppose each other. Nobody can just 'understand' without presupposing factual knowledge which could be stated explicitly as 'explanations.' On the other hand, no natural scientist can explain anything without participating in the intersubjective communication . . ." (1967, 23). The complementarity of subject and object is a principle reflecting the dialectical relationship between symbol and technique. The objective methods of the natural sciences, the hermeneutic methods of the cultural sciences, and the reflective methods of the critical sciences must stand in a close and compelling relationship.

While Habermas's presentation of the three cognitive interests shows the basic orientations of the human program, Bernstein suggests that the *categorical distinctiveness* of these areas is suspect: "It is a fiction—and not a useful methodological one—to suggest that there are categorically different types of inquiry and knowledge. But it is not a fiction—rather, it is the locus of the most important controversies about the nature and limits of human knowledge, as it pertains to social and political inquiry—to see how the battle of competing technical, practical, and emancipa-

tory cognitive interests continues to rage" (1976, 223). Apel is able to show
the relationship between the technical and practical interests, and, while
neglecting an orientation to critique, allows for the possibility of emancipatory development. A final quotation is illustrative of his thinking:

> Statistical methods, for example, are not the beginning of a statisti-
> cal science of man as a whole, but they are serving objective theories
> of motivation; the latter are, again, not the beginning of a causally-
> explaining science of human behavior, but they serve — as, for exam-
> ple, in psychoanalysis and the critique of ideologies — the ever new
> attempts to understand men better than they understand them-
> selves. These attempts to let "objectification" serve "disobjectifica-
> tion," i.e. that condition in which man is freed by knowledge to act
> responsibly, have to be judged according to whether the "objects" of
> the theory can become "subjects" who can incorporate that theory
> into their own language and self-understanding [1967, 57].

A model of the relationships would therefore look like the interpene-
tration of three circles, each one informing the other:

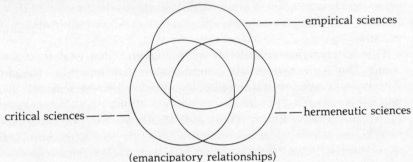

(emancipatory relationships)

The interrelationships of these three human interests are thus oriented toward discovering the possibilities of increasing personal and interpersonal freedom; toward avoiding an institutional dominance so severe
that it perverts rationality in the name of rationality.

. . . To Practice

Educational theorists tend to fall into one of three camps: first, those
who see in the development of an educational science the promise of a
positive utopia which, in adhering to the "end of ideology" thesis, sees the
completely rational potential of institutions; secondly, those who recognize the oppressive potential of institutions and can only see "negative
utopia"; thirdly, those who see no utopias at all but hope that systemic
changes may attenuate some of the ills. Into the first camp go those
whose belief in rational systems management, in management through
clarification, in precision and performance, and in the high technology of

control mechanisms ordains a future where control of systems is complete and the possibility of unforseen problems remote. Into the second camp go those whose vocabulary is limited to oppression, who see the demise of the state as imminent, and who attack not only scientism but also science. And into the third camp go those who can see the potential for reflective critique in exposing instances of real domination, who may argue against the contradictions of the system but yet may see factors of liberation in the system.

In other words, one need not be a certified Marxist to profit from much of what Marx and Marxians say; one need not abandon faith in a constitutional system of government in order to discuss the "evils of the class system"; and one need not have to call for a return to charismatic or patriarchical organizational structures in order to point out the limitations and dominations of bureaucracy.

Educational administrators can, in the same fashion, profit from a disciplined critique of their own institutions if they can portray the institution's role in affecting the lives of its charges; if, indeed, they can look somewhat beyond the instrumental obligations to the structure of the institution itself as a meaningful event which creates a certain reality for its membership.

There is one major objection to our thesis here which needs to be overcome. This is the charge that administration is a "practical" discipline with its own techniques and methodology and that engaging in critical theorizing and reflection is, ipso facto, not "doing administration" but rather "doing sociology" or "doing philosophy" or whatever other discipline comes to mind. There is indeed support for this charge, principally from Winch's (1958) Wittgensteinian notion of "games" which actors engage in and which, in fact, one needs to participate in before one can understand. Can one, for example, understand the "game" of educational administration without in fact being in, participating in, living in the field of educational administration? This is to say that the field — as a "practice" or way of life — lives by its own rules which define and limit the identifiability of the field, for if there were not these rules telling us what educational administration *is*, how could we then recognize it? Further, that recognition allows us to say that *this* field is not sociology, nor philosophy.

This objection can be countered through one of several related ways. In the first place, as Apel (1967) shows, Winch engages in a type of cultural relativism which denies the influence and interplay between many "games," if we retain that terminology. Now while it is true that we may know about administration without knowing how to actually administer, it is also true that the knowing *about* influences and interacts with the knowing *how*. Should we subscribe to the distinct and categorical separation of fields of knowledge, then we have essentially divorced theory from practice (*"praxis"*), a state of affairs which leads to the perpetuation of that which is.

A second point that can be made is that educational administration is a *sub*discipline, i.e., it calls to other fields for much of its major intellectual direction. Boyan has noted that there are three "central and salient conditions" that characterize contemporary administrative studies: "First, internal specialization has increasingly characterized inquiry. Second, the requirements do not exist for emergence of a new, single, synthesizing paradigm to guide research across the entire territory or even within any of the several major specializations. Third, improvement in the states of the several arts has moved unevenly and modestly" (1981, 12). The implication that can be drawn is that the practice of administration requires the integration of those ideas and concepts which, at another level, function as specializations, e.g., school finance, policy development, and organizational control. In practice, "doing administration" is often doing those things prescribed by the encompassing parent disciplines.

A third point is related to the above. Administration, as Weber shows us, "means fundamentally domination through knowledge" (1968, 225). The specialized functions of administration require, except in the simplest circumstances, the accumulation of staff and the distribution of authority, and lead to control through the exercise of knowledge to which all are not privy (Bendix 1966). But the power of knowledge is not limited to the functional demands of the situation; it extends to areas of interpersonal relations, leadership structures, and even personality. The knowledge of structure, again, is not categorical for administration though, of course, it could be analyzed as such.

Finally, limitations on the study of administration to the study of technical formulations ignore the life-role that administrators choose for themselves and dispute the reality that administrators integrate intellectual and socioemotional demands into their job performance. Administrators can be, and often are, politically conscious and sociologically aware, and both of these conditions are part of "doing administration."

The Empirical Arguments

Efforts to describe and understand the nature of organization and administration must reflect evidence of (1) the regular and orderly universe of structural relations and of (2) the moral universe of meaningful relations. In this sense we, on the one hand, look at the bureaucratic or the structural/functional or the coupling aspects of the school organization and of its participants, and on the other hand at the interpretation of subjective meaning and the social construction of shared realities. However, a comprehensive theory of educational administration (or theories), if it is to pursue a critical dimension, must look beyond the description and understanding of the present reality; it must engage in a self-reflective posture regarding the consequences of theory itself. But it does a disservice to critical theory to suggest that such reflection must remain limited to subjectivistic impressions: empirical verification is required; data are necessary.

If we can generally define "administration" as a set of practices concerned with the control, direction, and development of the institution, and administrative theory as the abstract classification and clarification of concepts related to this, then it would appear appropriate for both theory and practice to be concerned about data or interpretations which show that schooling, for many, is indeed an imperfect institution.

This is to say that a critical theory of educational administration must be grounded in an analysis of empirical regularities: what do educational organizations do *for* and *to* their membership? The development of administrative theory, rather than concentrating on its internal logic (i.e., its functions of planning, controlling, leadership, and so on) should also begin an analysis of itself as a method of legal domination (Weber 1968) with internal — classroom — and external — social structure — effects.

This orientation has historically largely been ignored in the field. Curti shared a general concern over education in 1935 and has yet to be fully answered: "Most educators advanced their arguments for increased public support and control of the schools, for certain types of instruction, for particular studies in the curriculum, and for given schemes of administration, without clearly defining or understanding how their proposed educational policies were to affect our social institutions" (1935, 581). Callahan's disturbing indictment of well-meaning educators who became "bookkeepers and public relations men" (1962, 259) is well known and need not be described here. Tyack (1974) and Tyack and Cummings (1977) continue in this vein, offering an interpretative classification of "administrative progressives" and the increasing urbanization and often estrangement of public schools, schools which "have rarely taught the children of the poor effectively — and this failure has been systematic, not idiosyncratic" (1974, 11).

More recently, of course, mainstream traditions of organizational theory and practice have been called into question not only by a circle of new-methodological scholars but also by mainstream theoreticians themselves, often in a rueful expression of disenchantment. Erickson writes that "a major reconsideration of what research on educational organization is, or *should* be, all about" is due (1979, 12). The underscored "should" reflects the dissatisfaction so many of the scholars have with the simple platitudes about the solely descriptive nature of educational research and theory. Griffiths, certainly a mover and shaper of the field, suggests that ". . . if educational administration is not in a state of intellectual turmoil, it should be . . ." (1979, 43).

Griffiths sees organizational theory as the parent of administrative theory; I would add that while the parent is analytic, the child must also be integrative. A useful theory of educational administration, if such could be found, would serve to integrate research on the relationship between internal school and classroom events and external social structure with a critical and dialectical appreciation of how one affects the other. By the internal characteristics, I think administration and organizational theory must begin to consider such items as how the level of decision-making affects quantity of time used for instruction (Harnischfeger & Wiley 1976); the relationship between a "strong" principal and "effective" teachers and their positive evaluation of the principalship (Rayder, Abrams, and Larson, 1978); the role and task orientation of the principalship (Mintzberg 1973; Sproul 1981) and the internal characteristics of classroom structure. Research into these areas has proceeded, yet it fails on the one hand to develop the particular value orientations inherent to the study of a subject such as this (e.g., definitions of "effective" and/or "good" teaching and administration) and, on the other hand, to specify clearly the effect of administration particularly.

However, while research into the internal characteristics is necessary, it is by no means sufficient. The quality and characteristics of the social/class structure of the society must also be considered when attempting to interpret the effects of education on pupils. To what degree does this intervening variable of status affect pupils' success in school, and if it does, then should we attempt to change the pupil or the social structure? Again, a critical theory of administration will also be concerned with the "incidental learnings" (Goldhammer 1969) that even so-called effective and traditional structures produce: Is there a dialectic between achievement and obedience and should a democratic society allow one in order to support the other?

In this regard, educational administration might well echo Ogbu's directive to an ethnography of education: ". . . an adequate ethnography of schooling cannot be confined to studying events in school, classrooms, the home, or playground. One must also study relevant societal and historical forces" (1981, 15). One need not completely accept the assertion that those forces compel a complete "correspondence between the social organization of schooling and that of work" (Bowles and Gintis 1977, 151) to be concerned about the often subtle ways that schooling may duplicate external social structure. Concurrently, administrative theorists must also wonder whether the nature of administration in schooling as it is presently constituted makes any difference at all to pupils' later occupation. Shea contends "that not everyone can go to college is one matter; that who does go to college is determined during the *initial stages of the life cycle* is another. Available research suggests early selection points for later attainments [emphasis added]" (1976, 514). Surely a finding such as this, given its accuracy, would compel administrative theorists to begin a rethinking of the nature and effects of their discipline.

The Administrative Response

Despite the many years of concern shown by educational philosophers over the nexus of school and society, the administrative response has largely and —perhaps—until recently been to develop a form of psychologism whose usefulness to practice is limited. It seems strange indeed that in a field whose concern lies primarily with the interrelationship of groups, the major sources of development concern themselves with theories of individualistic improvement. The mainstream approach to administrative theory is one which tends to concentrate on how the administrator can assure a successful psychological "fit" between institution and individual; thus, most preparation material tends to emphasize such concepts as "role," taken as "bundles of interpersonal definitions, rights and responsibilities" (Anderson 1974, 32); "motivation," taken as "motivation of subordinates and associates" (Owens 1981, 106); "leadership," taken as "an interactive process between the leader and the group," (Owens 1981, 146); "climate," taken "roughly as the personality of the school," (Hoy and Miskel 1982, 186); and "communication," whose key issue is taken as "whether administrators communicate effectively or poorly" (Hoy and Miskel 1982, 293). Perhaps the orientation to "Eupsychian Management" (Sergiovanni and Carver 1980, 50) as a model for the field best exemplifies the strong social psychological bias of the discipline.

It need not be disputed that these are indeed important topics for administrators; from a critical perspective, however, one must wonder whether these concepts become devices which tend to disguise under an ideology of change and progress the basic features of structural domination. Benson for example, claims that "even [organizational] studies which claim purely objective, scientific interests tend to pose research questions from an essentially technical-administrative point of view. The interest implicit in the research questions is typically one of administrative control" (1977, 6). Such control can lead to the institutional repression of personal freedoms or, to be discussed, to the distortion of communicative acts, and it is with this that our concern lies.

One's "role" in the institution can be examined, for example, from several perspectives: the most common is to consider how the idiographic dimensions must be accommodated to the nomothetic. But another perspective could ask why is it that many of the nomothetic characteristics of certain authority-centered roles require individuals who share idio-graphic likenesses? More eloquently, certainly, Griffiths gets to part of the issue here when he states that "one wonders why more attention has not been paid to the disregard for the plight of women and minorities by organizational theorists . . ." (1979, 46). Another aspect concerns the disbursement of organizationally specific knowledge to certain roles and prompts one to ask why and in what fashion. The role of "principal," for example, allows one to speak of certain things forbidden to the role of "teacher," particularly insofar as the teaching role is often circumscribed in such a way as to make it difficult for a teacher to provide an organiza-tionally approved critique of administration. It can be done, of course, but it takes either courage or foolhardiness.

The orientation to the issues of motivation, leadership, climate, and communication often takes the form of a set of technical procedures de-signed to initiate the recalcitrant member into the organizational view-point. An institutional leader is advised to jump between task and relation-ship depending on the needs of the situation, i.e., of the organization. The reliance on sociopsychological indicators of human performance, without a concommitant consideration of the ethical issue of manipulation possible to organizational leaders, is in itself disturbing.

The same concern presents itself when addressing motivational strate-gies. A cynic might consider this body of research to be one concerning how to get individuals to come to work in environments devoid of per-sonal authority and personal pleasure. While we are not cynics, the uses of the research are such that they seem to be a means of increasing indi-vidual employee satisfaction without allowing for actual employee in-volvement and dialogue on the nature of work: its alienating effects, its satisfying effects, and its distribution of rewards. As long as the literature here concentrates on providing sets of techniques to allow administrators to increase employee morale, without allowing for the critical evaluation of the nature of the institution itself, it will remain inadequate for the purposes of a critical theory.

In the areas of climate and communication the emphasis again lies on creating improvement which ultimately is to the benefit of the estab-lished structure of the institution. The theories neglect to mention the possibility of happy slavery, of people working together under condi-tions that they can't recognize as oppressive. This analogy is farfetched, yet makes the point that developing psychological mechanisms to allevi-ate the tensions of life in school is no substitute for consideration of the sociological defects of the institution. In the same way, one can have pre-cise and effective communication strategies which gloss over the content and intent of what is communicated. Distorted communication, in the sense that Mueller (1973) discusses this term, can yet be effective and efficient.

I see no reason why administrative theory in education cannot adopt a perspective consistent with the critical evaluation of empirical research for the purpose of developing administrators as concerned about the effects of school structure as about developing psychological states of mind conducive to institutionalism. Yet we tend to feel that if we admit the importance of critique we are in effect cutting our own throats. This attitude is changing, particularly with respect to developments in organizational theory. Perrow (1979), for example, is an organizational theorist in the mainstream tradition, yet one who can adequately and succinctly dissect that body of literature with a view toward its conceptual clarity. His analysis of some of the literature in leadership research is classic. How disappointing, then, it is to read an educational writer comment that ". . . work such as that of Perrow (a sociologist) probably reflects academic chutzpah as much as genuine theoretic or conceptual analysis . . . in that it essentially is an attack on the mainstream of contemporary organizational theory (which largely has become the province of social psychologists). Views such as Perrow expresses cannot be taken seriously until they are documented by empirical evidence derived from vigorous and rigorously designed research" (Owens 1981, 221). Ignoring the uncritical acceptance of what constitutes "empirical research," one is still tempted to ask 1) how such rigorous research will be done on a question not "taken seriously" and 2) whether an "attack on the mainstream" is *always* devoid of "theoretic and conceptual analysis"? Administrative theorists have an unfortunate tendency to turn theory into theology.

The last few years have developed "alternatives" to mainstream theory, principally the Marxist and the phenomenological approaches, sometimes combined into a term such as "ethno-Marxism." Although I am not currently aware of any strictly "Marxist" theories of educational administration (and I wonder indeed if this is at all possible), the Marxist tradition is certainly alive in organizational theory. Heydebrand is one who seeks to develop "a dialectical-historical conception [of organizations] based on a critical adaptation of basic Marxian categories and propositions" (1977, 103). Consequently, the intellectual framework adopted depends to a large degree on the interpretation of organizational activity in terms of "social relations or production," "alienation," and "contradictions" inherent in the structure of the capitalistic system.

The phenomenological approach is exemplified by the work of Greenfield who argues that "the basic problem in the study of organizations is that of understanding human intention and meaning" (1980, 26). The reality of organizations is subjective reality: "simply manifestations of mind and will" (1980, 27). This conceptualization of organizations has obvious implications for administrative development and traditional approaches to the methical analysis of organizations. By looking at organizations as subjectively created phenomena, attention is focused on how members create moral universes which have as a characteristic unequal power relations. The role of the administrator becomes one of recognizing the existential quality of such relations and, mindful of their Promethean struggle, to simply do what they can.

Benson has perhaps made the boldest attempt to reconcile these approaches by formulating multidimensional indicia. A competent organizational theory, he claims, ". . . must deal with (1) social production of organizational reality . . . (2) the political bases of organizational reality . . . (3) the connection of organizations to the larger set of structural arrangements in the society; and (4) the continuously emergent character of organizational patterns" (1977, 16). At the same time, Benson is critical of the normal approach to the study of organizations, the "rational, goal-seeking" model which assumes the organization to be bounded in space and time. By examining organizations as social constructions, yet still maintaining an analysis of structural and power elements, Benson identifies a program for research substantially different from the structural/functional model. Still, Benson doesn't develop so much a theory of organization as much as a justified critique of contemporary theory.

These newer approaches to organizational theorizing are both significant and helpful. However, they, too, are not completely adequate for the task. In the Marxist approach, for example, organizations tend to be seen as reified "actors" that maintain a direct relationship to modes of economic structuration. Little attention is paid to different kinds of organizations or to their possible emancipatory potential. The phenomenological perspective, in turn, suffers from its neglect of structural considerations with a consequent over-reliance on a transubjective idealism which cannot find a concrete location.

An integrated perspective seems to offer the most theoretically comprehensive account of organizational life. It would be one which incorporates "phenomenological perspectives, which typically focus at the micro level upon the intersubjective construction of meanings — traditional, ahistorical organizational analyses of structural regularities — and broader sociohistorical perspectives of economy and culture" (Ranson, Hinings, and Greenwood, 1980, 14). Yet if this integrated approach to organizational study is to be of any consequence to educational administration, it must add a critical dimension.

Toward a Critical Theory of Administration

A critical theory of administration should accept and build upon both the hermeneutic and the empirical viewpoints, utilizing analyses of phenomenological interactions, of structural regularities, and of social meaning and historical context. Critical theory should also maintain its concern for exposing the practical impediments to unifying theory and practice. One overarching framework for researching the critical relationship between administration and social structure, for the purpose of improving the educational impact of schooling, might lie in identifying and analyzing the most basic element which allows for the development of organizations and institutions, that of the human capacity for speech. The conception that educational institutions can be thought of as *speech communities* allows the incorporation of hermeneutic, structural, and critical elements. The phenomenological approach can be incorporated insofar as it allows one to investigate how meaning about the organization is intersubjectively communicated and created; the structural approach is necessary because it allows investigation of the "grammar" of the institution, or the structural features that hold the meaningful system together; the critical dimension is necessary because it asks in what ways does the institutional structure contribute to the distortion of communication between individuals.

Held (1980, 257) suggests that contemporary critical theory, particularly in Habermas's work, has moved from a critique of "capital," or political economy, to a critique of distorted communication. The conditions for total emancipatory relations, that is, must include the ability to engage in uncoerced, rational discourse; this, in turn, is to presuppose an "ideal speech situation" (Habermas 1979, 1970b). Ideal speech, in turn, is said to be based on norms of truth, freedom, and justice; these "underlie" the conditions for engaging in understandable and truth-presumptive dialogue.

If a purpose of critical theory is to expose "coercion and unequal social relations" (Seward 1980, 339) as they occur in respect to social institutions, then it is profitable to consider the relationship between given speech communities and the distribution of knowledge and power to those communities. This in turn would allow for the critical reflection by administrators on the methodology of removing distortions which either contribute to the external suppression of interest groups or the internal acceptance of current conditions by such groups. Theory and practice come closer together, and the rationality of institutions may be based on a substantive rationality founded on universal norms. The question then becomes to what degree does this administrative practice contribute to the development of truth or freedom or justice?

Weber long ago commented that ". . . the domination exercised in the schools stereotypes the form and the predominance of the official school language most enduringly and decisively" (1968, 941) and it is this nexus between institutional domination, institutional rationality as manifest in a school language, and the possibility of distortion-free discourse that is of particular consequence. Administration is communication and administrators form their own speech communities, as do teachers and pupils. Bates tells us that "administration is therefore as much a rhetorical activity as a technical one, directed toward the mediation of cultural reproduction through the coupling of the internal culture of the schools with specific external cultures" (1981, 19).

This framework allows us to develop an empirically researchable and critically valid understanding of how administrators behave in educational settings and how they indeed influence those settings. Thus, administrators must be familiar with three premises of their institution:

> . . . first, social interaction is a rule-governed system that is culturally and situationally determined; second, classrooms are emerging social systems in which teaching-learning events are not given but rather are constructed as part of the social interactions of participants as they work to achieve communicative, social, and academic goals; and third, classrooms are cross-cultural situations in which the teacher and students are seen as coming from different cultural groups . . . [Green 1981, 1].

Do institutions tend to introduce distortions into the communicative possibilities of the members of the institution? How, in fact, do institutions introduce class distinctions to children? Entering at one end of the institution is the biographically preclass child; coming out of the institution is the class-encoded child. How does administration function to reproduce elements of the class system if indeed it does? (see Foster 1980a, 1980b). These are certainly questions which need to be addressed in some manner if a critically adequate theory of administration — which is both organizational and emancipatory — is to be reached. Hurn suggests that "new research on linguistic codes and on classroom interaction will, I hope, eventually help us to specify in considerable detail the barriers that prevent children from achieving the kinds of intellectual skills that only a minority presently achieve" (1978, 275). Administrators must be part of such a movement, if only to understand the ways in which they react to the cultural dimensions of their charges and to reflect upon the rationale behind the forms of institutional domination. The ideal of distortion-free communication for the organization becomes one toward which the critical administrator can work.

For now, however, a critical administration must evidence a great concern for the relationship between external and internal structures, viewing schooling as a mediator between these and administration as a force which can serve a negative function in exposing contradictions and distortions *and* a positive function in attempting to develop an "objectively" rational basis for schooling. The external structure must be considered given the question "do we wish to construct a more just society?" The internal structure must be considered given the question "are all children given equal educational opportunity in the schools?" This in turn means abandoning an instrumentally rational approach to administration — how is control most effectively established? — in favor of a more substantive rationality — what and why do we administer? A critical theory of administration calls then upon positive knowledge concerning, for example, the nature of speech communities in education, and hermeneutic knowledge, concerning, for example, the interpretation of the meaningfulness of the educational experience by different communities and the critical interrelationships that exist between these two dimensions. This does not mean, in my view, abandoning the traditional content of administrative training programs, but of placing that content in a sociophilosophical and critical context.

REFERENCES

Anderson, Charles (1974). *Toward a New Sociology.* Homewood, Ill.: Dorsey Press.

Apel, Karl-Otto (1967). *Analytic Philosophy of Language and the Geisteswissenschaften.* Dordrecht, Holland: D. Reidel.

Arato, Andrew, and Eike Gebhardt (1978). *The Essential Frankfurt School Reader.* Oxford: Basil Blackwell.

Bates, Richard (1981). "Power and the Educational Administrator: Bureaucracy Loose Coupling or Cultural Negotiation?" Paper presented at the annual meeting of the American Educational Research Association, Los Angeles.

Bendix, Reinhard (1966). *Max Weber: An Intellectual Portrait.* London: Methuen.

Benson, J. Kenneth (1977). "Innovation and Crisis in Organizational Analysis." In J. Kenneth Benson, ed. *Organizational Analysis: Critique and Innovation.* Beverly Hills: Sage, pp. 5–18.

Bernstein, Richard J. (1976). *The Restructuring of Social and Political Theory.* New York: Harcourt Brace Jovanovich.

Bowles, Samuel, and Herbert Gintis (1976). *Schooling in Capitalist America.* New York: Basic Books.

Boyan, Norman (1981). "Follow the Leader: Commentary on Research in Educational Administration." *Educational Researcher* 10(2), 6–13.

Callahan, Raymond E. (1962). *Education and the Cult of Efficiency.* Chicago: University of Chicago Press.

Curti, Merle (1935). *The Social Ideas of American Educators.* New York: Charles Scribner's Sons; 1974 reprint, Totowa, N. J.: Littlefield, Adams & Co.

Edmonds, Ronald (1979). "Effective Schools for the Urban Poor." *Educational Leadership* 37(1), 15–24.

Erickson, Donald (1979). "Research on Educational Administration: The State of the Art." *Educational Researcher* 8, 9–14.

Foster, William (1980a). "The Changing Administrator: Developing Managerial Praxis." *Educational Theory* 30, 11–23.

_____ (1980b). "Administration and the Crisis in Legitimacy: A Review of Habermasian Thought." *Harvard Educational Review* 50, 496–505.

Goldhammer, Robert (1969). *Clinical Supervision.* New York: Holt, Rinehart & Winston.

Green, Judith (1981). "Context in Classrooms: A Sociolinguistic Perspective." Paper presented at the annual meeting of the American Educational Research Association, Los Angeles.

Greenfield, Thomas (1980). "The Man Who Comes Back through the Door in the Wall: Discovering Organizations." *Educational Administration Quarterly* 16, 26–59.

Griffiths, Daniel (1979). "Intellectual Turmoil in Educational Administration." *Educational Administration Quarterly* 15, 43–65.

Habermas, Jurgen (1970a). *Toward a Rational Society.* Translated by Jeremy Shapiro. Boston: Beacon Press.

_____ (1970b). "Toward a Theory of Communicative Competence." In Hans Dreitzel, ed. *Recent Sociology* 2, 115–48.

_____ (1971). *Knowledge and Human Interests.* Translated by Jeremy Shapiro. Boston: Beacon Press.

_____ (1974). "Rationalism Divided in Two." In Anthony Giddens, ed. *Positivism and Sociology.* London: Heinemann, pp. 195–224.

_____ (1975). *Legitimation Crisis.* Translated by Thomas McCarthy. Boston: Beacon Press.

_____ (1979). *Communication and the Evolution of Society.* Translated by Thomas McCarthy. Boston: Beacon Press.

Harnischfeger, Annegret, and David Wiley (1976). "The Teaching-Learning Process in Elementary Schools: A Synoptic View." *Curriculum Inquiry* 6, 5–43.

Held, David (1980). *Introduction to Critical Theory.* Berkeley and Los Angeles: University of California Press.

Heydebrand, Wolf (1977). "Organizational Contradictions in the Public Bureaucracies: Toward a Marxian Theory of Organizations." In J. Kenneth Benson, ed. *Organizational Analysis: Critique and Innovation.* Beverly Hills: Sage, pp. 85–109.

Horkheimer, Max (1972). *Critical Theory: Selected Essays.* Translated by Matthew O'Connell et al. New York: Herder & Herder.

Horkheimer, Max (1974). *Eclipse of Reason.* New York: The Seabury Press (first published 1947).

Hoy, Wayne, and Cecil Miskel (1982). *Educational Administration: Theory, Research, and Practice,* 2nd ed. New York: Random House.

Hurn, Christopher (1978). *The Limits and Possibilities of Schooling.* Boston: Allyn & Bacon.

Jay, Martin (1973). *The Dialectical Imagination.* Boston: Little-Brown.

McCarthy, Thomas (1978). *The Critical Theory of Jurgen Habermas.* Cambridge, Mass.: MIT Press.

Mintzberg, Henry (1973). *The Nature of Managerial Work.* New York: Harper & Row.

Mueller, Claus (1973). *The Politics of Communication.* New York: Oxford.

Ogbu, John (1981). "School Ethnography: A Multilevel Approach." *Anthropology and Education Quarterly* 12, 3–29.

Owens, Robert (1981). *Organizational Behavior in Education,* 2nd ed. Englewood Cliffs, N. J.: Prentice-Hall.

Perrow, Charles (1979). *Complex Organizations: A Critical Essay,* 2nd ed. Glenview, Ill.: Scott, Foresman.

Ranson, Stewart, Bob Hinings, and Royston Greenwood (1980). "The Structuring of Organizational Structures." *Administrative Science Quarterly* 25, 1–17.

Rayder, Nicholas, Allen Abrams, and John Larson (1978). "Effect of Socio-Contextual Variables on Child Achievement." *Journal of Teacher Education* 1, 58–63.

Shroyer, Trent (1973). *The Critique of Domination.* New York: George Braziller.

Sergiovanni, Thomas, and Fred Carver (1980). *The New School Executive: A Theory of Administration,* 2nd ed. New York: Harper & Row.

Seward, John (1980). "Jurgen Habermas's reconstruction of Critical Theory." In Scott G. McNall, and Gary Howe (1980). *Current Perspectives in Social Theory,* vol. 1. Greenwich, Conn.: JAI Press, pp. 323–56.

Shea, Brent Mack (1976). "Schooling and Its Antecedents: Substantive and Methodological Issues in the Status Attainment Process." *Review of Educational Research* 46, 463–526.

Sproul, Lee S. (1981). "Managing Education Programs: A Micro-Behavioral Analysis." *Human Organization* 40, 113–22.

Tyack, David (1974). *The One Best System.* Cambridge, Mass.: Harvard University Press.

Tyack, David, and Robert Cummings (1977). "Leadership in American Public Schools before 1954: Historical Configurations and Conjectures." In W. Hack Cunningham and R. Nystrand, eds. *Educational Administration: The Developing Decades.* Berkeley: McCutchan.

Weber, Max (1968). *Economy and Society,* vols. 1, 2, and 3. Translated by E. Fischoff, et al.; edited by G. Roth and C. Wittich. New York: Bedminster.

Wellmer, Albrecht (1974). *Critical Theory of Society.* New York: Seabury Press.

Winch, Peter (1958). *The Idea of a Social Science and Its Relation to Philosophy.* London: Routledge & Kegan Paul.

CHAPTER 14

Toward a Critical Practice
of Educational Administration

Richard J. Bates

Though misconceived and misdirected, the quest for a behavioral science of educational administration continues. Despite the revolution brought about in natural science by Heisenberg's uncertainty principle and by relativity and quantum theory, the scientific model propagated by mainstream theorists of educational administration is still firmly rooted in Newtonian physics. Despite the acknowledgement of philosophers of the impossibility of eliminating evaluative judgments from the interpretative frameworks within which facts are both sought and understood, mainstream theorists of educational administration continue to declare the incommensurability of fact and value. Despite the social theorists' large-scale abandonment of the quest for a value-free science of society, the mainstream theorists of educational administration still pursue positivistic attempts to develop generalizable laws and principles which will explain the structure and dynamics of organizations.

Perhaps the most outstanding example of this conservative and anachronistic approach to educational administration is the highly developed view of educational administration as rooted in the "theory moment" of the 1960s. Those who persist in this view remain blissfully unaware of the widely acknowledged revolutions in science, philosophy, and social theory mentioned above. The literature of this era, for example, is noticeably lacking in its attention to unique characteristics of educational organizations and to other contextual matters such as contemporary educational issues. The tendency of educational administrators to separate administrative issues from educational issues and to ignore the latter has been noted previously by Callahan (1962) in his discussion of

This chapter is based on a paper presented to the annual meeting of the American Educational Research Association, New York, March 1982.

the cult of efficiency. It is as though the administration of schools and school systems consists entirely of processes of motivation, leadership, decision-making, and communication conducted by professional bureaucrats who are responsible for organizational climate, effectiveness, and change. Readers may search in vain for reference to a single *educational* idea. There is, for instance, deafening silence concerning the fundamental message systems of schools: curriculum, pedagogy, and evaluation (Bernstein, 1975).

The pathology of such an approach to educational administration is surely indicated both by its neglect of contemporary science (Bates 1980a), philosophy (Hodgkinson 1978), and social theory (Tipton 1977), and by its exclusion of educational concerns (cf. Boyd and Crowson 1981). A theory of educational administration that divorces fact from value, theory from practice, rationality from common sense, and education from administration is unlikely to be capable of guiding the administrator's hand (Greenfield 1981).

Organization, Culture and Praxis

Greenfield, among others, has argued for some time now for an essentially phenomenological view of organizations. This view sees organizations as accomplishments, as consequences of human action directed by individual will, intention, and value which provide contexts for the negotiation and construction of meaning, moral order, and power. As such, organizations are essentially arbitrary definitions of reality "woven in symbols and expressed in language" (1980, 44).

Such a perspective does not deny the facts of organizational reality but interprets them within a wider context which sees them as "structures of consciousness as well as features of face-to-face settings" (Brown 1978, 365). Thus rationality, for instance, is seen not as a property of organizations or as an abstract standard by which behavior may be judged but as an achievement: ". . . rationality neither instructs us as to what action to take, nor is it a property inherent in the social system as such. Instead, rationality emerges in interaction and is then used retrospectively to legitimize what has already taken place or is being enacted" (Brown 1978, 369).

From such a perspective, rather than organizations being entities whose internal and external interactions are determined by the causal laws of behavioral and social science, "formal organizations are essentially processes of organizing enacted by persons" (Brown 1978, 371). Thus, "the study of reality creation in organizations is a study of power, in that definitions of reality, normalcy, rationality and so on serve as paradigms that in some sense govern the conduct permissible within them (1978, 371).

Moreover, as with scientific paradigms, organizational paradigms are not only formal structures of thought but are also constituted by the language, rhetoric, and practices of the organizational community. The power of such paradigms lies in their ability to define what shall be included or excluded from discussion, practice, and therefore consciousness (Brown 1978; Giroux 1981).

Paradigms, however, are both constructed and contested. They are subject to periodic overthrow or supercession. As with scientific communities, formal organizations construct defenses and mechanisms of suppression in order to protect and sustain dominant paradigms. These mechanisms are essentially symbolic, communicated through the language, rituals, and metaphors that define the nature and meaning of the organization and celebrate the purposive intentions of organizational life. In short, organizations are cultures rather than structures and it is the maintenance and contestation of what is to constitute the culture of organizational life that provides the dynamic of rationality, legitimation, and motivation in organizations. This dynamic is the praxis of administration.

The Cultural Analysis of Educational Administration

Foster (1980), Giroux (1981), Greenfield (1979, 1980), and Bates (1980a, 1981) have all argued the necessity of constructing a cultural analysis of educational administration as an alternative to the inherently sterile pursuit of a deterministic behavioral science. This is not solely because the dynamics of organizations can better be understood through such a perspective but also because educational organizations, above all, are committed to the maintenance, transmission, and re-creation of culture. Culture is, in fact, the prime resource of educational practice (Bates 1981b). Thus a theory of educational administration that ignores this central preoccupation can hardly be counted as a theory of educational administration in any very serious sense.

It is culture that gives meaning to life. The beliefs, languages, rituals, knowledge, conventions, courtesies, and artifacts—in short the cultural baggage of any group, are the resources from which the individual and social identities are constructed. They provide the framework upon which individuals construct their understanding of the world and of themselves. Part of this cultural baggage is factual. It is empirical, descriptive, and objective. Another part of this cultural baggage, perhaps the greater part, is mythical. It is concerned not with facts but with *meaning*, that is, the interpretative and prescriptive rules which provide the basis for understanding and action.

Malinowski, for instance, argued that "myth fulfills in primitive culture an indispensible function: it expresses, enhances and codifies belief;

it safeguards and enforces morality; it vouches for the efficiency of ritual and contains the practical rules for the guidance of man" (1948, 79).

At the other extreme, as Bailey points out, Sorel's definition is equally acceptable: ". . . men who are participating in a great social movement always picture their coming action as a battle in which their cause is certain to triumph. These constructions . . . I propose to call myths" (Sorel 1908, in Bailey 1977, 16).

While it is unlikely that many of the myths that give meaning and purpose to schools' activities approach the apocalyptic vision of a second coming or Marx's revolution, it can readily be seen that myths are not confined to great social movements but are a fundamental feature of everyday life in schools as elsewhere. Consequently schools, alongside other public institutions, are battlegrounds in which contending mythologies compete for the holy grail — control of the future.

Myths are, then, an important cultural resource in schools — they alone can give meaning and purpose to schools' activities. They are intimately built into the day-to-day life of schools and in an important sense they constitute the groundwork of belief, morality, ritual, and rules within which social and personal identity are managed. Any adequate theory or effective practice of educational administration must necessarily, therefore, be concerned with the nature of the myths that guide the organizational life of schools and with the characteristics of interpersonal life through which such myths are perpetuated and negotiated.

Three key aspects of the cultural myths of schools are particularly important: metaphors, rituals, and negotiations. These are the aspects of life in schools that provide the means through which individuals and groups attempt to manage the cultural reality of the school and shape it to fit their vision of the future. Administrators need to be sensitive to this process and aware of its importance in the processes of rationalization, legitimation, and motivation involved in schooling.

Metaphors and the Management of Meaning

It was Wittgenstein (1953) who spoke of the bewitchment of our intelligence by the means of language. He also spoke of the need for liberation from such bewitchment — the need for the fly to find his way out of the fly bottle. The directions for escape, he insisted, were not to be found in the dictionary but in the world of real experience where the meaning of words is revealed in their use. The language we use and the way in which we use it are the keys to our particular bewitchment.

We are often unaware of the associations that crowd in on us in our use of particular phrases. The images they conjure up may be commonplace; alternatively, the metaphors we employ may be, or may once have been, vivid. Nietzsche (1968) argued that the use of metaphor is basic to the intellectual processes we use to establish truth and meaning. Moreover, this impulse toward the formation of metaphor, linked as it is with the processes of categorization, classification, and association is identified with the "will to power" (Nietzsche 1968; Bowers 1980). Metaphors allow us to structure and create meaning out of experience. They may also act like fly bottles, to keep us trapped in invisible prisons. They can, moreover, mislead us when we apply inappropriate metaphors to situations better understood in other ways.

Shifts in the use of metaphor are not always trivial. They may, as Kuhn (1962) suggests, be basic to the nature of scientific revolutions and involve a major shift in world view. For instance, the shift from an animistic view of the universe to a mechanistic one brought about by Newton and his philosophical colleagues, Bacon and Locke, involves a major shift in attitude toward nature which became for the first time viewed as accessible, knowable, and controllable. The metaphor involved, that of the machine, allowed not only a transformation of production but also a transformation of society which could now be viewed as a mechanical system.

As Hamilton (1980) has shown, the metaphor of the machine or the mechanical system was rapidly applied to education. In this process the work of Adam Smith and his harmonization of the ideas of individual and collective self-interest through the metaphor of the invisible hand was crucial in the development and legitimization of simultaneous instruction. Such instruction was a key practice in the development of mass education.

Shifts in the fundamental metaphors which we use to explore and interpret the world of nature and the nature of society have far-reaching repercussions. The metaphor of the machine is frequently used in education and forms the basis of much of the language of systems engineers who use the metaphor in much the same way as Adam Smith. "Systems in many respects resemble machines. . . . A system is an imaginary machine, invented to connect together in fancy those different movements and effects which are already in reality performed" (in Hamilton 1980, 4).

Smith's legacy is still with us in the contemporary language of cybernetics. "Today the spokesmen for cybernetic systems theory argue that formal organizations are (or are like) a giant computer with its input and output, its feedback loops, and its programs. This machine—the organization—is in turn guided by a servomechanism—the techno-administrative elite" (Brown 1978, 375).

Such metaphors profoundly, and often unconsciously, determine our attitudes toward the world, people, events, and action. Teachers and administrators and their pupils use metaphors continually to represent relationships and to define the power structures which organize behavior. Metaphor is a major weapon in the presentation of self and the management of situations. Such metaphors not infrequently obscure the interests of dominating elites and present particular partisan views of the world as uncontestable descriptions of the way things are. Positivistic and mechanical accounts of social structure and process are frequently of this kind. Phenomenological or critical analysis however allows us

> to see this (cybernetic) imagery as a thing made, as a symbolic artifact rather than as the fact. (It allows us) to reject it as a literal description of how the organization "really" is and to unmask it as a legitimating ideology. By doing a close textual analysis, we can make it clear that in the paradigm of cybernetics the vocabularies of personal agency, ethical accountability, and political community have atrophied. In their place, the organization, initially conceived as serving human values, becomes a closed system directed by elites and generating its own self-maintaining ends [Brown 1978, 375].

A critical analysis of the metaphors that articulate (if indeed they do not constitute) our beliefs and actions is, therefore, one powerful way of ensuring that we do not remain trapped within the evidently transparent prison of the fly bottle.

Metaphors not only intrude on the processes of educational administration in a grand fashion as in the language of cybernetics, they also directly affect our negotiations and relations with each other at the most personal level. In the common, everyday language of schools metaphors about children and metaphors about schools exist and compete. They are frequently varied, contradictory, and powerful. Metaphors of the child as flower, enemy, cog, machine, chamelon, miniature adult, psychopath, gentleman, lady, or reasoner, are common currency in staffrooms as are our metaphors of the school as factory, clinic, or bureaucracy. The nature, occurrence, and emphases of such metaphors are vitally important to administrators for the "tone" or "climate" of the school has a lot to do with the metaphors employed and the relationships they bear to the reality of interpersonal relations. Parents and pupils are, for instance, particularly scathing in their evaluations of schools which use one metaphor (community) in their rhetoric and another metaphor (factory) to guide their activity.

Such conflicts of metaphor are sources of great debate and tension within educational systems and schools. But the tension is not simply a semantic one. The metaphors which people use are often representative of the kind of future—the social movement—to which they are consciously or unconsciously committed. Such cultural commitment is frequently passionate and contains views of man, society, and education which are closely related to the meaning and identity of the individual.

Metaphors carry both personal identity and social commitment. Schools are instrumental in the support or denial of such identity. They are, therefore, important cultural artifacts and the struggle to shape them is closely related, as Greenfield reminds us, to the values that are central and meaningful in people's lives.

The relationship between educational metaphors and individual and social identity is clearly and powerfully illustrated in the work and ideas of Paulo Friere. His work relies on a series of opposing metaphors: cultural domination versus freedom; the culture of silence versus cultural action; education as banking versus education as praxis. In each of the metaphors education is related to social organization. On the one side education as banking, the conspiracy of silence, and cultural domination are related to forms of social oppression of militarist, sexist, racist, class kinds. On the other side education is praxis, liberation, autonomy, cultural action for freedom. The form that education takes in schools is, he argues, intimately bound up with the personal and social identity of individuals (Friere 1972).

Friere's view is clearly developed within the context of Third World countries. The relationships between views of man, society, education, and the organization of learning do, however, apply to our contemporary society, for any systematic organization of learning incorporates into its structure not only content but also forms of relationship built on the metaphors which encapsulate our view of society and people.

Education systems are then, in a sense, a physical working out of the cultural metaphors and myths held by educators and administrators. Many of the metaphors we employ are, for instance, ritualized in the forms of organization, ceremony, and interaction which are typical of schools. Jackson (1968), for instance, shows how the organizational structure of schools emphasizes and demands certain kinds of relationships between teachers and pupils. The facts of crowdedness, praise, and power provide an essentially coercive environment in which relationships between teachers and pupils are ritualized. The metaphors of child as cog, machine, are translated into cultural reality through the rituals of classroom interaction.

Again Dreeben (1968), following Parsons (1959), argues that the organization of the school is devoted to creating social and psychological situations that encourage, when compared with the family, activities leading to the development of independence, achievement, universalism, and specificity in children. These metaphors or norms are constructed by the social organization of the school. The organization of time, place, and relationships shapes the consciousness of individuals through their structure and the treatment accorded to particular groups.

Jean Anyon (1980) has argued this position in more detail showing how the ways in which pupils' "work" is treated in schools — in terms of the content of their work, their relationships with teachers, the products of their activity — can be differentiated according to social class. The nature of the metaphors which are interpreted and enforced through the school's organization are different for different children. Moreover these differences apparently relate to the kinds of work relationships found in different occupational groups. Thus, for working-class children, conflictual relationships are predominant — child as inferior, child as enemy. This form of relationship in school is also borne out by the work of Willis (1977) and Birkstead (1976) among others. Middle-class children tend, however, to meet bureaucratized relationships in the school — child as cog, child as machine — and be subjected to rituals of evaluation, classification, and certification (Cicourel and Kitsuse 1963). Upper-class schools, Anyon argues, tend to define work relationships in terms of negotiation and symbolic capital where the dominant metaphors are those of manipulability, adaptability, and effectiveness — child as reasoner, child as adult. Thus, the metaphors we use to classify and interpret the world are translated into work structures which relate to wider social relations and to structures outside the school.

It would seem therefore that a critical practice of educational administration would necessarily involve observation, analysis, and reflection on the metaphorical currency negotiated and exchanged within the school. It might also on occasion involve the negotiation of a different currency.

Administration, Ritualization, and Control

Along with metaphors, rituals are a potent mechanism of control. Although the meaning of rituals may be redundant (i.e., no longer explicit) the relationships represented in those rituals are frequently both metaphorical and practical specifications of intergroup power. Ritualistic acts revivify the relationships which constitute particular forms of order in social situations. Schools are saturated with rituals. The management of ritual in schools is an important element in the maintenance of order for rituals celebrate both unifying and differentiating features in the social structure of the school (Bernstein 1975).

Rituals can often be so powerful as to take on a life of their own. Conformity to rituals may be so complete as to govern movement, place, time, language, sequences of activity, participant's response, and the use of artifacts. Their shape, the metaphors they utilize, and the symbols that guide responses are powerful means of control. These ritual structures of communication are rather obvious in churches, rallies, television interviews, cafeterias, and football games. They are also obvious to outsiders describing what goes on in schools. They are not always obvious to those who participate more or less permanently in the rituals of schools. Because the form and meaning of the rituals are so well known, their impact can be underestimated. Even the effect of new forms of social organization or innovation in curriculum structures and communication structures can be constrained by the habits derived from ritual.

For example, there are numerous instances of curriculum innovations being "turned" to fit the preexisting structures of schools' activities (Whiteside 1976). Even when not only curriculum but the whole organizational structure of the school is reformed through the introduction of an alternative technology, the capacity of schools to maintain their own ritual structures is very strong (Popkewitz 1981; Popkewitz, Tabachnik, and Whelage 1980).

This seems to happen despite the intentions of individual teachers or school administrators (Shipman 1974). Part of the reason for this is the threat to those ritualized forms of action and meaning which form a background to learning. As Shipman puts it, "Every change in routine is a threat to teacher-pupil relations and standard of work" (1974, 176). Routines as ritualized relations are both redundant and powerful. Redundant, because they are not consciously thought about, because they are accepted without examination or question. Powerful, because they are unconsciously followed and unquestionably accepted. Rituals and routines in fact facilitate the direct focusing of attention on learning. They are the major constituents of the hidden curriculum of schools.

This hidden curriculum and the metaphors it ritualizes in everyday, commonsense activity and understanding is in essence an administrative curriculum. The links between language, metaphor, and ritual and their celebration of particular social ideals or myths form the essential administrative culture of the school. The culture is a translation of myths into action and relationships.

A critical practice of educational administration would involve a reflective analysis and an active intervention and reconstruction of such ritual structures so that they celebrate the intended educational purposes of the school community rather than the redundant purposes of a previous administration.

Educational Administration and the Language of Negotiation

Administrative intervention in the metaphorical and ritual performances which form the texture of school life must, therefore, be conducted through the means of language. Language is not only a tool of critical reflection through which we may demystify our world but also the medium of action through which we shape it. As Gron suggests, "The administrative setting is a speech milieu which organization members enact in their talk with one another." Thus talk is "an instrument for accomplishing administrative control" (1982, 1). But, as Gron points out in his analysis of a school principal's administrative talk with his staff, this talk is by no means simply directive on the part of the administrator nor automatically compliant on the part of the staff. Indeed as Gron reports, "Contrary . . . to the image of the administrator in much of the management literature as 'directing,' 'commanding,' 'planning,' etc., as if administering is a unilateral and unidirectional action performed on a set of anonymous employees, here is an administrator seemingly caught in a mesh not of his own making. Prior to the staff meeting he is being controlled rather than being in control" (p. 15).

What emerges in the course of the administrative performance is a negotiation in which language, territory, and status are employed by the principal to gain advantage and shape agreement and consent over decision. Gron's analysis presents us with a picture of administration far removed from the tidy conceptual schemes of positivistic, behavioral, and managerial science. Indeed neither place, nor time, nor metaphor, nor language seems predictable.

> Administration can take place anywhere. It is timeconsuming and it observes no set time schedule. It follows no set order or format for it can arise out of a chance meeting and can include all kinds of matters that might be routine, spontaneous, trivial or highly eventful in character. The school principal free-wheels. He is a classic drifter moving in and out of different locations and areas, in and out of relationships and encounters. . . . the dynamics of this activity show it to be antithetical to the obsession with order and precision evident in (writings on) scientific management [1982, 21].

The dependence of administrators on the use of language to shape and determine action is the third major aspect of administrative culture. It is a dynamic process that bears some relationship to the organizational structure of the school but also has a degree of autonomy from it. This autonomy is a result of the necessary processes of negotiation that occur between groups or individuals who proclaim differing mythologies and who represent contending interests. One common example of such negotiation results from the widespread conflict between those holding representative and participatory views of democracy.

The representative view is readily compatible with forms of bureaucratic, centralized control. It is also compatible with banking education and with certain forms of social control. The participative view is often opposed to centralized, bureaucratic control and decision-making and embraces a liberationist, activist, constructivist view of learning and the learner. It is a view which argues, as Greenfield does, that only through participation in the struggle to shape institutions in their own image can people find purpose and meaning in their lives.

These ideas are both "large" ideas in that their opposed myths form the ideological structure of much contemporary political and economic debate and "small" ideas in that the myths are incorporated one way or another in the structure of our daily lives. An interesting illustration of the conflict and negotiation of these competing views is found in Hunter's (1980) discussion of the administrative culture of a secondary school and its conflict with the politics of participation. In particular Hunter's discussion is interesting because of its analysis of the headmaster's role in the negotiations which shows the way in which the power to determine the *forms* of negotiation, the rituals that will be adopted, allows the incorporation or exclusion of the myths held by other groups in the school. The backstage culture and the up-front culture of teachers are markedly different. Why? Because of the administrative ritualization of the negotiations and the acceptance of particular forms of power and authority as "natural."

Hunter's paper is an attempt to show how various differing definitions of participation and democracy operate alongside each other in schools and how partial negotiations of the conflicts between these definitions occur. It is also an attempt to show how administrative power affects such negotiations by excluding various groups from effective participation, and defining alternative proposals as technically impossible. This example is a paradigm case of the use of a technical definition of administration to exclude debate and discussion over normative issues. The power to define situations in particular ways is, then, not the least important attribute of administrative control. In particular, the power to define the ways in which culture is presented and structured in the school is of paramount importance.

These illustrations indicate that the third major component of a critical practice of educational administration revolves around the use of language as a mechanism of control in negotiations over action. The comparison of the use of language in the discourse of negotiations in the administrative context of the school with the conditions of ideal discourse outlined by Habermas (1971, 1973) may well prove very revealing of the ways in which certain forms of domination are imposed via the language of administering. A critical educational administration would be in part directed toward the clarification, examination, and redirection of such discourse.

Conclusion

Culture, as Bourdieu suggests, is the most important resource available to the school. The interiorization of cultural patterns is the most profound effect that the school has on both teachers and pupils. But culture is not a static set of values, beliefs, and understandings; rather, "it is a common set of previously assimilated master patterns from which, by an 'art of invention' similar to that involved in the writing of music, an infinite number of individual patterns directly applicable to specific situations is generated" (1971, 192). Thus the myths, metaphors and rituals of the school contribute to the reproduction of ways of thought in the individual. "Every individual owes to the type of schooling he has received a set of basic, deeply interiorized master patterns on the basis of which he subsequently acquires other patterns, so that the system of patterns by which his thought is organized owes the specific character not only to the nature of the patterns constituting it, but also to the frequency with which these are used and to the level of consciousness at which they operate" (1971, 193).

The fact that differing definitions of culture — competing myths and ideologies — exist in the school makes the determination of what is to count as culture in the school problematic. Which mythology is to prevail is not altogether a matter of reason but also a matter of social, moral, and political commitment and, most importantly for administrators, a matter of power and control.

Very little work has been done which explains the impact of administrative processes on the culture of schools. But the impact of administrative processes on the master patterns which are reproduced through schooling is obviously an area of great importance. As Bantock argues, "The basic educational dilemma of our time is a cultural one and affects the nature of the meanings to be transmitted by the school" (1973, 166). Moreover, administrative control of the central message systems of the school — curriculum, pedagogy, and evaluation (Bernstein 1975) — as well as processes of training and professionalization (Smith 1979) and the allocation of physical resources (Young and Whitty 1977, Grace 1978) ensure that constraints exist on the definitions of culture which are able to be reproduced through schools. These constraints, as Waller argued in 1932 (1967), ensure that schools act as conservative agencies of social control through their control of the cultural definitions of situations.

The schools may be viewed as an agency for imposing preformed definitions of the situation. Education, as has been truly said, is the art of imposing on the young the definitions of situations current and accepted in the group which maintains the schools. The school is thus a gigantic agency of social control. It is part of its function to

transmit to the young the attitudes of the elders, which it does by
presenting to them social situations as the elders have defined
them. . . . From a fact that situations may be defined in different
ways and by different groups arises a conflict of definitions of situations and we may see the whole process of personal and group conflict which centers about the school as a conflict of contradictory
definitions of situations. The fundamental problem of school discipline may be stated as the struggle of students and teachers to establish their own definitions of situations in the life of the school
[Waller 1967, 296].

The culture of the school is therefore the product of conflict and negotiation over definitions of situations. The administrative influence on
school language, metaphors, myths, and ritual is a major factor in the
determination of the culture which is reproduced in the consciousness of
teachers and pupils. Whether that culture is largely based on metaphors
of participatory democracy, equity, and cultural liberation or on metaphors of capital accumulation, hierarchy, and domination is at least
partly attributable to the exercise of administrative authority during the
negotiation of what is to count as culture in the school. A critical practice
of educational administration would, necessarily, be reflective concerning such negotiations, placing them within the context of a critique of
domination and a commitment to struggle in the interest of a better
world.

REFERENCES

Anyon, Jean (1980). "Social Class and the Hidden Curriculum of Work."
    Journal of Education 162 (1), 67–92.
Bailey, F. G. (1977). "Morality and Expediency: the Folklore of Academic Poli-
    tics." Oxford: Basil Blackwell.
Bantock, G. H. (1973). "Are We in the Wrong Struggle?" *Times Educational Sup-
    plement,* 5 October.
Bates, Richard J. (1980a). "Educational Administration, the Sociology of Science
    and the Management of Knowledge." *Educational Administration Quarterly*
    16(2), 1–20.
——— (1980b). "The Function of Educational Administration in the Processes of
    Cultural Transmission." Paper presented to the Conference on the Origins
    and Operations of Educational Systems, International Sociological Associa-
    tion, Paris.
——— (1981). "Educational Administration, the Technologization of Reason and
    the Management of Knowledge: Towards a Critical Theory." Paper pre-
    sented to the Annual Meeting of the American Educational Research Associ-
    ation, Los Angeles.
Bernstein, Basil (1975). *Class, Codes and Control Vol. 3: Towards a Theory of
    Educational Transmissions.* London: Routledge & Kegan Paul.

Birkstead, Ian K. (1976). "School Performance Viewed from the Boys." *Sociological Review* 24(1), 63–77.

Bourdieu, Pierre (1971). "Systems of Education and Systems of Thought." In Michael F. D. Young, ed. *Knowledge and Control.* London: Macmillan, pp. 189–207.

Bowers, C. A. (1980). "Curriculum as Cultural Reproduction: An Examination of Metaphor as a Carrier of Ideology." Paper presented to the Annual Meeting of the American Educational Research Association, Boston.

Boyd, W. L., and R. L. Crowson (1981). "The Changing Conception and Practice of Public School Administration." In D. D. Berliner, ed. *Review of Research in Education,* 9, 311–73.

Brown, Richard H. (1978). "Bureaucracy as Praxis." *Administrative Science Quarterly* 23(3), 365–82.

Callahan, R. E. (1962). *Education and the Cult of Efficiency.* Chicago: University of Chicago Press.

Cicourel, A. V., and J. I. Kitsuse (1963). *The Educational Decision Makers.* Chicago: Bobbs-Merrill.

Dreeben, Robert (1968). *On What Is Learned in School.* Reading, Mass.: Addison-Wesley.

Foster, W. P. (1980). "Administration and the Crisis of Legitimacy: A Review of Habermasion Thought." *Harvard Education Review* 50 (4), 496–505.

Friere, Paulo (1972). *Cultural Action for Freedom.* Harmondsworth: Penguin.

Giroux, Henry A. (1981). *Ideology, Culture and the Process of Schooling.* London: Falmer Press.

Grace, G. (1978). *Teachers, Ideology and Control.* London: Routledge & Kegan Paul.

Greenfield, Thomas B. (1979). "Organization Theory as Ideology." *Curriculum Inquiry* 9(2), 97–112.

———— (1980). "The Man Who Comes Back through the Door in the Wall." *Educational Administration Quarterly* 16(3), 26–59.

———— (1981). "Can Theory Guide the Educational Administrator's Hand?" Paper presented to the Victorian Council for Educational Administration, Melbourne.

Gron, Peter C. (1982). "Accomplishing the Doing of School Administration: Talk as the Work." *Educational Administration Quarterly* (in press).

Habermas, J. (1971). *Knowledge and Human Interests.* Translated by Jeremy Shapiro. Boston: Beacon Press.

———— (1973). *Theory and Practice.* Translated by John Viertel. Boston: Beacon Press.

Hamilton, David (1980). "Adam Smith and the Moral Economy of the Classroom System." *Journal of Curriculum Studies* 12(4), 281–98.

Hodgkinson, C. (1978). *Towards a Philosophy of Educational Administration.* Oxford: Basil Blackwell.

Hunter, C. (1980). "The Politics of Participation—With Specific Reference to Teacher-Pupil Relationships." In P. Woods, ed. *Teacher Strategies: Explorations in the Sociology of the School.* London: Croom Helm, pp. 213–36.

Jackson, Phillip W. (1968). *Life in Classrooms.* New York: Holt, Rinehart and Winston.

Kuhn, T. S. (1962). *The Structure of Scientific Revolutions.* Chicago: University of Chicago Press.

Malinowski, B. (1948). *Magic, Science and Religion and Other Essays*. Glencoe: Free Press.

Nietzsche, F. (1968). *The Will to Power*. New York: Vintage Books.

Parsons, Talcott (1959). "The School Class as a Social System: Some of Its Functions in American Society." *Harvard Educational Review* 29(4), 297–318.

Popkewitz, T. S. (1982). "Educational Reform as the Organization of Ritual: Stability as Change." *Journal of Education*, 164(5), 5–29.

Popkewitz, T., B. R. Tabachnick and G. Whelage (1980). *School Reform and Institutional Life: A Case Study of Individually Guided Education*. University of Wisconsin, Madison: Research and Development Center for Student Diversity and Schooling.

Shipman, M. (1974). *Inside a Curriculum Project*. London: Methuen.

Smith, Louis M. (1979). "An Evolving Logic of Participant Observation, Educational Ethnography and Other Case Studies." In L. Shulman, ed. *Review of Research in Education*, vol. 6. Itasca: Peacock Press, pp. 316–77.

Tipton, Beryl (1977). "The Tense Relationship of Sociology and Educational Administration." *Educational Administration* 5(2), 46–57.

Waller, Willard (1967). *The Sociology of Teaching*. New York: Wiley & Sons.

Wexler, P. (1976). *The Sociology of Education*. Indianapolis: Bobbs-Merrill.

Whiteside, T. (1976). *The Sociology of Educational Innovation*. London: Methuen.

Willis, Paul (1977). *Learning to Labour*. London: Saxon House.

Wittgenstein, L. (1953). *Philosophical Investigations*. Oxford: Basil Blackwell.

Young, Michael and Geoff Whitty (1977). *Society, State and Schooling*. Ringmer: Falmer Press.

CHAPTER 15

Developing a Relevant
Theory of Administration

Thomas J. Sergiovanni

We are at an important watershed in the development of thought and practice in administration. Mainstream thought continues the tradition of building a science of administration closely tied to the social science disciplines and aligned with the principles of logical positivism. This tradition was a driving force in educational administration during the "theory movement" of the fifties and sixties. But significant branches in the stream of scholarly inquiry in administration are becoming apparent. One branch is represented by a renewed interest in normative science. Questions of philosophy, values, and ethics, and images of the just and good life, are important to this branch. A second branch is represented by an interest in interpretive science and a renewed concern for practice. It is characterized by a regard for the idiosyncratic, the nuances of life and the cultural imperatives which are defined by specific contexts and practical issues and the actual drama of living and being.

At times these branches of thought seem forever destined to travel away from the mainstream of traditional science and indeed to become separate and competing entities. The watershed metaphor is a good one because it allows branches from the mainstream to develop individual identities and integrity but to still feed back, later on in the course of the stream, as tributaries, building new life in the body of scientific and practical knowledge. The further development of administration as a field of scholarly inquiry and professional practice requires that these seemingly independent and competing views of reality be brought together in a reasoned and integrated fashion (Sergiovanni 1980).

This chapter is a revision and extension of the Sir George Alexander Currie Lecture "Hermeneutics and the Science of Administration" given to the Australian Capitol Territory Institute of Educational Administration in Canberra, 12 October 1981.

The term "theory of practice" has been coined to reflect attempts to bring about a more integrated understanding of scholarship and practice (Culbertson 1979, 1980).

In this chapter the concept of theory of practice is examined as well as the possible contribution of hermeneutics to its development and implementation. Hermeneutics is the art of interpretation. It seeks to go beyond the objective identification of facts as "is" to understanding the facts given certain combinations of circumstances and to interpreting the facts in an attempt to render them meaningful.

The Nature of Science and Applied Science

What is our scientific heritage in Western society? The "experimenting society" is the metaphor Campbell uses to describe scientific activity. In his view the growth and development of knowledge results from a series of trial and error processes involving the comparison of hypotheses with experimentally induced results (Campbell 1974). Scientific inquiry seeks to ascertain and discover the facts on the one hand and to construct hypotheses and theories on the other. Theory building seeks to predict occurrences of events and outcomes of experiments and to explain facts which are discovered by establishing causal chains between and among them (von Wright 1971).

What is the aim of science? Simply, the aim is to establish truth and refute conjecture; to bring about hegenomy of thought through systematic experimental research; to find the right answer, the correct explanation, and the best way. The truth of fact is supreme in science. Throughout this process the scientist must be scrupulous in separating fact from value, and where values come to play they are to be treated as fact variables to be experimentally defined and manipulated as one would other variables. Herbert A. Simon makes this point as follows: "In the first place, an administrative science, like any science, is concerned purely with factual statements. There is no place for ethical assertions in the body of a science. Whenever ethical statements do occur, they can be separated into two parts, one factual and one ethical; and only the former has any relevance to science" (1957, 253).

What about the metaphor of applied science? Does this more adequately describe the administrative sciences? Applied science is the direct application of scientific truth and scientific theory to problems of professional practice. An assumption basic to applied science is that a one-to-one correspondence exists between scientific knowledge and professional practice. What is the aim of applied science? The aim is to establish the one best analysis of a problem, the one best way to practice given existing scientific knowledge. The truth of analyses and the truth of methods based on true facts is supreme in applied science.

Images of science and applied science have great appeal in our society. If one views educational policy and administration, for example, as sciences, then we need only describe, explain, analyze, and predict. We would do this by applying the scientific approach of accuracy, reliability, objectivity, and neutrality. We could then identify and articulate clear-cut and indisputable principles to guide administrative action. At last, we would get our work down to a "science." Administrators would need only to master a set of procedures and by repeating them get the desired results every time (Eisner 1982). Respect and power would come from such a development but, alas, this is not to be the case for neither administration as science nor administration as applied science is up to the task of mastering the ideographic complexities of administrative work and particularly administrative work in educational settings.

Educational Administration and Organizational Analysis as Unique Fields

Educational administration and organizational analysis are distinct enterprises. Two important characteristics of this distinctiveness are their applied nature *and* human activity. Having both an applied and a human characteristic places certain unique requirements on inquiry in these fields and on the development of prescriptions for practice. Applied fields typically rely on a fairly well developed knowledge base and are linked to one or more academic disciplines. In the case of educational administration, the political, economic, social, and management sciences have traditionally stood out as key disciplines. Applied suggests that knowledge from these disciplines is utilized toward some end. Further, in pursuit of this end action takes place; decisions are made and implemented. Thus applied fields can be described as having teleological and praxis qualities, as being concerned with practice toward some end.

Added to this applied nature is the characteristic of human activity. Unlike the study of natural phenomena, as might be the case in chemistry or physics, the human sciences are distinctly more artificial (Simon 1969). They are created by human conventions. The natural sciences are more concerned with how things are; the sciences of the artificial are concerned with how things ought to be and with designs which help to attain goals.

As a human science, educational administration is not merely concerned with ends in an instrumental sense but with *better* ends. Educational policy aspects of administration, for example, speak to what ought to be and direct their analyses toward uncovering and understanding the conditions under which this "ought" is to be realized. Educational administration is therefore the science and art of developing and implementing effective and satisfying ways to achieve desired ends. Improving the social order gives educational administration a normative quality which must of necessity become an important part of inquiry, analysis, and practice. In short, educational administration is a science of designing courses of action aimed at changing existing situations into preferred ones.

The human sciences are artificial in phenomenological and cultural senses as well. Despite the fact that objective reality exists and is worth pursuing, reality is also a state of mind whose validity and meaning are determined by the private worlds within which each of us lives. Reality is also created and validated in our interaction with others and this interaction network constitutes a cultural web of which we are a part.

In its scientific sense, for example, administrative behavior can be defined as actions identified and described beyond interpretive disputes. Mary, the school principal, might behave in a certain way, and after careful recording of this behavior indisputable conclusions might be reached, such as Mary was autocratic or task-oriented when she gave directions to teachers John and Bill. Behavior so described is brute data (C. Taylor 1971) — it has certain characteristics and configurations which can be documented and described fairly systematically. Mary tells John and Bill exactly what she expects and precisely what standards are to be met. The issue, of course, is exactly what Mary's behavior means. Meanings implicit in administrative behavior are beyond the reach of mere descriptions and objective measurements. Indeed, the very same act may have quite different meanings to different people or to the same people in different situations. John, for example, might view Mary's behavior as being a bit overbearing, bossy, or dictatorial and might feel that such behavior is out of bounds. Perhaps his professional ego is hurt for directive behavior, he maintains, is not an appropriate way to manage professionals. Bill, on the other hand, considers Mary's identical behavior to be courageous and responds with admiration. Mary, he concludes, has high standards, cares about the school and him, gives a great deal herself, and expects a great deal in return. He likes knowing where Mary stands and is motivated by her high standards and expectations.

In this case Mary's actual behavior is clearly secondary to the meanings raised to consciousness of John and Bill. When focusing on Mary's behavior in a descriptive sense, we are emphasizing the configurations of leadership but not its meaning; on the brute data which comprise events in action but not sense data imbedded in our consciousness; on descriptions of leadership but not understandings and interpretations. Key to the human sciences is that events have meanings. Understanding in the human sciences requires that brute events be interpreted and make sense.

Developing a Theory of Practice

Traditional conceptions of theory and practice have not been able to capture the complexity and sensitivity needed to accommodate to the teleological, praxis, and human qualities of educational policy and administration. Needed, nevertheless, is some theoretical framework, some systematic mode of analysis, some series of cognitive maps which can help in understanding and informing administrative practice. Recognizing the complexity of the problem and the shortcomings of traditional conceptions of theoretical science is not to eschew theory. Needed is a theory which can accommodate itself to practice. Such a theory would not seek truth in an effort to expand the knowledge base in a particular discipline but would seek informed practice. The concept of theory of practice represents a promising attempt to develop such a theoretical formulation.

Though I speak of theory of practice, I have in mind the development of a number of theories of practice, each different in scope, the dimensions from which they are comprised, and the sorts of problems they are able to illuminate. They would share, nevertheless, certain common characteristics and rest on similar epistemological assumptions. The following are suggested as some of the more critical characteristics and assumptions which would characterize a theory of practice. They are offered as guides to developing a relevant science of administration.

1. *A theory of practice would be integrative.* It would recognize the value and utility of both normative and descriptive science, positivism and moral science, explanation and understanding, causal inquiry and interpretation. Its strength and future would depend on linking these seemingly separate features together as both alternate and integrative ways of knowing.

2. *A theory of practice would emphasize increasing understanding and improving practice.* Such a theory would recognize and appreciate the ultimate goal of truth critical to traditional science but would accept as well that, in practice, truth is ultimately culturally and perceptually determined. A true knowledge of what is and a true rendering of causal relationships as defined by traditional theoretical science is but one dimension in the complex interaction of factors which should be considered. The ultimate goal of seeking truth as defined by traditional theoretical science is, therefore, replaced by the goals of increasing understanding, informing intuition, and improving practice. The pursuit of understanding as a mode of inquiry requires that practical reasoning gain prominence. Practical reasoning differs from that of proof reasoning which is characteristic of traditional theoretical science. Traditional theoretical science seeks verification

of fact beyond differences in interpretation. Theories of practice, on the other hand, are cast from an understanding, not verification, science. This is not to discount the importance of establishing what is, of accurately rendering the descriptive facts of the world. One must have some basis for understanding. The facts, however, are not ends in themselves but the shadow and substance of interpretations which increase understanding. Understanding, in turn, is a prerequisite to improved practice.

3. *A theory of practice would emphasize action toward some goal or series of goals.* This action emphasis requires that bounded rationality replace absolute rationality, that subjectivity and intersubjectivity be accepted as legitimate units of analyses, and that accommodations be sought in recognition that the world of policy and administration is dynamic. Decisions are made continuously, events are forever unfolding, and with each event completed comes changes in events anticipated. A theory of practice must work *in process.* The still camera and snapshot metaphors associated with traditional scientific inquiry need to be replaced by the motion camera metaphor.

4. *A theory of practice would focus on aspects unique to educational administration and organizational analysis.* Attention would be given to policy *qua* policy science, administration *qua* administrative science, politics *qua* political science and so on for these are important dimensions in support of a theory of practice. Prime attention, however, would be given to the particulars which make educational administration unique. A theory which seeks understanding does not shy away from drawing practical conclusions from its discoveries and from turning its theoretical analyses into social practice (Bauman 1978, 59). Essential to a theory of practice is attention, understanding, and sensitivity to the particular.

5. *A theory of practice would be concerned with what "is."* Of interest are accurate and reliable descriptions of the real world and how it works. With respect to administrative and organizational behavior for example, relationships would be explained, linked together, and predicted. Laws and rules which govern behavior would be sought. Thus traditional scientific inquiry plays an important role in developing a theory of practice. No progress can be made in developing a theory of practice if the themes of prediction and explanation, the hallmarks of traditional scientific inquiry, are not included. In a theory of practice, however, the ledger is incomplete without the normative side of science or the "ought" side.

6. *A theory of practice would be concerned with what "ought" to be.* What cultural imperatives should determine action? What values should be expressed? What qualities of life should be in evidence? What standards should be applied? Theories of practice are designed to improve things, to bring about higher standards, to strive for a better life. Much

debate exists about the role of normative assertions in any scientific endeavor. Skeptics point to the difficulty in establishing the truth of such assertions. Part of this difficulty is in the insistence that the same definitions of truth as used in traditional theoretical science be used for normative assertions. Paul Taylor points out, however, that the truth of normative assertions differs from the truth of factual assertions.

> The truth of normative assertions depends on human decisions; the truth of factual assertions does not. A factual assertion is true if it corresponds to the way the world is regardless of whether we want the world to be that way. . . . A normative assertion is true, on the other hand, only because we have decided to adopt a standard or rule as applicable to what we are making the assertion about. Unless we make such a decision, our assertion has no truth or falsity. And the way the world is does not logically determine what decision we must make. Our adoption of a standard or rule on which the truth or falsity of our assertion depends does not itself depend on the way things are. We must *decide* what ought to be the case. We cannot *discover* what ought to be the case by investigating what is the case [P. Taylor 1958, 248].

7. And finally, *a theory of practice could be concerned with what is and ought "mean."* If a theory of practice is concerned with usable knowledge, then it should be concerned as well with knowledge which makes *sense* to people. It is for this reason that a theory of practice should move beyond the mapping of reality in abstract to the mapping of reality as viewed in different contexts and as viewed by different actors. Such metaphorical analogies as photo replica, electronic portrait, and play script tend to characterize descriptive modes of inquiry. The photo collage, impressionistic painting, and play performance suggest the worlds of interpretation and meaning. No human event studied in abstract is the same as in use.

Meaning and Interpretation

Meaning is an essential ingredient in a theory of practice. Understanding is key to the pursuit of meaning and understanding comes from interpreting the shadow and substance of observed events. Human organizations and enterprises are cultural artifacts which require that inquiry into these fields move beyond description and explanation. "One needs to explain nature, but to understand culture; . . . to 'cognitively assimilate' natural phenomena one has to arrange them in causal chains, but to know cultural phenomena one has to grasp their meaning" (Bauman 1978, 84).

The art of interpretation is thus important to analysis in a theory of practice. Interpretation is an attempt to make clear, to make sense of an object, issue, or event being studied (C. Taylor 1971, 1). Objects, issues, and events studied as "is" yield brute data, brute inferences, and brute descriptions (C. Taylor 1971, 5). Brute data is removed from its context and studied antiseptically. Brute data is essential to establishing the social facts of a given issue, situation, or event. By contrast, "sense" data seek to uncover the meaning of brute data to different individuals and given different intents and contexts (C. Taylor 1971, 11). Touching the brow to brush a fly or to bid at an auction are examples of identical acts with different intents. The famed Italian pinch in a Roman plaza might be viewed differently by a woman than the same pinch in the darkened foyer of a theater in Chicago. Competitive behavior of children might be applauded by parents of one subculture living on the 400 block of San Antonio, Texas, but frowned upon by parents of another subculture just a block away. Recording the number of brow touchings observed, the frequency pattern of pinching, and the incidence of competitive behavior are social facts which tell us very little of the social meanings and social consequences these acts have for the principals involves. Brute data are yielded by careful observation. Sense data are yielded by careful interpretation. The teleological, praxis, and human characteristics of educational administration and organizational analysis require that inquiry and analysis go beyond brute to sense data.

Hermeneutics and the Science of Administration

Of interest to educational policy and administration is the interplay of three questions: what "is" fact and reality; what "ought" to be; and what do events which comprise the is and ought "mean"? Normative, descriptive, and interpretive science as reflected in the three questions, once integrated, become the basis and structure of a theory of practice. Hermeneutics can help in this integration by providing a cognitive map and a mode of inquiry and analysis by which the normative, descriptive, and interpretive sciences can come to play in addressing practical problems of educational policy and administration.

Hermeneutics in the social sciences is the art of interpretation. It is the theory of the operation of understanding in its relation to the interpretation of certain events and issues in context. Its history as a discipline is long and dates back to scholarly debates over the authenticity and true meaning of classical texts of Greco-Latin antiquity and of sacred texts such as the Old and New Testaments. From this technical origin hermeneutics evolved into a mode of philosophical inquiry addressed to epistomology in seeking an answer to the question, "How do we know?" (Ricoeur 1973). Of late, hermeneutics has taken on an ontological quality as it adds to its quest, "What is the mode of that being who only exists through understanding"? (Ricoeur 1973). It is this shift from a philosophy of science per se to a more action-oriented perspective concerned with actual meaning in a given context which makes hermeneutics attractive to an applied field such as educational policy and administration.

This action orientation is expressed in the triad situation-understanding-interpretation (Ricoeur 1973). Situation requires the explication of what is and provides the necessary substrata for further analysis of a practical problem or situation. Understanding asks the question why it is and attempts to explain causal relationships implicit in person or situation. Using art as an example, "to understand the work of art was to recover the artist's design" (Bauman 1978, 12). Interpretation asks what it means. Identifying implied purposes, intentions, and motives of an actor and learning of the reactions of others to same are important to interpretation. Interpretation "recreates the actor's web of motives and intentions" (Bauman 1978, 12).

Certainly important limitations exist in adopting the hermeneutical mode to applied and action-oriented fields such as administration and organizational analysis. Hermeneutics, for example, seeks as its goal ever clearer interpretations. As an epistomology it is a mode of knowledge which seeks perfection in understanding but never finds it. Hermeneutics is likely to be more successful where praxis is not a characteristic of the objects of study. Historical events, for example, lend themselves to hermeneutical inquiry because they remain done, fixed in time. Post hoc analysis of events reveals new insights and illuminates more vividly the meaning of these events, but the events themselves as facts of occurrence do not change. Contrast history with the fastpaced, everevolving, and dynamic nature of educational policy and administration. In these fields we are concerned with events occurred, presently occurring, and likely to occur. The necessity for understanding and meaning in studying these events remains important but is tempered by the bounded rationality of time unfolding and the necessity for action.

The famous hermeneutical circle, for example, refers to the endless analysis of object within objects, event within events, and item within context seeking everenriched meanings.

> The circle can also be put in terms of part-whole relations: we are trying to establish a reading for the whole text, and for this we appeal to readings of its partial expressions; and yet, because we are dealing with meaning, with making sense, where expressions only make sense or not in relation to others, the readings of partial expressions depend on those of others, and ultimately of the whole [C. Taylor 1971, 4].

> Understanding means going in circles: rather than a unilinear progress toward better and less vulnerable knowledge, it consists of an endless recapitulation and reassessment of collective memories —

evermore voluminous, but always selective. It is difficult to see how any of the successive recapitulations can claim to be final and conclusive; still more difficult would be to substantiate this claim [Bauman 1978, 17].

Each revolution within the hermeneutical circle stirs the analyst on to further analysis in a seemingly neverending search for more lucid, intense, and complete meanings. "One would rather speak of a hermeneutic spiral, to be sure: in our search of the lost affinity, in our urge to reappropriate fully estranged creations of the kindred Spirit, we never really finish our job. But we move from the particular to the universal and back in ever-widening circles, ever closer to the ideal of the Spirit once again, but this time self-consciously, unified" (Bauman 1978, 28).

Educational administration and organizational analysis, by contrast, do not seek ever-clearer meanings and understandings as ends. Their purpose is to inform and improve practice. They seek a qualitative difference in the social order by altering present circumstances for the better. The praxis qualities of educational administration and organizational analysis, therefore, make it difficult for them to become hermeneutical sciences in their own right. Yet, the teleological and human characteristics of their fields lend themselves to hermeneutical inquiry and analysis. Can educational administration and organizational analysis become hermeneutical sciences? The answer is probably not, but hermeneutical inquiry and analysis can play an important role in developing theories of practice in these fields.

Using the Theory of Practice Perspective

I now turn to applying some of these ideas to the practical problems of conflict within an organization. A theory of practice model is proposed to show how hermeneutical thinking can help in analysis. In this context, understanding and meaning are not ends in themselves but roadways to more informed intuition and improved practice. One might characterize the analysis, therefore, as more like hermeneutical thinking than hermeneutical science and of using hermeneutical cycles rather than the seemingly endless hermeneutical circle or spiral.

Of interest to analysis in administration are events occurred, events occurring, and future events or deciding what to do. To illustrate the theory of practice approach, conflict management will be used to evaluate events occurred and occurring. The problem of centralization-decentralization will be used to suggest a mode suitable to deciding what one should do.

Two key distinctions have been made in this chapter: descriptive knowledge or knowledge of what "is" as being different than normative knowledge or knowledge of what "ought" to be; and, viewing the world from a theoretical perspective as opposed to a practical perspective. The integrative criterion suggested for a theory of practice requires that all of these dimensions not only come to play as important separate aspects of analysis, but that they be integrated into a unified analysis. We can, therefore, speak of descriptive knowledge and normative knowledge on the one hand and viewing events from a practical perspective and theoretical perspective on the other.

Four combinations are suggested by this interplay: practical-descriptive, theoretical-descriptive, practical-normative and theoretical-normative. The four can be displayed in grid form as illustrated in Figure 1. Within this grid, quadrant 1 (practical-descriptive) focuses attention on the concrete facts which exist in a situation; quadrant 2 (theoretical-descriptive) focuses attention on the scientific laws and relationships which help explain these facts and other facts of this genre; quadrant 3 (practical-normative) focuses attention on the stated and implied intents and platforms of individual actors; quadrant 4 (theoretical-normative) focuses attention on the stated and applied cultural norms, ideals, and standards which bear on the situation under analysis. Each of the four quadrants represents sources for establishing certain social facts which describe and explain the situation of issue. As hermeneutical inquiry (represented by the "spiral-cycle" in the center of Figure 1) proceeds, social facts become closer to social meanings. Until this progression from social fact to social meaning begins, true understanding is suspect and presumably the intuitions of analyst and administrator are not adequately informed.

Consider, for example, a situation in a school or college where certain departments or units are involved in serious conflict with each other. In examining the avenues of inquiry suggested in Figure 1, certain key questions might be asked:

Quadrant 1. What is the nature of conflict which exists in this school or college? How can this conflict be objectively and accurately described? Who are the principals involved in this conflict? What do they do and say?

Quadrant 2. What cognitive maps, models, and theoretical frameworks exist which help explain and tie together observed events? Can causal links among events be theoretically established? What research exists which substantiates these theoretical speculations? Can future actions be predicted?

Quadrant 3. What are the hopes, aspirations, and intents of the individual actors involved in the conflict? What do they seek? What do they want to happen? What are they trying to accomplish? Can these intents be separated into those espoused and those inferred from actions, attitudes, and language systems used?

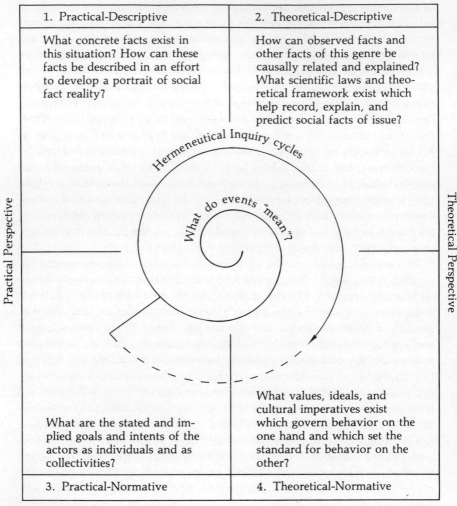

Figure 1. Suggested avenues of inquiry in a theory of practice.

Quadrant 4. What norms, values, and standards exist which help to develop a set of ideal criteria to which groups involved in the crisis might strive? What cultural imperatives exist in this situation which govern behavior of individuals involved? How do such considerations as justice, equity, free expression, and democratic ideals come to play? Are there images of how schools and colleges should be organized and how groups should behave which in the ideal are most suited to educational quality?

From Q1 observations we might observe that individuals within each of the competing groups are becoming more closely knit and disciplined and that demands for loyalty are increasing. We might also learn that some individuals involved have no interest in the conflict per se but are responding to increases in pressure to express loyalty to the group. From a Q2 review of traditional social science literature (i.e., Sherif, et al. 1961; Blake and Mouten 1961) on the topic, we might note that as intergroup conflict increases intragroup conflict decreases. Members begin to overlook individual differences and emphasize commonalities. Further, the group becomes more structured and the leader more powerful as group members become more willing to accept autocratic leadership. Finally, the group works harder and is willing to sacrifice personal interests on behalf of group goals. All of these factors are thought to contribute to intragroup effectiveness but seem also to have negative consequences for intergroup effectiveness. Thus, while individual departments may seem to be more productive and display higher morale, the college or school as a whole may actually be less effective.

This sort of analysis can be very useful in developing a framework for understanding some of the forces which might be at play in this particular conflict situation. But the analysis suffers from objectivity, abstractness, and universalism. Theories of practice are concerned with the *particulars* of given situations and specific problems. Key to providing an analysis which would be helpful in actually managing conflict in a specific situation is *understanding*, which comes from the particular. Q3 can help in this effort to understand by charting what it is that motivates individual actors actually involved in the conflict. We are not concerned with individual behavior in the abstract but individual behavior as defined by a particular context. We might learn, for example, that this particular college or school faces serious problems not at stake in the conflict under study (deteriorating work conditions and prospects of low salary increases, for example) and that the principal or dean intends to use the present conflict as a means to distract faculty from other issues. Or perhaps the majority of those involved are not interested in the substance of the conflict but are caught up in the psychological effects or are responding to group pressures in a desire to belong. Whatever the case may be, as these facts of the situation change, they cast the more theoretical and descriptive facts yielded by quadrants 1 and 2 in different lights; in other words, their meanings and relevance change. From Q4 come certain ideal images of how a school or college might fully function in quest of excellence (i.e., Likert 1967; Sergiovanni and Carver 1980) and certain ethical criteria (democratic ideals, justice, cooperation, etc.) which become standards for evaluating behavior or for determining what is good and what isn't.

Now that the territory of analysis has been briefly sketched, each of the quadrants would be examined in connection with others. Quadrant 1, for example, would be compared with Q2 in an effort to develop keener descriptions of reality and more powerful causal explanations of events and activities. Actor intents (Q3) would be compared with observations of actual behavior (Q1) in an effort to determine discrepancies between "espoused theories" and "theories in use" (Arygris and Schön 1974). Both theories would be held up against ideal images and standards which emerge from Q4. This "cycle" of analysis would be repeated and, with each repeat, understanding would presumably increase.

Ultimately, the pace of the analysis would shift from examining quadrants as separate entities to overlapping; from quadrants being viewed as four independent but related snapshots to one multiple exposure. And gradually, the social facts which comprise each of the four quadrants would become social meanings with relevance to the particular problem at hand. As this progression from social facts to social meanings occurs, the intuitions of both analyst and practitioner become more informed and presumably more reasoned, and relevant action is made possible.

Since the nature of educational administration and organizational analysis requires that practical issues be addressed, immediacy becomes a problem and bounded rationality a reality. One cannot, for example, take the "best" solutions to a problem and hold on to them until the world is ready to accept them. Rather, decisions must be made in the face of reality. Changes are evolutionary and progress gained today added to that of tomorrow moves one closer to the ideal. The pluralistic framework offered here seeks to test the tension between and among opposing forces with the intent that this ideal is approached a little more with each decision that is made.

Hermeneutics, as a science of interpretation, cannot substitute for a theory of practice anymore than can descriptive or normative science. These sciences exist not as ends in themselves but to serve the decision process in the practice of educational policy and administration. Deciding what to "do" is the sine qua non of a theory of practice. Yet informed doing requires that one consider what is (descriptive science), what ought to be (normative science), and what events mean (interpretative or hermeneutical science).

Avoiding Errors of the Third and Fourth Type

By suggesting that educational administration and organizational analysis should not be exclusively characterized by either traditional science or hermeneutical sciences, I propose a worsening dilemma. One might reasonably ask, how can we as administrators accept the ambiguity of seeking a reasonable amount of rationality, objectivity, and certainty in our scholarly investigations and professional practice on the one hand and of being forced to adopt the elusive modes of inquiry and analysis suggested by hermeneutics and theory of practice on the other? Faced with this dilemma one is tempted to seek the certainty and comfort of traditional scientific views of administration regardless of their appropriateness. Rationality in method, clarity in model building, precision in technique, and certainty in subsequent conclusions are norms so powerful in our Western academic and professional cultures that they often obscure substantive issues of importance, accuracy, and relevance. What are the risks of following such a comfortable course?

Threats to knowledge claims can result from both doubtful cogency and doubtful relevance (Dunn 1980). Important distinctions can be made between misplaced and misjudged cogency on the one hand and misplaced relevancy on the other. Misjudged cogency is the best known of these distinctions and refers to errors in practical judgments which result when statistical limits are set too high (commonly known as Type I error) or too low (Type II error). Misplaced cogency, less considered in our scientific tradition, refers not to errors of measurement or method but to the adequacy of problems addressed. Addressing the wrong problem, regardless of ardor and cogency of method, can be referred to as a Type III error (Mitroff 1974). This is the error type we face by yielding to the temptation of business as usual in administrative science and practice regardless of the appropriateness of our theories and methods to the tasks and problems they are presumed to address. John Tukey's admonition is important here: "Far better an approximate answer to the right question, which is often vague, than an exact answer to the wrong question, which can always be made precise" (quoted in Rose 1977, 23).

Given the teleological, praxis, and human characteristics of administrative study and practice, it is far better to adopt the concept of theory of practice and the hermeneutical mode of inquiry, no matter how difficult this task, than to continue with the more comfortable but less appropriate methods and images of traditional science. To do otherwise is to commit the Type III error.

Misplaced relevance refers to the development and application of cogent knowledge which is relevant to one type of problem but not another. Misplaced relevance can be referred to as a Type IV error (Dunn 1980). The practical problem of "doing," the making of professional decisions and the daily conduct of administrative affairs, is very different from the problem of determining what is, from providing accurate and reliable description of situations. Misplaced relevancy occurs when our analysis moves from what is to what one should do (from descriptive science to professional practice) without adequate consideration of what ought to be (normative science) and what is and ought mean in a given context and to particular people (interpretive science). When we do this, we commit the Type IV error.

This analysis will undoubtedly not please those who are wed to the canons of traditional science. But if scholars of administration and organizational analysis and professionals who practice the art of administration wish to avoid errors of the third and fourth kind, they are left with no other alternative but to proceed in these murky waters. This dilemma represents the challenge we face. If we desire a relevant science of administration, then the worlds of descriptive, normative, and interpretive science must be brought together to bear on the problem of professional practice. In this effort the role of science is not that of surrogate to the administrator's intuition but serves to inform that intuition. Indeed, the art of administration is celebrated in actions born of informed intuition.

REFERENCES

Arygris, Chris, and Donald A. Schön (1974). *Theory in Practice: Increasing Professional Effectiveness.* San Francisco: Jossey-Bass.

Bauman, Zygmunt. *Hermeneutics and Social Science* (1978). New York: Columbia University Press.

Blake, Robert R., and Jane S. Mouton (1961). "Reactions to Intergroup Competition Under Win-Lose Conditions." *Management Science* 7, 420–35.

Campbell, P. J. (1974). "Evolutionary Epistemology." In P. A. Schlipp ed. *The Philosophy of Karl Popper.* LaSalle, Ill.: Open Court Press, pp. 413–63.

Culbertson, Jack (1979). "Some Key Epistemological Questions about a Theory of Practice.' " Symposium presentation, American Educational Research Association, San Francisco,

_____ (1980). "Educational Administration: Where We Are and Where We Are Going." In Robin Farquhar and Ian Housego, eds. *Canadian and Comparative Educational Administration.* Vancouver: University of British Columbia Press.

Dunn, William N. (1980). "Reforms as Arguments." Paper presented to the International Conference on Political Realization of Social Science Knowledge and Research, Vienna.

Eisner, Elliot (1982). "An Artistic Approach to Supervision." In T. J. Sergiovanni, ed. *Supervision of Teaching.* 1982 Yearbook of the Association for Supervision and Curriculum Development. Arlington, Va.:

Likert, Rensis (1967). *The Human Organization: Its Management and Value.* New York: McGraw Hill.

Mitroff, Ian I. (1974). *The Subjective Side of Science.* New York: Elseurer.

Ricoeur, Paul (1973). "The Task of Hermeneutics." *Philosophy Today* 17(2). 112–82.

Rose, R. (1977). "Disciplined Research and Undisciplined Problems." In Carol H. Weiss, ed. *Using Social Research in Public Policy Making.* Lexington, Mass.: D. C. Heath.

Sergiovanni, Thomas J. (1980). "A Social Humanities View of Educational Policy and Administration." *Educational Administration Quarterly* 16(1), 1–20.

Sergiovanni, Thomas J., and Fred D. Carver (1980). *The New School Executive: A Theory of Administration,* 2nd ed. New York: Harper & Row.

Sherif, M., O. J. Harvey, B. J. White, W. R. Hood, and C. Sherif (1961). *Intergroup Conflict and Cooperation: The Robbers Cave Experiment.* Norman, Okla.: University Book Exchange.

Simon, Herbert A. (1957). *Administrative Behavior,* 2nd ed. New York: Free Press.

_____ (1969). *The Sciences of the Artificial.* Cambridge, Mass.: MIT Press.

Taylor, Charles (1971). "Interpretation and the Sciences of Man." *The Review of Metaphysics* 25(1), 3–51.

Taylor, Paul W. (1961). *Normative Discourse.* Englewood Cliffs, N.J.: Prentice Hall.

von Wright, George Henrik (1971). *Explanation and Understanding.* Ithaca, N.Y.: Cornell University Press.

PART IV

Theory into Practice

It is fitting that this volume concludes with a specific effort to relate theory and practice using the action word "into" rather than the more bland connecting "and." There is, of course, no law nor rule which requires that theory be put into practice. Theory may be used to analyze or to explain or to evaluate practice rather than to govern practice. Seemingly random findings, for example, keep confirming that Einstein was in fact correct in his theory of relativity, but the theory has not really guided the practice of physics or any other related science.

There is merit — if not necessity — in providing for a practitioner's view of theory just as the theoretician depends upon some view of practice for his or her work. It is to that end that the possibilities of putting theory into practice are explored here. It is not that theory is only good when it guides practice, only that it is good to consider whether a given theoretical framework might guide or otherwise relate to practice.

The three essays which comprise Part IV provide critical summaries of the book's chapters. One might fairly ask, why three such critical summaries for the book? Key to the cultural perspective is that the same events have different meanings as individuals and settings change. The individuals (Martin Burlingame, Hugh G. Petrie, and John E. Corbally) and the settings (educational administration, educational policy analysis, and higher education administration), therefore, provide different interpretations of the book's contents. Though the summary essays agree on certain key aspects of the cultural perspective, all are quick to cite reservations and raise issues as the perspective is articulated into practice.

One is tempted to summarize the summaries and thus offer a fourth interpretation. We choose, instead, to let the essays of Part IV stand as independent summaries to the book and indeed as an invitation for readers to add still a final chapter outlining their own understandings. In books of this sort, endings are really beginnings. Our purpose will have been fulfilled if we have succeeded in portraying the cultural perspective on administrative leadership and organizational analysis as a viable and needed alternative to other perspectives, and if we have enticed readers to join with us in continuing to map out this perspective in pursuit of a viable theory of administration and framework for practice.

CHAPTER 16

Theory into Practice: Educational Administration and the Cultural Perspective

Martin Burlingame

What do these scholarly essays say collectively to those currently practicing school administration? The (deceptively) simple charge of this chapter is to make sense of these presentations and their perspectives, for example, to elementary school principals or superintendents of middle-sized districts. The (deceptively) simple answer might be that these essays really have nothing to say to practitioners. At their very best, they are the prattle of scholastics, not the hardheaded praxis needed by administrators. But such a curt dismissal ignores the strenuous efforts of the essays to move from scholarship to practice. For the moment, then, we shall act "as if" these essays as a collectivity have something of value for school administrators.

Two characteristics of the essays complicate, if not confound, fulfilling even a simple charge. First, they are not neatly integrated around a single notion or even a restricted set of notions. They do seem to be in the neighborhood referred to in the book as "culture." But as Taylor warns, that word has ambiguous meanings. Second, as Sergiovanni notes, these essays reflect an emerging, not a mature perspective. They do not illuminate a state of the art capable of telling either researchers or practitioners if certain notions or certain relationships are especially fruitful or dreadfully dull. Hence, the essays provide a menu of ideas but delineate neither whether separate items are appetizer or main course nor whether one or four star in quality.

One way to get some sort of handle on these essays is to argue that practicing administrators know that they fulfill several roles in their schools, and that certain problems persistently bother them. We will use these intuitive bits of knowledge from practicing administrators to "test" the notions presented. Such an approach may suggest whether in fact these essays provide not only helpful guides for practicing administrators but also some understanding of the general perspective and emerging notions of the cultural perspective. Such a strategy, that is, suggesting a framework which is useful but where development in detail is beyond the scope of this chapter has some obvious costs. But this effort at macrolevel analysis of the school as an institution in its culture may stimulate others, both researchers and practitioners, to puzzle about the strengths and weaknesses of this new and different perspective.

Administrators in schools know they fulfill several managerial roles. Following the notions of Mintzberg (1973), for instance, we can ask, what do these papers say about the interpersonal, informational, and decisional roles of school managers? Briefly, Mintzberg argues that interpersonal roles involve figurehead, liaison, and leader activities. These activities are grounded in the formal authority and status of managers. The informational role includes monitor, disseminator, and spokesperson activities. All depend upon managers being the nerve center of organizational information. Finally, managerial activities such as entrepreneur, disturbance handler, resource allocator, and negotiator denote their decisional role. Managers are at the central point where organizational decisions are made.

Administrators in schools face a number of persisting problems. Following Eliot (1959), we can ask, what do these papers say to school managers about the problems associated with curriculum, facilities, district organization, personnel, and financing? Eliot argues that these five topics are among the most significant for school administrators. They are the topics that generate the most discussion, that produce the most emotion, and that carry the most impact on schools and their operators. These two dimensions of roles and problems suggest an analytic matrix (Figure 1) which may help in ordering the diversity of notions found throughout the book. After using this matrix as a tool to examine what these papers may be saying, the final section speculates about the implications of these papers for practicing administrators.

Figure 1: Matrix of school problems and managerial roles.

		Curriculum	Facilities	District Organization	Personnel	Finances
Managerial Roles	Interpersonal					
	Informational					
	Decisional					

A Matrix of Roles and Problems

Before turning to the first topic, curriculum, it will serve us well to see if we can create some larger image of what these essays seem to be arguing. By picking and choosing, by hopping and skipping, we may be able to start from a reasonably coherent "big" picture. To begin, according to Taylor, there are prime objects and replications which seem to predominate in certain periods of time. At some point in time this system of prime objects and replications becomes a "replica-mass." These replica-masses are identifiable and capable of classification, thus enabling us to sort accurately ancient Greek from ancient Roman artifacts or to segregate correctly organizations such as universities from armies.

These replica-masses appear for Schön to be metaphors about what we should consider to be for a particular group or organization the central questions of life and the range of acceptable answers for such questions. A replica-mass then provides the key generative metaphor for a culture or an organization. In much the same vein, prime objects and replications for Hirsch are the normal symbol systems of organizations. According to Meyer, the replica-mass provides the rationale for what we "believe" is happening.

The cultural perspective, hence, argues that there are identifiable themes or replica-masses which predominate certain periods of time or certain social institutions. But, if Hirsch is correct, this perspective argues further that the prime objects of a period may be challenged by crises such as shifts in the environment. Under such conditions, conflicts occur about what the prime objects or replications truly are. If Meyer is correct, many times we strive to slow down, if not completely extinguish, these conflicts by pointing proudly to institutions certified to carry out the replications of prime objects even though, in fact, these certified institutions may be failing miserably to produce replications.

This sense of conflict not only feels reasonably "life-like" to administrators but also suggests one last theme in the cultural perspective. Both Hirsch and Meyer seem to be pointing to the fact that at any particular moment in any particular culture there will be conflicts about what constitutes the prime objects. In contrast to Vaill's high-performing system, this line of reasoning suggests that at any current moment in complex, literate, and industrial systems there should be low performance because of strenuous debates about prime objects. Replica-masses, then, seem reasonably clear and distinct at a distance. The closer one approaches, the more struggles over prime object should be evident.

Curriculum

From the perspective of a practicing administrator, the "official" school curriculum is the certified story, the replica-mass of prime objects and replications, the school is licensed to present to the young. Much as the old men or women in preliterate tribes, school teachers tell the young the stories of the tribe. These stories are made up of "acceptable" questions and answers intimately linked in ways that mark off the "valuable" from the "worthless." For instance, these stories in America suggest how our nation was founded, how it has developed, and what its future should be. During this national development, certain values have helped and certain wrongs have hindered the realization of our destiny. Such tribal stories present to the young a world of important understandings, understandings to be reenforced by the actions of teachers and classmates. These stories, these metaphors of life, are the school's curriculum. Stories thus provide for the young a beginning, a middle, and an end which link them to their peers and to prime objects and replications which are their immediate culture.

As with most tribes, these stories may often change in the telling, may be challenged by shifts in the environment, or may be slowly transformed by contact with different stories. Hence, the practicing school administrator is confronted almost daily by proponents of differing stories. Some of these accentuate the values of yesterday, others anticipate what the future may hold, and still others hope to change the questions and answers of today. In turn, the school administrator must choose whether to act in ways which facilitate or hinder communication among competing storytellers, to share or hide various stories, and to decide which stories are to be told or are to be denied a hearing in classrooms.

At any particular moment there seem to be countless stories. A few which American schools tell students come to mind: stories about the life and value of becoming a (1) doctor or lawyer, (2) common laborer, (3) husband/wife/mother/father, (4) athlete, (5) singer/dancer/actor, (6) soldier, (7) good citizen, and so on. As stories, these prime objects provide images of a beginning, a middle and an end (a career), offer criteria for assessing the goodness or badness both of the career choice and the career itself, e.g., doctors get up at night but make a lot of money, and provide a powerful rationale for social mingling and segregation. For example, some people are interested in fine wines and classical music, others in beer and baseball.

The cultural perspective highlights that most in society will see the school as a powerful agent for inculcating important tribal stories. But since there are several competing tribal stories, and several possible levels of critical understanding of these stories (the unquestioning loyalist, the disinterested or the passionate critic), school administrators should anticipate curriculum conflicts about content ("what"), storyteller ("who"), amount ("how much"), and timing ("when"). In such conflictual situations, some administrators may choose to follow a single story and create a high-performing school as suggested by Vaill or may choose to present themselves as constructively and creatively single-minded. Others, as Staw noted, may see themselves "trapped" by older stories and commitments, unable to pull back from impending disaster but applauded for this constancy by colleagues. Still others may seek symbolic realignment, as hypothesized by Hirsch, or shifts in predominant metaphors (Schön). Others may blighthly sail along, unaware of what is happening, but continuing as Meyers believed to play their roles with zest, while others may note as Allison did that their past experiences and stories do not help this new and "different" situation.

Such a rendering of administrative actions suggests not only the wide catalog of possible problems and responses but also the bond between response and story most favored by the administrator. The preferences of an administrator indicate both which story the administrator values and the level of critical comprehension the administrator has of this, and other, stories. Not only do these preferences color choices, they suggest to Sergiovanni the boundaries of legitimate political behavior for an administrator. Certain issues may be amenable to discussion but others may be at the core of personal meaning. Some school leaders may even face issues which necessarily lead to their "symbolic martyrdom" (Burlingame 1981).

A contrived situation may clarify this discussion. Imagine that you as the principal of a high school are directed by the superintendent to release one of two teachers and to provide the superintendent and school board with a brief statement explaining your action. The superintendent will accept retaining either (1) the only art teacher or (2) the only advanced math and science teacher. You have no other faculty capable of "filling in" for either of these teachers. What do you do, and why? While contrived, such a situation helps illuminate conflicts among several stories that could be told to the young and how the preferences of the individual administrator may influence certain acts. (How many opted, for instance, for a firm letter to superintendent and board suggesting the choice was impossible?)

Facilities

A second area is the facilities of the school. Are school buildings statements of the preferred stories of the educators and community just as Greek statues or Roman buildings exemplify their ages? These papers would suggest that indeed they are significant cultural artifacts. These artifacts suggest critical insights into their replica-masses. For example, what is the relationship between the size and investment in equipment in gyms versus size and investment in books in libraries? What "creature comforts" are seen as necessary for students, e.g., recreation rooms, lounges, carpeting, and paved parking lots or playgrounds? Are there special offices or lounges for teachers? How big is the principal's office? All these tells us much about preferred stories.

Furthermore, in districts with several schools the evolution of changes in school facilities may be traced. Schools should be approached as if they are temples, filled with artifacts reflecting important images of their time. For instance, the naming of schools may link them to particular national heroes (the everpresent Washington, Jefferson, Lincoln, or Roosevelt) of specific eras. Equally, names of present giants in the field of education that grace the buildings of our era may never appear again. Upon entering the school the architecture often illuminates assumptions about the nature and characteristic of the young. For example, is the school built in such a way that there are no places to hide or to gain privacy? Many have noticed that the usual school building features several prime points for surveillance of youth. Equally, the shape and size of classrooms reveals much about what we believe (what our story tells us) about the characteristics of the young (Getzels 1974).

Again, the locations of schools within larger communities may tell us about the power of their home neighborhoods. Are the young of a particular neighborhood, a neighborhood often consciously selected by their parents, to be kept close to home and with their same kind, or to be bused to a larger facility where they may encounter different sorts of children and different ways of dealing with the world? Such decisions provide clues to preferred stories.

Hence, the facilities of schools provide insights into topics such as evolution of preferred stories, dominant metaphors about the young, preferred means of inculcation into society, and relationship of neighborhood to school. These insights provide clues, for example, to how administrators represented the school system to others, to what information was seen as valuable or misguided, and to grounds that were used to make such decisions. In this way, facilities are both opportunities for outsiders to "view" the preferred stories and embodiments of the preferred story for insiders. Much as the stained glass windows and arches of Gothic cathedrals told important stories of that age to worshipers, the classrooms and corridors of schools tell the young and represent to elders much about the preferred stories of their time and community.

District Organization

The structuring of the school district as an organized entity — the number of schools, the size of schools, the number of students in a district, and the size of a district (both demographically and geographically) — provides further clues to the preferred story. Since the 1900s, for example, there have been consistent professional stories stressing the flaws of small school districts. Such districts, the story goes, lack adequate curriculum and facilities, hire less than competent teachers, and provide too few funds for efficient education of children. In contrast, the local control story of many smaller communities' residents, and their few professional friends, has stressed the power of intimacy between schooling and locale, the importance of continuity among several generations, and the willingness of communities to spend monies for results the local citizens can see firsthand.

These conflicting stories color the roles that practicing administrators play. The interpersonal styles of superintendents have often meant that they were accepted by the locals as a "good ol' boy" (Peshkin 1978) or rejected as a "city slicker" bent on destruction of the local school. The genre of expert information provided by "good" superintendents underscored the story preferred in that community. Thus, the virtues of localism (or of consolidation to larger units) became the theme of speeches to local groups who generally favored the story already.

One interesting outcome of these preferred stories was the inherent tribalism of school administrator associations. At the national level, these organizations seemed schizophrenic about topics such as district organizations because the various subgroups within the association lobbied for their particular story. The outcome of such struggles was inevitable: the careful compromise producing glittering generality platforms. Such nebulous nonsense, such patent patchings provided an air of unanimity and a sense of a common preferred story where, in fact, deep disagreement existed. While both sides honored education, the exact nature of that enterprise was sharply different for the competing factions.

Personnel

The qualifications of the people hired to run the schools, to teach the classes, and to maintain the school, e.g., janitors, secretaries, and bus drivers, provide important avenues to the preferred story of a community at a particular moment in time. The "class" of teachers hired at a particular time, for example, tells us whether outsiders are being brought in to stimulate change or insiders are being hired to maintain the status quo. However, the personnel of a school system may be hired at the same time but leave at different times; hence school personnel are rarely a uniform batch. They instead reflect stories which dominated certain eras. Put another way, comings and goings of personnel create the problem of generational conflict within schools.

What is important to grasp is that the stratified nature of personnel offers multiple opportunities for conflicts to erupt over stories. Teachers holding different stories about children may exhibit these stories in discussions, for example, about discipline, about what ought to be learned, and about the mix of responsibilities for parents and schools. Such topics provide constant sources of irritation and excitability, or of commonness and unanimity. We can also anticipate that individuals and organizations will develop mechanisms to reduce the possibilities of conflict (Fernandez 1965). Groups or individuals, for instance, may be deliberately segregated from each other (elementary from secondary teachers); differences may be simply overlooked to avoid tension, e.g., "everybody wants the same things from schools for their children"; and glittering generalities and senseless slogans may be proposed which gloss such differences as, for example, "equal educational opportunity."

Practicing administrators, therefore, may become adept at finding simplifying devices, as noted by Vaill, or specific and powerful images which accentuate commonality of school goals and personnel. In fact, little of what they say may in fact truly exist, if we are to believe Meyer. In this sense, the symbols and trappings of school administration often serve to accentuate the commonality of the preferred story being told about schools. In reality, these symbols and trappings may hide from public view the diversity of stories being told by personnel, the wide variations in depth provided by these storytellers, and the almost absolute necessity for students ultimately to build their own story of what is happening. Public schools, then, are institutions in which multiple groups compete to see what "public" means, and, as Allison noted, administrators of such institutions are attentive to these conflicts about stories.

Financing

The financing of schools provides constant headaches. From the perspective of the papers, these headaches for administrators spring from two diverse sources. First, various groups within the community wish to invest differing amounts of dollars into different categories of human capital. Some want to invest, for example, in the development of artistic talents, others in the training of passive blue-collar workers. Second, these decisions about funding expose clearly the match between the preferences of professional educators and differing citizens groups. Many of the programs that educators wish to add or delete can be examined and then rejected by public vote.

The initial studies of the financing of education stressed the political nature of decision-making as described by Sergiovanni. Some of these papers, for example Taylor, Meyer, and Hirsch, suggest that the issues involved in financing schools are better viewed as struggles among various symbol systems which may be either abated momentarily by political compromise or resolved by the emergence of newer symbolic patterns (Turner 1974). These symbolic "revolutions" may provide "new" and "different" stories and constellations of values, creating a "new" and "different" situation. Note, for example, how the 1970s voucher experiment of the Office of Economic Opportunity and the National Institute of Education provided a "different" view of parental and student rights and opportunities, offered a "new" role to schools as competitors for students, and financed schools by student choice not obligation. The voucher experiment provided a different story of American education — a story vigorously attacked by educational groups.

Financing offers at least one other insight into the cultural perspective on schools. Much of the financing of schools and the distribution of funds has been done by formulas. These formulas are often based on the number of students in school or the average ratio of students to teachers. Such formulas are the artifacts of some particular preferred story. One such story, for example, stresses that the fewer students taught by a single teacher, the better the students will be taught. Disputes, e.g., is it the case that the fewer students the better, illuminate clashes among various and competing stories. At times these clashes may be heated and public. They capture the attention and mood of various groups that hope to gain advantage or resist disadvantage. At other times these formulas are unchallenged, dominating the activities of schools. Until the advent of declining enrollments, for instance, most school district personnel and most publics accepted linking dollars to number of students. This tight coupling of student and dollar worked to bring more monies to schools and was unchallenged in many legislative arenas until the number of students began to drop. What we can anticipate is that various pieces of the school system, often formulas as artifacts of different stories, will rest undisturbed until environmental conditions or some new and challenging story upsets this peaceful bliss. Systems, seen from this perspective, are much like Christmas fruitcakes. They are made of many different elements from various times and parts of the world.

For practicing administrators, the roles that they play in the area of finance are shaped by efforts to dampen such conflict. Strategies include efforts to show that schools provide at low costs many benefits to the entire community, e.g., schools not only educate, they keep students off the streets; that schools serve the special interests contained in the preferred story of the group they are now addressing, e.g., they help train business leaders to fill the roles of the chamber of commerce; and that the general uncertainty between present schooling and future activities of students necessitates a program with many alternatives, e.g., they provide opportunities for Johnny and Mary to succeed. In this fashion, practicing administrators must argue that while they now have enough funds to almost achieve these goals, more funds would make for the complete fulfillment of goals. At other times, administrators must seek new funds as new stories impose different tasks on the schools. In all these cases, nonetheless, practicing administrators seek to avoid publicly picking one preferred story over another preferred story. While they may in fact privately do just that, more frequently they seek politically to provide something for everyone. Doing something for everybody means a full agenda for most of the days of practicing administrators.

Summary

In this all too busy and sketchy overview, I have endeavored to see if the essays in this book had anything to say to practicing school administrators. Using an analytic matrix of managerial roles and persistent problems, I examined the ways these papers might cast light on managerial activities. Three points seem to emerge.

First, these essays suggest we may insightfully view schools as not only the creators of our future culture but as artifacts of our past culture. What goes on in schools is as much the product of past decisions as it is about future priorities. The locations of buildings, generations of teachers, and texts suggested by curriculum guides are instances of past decisions shaping — both implicitly and explicitly — the future.

Second, these essays suggest that we are both conscious of the amount of conflict possible in and about schools and deliberate in our attempts to keep this conflict manageable. The heavy stress found on allegiance and the willingness to overlook frequent gaps between promise and practice suggest that conflict avoidance is an important notion for practicing administrators to understand and use, and those of a more scholarly bent to investigate.

Third, and finally, these essays suggest the rather limited power of technical solutions to administrative problems. The roots of an administrator's day-to-day hassles are grounded firmly in the large issue of which cultural story is to be preferred. Put in rather typical sociological jargon, the manifest appearance of technical administrative problems nearly always masks latent cultural conflicts. If these papers are on target, practicing administrators would be well served to study the anthology of stories of their community.

Speculations

In working through the analytic matrix, several odd, but seemingly important, points surfaced. In this section these eye-catching notions will be elaborated as follows: cultural pluralism; cultural sense-making; cultural distortion and change; and cultural remembering and forgetting.

Cultural Pluralism

One point that emerged consistently is the fact that at any particular moment in time any particular culture is made up of multiple stories. In a sense, we should think of a particular culture as an anthology of competing stories. From a distance, these stories appear to be reasonably clustered around certain major prime objects. Up close, any particular point could be seen as a jumble of highly competitive stories seeking to gain an advantage. The issue of perspective, of distance from, seems an important one to consider.

This imagery suggests that practicing administrators (and others such as researchers) would be well advised to read the many stories, to enunciate the main themes to be found in schools at particular times, and to assess with great care their own proximity to these stories and themes. Reading the themes seems to involve looking closely at the curriculum, personnel, facilities, organization, and financing of the district to find deeper meanings. Moreover, administrators need to be sensitive to shifts in public moods, as well as to the persistent concerns of those who seem out of step with what is happening. Enunciating these contra-themes may result in administrative activities as diverse as simple private comprehension to use of such themes in public arenas to support or to attack the stories of various groups. Finally, it seems clear the administrators are *not* value-neutral. What they chose to recommend or to argue against provides advantages for some, disadvantages for others. We are not only users of our stories, we are their advocates.

In terms of schools, awareness of the pluralism within the culture could lead administrators to many courses of action. Some administrators may wish to accentuate the uniqueness of the many stories told. At other times, these same administrators may seek to hide this multiplicity behind the rhetoric of a singular and all-encompassing story, as Meyer "suggests." Such a contingency approach also highlights the importance of stories used by practicing administrators. These administrative stories may accentuate, for example, the technical nature of administration, the human relations approach, or the political approach as discussed by Sergiovanni. Each of these "schools" of administrative thought may be seen as competing stories, arguing for their particular versions of beginnings, middles, and ends, and offering criteria for assessment of worth from trash.

The notion of a culturally pluralistic school and administration also highlights the importance of knowing the exact time enveloping these events. We should expect that the particular climate of the times (the preferred stories) and the sophistication of administrators (their grasp of the depth and complexity of stories) should deeply influence actions taken.

Some administrative actions may be highly ritualized because of the need to maintain certain stories and to demonstrate the administrator's acceptance of these stories, e.g., graduation. Other actions may be unique occurrences shaped by a one time only constellation of stories and understandings. It seems wise, thusly, to highlight the pluralism that administrators face and often act upon.

Cultural Sense-making

A second point highlights the fact that practicing administrators must "make sense" of the multiple stories available at a particular time and deal with other stories as they develop later. A good example of an emergent stories is that of federal support for the needs of handicapped children (PL 94–142). This "new" story about the relationship between schools and special children accentuates the importance of understanding how we "fit" the old and the new into reasonably coherent patterns.

The task for the individual administrator is to fashion a story which makes sense of what is happening. We might suggest that such a holistic process could involve (1) basic understandings which serve as the major interpretive themes (Taylor), (2) mechanisms for dealing with day-to-day events to "fit" them to the predominant themes (Meyer), and (3) processes for altering or changing major themes (Hirsch). For many current practicing administrators, we might suggest a major and current educational story which highlights the importance of education for all youth, mechanisms which allow for "fitting" the actions of children in schools to this theme, and assessment which stresses that today's children and their schools are really better than yesterday's children and schools.

Individual stories may be collected and studied — what are the stories of teachers? — but the perspective of these papers suggests that generalizations may be of limited scope. Stories of teachers, to continue that example, may be comprehended by individual teachers at different levels of complexity and may merely be aped to avoid conflict. This avoidance of conflict produces "social desirability" effects in teacher interviews and questionnaires, for example. Hence, larger generalizations about schools need to be sensitive to the context (the preferred stories) of the teachers in that locale.

We should also anticipate that the sense-making process produces stories which are important to individuals as persons, not just as educators. While some of the stories may be tried on for size ("window-shopping" for an image or "daydreaming" about success), the major interpretative themes may well constitute the key definitions of self. These themes thus become the deep structures of the self, fraught with value and emotion. Even though they may seem to others both inconsistent and shoddy, these deep structures validate one's self and vision of the world. These become the individual's vision of his or her culture. Put in educational terms, when an outsider belittles the role of a teacher, the response by that teacher may expose the fundamental story a teacher is trying to "act out." That teacher's story often involves, for example, commitment to young children, to improving their lot in the coming world, and to creating a life of devoted service — and may well be symbolized in the beloved legend of Mr. Chips.

When individuals who use different stories confront each other, we should anticipate conflict. The volatility and intensity of conflicts among individuals or groups may depend upon how vigorously one group seeks to change the story of another group. In educational terms, the war between teachers and students may be more heated and intense as teachers strive to imprint their stories on the young, and as teachers ignore the stories that youth tell about their own images of the future. As Hirsch notes, these symbolic wars may be extremely intense. Such heated conflicts should be anticipated by the practicing administrators and strategies considered for resolving such disputes. These conflicts underscore the importance of understanding that administrators, teachers, and students, as well as others, must make sense of their culture.

Cultural Distortion and Change

A moment's reflection suggests that the individualistic nature of making sense of stories means that distortions and changes in stories are inevitable. Some individuals are more subtle, for example, and see deeper meanings and connections. Other individuals are better storytellers, making modifications and adding nuances to enhance the telling, not the story. Over time, then, the collective stories offered by groups to individuals become distorted and change. Stories, as Topsy did, "just grow."

This evolutionary process may be explored profitably in training institutions where notions such as "individual differences" or "motivation" seem in perpetual reconsideration. It may also be studied in the local contexts where notions such as "neighborhood school" or "teacher contract" seem to slip and slide constantly. What these examinations display are not only the struggles among individuals or groups to provide "the" story that best deals with the context but also the subtle shifts and shadings which seem to happen to stories "in the nature of things." In this natural shifting and sliding, elements are dropped or added as conscious (or unconscious) efforts are made to keep the story powerful enough to explain the past and fruitful enough to generate an interesting future.

These natural distortions and changes may be important to practicing administrators as ways of linking diverse groups to cool conflictual situations or as warning signs for the creation of new, yet highly improbable coalitions. New symbols may be distortions or changes of formerly conflicting symbols valued by divergent groups (Turner 1974). Hence, the closing of local neighborhood schools may be the "front" used to achieve desegregation of blacks and whites in a community. Such a strategy may link former foes in support of or opposition to such change. Other symbols, e.g., "sex education," may link highly divergent groups into powerful coalitions whose members share only small, but now common, fragments of diverse stories. Distortion and change, then, are normal processes to be anticipated by practicing administrators.

Cultural Remembering and Forgetting

These papers trigger a final speculation. The notions of story, sense-making, and distortion and change suggest the importance of remembering and forgetting stories.

When, if ever, do stories die? Certainly they seem embodied in the lives of individuals and in the major symbols of groups. But in the retelling, stories seem inevitably changed and distorted, often to meet the needs of the moment and perhaps just as often by the skills and whims of the storyteller. (Boredom may induce change just as frequently as need.) Some of the papers, e.g., Taylor, Hirsch and Andrews, and Sergiovanni, imply that changes do occur over centuries, in crisis, or as part of multiple perspectives.

For the practicing administrator, remembering and forgetting may be important in dealing with others. The nature of "pertinent" information, for example, may be shaped by remembering or forgetting. Thus, superintendents would do well to forget what teacher associations were like in the 1950s or to remember the financial hardships of the 1930s. Equally, the kinds of problems and solutions brought to a particular community group may be influenced deeply by an administrator's grasp of what that group remembers or forgets. Contexts where stories may be remembered or forgotten may well become arenas for social conflict. Practicing administrators may wisely urge researchers to explore with care remembering and forgetting, even though these processes seem esoteric.

Summary

This brief set of speculations concludes efforts to see if these essays in toto have anything to say to practicing school administrators. I believe these essays will be of great interest to practicing administrators. Their suggestions about controlling conflicts, anticipating changes, and being conscious of one's own values will not only bear the ring of truth to but also trigger some thoughtful new approaches for administrators. These essays are a good start for a longer-run attempt to perceive the school and its administration from a cultural perspective.

REFERENCES

Burlingame, Martin (1981). "Superintendent Power Retention." In Samuel B. Bachrach, ed. *Organizational Behavior in Schools and School Districts.* New York: Praeger.

Eliot, Thomas H. (1959). "Toward an Understanding of Public School Politics." *American Political Science Review* 52, 1032–51.

Fernandez, James W. (1965). "Symbolic Consensus in a Fang Reformative Cult." *American Anthropologist* 67, 902–29.

Getzels, Jacob W. (1974). "Images of the Classroom and Visions of the Learner." *School Review* 82, 527–40.

Mintzberg, Henry (1973). *The Nature of Managerial Work.* New York: Harper & Row.

Peshkin, Alan (1978). *Growing Up American: Schooling and the Survival of the Community.* Chicago: University of Chicago Press.

Turner, Victor (1974). *Dramas, Fields, and Metaphors: Symbolic Action in Human Society.* Ithaca: Cornell University Press.

CHAPTER 17

Theory into Practice: Educational Policy Analysis and the Cultural Perspective

Hugh G. Petrie

The central theme of this book is the place and role of concepts like "culture" in studies of administrative leadership in education. The theme crops up time and again. Graham Allison paints public management in terms evocative of cultural analysis. Thomas Sergiovanni lists the cultural as a new emerging model for thinking about administration and policy. James March's contribution calls our attention to the enculturation processes by which administrators get chosen. Donald Schön notes the difficulties when different cultural expectations clash. Warren Bennis's descriptions of leaders suggest images of their positions as central figures in a culture. Barry Staw's concept of commitment can be placed easily into the framework of cultural values and images. Peter Vaill's high-performing systems are patently groups with a cohesive culture. Paul Hirsch and John Andrews's view of symbols reflects the cultural truism that symbols help bind cultures together. John Meyer explains how structures "celebrate" a given rationality as well as promoting it. Thomas Greenfield treats organizations as specific cultural artifacts. William Taylor borrows the concept of "prime object" from art history to apply to his analysis of British higher education. Richard Bates is concerned with the cultural analysis of educational administration. William Foster argues for bringing together the hermeneutic methods of the cultural sciences with the reflective methods of the critical sciences in analysis of administrative problems. In short, the concept of culture as important to administrative theorizing is *the* contribution of this volume.

I personally welcome the emphasis. My own work (Petrie 1981) reflects the strong belief that the basic features of human thought and action can only be understood with reference to cultures and communities and the ways in which these cultures and communities socialize and educate their members.

My particular goal in this paper will be to say something about how this emphasis on culture is to be understood in the area of educational policy analysis. First, by contrasting the cultural perspective with other perspectives I will illustrate how very different educational policy analysis looks in the different perspectives. Second, I will suggest that the emphasis on culture harbors a great danger for policy analysis — what I will call the danger of pluralistic paralysis. Third, I will point out that if we supplement the cultural perspective with an emphasis on cultural adaptation and change, we can guard against the danger of pluralistic paralysis. Finally, I will try to illustrate the usefulness of the cultural perspective for educational policy analysis by examining a current policy debate through the cultural lens — James Coleman's 1981 report on public and private schools.

Thought and Action in Policy Analysis

Sergiovanni calls our attention in this volume to four perspectives on administration — management science, human relations, political, and cultural. The importance of this comparative view is that it focuses our attention on the very different ways in which these models characterize human thought and action.

The management science perspective views organizational behavior as essentially a series of tasks to be performed. These tasks are analyzed into smaller subunits and structures, usually bureaucratically devised, to implement the tasks. Organizational structures are viewed as systems of rules, rewards, and sanctions. These devices get people to perform the appropriate tasks. Policy analysis on this model involves a careful specification of the tasks to be performed in the system and then the provision of bureaucratic rules and policies intended to ensure compliance. As little as possible is left to individual judgment and initiative. Policies are written as specifically as possible and compliance ensured through rewards and punishments. The rules and regulations surrounding compulsory attendance in any given school district tend to be a good example of educational policy devised with the management science model in mind.

The human relations model views organizational behavior as essentially a group of persons interacting with each other in a social setting defined by the organization. That people in such a setting perform certain organizational "tasks" is derivative from their basic social interaction. Rather than the organization being conceived as primary with the people as more or less replaceable parts as in the management science view, in the human relations model the individuals are the primary units of analysis with the organizational goals a by-product of the goals of the individuals. One acts on this kind of organization through arranging conditions for personal growth and development of the members. Their growth becomes the organization's growth and vice versa. Policy analysis in this model involves an appreciation of the goals of individual organizational members and an effort to see how those goals can be melded into the goals of the whole. The more or less informal consultative arrangements often found in team-teaching situations exemplify the human relations model of educational policy analysis. Each member of the team is assumed to be committed to the growth and learning of the students, and collaborative interaction is used to decide on the policies needed to promote both student and teacher growth.

The political model views organizational behavior as essentially the result of competing interest groups, both internal and external. Bargaining, authority, and the sheer power to enforce certain behavior are the key concepts. Organizational structures are neither systems of rules nor quasi-informal social groupings of people. Rather, different groups have different needs and resources which they use to bargain with other such groups. Policy analysis becomes political analysis. Who has the power to do what in which circumstances? What coalitions are made and how do they operate? Whose interests would be served by a given policy? The obvious political haggling over state school aid formulas is a paradigm case of educational policy viewed through the political lens.

With the cultural perspective, the unit of analysis changes to that of the natural community. The natural community is one whose members share basic values, meanings, and understandings. The team of teachers described above as an example of the human relations perspective can also be viewed as in the process of trying to create a team "culture." The grouping of, say, mathematics teachers from all of the teams in a given school would come close to forming a natural community and, hence, a culture. Organizational behavior in this view is at bottom exemplary of the natural values which bind the community together. One need not make the rules and procedures explicit as in the management science approach. Nor need one concentrate on individual growth and development as in the human relations model. Nor does the political approach recognize that natural communities may be a far more potent form of association than political interest groups — although the two can overlap. If one's basic view of reality depends deeply upon the natural community in which one has grown up, then neither rewards and sanctions, nor personal growth, nor even political power are likely to make much more than superficial changes in the way in which one behaves.

The only organizational theorists who have taken this view seriously have been those who have explicitly set out to change entire cultures — such as the Chinese communists. In our society such activity aimed at deep-seated cultural changes tends to be highly suspect, and this leads to a somewhat interesting result. If one forswears cultural change, then the organizational activity which is possible on the cultural model is quite limited. The best that we can do is try to understand the different cultures and lay bare their meanings. Anything else would be cultural intrusion.

Policy analysis in the cultural model is primarily a description of basic meanings and values. Its goal is understanding. The movement known as bilingual education is a good example of educational policy analysis in the cultural model. Language, it is claimed, is central to culture. The ways in which we speak about our world structure the ways in which we experience it. To force a student not only to learn something new, but also to learn it in another language is to put an impossible burden on the student. It violates the student's very being and is, thus, morally indefensible. At a minimum, it is argued that we must teach, at least in the beginning, in the student's own language.

Notice, too, how different the bilingual example would look under the other three models. Under the scientific management model, the question would be simply one of how efficiently we can teach students who do not know English. Should we force them to learn English on their own, teach them English first, or teach them regular subjects in their native tongue. From the human relations view, we would need to show the student how his or her own goals could more effectively be pursued by learning English — and we would, of course, be presuming that those are the goals of the dominant culture. In the political model, the policy question would be one of who has the votes to enact what form of bilingual education. None of the foregoing acknowledge the alleged impossibility, short of cultural conversion, of teaching children from different cultures with standard approaches. The cultural approach reminds us forcefully that our very mode and manner of experiencing the world may well depend upon the culture in which we grew up.

Cultural Policy Analysis and Pluralistic Paralysis

The great strength of the cultural perspective is that it reminds us how intimately involved in our human experience is our cultural background. Members of different cultures simply look at the "same" world and see things very differently. We have any number of examples of this in education. As bitter experience has shown, desegregation of schools is not the same thing as integration. Traits highly prized in the black community are objectionable in the dominant white culture and without teachers understanding this, no mere "body-mixing" can work. Or consider the question of whether Americans are "over-educated." For a culture which views education as job training, the lack of positions for college-trained people is a clear indication that we must cut back on our educational investment. For those who view education as part of what it *means* to become a civilized person, the lack of jobs for college graduates is, at worst, a minor irritant and touches not at all the continued need for higher education.

And so it goes. Most extant models of policy analysis treat as *given* the basic values and meanings of the culture. The analysis then typically concerns the means necessary to achieve these ends. This is why "value-free" social science has been so heavily touted in policy analysis. If we are not allowed to debate the goals of education, if these are simply assumed, then we will indeed spend our time arguing over whether this or that program will more likely lead to these goals.

As noted above, however, even the programs themselves are not value-free. Desegregation is not the same as integration although both may involve busing children. Bilingual education is not the same as English as a second language, although both may involve teaching English to the non-native English speakers. Nor is aptitude testing simply an efficient way of tracking students for individualized instruction. The question always remains, "Aptitude to do what?" And the answer is always in terms of basic cultural values. Thus, one of the tenets of standard educational policy analysis is shown to be a chimera. Policy analysis is not and cannot be value-free. Policies always depend upon and reflect the basic values of the cultures in which they are evolved. Such policies may *appear* value-free when there is widespread consensus on the basic operative values, as, perhaps, in the case of compulsory attendance laws. But the fact that we do not always question the underlying values does not make the analyses any less dependent on the values.

When we do happen to expose the underlying values in a given policy area, traditional wisdom tends to relegate the value question to the political arena. This move brings political analysis to bear, but analysis largely on the level of what is, in fact, the case. An analysis of what ought to be the case is seldom attempted. Values become alternative springs of action rather than guides to the good life. A political analysis of state aid formulas may enlighten us as to the relative political strengths of urban and rural, rich and poor constituencies, but it seldom tells us what the fairest formula would be.

Even more critically, a political analysis will be unable to tell us why groups of people keep pressing for certain educational goals in the face of all political odds. A cultural analysis, however, by exposing the meanings and basic values behind a given policy position, can help us to "feel" what it would be like to hold that position and to try to get it adopted. A successful cultural policy analysis will probably use many of the tools of the humanities to get us to see the world as others see it. This is, no doubt, why some of the "popular" essays and books on, say, the horrors of urban schools have so much more impact than a dozen scholarly analyses. Through the popular accounts we can experience and understand the culture firsthand, and we react to it with our whole being.

So the tools of cultural policy analysis will be the sketch, the novel, the portrait, the case study, the documentary, persuasive journalism, and the symbolic demonstration. These are examples of the forms which can engage us at a level deep enough to fuse thought and action and feeling. These are the ways in which we come to understand a culture, and until we understand a proposed educational policy from within a culture, we have not understood it. The complaint that educational policy makers do not understand the implications of their policies is not, then, something which could be remedied by more sophisticated conventional analyses. It is rather a complaint that the policy makers do not understand the ways in which their policies affect the culture and very being of the constituencies. It is clearly a great strength for the cultural view to have made respectable the necessity for *understanding*, in the deepest sense, the implications of a given policy.

But this strength is also a weakness, for it is too often assumed that understanding is enough. Despite having pointed out the critical importance of cultural values in policy analysis, the partisans of cultural analysis often refuse to take a stand on those values. Indeed, they often explicitly embrace a cultural relativism, and a noncommital subjectivism is often but a step beyond. What such people fail to realize is that an uncritical acceptance of cultural pluralism *is itself the value of a particular culture.* It may or may not be appropriate upon analysis.

I am not, of course, advocating intolerance. I am rather pointing out the logical implications of an extreme cultural pluralism. These implications may or may not be desirable — that remains to be determined. What must be realized, however, is the potential limitation for educational policy analysis which is imposed by the cultural viewpoint. The danger is that having appreciated the critical importance of the cultural and having analyzed and understood a given educational policy from the standpoint of the various affected cultures, we will abandon any further efforts. After we have truly understood the plight of a Latino going to school where people constantly talk in a foreign language, and after we have truly understood the necessity for that Latino to learn English to survive in our society, we still do not know what we ought to do.

Notice that I said that we do not know what we "ought" to do, not that we do not know what we "will" do. The latter could, conceivably, be revealed by further political analysis. The former remains a question even given the cultural perspective on policy analysis. Ought we to force the Latino to learn English? Why? Ought we to become largely a multicultural and multilingual nation? Why? There are no easy answers and the difficulty of the situation is matched only by the obvious necessity for making *some* sort of choice.

I am urging that we cannot rest content in exposing and pointing out the importance of cultural values in educational policy analyses. If we cannot pursue policies which allow *all* cultural values to be pursued, and often we cannot, then we must make choices. Cultural policy analysis allows us to understand the choices we must make, but the danger is that in its emphasis on cultural pluralism, it will effectively counsel doing nothing. Yet the counsel of cultural pluralism is itself a cultural value and clearly could conflict with a culture, say, which claims that only *it* has the access to the truth. Cultural policy analysis is in grave danger of leading to pluralistic paralysis. This is a paralysis which comes from recognizing the relative independence and the relative completeness of various cultures, along with the impossibility of attaining a neutral stance from which to evaluate the various cultures.

Are the virtues and vices of different cultural perspectives really no different than different tastes in ice cream? It seems highly unlikely, and in any event, we are often faced with the situation in education in which we have only enough resources to make chocolate or vanilla, but not both. Nor is our puzzle solved if we really understand and have experienced the taste of both chocolate and vanilla. *Which* ought we to make? If we give in to pluralistic paralysis, we may well end up with neither.

Educational Policy Analysis from a Cultural Perspective

Pluralistic paralysis can, however, be avoided if one shifts from thinking of cultures as static entities and takes, instead, a dynamic view. The dynamic view of cultures is one which recognizes that a culture is a particular way of dealing with an environment successfully, either by assimilating the environment to the cultural norms, or by accommodating the cultural norms to the environment, or by a combination of the two. Ecological adaptability thus becomes a way of evaluating various cultures and avoiding pluralistic paralysis. The first question to be asked of any culture is whether or not its characteristic modes of behavior are appropriate for the ecology in which it finds itself. If so, there is really no standpoint from which to criticize the culture. If not, the second question concerns whether the culture can adapt to its ecology. If not, it is justifiably criticizable — and this criticism is *not* cultural intrusion, for it is the culture itself which is not adaptable.

Let me try to illustrate the advantage that this dynamic perspective gives to the cultural model of policy analysis. My example comes from current discussions regarding the teaching of mathematics. For generations calculus has been the basic mathematics course to be taken by most technically oriented students, especially engineers. The educational policy consideration underlying this decision had to do primarily with the types of problems most applied students had to solve. However, as time went on, calculus, as the first mathematics course, took on a fundamental position in the culture of mathematics teachers.

What appears to have happened, however, is that with the twin advent of the computer and powerful statistical techniques, the methods of calculus for solving practical problems seem to be of the horse and buggy variety. Yet, teaching calculus persists. If we leave aside the interest of calculus to pure mathematicians and historians of mathematics, we are left with the educational policy question of what to teach as a first mathematics course.

A static cultural policy analysis will describe the culture of existing mathematics departments and their commitment to calculus. It will be seen as important and meaningful, with, no doubt, a few crumbs thrown to the importance of statistics and computer analysis. Nevertheless, we will come to understand the meaning of calculus. A similar analysis would be done for the culture of the applied statistician. Unless we look further, at the relative abilities of the cultures to adapt to the changing circumstances, we would be faced with pluralistic paralysis. I am suggesting that an essential part of cultural educational policy analysis would be to focus on the processes by which the two cultures approach the problem. I am not implying that all the fault will necessarily lie with the moss-bound classical mathematicians. The statisticians may well be missing from their cultural perspective crucial features pointed out by the classicists. Only an analysis of the dynamics will tell for certain.

Accordingly, cultural educational policy analysis should have at least the following features:

1. *The analysis will always be constrained by and in terms of a presupposed culture.* This is a logical point. The very considerations which count in favor of cultural analysis make it clear that there is no "neutral" ground upon which to stand in performing a policy analysis. For this reason, the most important consideration is to try to understand the particular case from inside of the culture in which it occurs.

2. *The analysis should be critical.* The basic values and goals of both the culture being analyzed as well as the culture of the analyst (if different) should be carefully examined and illuminated. Hidden agendas, unspoken assumptions, and constitutive values must be critically assessed in terms of their contribution to the ecological stability of the culture.

3. *The analysis cannot be "value free."* This point follows from one and two. Since any analysis must always be in terms of a given culture, the values of that culture will necessarily condition it. If, however, as

urged in point two above, the values are made explicit, their influence can be better gauged.

4. *The analysis should avoid pluralistic paralysis.* Cultural analysis of static structures at best leads to understanding. Although this is very important, it should not lead to subjectivism and paralysis. Policy analysis must be concerned with action as well as understanding.

5. *The analysis should be ecological.* The way to avoid pluralistic paralysis is to remember that cultures are social ways of dealing with the ecology. The analysis must look not only at the meanings which the culture gives to events, but also at the adequacy of those meanings for the culture's ability to adapt to the environment.

6. *The analysis should include an examination of the policy processes as well as of the culture's structures.* If a given culture becomes less and less able to deal with a changing ecology, an examination of the processes by which the culture tries to accommodate to the changed environment will also be instructive. A culture which can shift its basic meanings and values as necessary can have numerous effects on just what consequences a given educational policy will actually have.

Public and Private Schools

One of the more interesting and timely educational policy issues currently on the scene involves James Coleman's study of public and private schools (1981a, 1981b). This study represents one of several analyses being done of the very large data base, *High School and Beyond*, collected by the national center for educational statistics in 1980. Without going into a great amount of detail, the major results of the study are, according to Coleman:

a) There is higher academic achievement in basic cognitive skills among private school students (especially Catholic students) than among public school students, even when family backgrounds are held constant.

b) Aspirations for higher education are higher among Catholic school students than among comparable students in public schools.

c) The gap in achievement between minority students and other students is less in Catholic schools than in public schools.

d) the gap in aspirations for further education between minority students and other students is less in Catholic schools than in public schools.

e) Catholic schools are less segregated by race than public schools.

In addition to these results, Coleman (1981b) draws four major conclusions regarding the implications for certain long-standing ideals of American public education.

1) The ideal of the common school has failed because of the great deal

of residential mobility in American leading to de facto segregation.

2) The concept of local control of schools has been eroded by the increasing policy-making and fiscal control being exercised at the state and federal levels.

3) Local financing of education has shifted significantly to state and federal governments in response to calls for greater equality and more specialized services for special populations such as the handicapped.

4) The idea that schools should act in loco parentis has become less and less accepted and less and less possible.

As would be expected of such findings, they have generated considerable discussion and criticism. In the remaining pages, I will comment on this discussion under the headings developed above concerning cultural educational policy analysis.

Analysis in Terms of a Given Culture

Coleman's own analysis clearly exemplifies this maxim. He assumes without question the traditional twin goals of American education, quality and equality. Indeed, they form the framework for the results concerning achievement, integration, and the like. There is no serious attempt to explore the possible contradictions inherent in trying to pursue excellence and equity. Furthermore, what excellence *means* is not questioned. Achievement in basic cognitive skills is excellence and that, of course, is quite obviously central to American culture. It is not so central to Chinese communist culture. Equity is likewise dependent on a definition of integration which concentrates on the pool of minority students available at each level and says nothing about access to that pool.

Radical critics also point to the fact that the present Coleman study seems to contradict his earlier work (1966). In the earlier study Coleman appeared to conclude that schools do not matter much, but classmates do. This was at a time when policy makers appeared to want information supporting their desire to integrate schools. The public and private schools study appears at just the time when voucher systems providing federal and state assistance for parents who choose private schools are much discussed. Whatever else Coleman is, he is "timely."

Further examples of the structuring role played by cultures can be found in the discussions of the ethos of private schools, the difficulty of finding a single mission in public schools, and the like. Coleman (1981a) insists that he is not allowing the data to speak for themselves but is rather presenting a conception of reality consistent with the data and challenging others to present alternative conceptions. This approach clearly recognizes the structuring effect of a given culture's view of things.

Critical Analysis

Coleman's (1981b) attack, noted above, on the current cultural ideals and assumptions of American public education is a good example of the critical analysis of basic values. On the other side, there have been few critical analyses thus far of the twin goals of excellence and equity espoused by Coleman.

The possible political agenda of Coleman has been pointed out by several critics. Several of his defenders, however, view this criticism as "unscientific." They claim that it is the *use* to which the analysis is put and not the scientific analysis itself which should be the subject of political debate. Coleman himself seems to vacillate on this point — occasionally relying on the "use" ploy and occasionally admitting the appropriateness, if not the success, of attacks on his political agenda.

Perhaps most important here is the discussion of the problem of self-selection. Coleman's critics suggest that the methodological "matching" by family background cannot in principle account for the fact that private school parents have *selected* their children's schools. The characteristics accounting for this selection, it is claimed, also provide powerful background and motivational characteristics for the children to succeed in these schools. Although Coleman does not directly address this issue, he appears to concede its importance when he speaks of the clear "mission" orientation of private schools compared to public schools and hypothesizes that this is important for their success. After all, parents choose these schools because they perceive them as embodying certain important educational values — in short, as providing a cultural milieu congenial to the parents for their children's education. On the other side, apologists for public education suggest that the requirement to be all things to all people in public education provides a significant obstacle to having clear values guiding public education's efforts. Thus, the whole issue of public and private schools places great emphasis on the cultural values present or absent in these institutions. At the same time the critical analysis of these values has only just begun. We are not very practiced at analyzing values in policy discussions.

No "Value-free" Analyses

Despite his occasional obeisance to the fact that his analysis does have value implications, Coleman continues to believe that "the appropriate role of policy research is to inform the various interest groups" (1981a, 543). This stance shows that he still clings to the myth that at least policy research can be value-free. The values are then supplied by the relevant interest groups.

I have already noted above several instances in which cultural values necessarily inform Coleman's policy research. More important, however, is his implicit acceptance of the political model of policy analysis. Interest groups must decide the value issues through the political process. Policy research can, at best, illuminate these issues for the decision-makers.

Avoid Pluralistic Paralysis

Perhaps, however, Coleman's insistence on informing interest groups through policy research is actually much more compatible with the cultural model's emphasis on understanding and elucidating meaning. If this is so, then Coleman avoids paralysis only by embracing pluralism with a vengeance. He argues (1981b) for an educational pluralism based on federal and state support for a variety of communities (cultures?) defined by their separate interests, values, and missions. Clearly this conception recognizes the importance of separate cultures. It lacks, however, any way of deciding among competing claims. It gives over to the marketplace the task of choosing among competing cultures. While such a move exhibits a great deal of faith in the marketplace, it abdicates the responsibility for fostering any commitment to the common good. Unfortunately, our history is as full of examples of cultures fostering narrow prejudices as it is of truly adaptive cultures emerging from a free competition.

Is Coleman really advocating that our educational policy be one of having *no* educational policy other than encouraging a multitude of educational policies? I am not sure, but it is clear that one way of interpreting him is as exemplifying the phenomenon of pluralistic paralysis. At the same time he does raise a critical challenge to those who would try to foster some conception of the common good. What is it, and how can it be achieved? Cultural analysis cries out for an analysis of the culture of the public schools as well as the private schools and how, if at all, those cultures can be influenced.

Ecological Analysis

The foregoing considerations lead naturally to the idea that the various cultures must be evaluated with regard to their adaptability to the ecology. There are two clear examples of this necessity in the public and private schools debate.

First, there is the question of whether it is the type of school itself, with its selection phenomena and the like, which is primarily determinative of the results, or whether it is the policies and procedures which are followed in these schools and which might be emulated elsewhere which are determinative of the results. In short, how do the various schools deal with their ecologies?

To be more specific, the analyses seem to suggest that emphasis on academics, a high level of homework, and strong discipline characterize the private schools. Are these directly responsible for the improved achievement? If so, could they be implemented in public schools? Or is it the case, as some suggest, that the mandates for diversity in public education, the restrictions on discipline, the lack of a unified parental culture, all conspire to limit the ability of public schools to pursue such policies? These are clear ecological issues and have scarcely been raised in the debate, let alone systematically explored.

Under the cultural model, the important questions would be the ability of a given culture to adapt to its ecology. The data used by Coleman just barely allows the raising of such questions. The data on achievement scores, aspirations, and family background are data collected from a quite different paradigm, probably the scientific management one in which the crucial variables are task-oriented. It is extremely risky to try to use that kind of data for a cultural analysis, and yet that is exactly what Coleman has done. A study performed with the cultural model of policy analysis in mind from the outset would look at cultural phenomena — parental expectations, parental involvement in school, public schools with missions (e.g., magnet schools), governmental and legal constraints, and so on.

The second place in which ecological considerations are paramount in the public and private school debate is in the area of supply response and regulation. We have no idea how existing private schools might respond to a plan of tuition vouchers which would allow parents to select among schools. Nor do we know whether new schools would emerge in an effort to make money. Would they retain the apparent benefits of the existing private schools or would they become diploma mills? We do not know if public schools might yet successfully adopt the curricula and discipline of the successful privates. With regard to regulation, government funds usually bring government regulation in their wake. Would such regulation destroy the hypothesized advantage of private schools to pursue their independently defined ethos? Again such ecological questions are barely being raised in the current debate. They would be commonplace under the cultural model.

Examination of Policy Processes

Finally the cultural model urges a dynamic view of policy analysis. The necessity for this view is implicit in the foregoing. We cannot begin to answer supply-response questions without knowing more about how policy is formed. We will have no idea about whether public schools can adopt new policies without understanding how policy formation proceeds. The dynamic effects of regulation must also be traced and understood so that we can see how public and private schools adapt to regulation. What are the determinants in the process of parents choosing a particular school or a particular neighborhood so that their children can attend a particular school? How do schools adjust to parental and student expectations? How do parents and students adjust to the expectations of the schools? These process questions are critical for a cultural analysis.

In summary, while I have generally applauded the emergence of the cultural model of educational policy analysis, I have also tried to point to a potential danger in its use and to suggest ways of avoiding the danger. The danger is that in following the model's injunction to understand the importance of basic meanings of a culture, one may be led to pluralistic paralysis. Pluralistic paralysis is the abdication of the responsibility for evaluating the success of various cultures in adapting to their environments. The antidote is to expand the cultural model to include an emphasis on ecological analysis and the policy-making and implementing processes of the cultures under investigation. These additions to the cultural model should help in establishing it as one of the most fruitful forms of policy analysis ever to emerge, for it is, of the models considered, one of the few which takes seriously the theory of practice.

REFERENCES

Coleman, J., E. Campbell, C. Hobson, J. McPartland, A. Mood, F. Weinfeld, and R. York (1966). *Equality of Educational Opportunity.* Washington, D.C.: U.S. Government Printing Office.

Coleman, J., T. Hoffer, and S. Kilgore (1981a). "Questions and Answers: Our Response." Part of "Report Analysis: Public and Private Schools." *Harvard Educational Review* 51(4), 481–545.

Coleman, J. (1981b). "Quality and Equality in American Education: Public and Catholic Schools." *Phi Delta Kappan* 63(3), 159–64.

Petrie, Hugh G. (1981). *The Dilemma of Enquiry and Learning.* Chicago: University of Chicago Press.

CHAPTER 18

Theory into Practice: Higher Education and the Cultural Perspective

John E. Corbally

The joy of a collection of essays such as this volume is that each author can reveal self and views in ways not appropriate for a textbook or for a scholarly report. This author approaches the subject as a one-time high school principal, a one-time professor of educational administration, a long-time administrator at various levels and places in higher education, and a short-time professor of higher education. I have, with James March, worried about "round theories and flat experience." I note that with his bent toward theory, he perhaps inadvertently credits the practitioner with the view that the world is flat — it was, after all, Christopher Columbus and Magellan and other sailing practitioners who were willing to act as if the world was round. But the fact that individuals who do different work have (and need) different views of the world is important. I may not agree with March and Cohen's "garbage can theory," (1974) but I profit from thinking about it.

As a practitioner, I had always felt it was important to know where I, at least, thought the institution or unit should be headed. Vaill's discussion of and research into high-performing systems provides a new emphasis to that sense of importance and provides a new framework within which to think about purpose.

As a practitioner, I have enjoyed sitting with colleagues at various meetings discussing the mythology of institutions and of leadership. John Meyer forces us to convert these hallway discussions into an orderly way of thinking about what organizations are and what they do. He accepts mythology as a given and makes it necessary for us to deal with mythology as a concept rather than as an idle topic with which the "old timers" regale the "newcomers."

Each of the essays in this volume could be cited and discussed in terms of the ways in which it stimulates and provides a framework for thinking about practice. Too often practitioners criticize theory because "it does not provide answers." Theory generally does not provide answers; primarily theory describes relationships and reduces variables. Theory is often just like the consultant in the old story in which the consultant's recommendation was to change a monkey into an elephant. It was the consultant's task to recommend, not to tell one how to accomplish the recommendation.

Consider $E = mc^2$. That mathematical expression of the theory of the relationship between energy and mass is increasingly being demonstrated to be precisely correct. It means that there is no energy problem in this world, for the conversion of a tiny mass into energy creates huge amounts of energy. But how to do it? How to control it? How to transmit it? How to do it safely? These are practice questions and we are not doing too well in answering them. In spite of the constant threats of shortages and of even the ultimate disappearance of fossil fuels, polls taken in late 1981 indicated that over half of the American people opposed the further development of nuclear energy. So obviously, $E = mc^2$ is worthless. Of course not, and someday the practitioners will discover how to work within the framework of that theory to produce safe and necessary energy.

But isn't this all a bit far afield from higher education? Only in terms of the subject matter. We practitioners in higher education have more good theory than we have learned how to use and because we do not know how to use it we often tend to reject it. And, as Sergiovanni points out in Chapter 15, we complicate our ability to use theory by adding factors of "what ought to be" or "what would be better." It is clear, for example, from a whole half-century of psychological research dealing with stimulus-response mechanisms that if we chose to use certain stimuli based upon fear of deprivation or of harm, we could produce certain results. These approaches, however, are not democratic, are not humanistic, are not collegial, are not fulfilling, do not honor the integrity of the individual, and so on. And so, in general, these approaches are not used. Interestingly enough, however, there are universities in which punishment-reward mechanisms of a rather simplistic nature are used and in which institutional purposes appear to be achieved. Outside observers are critical of both the style and substance of such institutions, but generally have to be critical in terms of values rather than in terms of institutional goals.

"They may be increasing their enrollment, but I sure wouldn't want to work there!"

"That guy pays well, but I sure wouldn't want to work for him!"

Leadership theory has some trouble with values just as does our science example, $E = mc^2$. In spite of the fact that several of the papers in this volume speak to the question of values in institutions, one problem in moving theory into practice relates to values. It is interesting to note, however, that many of the papers speak of "culture" and value is a key factor in describing a culture. Practice, however, must deal with both an overall institutional culture and with a variety of different subcultures within the institution.

To what extent, for example, does the theory of organizational behavior need adjustment when speaking of faculty members or students or physical plant staff within an institution? Is there a capital-P Purpose or a capital-R Rationality to which all subgroups will pledge some major degree of loyalty? Or, is an institution — as several papers either state or hint — actually a set of discrete subunits with only minimal overlap or agreement about purposes or about the "real world"?

The problem, then, with either theory about or practice in complex organizations is that we tend to talk about thin slices of behavior viewed over small periods of time. Neither the theorist nor the practitioner is satisfied with this necessity nor with what results. There are too many variables and too few controlled variables to lead easily to the construction of theories; there are too many variables and too few controlled variables to permit any single theory to govern practice. In my practitioner role — my more comfortable role — I am pleased when a man of Allison's stature describes theories which reflect the complexities of my kind of organization. Too often, however, I find the theorist explaining why this or that theory only works part of the time and not explaining which is the time it will work and which is the other. Why, I sometimes wonder, isn't there a theory which describes the precise conditions under which any given theory will work? In physics, again, I know that heat increases pressure only if there is a control upon volume, but when is the idiographic dimension of social behavior more crucial than the nomothetic dimension? And why, I ask in a sort of practitioner's lament, do they (the theorists) use so many different and long words to mean the same simple thing? It is so much easier to remember that the administrator has to worry about the university and about its people rather than to try to remember which worry is nomothetic or idiographic or normative or personal or whatever.

These comments are, of course, at the heart of papers such as that by Hirsch, and Schön has constructed a scheme in which the practitioner becomes the scientist. To me, both my own views gained over a number of practitioner years and those views I read in this volume reinforce the danger of thinking that there is "a" theory of university administration or "a" theory of university organization.

What I think is that there are a variety of frameworks developed by men and women who devote the major part of their time and intellectual effort to the examination of administrator behavior and of administrative organization. Their work enables the practitioner to discover ways of thinking about what he or she has done, is doing, and must do in the future. Their work helps the practitioner choose courses of action from among organized categories or sets of alternatives and helps the practitioner understand the experiences of others expressed in objective ways.

Part of the problem involved in practitioners explaining "how to do it" or "how I did it" to other practitioners is that their explanations are always incomplete. I am told that when I describe how I overcame a particularly difficult organizational problem, my behavior as I describe it always sounds more decisive and more brilliant than my colleagues who were with me thought it was at the time. I tend, they say, to overstate the problem and to overlook luck. That may be true—at least I note the same tendencies when my colleagues describe their triumphs. I—as a practitioner—even have trouble describing actions of my administrator colleagues because I tend to read in my own reactions and my own tendencies. But as I read Vaill or Schön, I begin to see myself within a framework, and I can analyze and think more clearly because of the fact that people like them devote their careers to analyzing and thinking.

So what would I say to my practitioner friends in higher education if they asked about this volume and about its value to them? I would suggest that they read it with care—not for its answers, but for its questions and for its orderly approach to those questions. It might lead them—as it has led my colleague Martin Burlingame—to think about the ways in which cultural anthropology might contribute to their understandings of their institutions. During the late 1960s and early 1970s, I found myself in some strong disagreement with Margaret Mead and her "generation gap," but her way of thinking about our current situation is valuable even if one believes her conclusions to be wrong.

It would be heartening for them to discover that some of the same uncertainties which plague the practitioner also plague the theorists. One reason the practitioner tends to dislike the theorist is because the theorist sometimes seems to act as if he or she really does have all the answers and the practitioner is not smart enough to understand or to use them. But these papers contain many words like "perhaps" or "it might be" or "on the other hand" and do not appear to belabor the practitioner.

Finally, I would argue that the theorists represented here and their work are practical. They speak to real problems, they generally use understandable words, and they recognize the limits and the complexities of reality. They present theoretical frameworks which really do fit into practice and their work can contribute to our work in meaningful ways.

REFERENCE

Cohen, Michael, and James March (1974). *Leadership and Ambiguity*. New York: McGraw-Hill.

CONTRIBUTORS

GRAHAM ALLISON is Dean of Harvard University's John F. Kennedy School of Government and Don K. Price Professor of Politics. Educated at Harvard and Oxford University, Professor Allison joined the Harvard faculty in 1968. In 1974–75, he served as Director of Defense and Arms Control Studies for the Commission on the Organization of the Government for the Conduct of Foreign Policy (the "Murphy Commission"); he has also been a consultant to various government agencies. Professor Allison's teaching and research concentrates on political analysis, American foreign policy, and ethics and public policy. He is the author of numerous books and articles, including *Essence of Decision: Explaining the Cuban Missile Crisis* (1971) and *Remaking Foreign Policy: The Organizational Connection*, with Peter Szanton (1976).

JOHN A. Y. ANDREWS is a Ph.D. candidate in the Department of Sociology at the University of Chicago. He is also Associate Editor of the *American Journal of Sociology* and co-author (with Paul M. Hirsch) of "Ambushes, Shootouts, and Knights of the Roundtable: The Diffusion and Normative Framing of Corporate Takeovers," in L. Pondy et al., eds., *Organizational Symbolism* (forthcoming).

RICHARD J. BATES is Associate Professor of Educational Administration, Deakin University. Prior to his current appointment, he was Senior Lecturer in Education, Massey University, New Zealand. Dr. Bates was involved in the establishment of programs in sociology of education and graduate training in educational administration at Massey University and in the establishment of the New Zealand Educational Administration Society and the New Zealand Association for Researchers in Education. His current interests are the development of a critical theory of educational administration and the application of ethnographic techniques to the analysis of schooling. Recent publications include "Educational Administration, the Sociology of Science and the Management of Knowledge" in *Educational Administration Quarterly* (1980) and "New Developments in the New Sociology of Education," *British Journal of Sociology of Education* (1980).

WARREN BENNIS is the Joseph DeBell Distinguished Professor of Management and Organization at the University of Southern California's

School of Business Administration. He has served as President of the University of Cincinnati and Provost of SUNY/Buffalo. Prior to that he was the chairperson of the Organizational Studies Department at M.I.T.'s Sloan School of Management. He is a leading scholar in the areas of leadership and organizational behavior. His major publications include *The Unconscious Conspiracy* (1977), *The Planning of Change*, (4th ed., 1983), and *The Temporary Society*, (1968).

MARTIN BURLINGAME is Professor of Educational Administration and Research Associate, Bureau of Educational Research, University of Illinois at Urbana-Champaign. He served as a Senior Associate at the National Institute of Education from 1973 to 1975. He is particularly interested in the local level politics of education, problems of power in educational organizations, and cultural studies of organizations. He is one of the authors of *Educational Governance and Administration* (1980) and has recently published "Superintendent Power Retention" in *Organizational Behavior in Schools and School Districts*, ed. Samuel B. Bachrach (1981).

JOHN E. CORBALLY is President and a Director of the John D. and Catherine T. MacArthur Foundation, Chicago. He is President Emeritus and Distinguished Professor of Higher Education Emeritus, University of Illinois. He was President, University of Illinois, from 1971 to 1979 and of Syracuse University from 1969 to 1971. His publications include *Introduction to Educational Administration*, with R. F. Campbell and J. A. Ramseyer (6th ed., 1983); *Educational Administration: The Secondary School*, with T. J. Jenson and W. F. Staub (2nd ed., 1965); and *School Finance* (1962).

WILLIAM FOSTER is Assistant Professor of Education at the University of San Diego. He served in a similar position at the University of Delaware from 1978 to 1981. His scholarly interests lie in the analysis of administrative theory from sociological and philosophical perspectives. His publications include "Administration and the Crisis of Legitimacy," *Harvard Educational Review* (Nov. 1980) and "The Changing Administrator: Developing Managerial Praxis," *Educational Theory* (Winter, 1980).

THOMAS B. GREENFIELD is Professor of Educational Administration at the Ontario Institute for Studies in Education and the University of Toronto. He was formerly Director of Research for the Canadian Teachers' Federation and has been President of the Canadian Society for the Study of Education. His writings over a decade have established a body of critical comment on systems metaphors in organization theory and on empiricism in research methodology. Recent articles include "The Man Who Comes Back Through the Door in the Wall: Discovering Self, Discovering Truth, Discovering Organizations," *Educational Administration Quarterly* (1980) and "Against Group Mind: An Anarchistic Theory of Organization," *McGill Journal of Education* (1981).

PAUL HIRSCH is Associate Professor of Sociology at the Graduate School of Business, University of Chicago. He also has taught at Indiana and Stanford universities, and served as Acting Director, Center for the Management of Public and Nonprofit Enterprise, University of Chicago Graduate School of Business, and as Assistant Program Director, University of Chicago National Humanities Institute. His research interests include organizational analysis, corporate and nonprofit boards, culture, and communications. He has published widely in such journals as *American Journal of Sociology, Administrative Science Quarterly, School Review, Communication Research,* and *The American Sociologist.*

JAMES G. MARCH is Fred H. Merrill Professor of Management at Stanford University and Senior Fellow at the Hoover Institute. He is a member of the National Academy of Sciences, the National Academy of Education, and the American Academy of Arts and Sciences. His major books include *Organizations,* with Herbert A. Simon (1958); *A Behavioral Theory of the Firm,* with Richard M. Cyert (1963); *Handbook of Organizations* (1965); *Leadership and Ambiguity: The American College President,* with Michael D. Cohen (1974); and *Ambiguity and Choice in Organizations,* with Johan P. Olsen (1976).

JOHN W. MEYER is Professor of Sociology at Stanford University. He is also a member of the Institute for Research on Educational Finance and Governance there. He has worked on a number of problems in organizational theory, in particular on educational organizations. He is one of the authors of *Environments and Organizations* (1978) and of a series of macrosociological studies reported in his *National Development and the World System,* with Michael Hannan (1979).

HUGH G. PETRIE is Dean of the Faculty of Educational Studies at the State University of New York at Buffalo. From 1977 to 1980, he served as Associate Vice-Chancellor for Academic Affairs and Director of the Office of Program Evaluation at the University of Illinois. His recent work has concentrated on the problems of both individual and organizational learning, with special attention to adaptive processes. His publications include *The Dilemma of Enquiry and Learning* (1981) and, with Daniel A. Alpert, "What *Is* the Problem of Retrenchment?" in *Journal of Management Studies* (1983).

As an industrial consultant, a government administrator, and a former president of Organization for Social and Technical Innovation, DONALD

A. SCHÖN has worked as a researcher and practitioner on the problem of organizational learning and professional effectiveness. He was invited in 1970 to deliver the Reith Lectures on the BBC. His books include *Invention and Evolution of Ideas* (1963); *Technology and Change* (1967); *Beyond the Stable State* (1971); *Theory in Practice: Increasing Professional Effectiveness*, with Chris Argyris (1974); and *The Reflective Practitioner* (1983). He is currently Ford Professor in the Department of Urban Studies and Planning and the Division for Study and Research in Education at M.I.T.

THOMAS J. SERGIOVANNI has been a member of the faculty in Educational Administration at the University of Illinois since 1966. He is now Professor and Chairperson of the Department of Administration, Higher and Continuing Education. His recent work has emphasized the limits and uses of scientific knowledge in professional practice. Among his publications are "A Social Humanities View of Educational Policy and Administration," *Educational Administration Quarterly* (1980) and "Hermeneutics and the Science of Administration," *Review Journal of Philosophy and Social Science* (1982). His books include *The New School Executive: A Theory of Administration*, with Fred D. Carver, (2nd. ed., 1980), *Some Theoretical Issues in Educational Organizations and Administration* (1980), and *Supervision: Human Perspectives*, with Robert J. Starratt (3rd ed., 1983). In August of 1984 Sergiovanni will be Lillian Radford Distinguished Professor of Education at Trinity University, San Antonio, Texas.

BARRY M. STAW is Professor of Organizational Behavior and Industrial Relations at the University of California, Berkeley. He is co-editor of the annual series *Research in Organizational Behavior* and also serves on the editorial boards of *Administrative Science Quarterly*, *Organizational Behavior and Human Performance*, and *The Journal of Applied Psychology*. Professor Staw has conducted research in the areas of individual motivation, perception and commitment, and, in the past few years, he has worked extensively on the issue of how individuals and organizations became locked-in to courses of action. He has taught at Northwestern University, the University of Illinois, and the University of Iowa in addition to his present position at Berkeley.

WILLIAM TAYLOR is Principal of the University of London. Formerly, he was Director of the Institute of Education at the University of London and Professor of Education at the University of Bristol. He is a Fellow of the Commonwealth Council for Educational Administration. His books include *The Secondary Modern School* (1963); *Society and the Education of Teachers* (1969); *Towards a Policy for the Education of Teachers*, ed.

(1969); *Educational Administration and the Social Sciences*, ed. with G. Baron (1969); *Heading for Change* (1972); *Research Perspectives in Education*, ed. (1973); *Research and Reform in Teacher Education* (1978); *Education in the 'Eighties: The Central Issues*, ed. with B. Simon (1981); and *The Metaphors of Education* (forthcoming).

PETER B. VAILL is Professor of Human Systems in the School of Government and Business Administration, George Washington University. He was Dean of this school from 1977 to 1978. His special fields of teaching and research include strategic management, organizational development, and the philosophy of science, as well as his work on high-performing systems. A previous article on a subject related to this volume is "Toward a Behavioral Description of High Performing Systems," in *Leadership: Where Else Can We Go?*, ed. Morgan McCall and Michael Lombardo (1978).

INDEX

Administration: theory of practice in, 207, 212; science of, 207, 212, 213, 275; as applied science, 212, 276. *See also* Administrative theory; Leadership

Administrative theory: contrasting views of, 1–7, 36–42, 246–48, 260, 275–79; the cultural perspective, 1, 2, 7–10; assumptions in, 2, 19; administration as artificial science, 2, 276, 277; the efficiency perspective, 3, 4, 105; the person (human) perspective, 5; the political perspective, 6, 7; conceptions of, 28, 29; contrasts between actual and ideal administration, 32–35; Model I theories-in-use, 56; building a reflective science of administration, 61, 62; Theory X, 70; Theory Y, 70: and critical theory, 249–57; as ideology, 251. *See also* Educational administration; Human relations movement; Human resources theory; Leadership; Organizational behavior

Administrators: ambitions of, 26–29; evaluation of, 27; competencies of, 27, 29; incentive for, 28; characteristics of effective, 65, 66, 93–97; characteristics of higher education administration, United Kingdom, 136, 137; school principals as, 161–62; problems faced by, 198–201; public and private compared, 219–26; the training of, 234–37. *See also* High-performing systems

Alexander, Chris, 39

Anthropology, 7

Apel, Karl-Otto, 245, 246

Authority: in organizations, 176–82; symbols as a source of, 176

Ball, George, 74

Barnard, Chester, 38, 88, 164, 219

Bauman, Zygmunt, 143, 148

Bennis, Warren, 93, 149

Benson, Kenneth, J., 251, 254

Bernstein, Richard, J., 240, 245

Blake, William, 153

Blumenthal, Michael, 231

Bok, Derek, 234

Bourdieu, Pierre, 271

Brown, David, 95

Brute data, 150, 151, 278

Burns, James MacGregor, 215

Callahan, Raymond, E., 249

Campbell, D. T.: "experimenting society", 78

Cartesian thought, 143, 144, 145, 148

Chandler, Alfred, 235

Change: organizations and, 20–23; reactions to, 170–71; impact of changing values and ideologies, 171–73

Chapin, Roy, 208, 228–33

Civil Service Reform Act of 1978, 233

Clark, Bob, 130

Coleman, James, 320, 321, 322

Comte, Auguste, 143, 144

Conflict resolution, 7

Contingency theory, 106

Costle, Doug, 208, 227–33

Critical theory: analysis of, 7, 209, 210, 240–54; critical theory of educational administration, 254–57; critical practice of educational administration, 260. *See also* Hermeneutics; Marxian thought

Cultural artifacts, 154

Cultural pluralism, 305

Decision-making: "garbage can" metaphor for, 14, 324; actual